Ethnicity and Integration

Understanding Population Trends and Processes

Volume 3

Series Editor

J. Stillwell

In western Europe and other developed parts of the world, there are some very significant demographic processes taking place at the individual, household, community and national scales including the ageing of the population, the delay in childbearing, the rise in childlessness, the increase in divorce, the fall in marriage rates, the increase in cohabitation, the increase in mixed marriages, the change in household structures, the rise in step-parenting, and the appearance of new streams of migration taking place both within and between countries. The relationships between demographic change, international migration, labour and housing market dynamics, care provision and intergenerational attitudes are complex to understand and yet it is vital to quantify the trends and to understand the processes. Similarly, it is critical to appreciate what the policy consequences are for the trends and processes that have become apparent. This series has its roots in understanding and analyzing these trends and processes.

This series will be of interest to a wide range of individuals with interests in demographic and social change, including demographers, population geographers, sociologists, economists, political scientists, epidemiologists and health researchers and well as practitioners and commentators across the social sciences.

For further volumes:
http://www.springer.com/series/8113

Ethnicity and Integration

Understanding Population Trends and Processes – Volume 3

Edited by

John Stillwell
University of Leeds, UK

and

Maarten van Ham
University of St. Andrews, UK

Springer

Editors
Professor John Stillwell
University of Leeds
School of Geography
Fac. Earth and Environment
Woodhouse Lane
Leeds LS2 9JT
United Kingdom
j.c.h.stillwell@leeds.ac.uk

Dr. Maarten van Ham
University of St Andrews
School of Geography and Geosciences
Centre for Housing Research
Fife KY16 9AL
United Kingdom
maarten.vanham@st-andrews.ac.uk

ISBN 978-90-481-9102-4 e-ISBN 978-90-481-9103-1
DOI 10.1007/978-90-481-9103-1
Springer Dordrecht Heidelberg London New York

Library of Congress Control Number: 2010930915

Printed on acid-free paper

Springer is part of Springer Science+Business Media (www.springer.com)

Foreword

Robust and forensic analysis of relevant data supported by scientific methodologies is key to challenging contemporary debates around the use and abuse of race statistics. Controversies surrounding the collection, interpretation and use of race, ethnicity and ethnic group data have a long history. Being rooted in Eugenics, this area of study has sparked intense reactions over the years. The abuse of 'race' statistics is not only apparent during times of uncertainty but has been entrenched in social policies and political discourses in Britain since the 1950s. The collection of research studies in this book is therefore much needed and timely, not least because of recent debates surrounding the nature and interactions of minority ethnic populations in Britain.

The numbers game is not new in British political discourses but took a nasty turn post 9/11 and peaked post 7/7 with diversity being negatively associated with concerns in relation to population segregation, community conflicts and terrorism. This book effectively debunks several myths and misinterpretions pertaining to population diversity, spatial density and the nature of social relationships between minority and majority groups. More importantly, armed with scientific evidence, it challenges the claim that spatial segregation along ethnic and racial lines is necessarily an indication of community tensions, social fragmentation and community conflicts.

Despite the obvious benefits of valid and reliable data on population diversity for understanding social change and improving social conditions, there was little appetite on the part of the British Government to formally collect national statistics on ethnicity until 1991. Notwithstanding this, the chapters in this book demonstrate that data from the 1991 and 2001 Censuses can, despite their limitations, provide

---

Kay Hampton (BA Hons, MA, PhD, FRSA, FHEA) is Professor in Communities and Race Relations at the Glasgow Caledonian University. She was Chair, Deputy Chair and Scottish Commissioner on the Commission for Racial Equality (2003–2007) and Commissioner on the Equality and Human Rights Commission (2006–2009). She is currently a Commissioner for the Scottish Human Rights Commission.

[1]The bombings of the Twin Towers in New York on 9 September 2001 and the London bombings on 7 July 2005.

useful baseline statistics for conducting in-depth, analytical studies in contested areas of 'race' and ethnicity.

A significant contribution of this book is that it reports on a wide range of contemporary issues relating to diversity, segregation, integration, multiculturalism, immigration and population growth, and puts to rest uncertainities surrounding the careless claims made in this regard. The last five years have seen political leaders and power elites make unfounded pronouncements about the relationship between diversity and social instability, many demanding that we socially engineer integration by imposing a so-called sense of 'Britishness'.

Indeed, a previous chair of the Commission for Racial Equality (now Chair of the Equality and Human Rights Commission) has notably painted a dramatic picture of widespread fragmentation along racial and ethnic lines. Whilst using some relevant data, creative interpretation of its implications served to create a sense of urgency and the establishment of an entire Government department to promote 'community cohesion' so that the country may be protected from acts of 'home grown' terrorists. Contrary to these alarmist predictions, this book provides solid evidence which paints a much more realistic and positive picture of the state of our communities in Britain.

In this regard, Sabater (Chapter 3) demonstrates clearly that despite the growth of certain ethnic minority groups between 1991 and 2001 in England and Wales, ethnic residential segregation has reduced for all groups over time and age cohorts. Similarly, Simon (Chapter 7) provides solid evidence to challenge the misconception that people from ethnic minority groups in Britain, self-segregate. She argues instead that there is a strong tendency to move away from areas with high concentration of their own group and, as a consequence, major cities are becoming more diverse.

This book proves that headline grabbing sound bites relating to the so-called 'end of multiculturalism'; 'sleepwalking to segregation'; 'rural apartheid'; 'fully fledged ghettos'; and 'White flight' are often based on patchy knowledge and careless interpretation of data. Indeed, they serve to inflame and create community tensions where often none exists. This is then followed by benign suggestions as to how these may be addressed by Government. Often voiced in times of social crisis, power elites attempt to appease community fear and insecurity. These announcements often arise from an inability to appreciate the homogeneity of ethnic groups as reflected in Mitton and Aspinall's Chapter (9) and the impact of broader social influences highlighted by Higgins and Dale (Chapter 10). In effect, this book not only provides comprehensive insights into the spatial distribution of population groups in Britain (Stafford et al., Chapter 11), but also provides a better understanding of how minority groups interact with majority groups.

In the context of contemporary political pressure to 'integrate', the drive for a universal British identity is unlikely to be easily achieved given the complexities discussed by Stillwell and van Ham (Chapter 1) and therein lies the strength of this collection of research. It is grounded in evidence and makes clear that any advancement towards building stable communities must include considerations of population distribution and density; and of political structure, culture and clarity of conceptual meaning. Inconsistent analysis of these critical factors will inevitably result in flawed understandings and unrealisable outcomes.

As we move towards the next census (2011), the contributions here give us much food for thought. In addition to demonstrating the complexity around the analysis of ethnicity, diversity and density data in contemporary societies, it is a sharp reminder of the folly of creating national policy on misinformed and headline grabbing sound bites.

Glasgow
December 2009

Kay Hampton

Preface

Views on the changing ethnic composition of the British population and its implications are divided. Some people consider that the fragmentation of our society by race and ethnicity is a catastrophe resulting in spatial segregation and community breakdown; for others, the cultural diversity associated with ethnic pluralism is something positive to be celebrated and enjoyed as we move towards a more integrated society. There is unanimity in thinking that integration has to be a two-way process, in which the settled communities accept that new people will bring change with them and newcomers realise that they too will have to change if we are to move closer to an integrated society. Trevor Phillips, chairman of the Equality and Human Rights Commission, favours policies that will stress sameness rather than distinctiveness and promote common British values.

The research that is reported in the chapters of this book addresses many of the key issues associated with ethnicity and integration that challenge social scientists, including a better understanding of ethnic population change and residential concentration, ethnic household dynamics such as fertility and mixed-ethnic unions, internal and international migration, the relationship between ethnicity and health, crime, identity and language, as well as ethnic population projection. Collectively, the findings of the different research projects constitute an evidence base upon which policy makers and practitioners can draw when formulating solutions to the range of problems at local, regional and national level that are associated with an increasingly multi-ethnic society.

This volume is the third in a series on 'Understanding Population Trends and Processes', which is based on research contributions to our knowledge of different aspects of population structure and distribution, involves the quantitative analysis of secondary data from censuses, surveys or administrative records, and reports results for Britain and, in some cases, elsewhere in Europe.

Leeds, UK — John Stillwell
St Andrews, UK — Maarten van Ham
December 2009

Acknowledgements

All the research projects reported in this volume have been funded by the UK Economic and Social Research Council (ESRC) as part of the 'Understanding Population Trends and Processes' (UPTAP) programme (2005–2009). The editors would like to express their thanks to all the chapter authors for submitting their initial manuscripts on schedule, responding positively to comments and suggestions from the editors and delivering final versions of chapters with minimum delay.

Lisa Youngman, the UPTAP administrator, has undertaken the task of proofreading the final manuscript and David Appleyard, the graphics technician in the School of Geography at the University of Leeds, has redrawn all the graphs and maps. The editors are very grateful to both Lisa and David for their efforts.

Contents

Contributors

Peter Aspinall Centre for Health Services Studies, George Allen Wing, University of Kent, Canterbury CT2 7NF, Kent, UK, peter.petjasp@googlemail.com

Laia Bécares Department of Epidemiology and Public Health, University College London, London WC1E 6BT, UK, l.becares@ucl.ac.uk

Peter Boden School of Geography, University of Leeds, Leeds LS2 9JT, UK, p.boden@leeds.ac.uk

Paul Boyle School of Geography and Geosciences/Longitudinal Studies Centre – Scotland (LSCS), University of St Andrews, Fife KY16 9AL, Scotland, UK, p.boyle@st-andrews.ac.uk

Angela Dale The Cathie Marsh Centre for Census and Survey Research (CCSR), School of Social Sciences, The University of Manchester, Manchester M13 9PL, UK, angela.dale@manchester.ac.uk

Sylvie Dubuc Department of Social Policy and Social Work, University of Oxford, Oxford OX1 2ER, UK, sylvie.dubuc@socres.ox.ac.uk

Zhiqiang Feng School of Geography and Geosciences/Longitudinal Studies Centre – Scotland (LSCS), University of St Andrews, Fife KY16 9AL, Scotland, UK, zf2@st-andrews.ac.uk

Nissa Finney School of Social Sciences, The Cathie Marsh Centre for Census and Survey Research (CCSR), The University of Manchester, Manchester M13 9PL, UK, Nissa.Finney@manchester.ac.uk

John Haskey Department of Social Policy and Social Work, University of Oxford, Oxford OX1 2ER, UK, john.haskey@socres.ox.ac.uk

Vanessa Higgins The Cathie Marsh Centre for Census and Survey Research (CCSR), School of Social Sciences, The University of Manchester, Manchester M13 9PL, UK, vanessa.higgins@manchester.ac.uk

Serena Hussain School of Geography and the Environment, University of Oxford, Oxford OX1 3QY, UK, serena.hussain@gmail.com

Paula Kautt UCL Jill Dando Institute of Crime Science, University College London, London, WC1E 7HN, UK, p.kautt@ucl.ac.uk

Lavinia Mitton School of Social Policy, Sociology and Social Research, University of Kent, Canterbury CT2 7NF, Kent, UK, L.Mitton@kent.ac.uk

John Mohan Division of Sociology and Social Policy, School of Social Sciences, ESRC-OTS Third Sector Research Centre, University of Southampton, Southampton SO17 1BH, UK, J.F.Mohan@soton.ac.uk

James Nazroo School of Social Sciences, University of Manchester, Manchester, UK, james.nazroo@manchester.ac.uk

Paul Norman School of Geography, University of Leeds, Leeds LS2 9JT, UK, p.d.norman@leeds.ac.uk

Gillian Raab School of Geography and Geosciences/Longitudinal Studies Centre – Scotland (LSCS), University of St Andrews, Fife KY16 9AL, Scotland, UK, gillian.raab@st-andrews.ac.uk

Philip Rees School of Geography, University of Leeds, Leeds LS2 9JT, UK, p.h.rees@leeds.ac.uk

Albert Sabater Centre d'Estudis Demogràfics, Universitat Autònoma de Barcelona, Edifici E7, Bellaterra (Barcelona), 08193, Spain, asabater@ced.uab.es

Marina Shaginyan-Shapira Centre for Educational Sociology, Edinburgh University, Edinburgh EH8 8AQ, UK, mshapira@staffmail.ed.ac.uk

Antonia Simon Thomas Coram Research Unit, Institute of Education, University of London, London WC1H 0AA, UK, A.Simon@ioe.ac.uk

Mai Stafford Department of Epidemiology and Public Health, University College London, London WC1E 6BT, UK, m.stafford@ucl.ac.uk

John Stillwell School of Geography, University of Leeds, Leeds LS2 9JT, UK, j.c.h.stillwell@leeds.ac.uk

Joanna Taylor Department of Geography, University of Portsmouth, Portsmouth PO1 3HE, UK, Joanna.Taylor@port.ac.uk

Liz Twigg Department of Geography, University of Portsmouth, Portsmouth PO1 3HE, UK, Liz.Twigg@port.ac.uk

Maarten van Ham School of Geography and Geosciences, Centre for Housing Research, University of St Andrews, Fife KY16 9AL, Scotland, UK, maarten.vanham@st-andrews.ac.uk

Pia Wohland School of Geography, University of Leeds, Leeds LS2 9JT, UK, p.n.wohland@leeds.ac.uk

Chapter 1
Ethnicity and Integration

John Stillwell and Maarten van Ham

Introduction

Ethnicity and integration, together with a range of associated concepts, have become central in demography and population studies. However, as Hargreaves (1995) pointed out, it is rather unfortunate that the discourses surrounding both these concepts in the English-speaking world are characterised by a certain amount of confusion and disagreement. In this first chapter, we aim to provide some clarity through brief examination of the concepts of race, ethnicity, immigration and integration before illustrating selected measures of ethnic evenness, isolation, diversity and density that are used later in the book. These initial sections, together with a brief synopsis of the structure and spatial distribution of ethnic populations in Britain, serve to set the scene for the chapters that follow and which are introduced in the second half of this first chapter.

There is no doubt that matters of ethnicity and integration have received major attention from the policy making community, particularly in light of the riots that took place on the streets of Bradford, Oldham and Burnley during the summer of 2001 and the attacks in London on 7th and 21st July 2005. Since then, a comprehensive framework for action has focused on the need for increased ethnic integration and an effort to re-think British multiculturalism as a means to combat terrorism. Trevor Phillips, when Chairman of the Commission for Racial Equality (CRE), called for controversial measures to prevent Britain from 'sleepwalking' into racial and religious segregation.

Race and Ethnicity

Race and ethnicity are both concepts for which there is no single universally accepted definition. The concept of race emerged in the fifteenth century when global explorations of discovery brought Europeans into contact with those of

J. Stillwell (✉)
School of Geography, University of Leeds, Leeds LS2 9JT, UK
e-mail: j.c.h.stillwell@leeds.ac.uk

J. Stillwell, M. van Ham (eds.), *Ethnicity and Integration*, Understanding Population Trends and Processes 3, DOI 10.1007/978-90-481-9103-1_1,

different physical appearance to themselves. Thus, we conceive races as referring to the variety of human species, consisting of distinct populations with anatomical traits that distinguish one race clearly from another. However, this biological definition of race does not fit the contemporary knowledge of human genetic variation and it is now clear that human races are primarily a cultural creation. Attempts to scientifically divide humanity into biological races based on anatomical characteristics, such as skin colour and specific facial characteristics, have proven unsatisfactory since mixing has meant that 'Black', 'White' or 'Other' racial categories are no longer distinct. We also recognise that historically the concept of race was closely associated with ideas of social inequality, supremacy and subordination which have led to the stereotypical images of others that some people still hold today and the concept of racism denoting particular attitudes, beliefs, ideologies, social actions and structures. In summary, race has come to mean a social relationship in which structural positions and social actions are explained by reference to systems of symbols and beliefs which emphasise the social and cultural relevance of biologically rooted characteristics. The collection of essays edited by Jackson (1987) was particularly useful in developing our understanding of the geography of race and racism in Britain in the 1980s, stimulating further work including, more recently, the volume of studies edited by Dwyer and Bressey (2008) which considers the intersection of race with religion and ethnicity.

In contrast to race, *ethnicity* refers to selected cultural and sometimes physical characteristics used to classify people into groups or categories considered to be significantly different from others. In some cases, ethnicity involves merely a loose group identity with little or no cultural traditions in common. On the other hand, some ethnic groups are coherent subcultures with a common place of origin, language, religion, ancestry and cultural traditions. Newly arrived immigrant groups often fit this pattern. It is important not to confuse the term ethnic minority with ethnic group. Ethnic groups may be either a minority or a majority in a population and most academic commentators stress some sort of cultural distinctiveness as the mark of ethnic grouping whilst emphasising the difficulty in distinguishing the boundaries between ethnic groups. An ethnic question was introduced for the first time in the 1991 Census and the four-volume series of books edited respectively by Coleman and Salt (1996), Peach (1996a), Ratcliffe (1996) and Karn (1997) represent the first comprehensive set of analyses of a variety of aspects of different ethnic minority populations in Britain.

One pragmatic issue that complicates comparative analysis across the United Kingdom (UK) is that each of the respective census offices for England and Wales, Scotland and Northern Ireland uses a slightly different ethnic classification. Thus, as shown in Table 1.1, four 'Mixed' categories were used in the 2001 Census for England and Wales but only one in the 2001 Censuses in Scotland and Northern Ireland.

It is possible to aggregate the population counts for the non-White groups into the ten broad categories shown in Fig. 1.1, which allows comparison of the national population shares of each ethnic minority between the four UK countries. It is clear that, apart from the Chinese, over 92% of each ethnic group live in England. The

Table 1.1 Ethnic group classification systems for countries of the UK, 2001

England and Wales				Scotland			Northern Ireland		
Ethnic group Table KS006 (KS006a for Wales)		England	Wales	Ethnic group and language (Scotland) Table KS006			Ethnic group Table KS006		
Code	Variable	Population	Population	Code		Population	Code		Population
ks0060001	All people	49, 138, 831	2, 903, 085	ks0060001	All people	5, 062, 011	ks0060001	All persons	1, 685, 267
ks0060002	White British	42, 747, 136	2, 786, 605	ks0060002	White Scottish	4, 459, 071	ks0060002	White	1, 670, 988
ks0060003	White Irish	624, 115	17, 689	ks0060003	Other White British	373, 685	ks0060003	Irish Traveller	1, 710
ks0060004	Other White	1, 308, 110	37, 211	ks0060004	White Irish	49, 428	ks0060004	Mixed	3, 319
ks0060005	Mixed:White and Black Caribbean	231, 424	5, 996	ks0060005	Other White	78, 150	ks0060005	Indian	1, 567
ks0060006	Mixed:White and Black African	76, 498	2, 413	ks0060006	Indian	15, 037	ks0060006	Pakistani	666
ks0060007	Mixed:White and Asian	184, 014	5, 001	ks0060007	Pakistani	31, 793	ks0060007	Bangladeshi	252
ks0060008	Mixed:Other Mixed	151, 437	4, 251	ks0060008	Bangladeshi	1, 981	ks0060008	Other Asian	194
ks0060009	Asian or Asian British: Indian	1, 028, 546	8, 261	ks0060009	Other South Asian	6, 196	ks0060009	Black Caribbean	255
ks00600010	Asian or Asian British: Pakistani	706, 539	8, 287	ks00600010	Chinese	16, 310	ks00600010	Black African	494
ks00600011	Asian or Asian British: Bangladeshi	275, 394	5, 436	ks00600011	Caribbean	1, 778	ks00600011	Other Black	387
ks00600012	Asian or Asian British: Other Asian	237, 810	3, 464	ks00600012	African	5, 118	ks00600012	Chinese	4, 145

Table 1.1 (continued)

England and Wales				Scotland			Northern Ireland		
Ethnic group Table KS006 (KS006a for Wales)		England	Wales	Ethnic group and language (Scotland) Table KS006			Ethnic group Table KS006		
Code	Variable	Population	Population	Code		Population	Code		Population
ks00600013	Black or Black British: Caribbean	561, 246	2, 597	ks00600013	Black Scottish or other Black	1, 129	ks00600013	Other Ethnic Group	1, 290
ks00600014	Black or Black British: African	475, 938	3, 727	ks00600014	Any mixed back-ground	12, 764			
ks00600015	Black or Black British: Black Other	95, 324	745	ks00600015	Other ethnic group	9, 571			
ks00600016	Chinese or other ethnic group: Chinese	220, 681	6, 267	ks00600016	Born in Scotland[a]	82, 221			
ks00600017	Chinese or other ethnic group: Other	214, 619	5, 135	ks00600017	Not born in Scotland[a]	10, 175			
ks00600018[b]	People identifying themsleves as Welsh		417, 820						

[a]People aged 3 and over, who understand, speak, read or write Gaelic will appear in other ethnic groups.
[b]People identifying themselves as Welsh will appear in both a specific standard ethnic group and in the Welsh group.
Source: Census (2001).

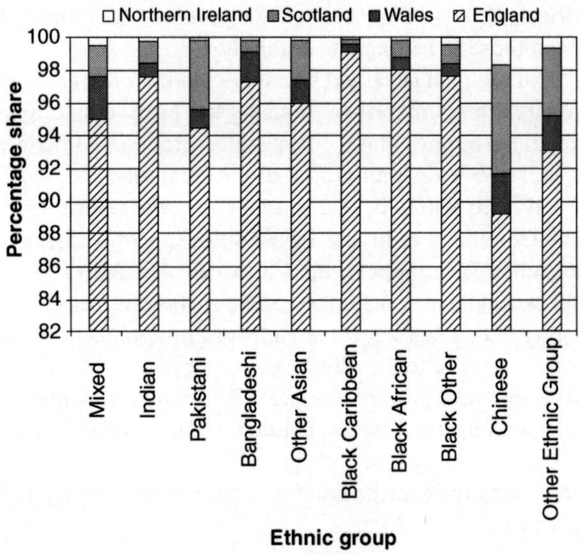

Fig. 1.1 Shares of ethnic group population by UK country of residence, 2001 (Source: Census, 2001)

Chinese and, to a lesser extent, the Other ethnic group, have higher shares of their populations resident in Scotland, Wales and Northern Ireland than the remaining groups with the Black Caribbean, Black African, Black Other and Indian groups being particularly concentrated in England in 2001.

It is also the case that ethnic group classifications change over time. The 16 groups shown for England and Wales in Table 1.1 in 2001 evolved from eight groups in 1991 with the introduction of four Mixed categories and the breakdown of the White category (Bulmer, 1996; Rankin and Bhopal, 1999), whereas in 1981 there was no ethnic classification. Following the consultation questionnaire on ethnic group for the 2011 Census that was tested in May 2007, the ONS Census Advisory Group (2008) has recommended the addition of Gypsy or Irish Traveller and Arab categories and the renaming of the British as English or Welsh categories, giving 18 tick boxes on the 2011 Census form following the 'What is your ethnic group?' question.

Not only does a classification have to deal with the problem of ethnic mixing but there are important issues of self identification as well as citizenship and belonging that need to be considered. Another Census Advisory Group recommendation for 2011 is the inclusion of a new question about national identity, thereby allowing ethnic minorities to choose one national identity within the UK: English; Welsh; Scottish; Northern Irish; British; Other. Ethnicity also depends upon circumstances. A man born in England to White parents may consider himself to be White English, White British or White European in different situations whereas a woman of Indian parentage living in England, might classify herself as Indian, Gujerati,

Hindu, East African Asian or British, depending on her background and her current circumstances and those of her parents or family.

In 2001, 8.1% of the total usually resident population of Great Britain were classified as non-White ethnic minorities. In using the term 'ethnic minority' there is a danger that the term implies that the designated group is numerically, and hence politically and morally, less significant than the 'majority'. Moreover, the term is widely understood in Britain to denote those people whose origins lie in the countries of the New Commonwealth and Pakistan; in other words, in former British colonies in the Indian subcontinent, the Caribbean and Africa as well as the Far East, parts of the world from which many of the first waves of post-war immigrants arrived. The reality is that subsequent streams of immigrants have resulted in what has been referred to by Vertovec (2006) as 'super-diversity', with London being *by far the most super-diverse representing 179 nationalities and 300 languages.* Languages, along with names, have been used by Mateos (2007) to develop a name-based ethnic classification system for the capital city that demonstrates the wide range of ethnic groups resident in London whose heterogeneity is hidden by the classification used in the 2001 Census.

Immigration and Integration

Since the 1970s, Britain has experienced a transition from being a country of net emigration to one of net immigration with substantial numbers of British and foreign citizens arriving in the early years of the twenty-first century. Figure 1.2 shows the ONS Total International Migration (TIM) estimates of arrivals and departures of international migrants (leaving or staying in the UK for over 12 months) from 1998 to 2007. The net balance has been around 200,000 for the last 4 years with an estimated 577,000 people arriving to live in the UK in 2007, of which 502,000 (87%) were non-British citizens. An estimated 96,000 Polish citizens migrated into

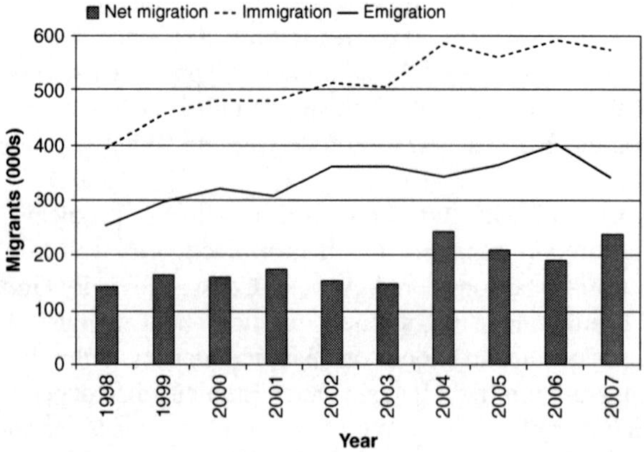

Fig. 1.2 Total international migration to and from the UK, 1997–2007 (Source: ONS Total International Migration (TIM) estimates)

the UK in 2007, the highest inflow of any individual citizenship. It is these international migration flows, together with the ethnic diversity resulting from mixed ethnic unions, which have created the super-diversity referred to by Vertovec (2006). Economic explanations of the variations in net international migration point to the selection effects of differing income distributions at home and abroad (Hatton, 2005).

The TIM estimates are mainly based on the International Passenger Survey (IPS) with adjustments for those whose intended length of stay changes so their migrant status changes (migrant/visitor switchers), for asylum seekers and their dependants not identified by the IPS, and for flows between the UK and the Republic of Ireland. The TIM statistics do not contain other groups of migrants classified in Fig. 1.3, such as migrant workers (who stay less than 12 months), trafficked persons or undocumented migrants. Figure 1.3 illustrates the increasingly complex task of defining different types of international immigrants whose arrival adds to the increasing ethnic diversity of the UK population.

Whilst immigration has been a key driver of ethnic population growth in the UK and mixed ethnic unions have led to further ethnic diversity, ethnic minority populations have also grown as first generation post-war immigrants have been followed by subsequent generations of children born in the UK or overseas. ONS announced in August 2009 (Whitehead, 2009) that for the first time in a decade, immigration has been exceeded by natural change due to increasing fertility, the majority of which (56% in the 12 months to June 2008) was accounted for by foreign-born mothers giving birth to 2.5 children per mother compared to UK-born women's fertility rate of 1.84 children per mother.

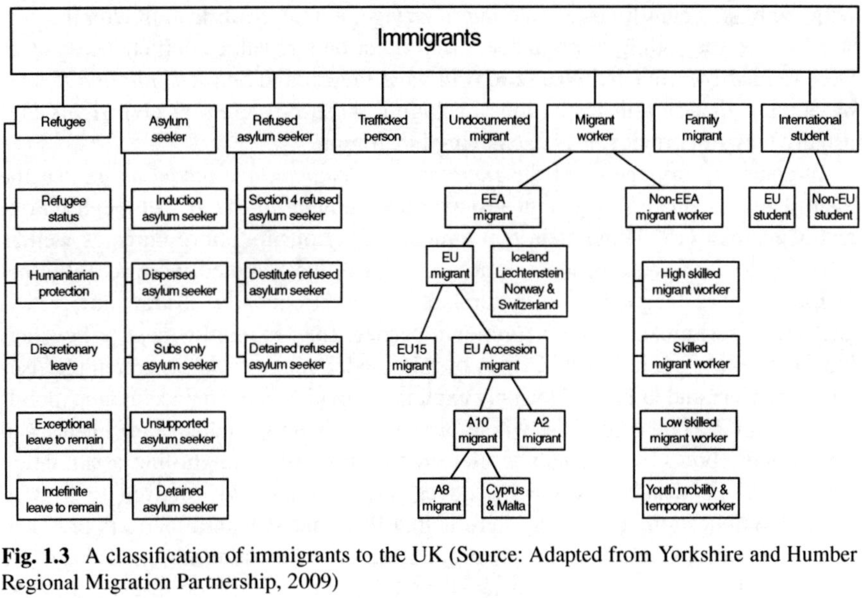

Fig. 1.3 A classification of immigrants to the UK (Source: Adapted from Yorkshire and Humber Regional Migration Partnership, 2009)

The growth of ethnic minorities and the changes in the ethnic complexion of the UK population have raised many questions for politicians, policy makers and academics as well as for members of the general public about the process of ethnic integration, the two-way process of new residents and host communities adapting to each other. Organisations like Migrationwatch UK have continually draw attention in recent years to the speed and scale of migration which, when combined with the shortcomings of official population figures on immigration (UK Statistics Authority, 2009), is placing considerable pressures on funding for services like housing and schools. There is, of course, the much wider debate about the economic as well as the social impacts of immigration and how to deal with it successfully which has commanded much time and space in the popular press but has also been given much attention by the academic community. Geographers have played an important role in the spatial analysis of ethnic settlement patterns encompassing the study of ethnic residential neighbourhoods (e.g. Peach 1996b; Peach et al., 1981) and school education (e.g. Johnston et al., 2006) whilst economists (e.g. Li and Heath, 2009, in the second volume of the UPTAP series) have documented changing employment and class positions of minority ethnic groups in Britain since the early 1970s.

Much of the theory underpinning the process of integration, or assimilation as it is sometimes called, comes from work in the USA where a number of theoretical models have been developed. *Classic assimilation theory*, which dates back to the Chicago School in the 1920s and, more recently, to the work of Alba and Nee (2003) regards immigrant/ethnic minority and host majority groups as following a straight-line convergence, becoming increasingly similar in norms, values, behaviours and characteristics over time. In 1964, Gordon suggested a number of stages that follow the acquisition of culture and language: structural assimilation (close social relations with the host society); large-scale intermarriage; ethnic identification with the host society; and the ending of prejudice, discrimination and value conflict. These ideas were refined by Alba and Nee (2003) in what they called *new assimilation theory*, by arguing that certain institutions, including those bolstered by civil rights law, usually play important roles in achieving integration.

In contrast, proponents of the *racial/ethnic disadvantage model* argue that the assimilation of many immigrant groups often remains blocked. Although Glazer and Moynihan (1963) maintain that ethnicity can constitute a resource as well as a burden for achieving economic mobility, others have argued more recently that factors such as language and cultural familiarity frequently obstruct integration and both discrimination and institutional barriers (e.g. in employment or housing) block complete assimilation. Critics of this model suggest that it overemphasises ethnic barriers and fails to adequately explain the evidence of socioeconomic mobility. Gans (1992) describes the whole process as 'bumpy' rather than 'linear' and Portes and Zhou (1993) combine elements of both the straight-line assimilation and the ethnic disadvantage perspectives into a framework referred to as *segmented assimilation*. The theory here is that there are structural barriers (e.g. bad schools, poor jobs) that have the greatest impact on the most disadvantaged and this produces alternative pathways to social mobility and integration or even negative assimilation, a process known as structural acculturation (Portes and Zhou, 1993). The obstacles along the route to occupational mobility and social acceptance, particularly as a consequence of racialization (Portes et al., 2005), may impact adversely on immigrant children's identities, their aspirations and their academic performance. Others suggest that it is factors such as family financial obligations or the lack of jobs due to poor industrial performance that are the major constraints rather than racialisation.

Measuring Ethnic Integration, Diversity and Density

One of the difficulties relating to integration is measurement of the phenomenon: to what extent is a particular ethnic group integrated with its host community or how much progress has been made towards integration? Questions like these are complicated because the concept of integration is multidimensional and the measurement of integration across a residential neighbourhood is different from integration at school or in the workplace, for example. Geographers have developed measures of spatial integration where, no matter what scale or focus, the approach typically highlights the difference between the geographies of the ethnic minority group and a reference group, usually those born in the host country or the rest of the population. Massey and Denton (1988) used an extensive literature search and cluster analysis to identify twenty different indices of segregation and classify them into five key dimensions of segregation: evenness, exposure, concentration, centralisation and clustering. The complete range of measures classified by Massey and Denton is not discussed here; instead we exemplify by selecting two indices that appear in chapters later in the book and which are amongst the most well used statistical measures for computing spatial integration: the index of segregation measuring evenness and the index of isolation measuring exposure.

The *index of segregation* (*IoS*) (Gorard, 2000) is a variant of the index of dissimilarity (Duncan and Duncan, 1955) and is usually computed by subtracting the percentage of one ethnic group *e* living in one area *i* from the percentage of the host population (or the rest of the population) that lives in that area. The absolute value of the difference is summed across all areas and the sum is multiplied by 0.5 in order to fix the range of values between 0 and 100.

$$IoS = 0.5\Sigma|(P_{ei}/P_e) - (P_{hi}/P_h)| \tag{1.1}$$

where P_{ei} is the population of group *e* in area *i*, P_{hi} is the host/rest of the population in area *i*, P_e is the total population of group *e*, and P_h is the total population of the host/rest of the population.

Whilst the index of segregation/dissimilarity measures how evenly distributed a population subgroup is compared to the host/rest of the population across areas in a city, the *index of isolation* (P^*) describes a group's exposure to all ethnic groups and has been used to determine the ethnic composition of the neighbourhood of the average person of a given ethnic group. The isolation index reflects the probabilities that a minority person shares a unit area with a majority person or with another minority person or *the extent to which minority members are exposed only to one another* (Massey and Denton, 1988, p. 288) and is computed as the minority-weighted average of the minority proportion in each area:

$$P^* = \Sigma(P_{ei}/P_e) - (P_{ei}/P_{*i}) \tag{1.2}$$

where P_{*i} is the total population of area i. When isolation indices are compared for different parts of a city (for example, the suburbs) with the city as a whole, we can see whether an ethnic group is evenly distributed across all areas or whether the group is concentrated in particular areas. There has been considerable debate in the literature about how to measure segregation and the extent to which British cities have experienced American-style ghettoisation. Index-based measures have been used by Simpson (2004, 2007) and Peach (1996b, 2007), for example, to suggest declining segregation whereas Poulsen et al. contend that a threshold approach presents a better way of assessing the extent to which ethnic groups live apart from each other (Johnston et al., 2002, 2005; Poulsen, 2005; Poulsen et al., 2001, 2009; Poulson and Johnston, 2006).

Two other ethnicity measures are introduced here since these appear in later chapters of the book. Firstly, reference is frequently made to ethnic heterogeneity or diversity. One of the most familiar measures of diversity is the index that reports the probability that two randomly selected people in a particular area would be from different ethnic groups (Brewer and Suchan, 2001). The *diversity index* for an area is computed by calculating the proportion of the population of the area in a particular group, squaring this proportion and then summing up the squared values across all ethnic groups and subtracting the total from unity. Thus, high values of the index represent greater ethnic diversity whereas lower values suggest more uniformity. Secondly, there is the concept of *ethnic density* calculated as the proportion of residents from a particular ethnic minority group in a given area. Studies indicate an ethnic density effect, whereby an increasing proportion of individuals of the same ethnicity (co-ethnics) in an area of residence is associated with reduced risk of morbidity among those ethnic populations, though evidence is mixed. Measures of ethnic density are commonly taken from small-area census data using predefined categories of ethnicity. In a recent study, Stafford et al. (2009) compared these measures with perceived ethnic density, based on self-reported proportion of co-ethnics in the area. Chapter 11 of this volume reports further on this work.

Structure and Spatial Distribution of Ethnic Populations of Britain

The populations of ethnic minority groups in Britain are spatially concentrated and we can use location quotients to quantify the extent of this concentration. A location quotient (*LQ*) is defined for each ethnic group *e* in each district *i* as:

$$LQ_{ei} = (P_{ei}/P_i)/(P_e/P_*) \times 100 \quad (1.3)$$

and is a measure of the under-representation (less than 1) or over-representation (greater than 1) of the ethnic group in each district when compared with the national average. Using data from the 2001 Census, the Isles of Scilly is the district of Great Britain with the highest LQ for the White population at 1.085 and Newham is the district with the lowest White LQ at 0.429. The districts with the highest LQs for aggregate ethnic groups are as follows: Leicester for Indians (13.97); Tower Hamlets for the Pakistanis and Other South Asians (15.69) and for Blacks (12.89); Westminster for the Chinese (5.28); Lambeth for Mixed (4.09) and Westminster for Other non-White (10.2).

Figure 1.4 provides a summary of ethnic geographical concentration by presenting, for seven aggregate ethnic groups, the percentage of the population that is contained in the top two deciles when the 408 local authorities in Britain are ranked on the basis of their ethnic group LQs. The figure shows that 6.7% of the White population reside in the top decile of districts with the highest White LQs, and 7.5% are in decile 2; over 80% of the Black population are in the top decile of districts based on Black LQs and 91.3% in the top 20%. Over 85% of Indian and Pakistani and Other South Asian (POSA) populations are located in the top 20% of districts whereas the remaining three groups are more widespread, with the Chinese having the lowest percentage of its population living in the districts with the highest LQs but having the highest percentage living in districts that comprise the second decile.

The locations of those districts in Britain in the top and bottom deciles of the districts ranked by the LQ for each of the four largest ethnic groups are shown in Fig. 1.5 and demonstrate the inverse relationship between the locations of White and

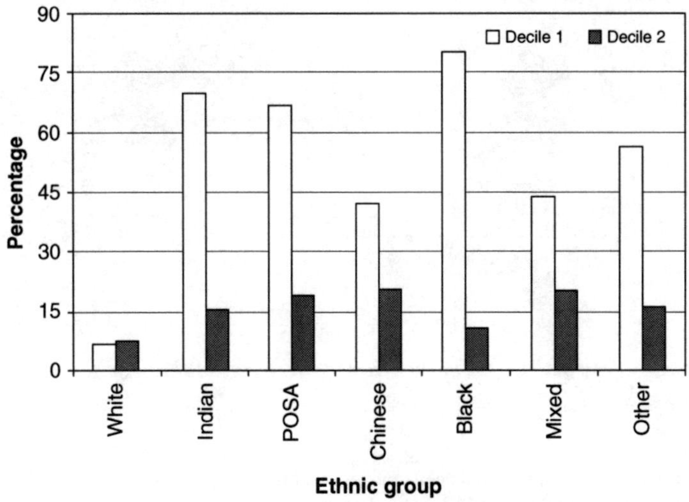

Fig. 1.4 Percentage of ethnic populations in the top two deciles of districts ranked by location quotient, 2001 (Source: Authors' calculations based on 2001 Census data)

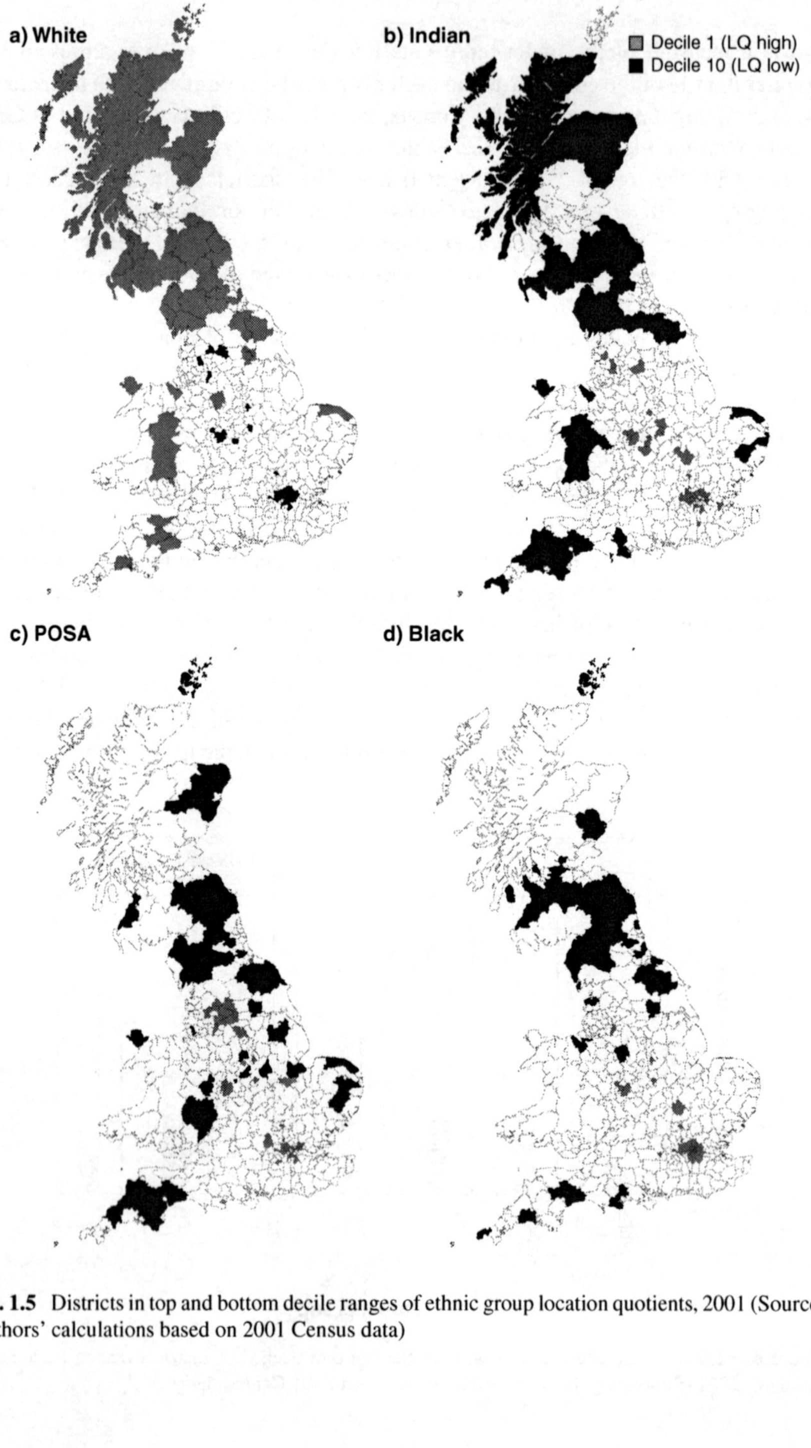

Fig. 1.5 Districts in top and bottom decile ranges of ethnic group location quotients, 2001 (Source: Authors' calculations based on 2001 Census data)

non-White groups as well as the overlap in the locations of the latter. Indians have over-representation in several districts in the Midlands whereas the POSA group have a more northern orientation. In all cases, London boroughs feature strongly as districts in the top decile, particularly so for Blacks; in fact 68% of the Black population of Britain live in London.

Book Structure and Contents

Ethnic Population Change and Residential Concentration

Much concern in twenty-first century Britain has been felt about the trends towards more social and familial fragmentation, the erosion of social capital and the lack of knowledge of how to build sustainable communities and promote community participation. The level of integration of ethnic minorities is clearly an important dimension of community development. Much of the debate has revolved around whether ethnic minorities are becoming more or less spatially segregated in terms of their residential location as well as the degree to which their integration across a range of contexts (e.g. employment, housing, education) has been impacted by the negative overtones resulting from the anti-social incidents highlighted by the popular press. An important consideration is how little we know, in quantitative terms, about the ethnic complexion of our neighbourhoods, cities and regions in 2009 and the dynamics that have led to the current complexion. Research focuses on measuring changes over time in the ethnic composition of areas, but also on understanding the mechanisms behind change: natural population change and migration. The most authoritative source of information at a small area scale remains the 2001 Census and we eagerly await the forthcoming 2011 Census to identify what changes have occurred over the last decade. In fact, the research community is still working towards a much better understanding of what has changed between the censuses of 1991 and 2001 and this is the focus of the first two chapters following this introduction.

In Chapter 2, *Nissa Finney* investigates to what extent natural change and net migration contribute towards changes in the ethnic population composition of wards across England and Wales. Births and deaths are both estimated initially and used with consistent estimates of ward population by age and sex (Sabater and Simpson, 2009) to give residual estimates of net migration between 1991 and 2001 for each ward in the country. At a national level, it is the Black Africans and Chinese that have net in-migration rates that exceed rates of natural increase whereas the Asian groups all have relatively high natural increase in contrast to net migration. Finney shows how rates of net migration by ethnic group also vary by age before presenting a case study of the dynamics of population change in the ward of Southall Broadway in London. This is the ward with the highest percentage of non-White residents in 2001 in the whole of England and Wales and a concentration of Indian Sikhs whose families originate from the Punjab. It is particularly interesting to note how Southall

Broadway experienced a net dispersal of over 2,000 of its Indian population during the inter-censal period whilst attracting young adult in-migrants of White and non-White Other ethnicity. In the final part of her analysis, Finney presents components of population change for wards grouped in quintiles according to their concentration of ethnic minority population. The results suggest a process of dispersal for Whites and minority groups which aligns with the results presented in subsequent chapters by Stillwell and Hussain and by Simon.

The study of changing residential patterns of ethnic groups is a key area to inform debates on residential segregation and diversity in urban areas. Chapter 3 by *Albert Sabater* presents analyses of changing ethnic residential segregation for cohorts in England and Wales. The first part of the analysis provides empirical evidence of clear declines in ethnic residential segregation between 1991 and 2001 using both census data as published and complete mid-year estimates for the same years. The outcomes highlight marginal changes when complete mid-year estimates are used, primarily as a consequence of census non-response and the harmonisation of the population definition and census geographies in the latter. The second part of his analysis traces changes in ethnic residential segregation for various age cohorts. This approach highlights the importance of residential segregation at some life stages more than others as well as the significance of a life pattern of segregation for all groups. The analyses show that using uncorrected census output can lead to incorrect conclusions about population change in small areas.

Ethnicity and Household Dynamics

Although it is apparent that total fertility in the last few years has been rising, there is plentiful evidence of trends towards lower and later fertility in the UK over recent decades. Fertility has remained below replacement level since the 1970s (Smallwood and Chamberlain, 2005) and the total fertility rate has remained around 1.7 children per woman in the last two decades. The pronounced rise in fertility since 2002 in White British women can most likely be attributed to catch-up behaviour after initial postponement of child bearing. In the first volume of the *Understanding Population Trends and Processes* series (Stillwell et al., 2009), the extent of delayed childbearing and increased childlessness was documented by Simpson (2009) and the role of education on childbearing was investigated by Smith and Ratcliffe (2009). In neither case, however, was any attention paid to the ethnic dimension of fertility and the timing of childbearing amongst different ethnic groups.

Data on births by ethnic group are not readily available in the UK and, as a consequence, ethnic fertility needs to be estimated. In Chapter 4, *Sylvie Dubuc* and *John Haskey* employ the 'own-child method' to obtain estimates of age-specific fertility rates by ethnic group from Labour Force Survey (LFS) data. This methodology was developed by the East-West Center, Hawaii (Cho et al., 1986). Their computer program, EASTWEST, enables survey data from the LFS to be turned into data on children ever-born by the calendar year of the birth of the child, and the age of the mother, and the numbers of mothers by age and calendar year at risk of producing the children. Age-specific fertility rates (ASFRs) can be derived from these data for each calendar year, by 1-year or 5-year age-groups of mothers, which are then used to compute total fertility rates (TFRs) and to investigate the 'quantum' and 'tempo' of childbearing over time. On average, the TFR of foreign-born women is greater than that of the women born in the UK and the varying proportions of immigrant (foreign-born) women amongst the different ethnic groups contribute some variability in their TFRs. Pakistani and Bangladeshi women have maintained the highest TFRs over the last two decades and Chinese women have the lowest rates. The results presented in Chapter 4 support the hypothesis that a convergence of fertility levels across ethnic groups has occurred, although at a decreasing pace since 2001. The results also suggest that childbearing has been delayed amongst ethnic minority women since 1998, a trend likely to be associated with women's involvement in higher education and paid employment as Smith and Ratcliffe (2009) and Hansen et al. (2009) have indicated.

The changing ethnic composition of the UK also impacts patterns of household formation, which is the focus of Chapter 5 by *Zhiqiang Feng, Paul Boyle, Maarten van Ham* and *Gillian Raab*, who consider ethnic mixing within the household. They acknowledge the increase in mixed-ethnic unions and study whether those who live in a mixed-ethnic neighbourhood will have a higher probability of ending up in a mixed-ethnic union. The authors use longitudinal data from the ONS Longitudinal Study to explore the likelihood that minority ethnic individuals choose a White partner in different geographical contexts. The results that are presented make interesting reading, not least because they support the hypothesis that increased spatial concentration has a negative effect on the formation of mixed-ethnic unions and that 'out-partnering', forming a union with someone from another ethnic group, is more likely in areas with low concentrations of those in the same ethnic group than in areas of greater co-ethnic concentration. More specifically, the authors show that, for Blacks, South Asians and Other Asians, the probability of having formed a partnership with a White person by 2001 is higher in the areas of least co-ethnic concentration in 1991 than in areas of highest co-ethnic concentration. This suggests that policy measures taken to support more spatial deconcentration of ethnic minorities are likely to result in more mixed-ethnic unions and have a positive impact on integration at the household level. One possible way in which spatial concentration of ethnic minorities is reduced is through migration and this is the focus of the next three chapters.

Internal and International Ethnic Migration

Secondary data on the geographical distribution of ethnic populations and on the migration of ethnic minorities is difficult to come by other than from the census of population carried out at the beginning of each decade. In order to explore the spatial patterns of ethnic migration, *John Stillwell* and *Serena Hussain* in Chapter 6 utilise a special table of origin-destination migration flows commissioned from the Office of National Statistics that provides counts of migrants in specific age and ethnic groups. The data have been released through a process of negotiation with the providers and unfortunately, for statistical disclosure reasons, do not allow the migration intensities and spatial patterns to be distinguished in detail beyond that of White, Black, Indian, Pakistani and Other South Asian, Chinese, Mixed and Other groups. Nevertheless, this broad categorisation of ethnicity combined with a breakdown of the counts into seven age groups is sufficient to confirm some significant variations in migration propensities between ethnic groups. The data also uncover some geographical patterns of net migration that demonstrate 'Urban London' is experiencing net losses of migrants in all ethnic groups, not just Whites. Urban London is one of four 'families' of districts that constitute the national area classification developed by Vickers et al. (2003) which the authors use as a framework for summarising the inter-district flows taking place in the 12 month period before the 2001 Census. The classification is used to show that Whites and Indians are also leaving provincial 'Urban' districts whereas these areas are gaining migrants from all the other ethnic groups. In order to set the scene for the migration analysis, the authors present a short review of some of the key debates in ethnic population and migration research and a synopsis of the ethnic complexion and distribution of population in England and Wales.

In Chapter 7, *Antonia Simon* reviews the theoretical and empirical work in the USA on ethnic minority concentration and the role of migration, and explains the difference between 'White flight' (Farley et al., 1994; Galster, 1990; Zubrinsky, 2000) and 'White avoidance' (Georing, 1978; Lee and Wood, 1991) whilst recognising that intolerance is not necessarily a phenomenon associated with race or ethnicity – but more with social conditions such as poverty and crime. Moreover, there are frequently important pull factors, such as housing opportunities, that influence White out-movement from areas where non-Whites concentrate, as well as the desire by Whites to live with members of their own ethnic group – although Krysan (2002) finds little evidence for this from the data on four major cities across the US. In Britain, ethnic migration has remained relatively unexplored until recent years when a number of researchers have begun to document patterns (Finney and Simpson, 2007, 2009; Hussain and Stillwell, 2008; Stillwell and Hussain, 2010) and to explain the underlying processes using 2001 Census data at different spatial scales. By analysing data across England and Wales at ward level from a commissioned table, Simon contributes further to the 'White flight' and 'self-segregation' debates by demonstrating how non-White migrants are leaving areas where their populations are concentrated and moving to areas of lesser concentration, where ethnic concentration is measured as the percentage of total population of each ward that is classified in each ethnic group.

Chapter 8 by *Marina Shaginyan-Shapira* is concerned with migration into Britain from overseas and the question of whether immigration has affected the wages and jobs of the native population. This is another very topical question; on Friday 30th January 2009, a series of unofficial strikes broke out around the UK over construction jobs awarded to European workers. The political editor of the Guardian reported that *as anger intensified over plans by oil companies to employ Portuguese and Italian workers, the Prime Minister said that he understood people's concerns*

(Summers, 2009). Whilst the popular press displayed pictures of the strikers with placards depicting the phrase *British jobs for British workers*, the controversial text used by Gordon Brown at an address to the GMB union in June 2007 was branded racist and illegal by critics. The Prime Minister insisted that his Government was *putting in place measures that ensure British workers can have access to the vacancies in the system.*

This strike exemplifies what has been a key political issue over the last decade – that of the impact of immigration on local labour markets in Britain – and one over which concerns have risen with the rapid transition to economic downturn in 2008. Salt et al. (2009) have argued that evidence from past recessions casts doubt on the widely held assumption that migrants to the UK return home when unemployment rises in the UK, which would free up jobs for the non-migrant population. They conclude that migration flows are likely to remain more stable than most people think over the course of the current economic downturn. They suggest that during the past three recessions that have affected Britain, migrant inflows began to pick up quickly, even before a noticeable improvement in the country's employment situation. While immigration has tended to fall and out-migration rise when unemployment increases, this pattern only lasts for a limited period. Chapter 8 addresses the question of whether spatial concentrations of immigrants – distinguishing those who had arrived before and after 2004 – have had a negative impact on the job opportunities (odds of entry into employment, and odds of entry in more prestigious occupations) and wages of non-migrant British workers. Using data from the Annual Population Survey (APS) for 2006, it appears that overall, immigrants do not have a negative effect on the labour market outcomes of British workers. The evidence suggests, in fact, that in local labour markets with larger concentrations of immigrants, the wages of non-migrant workers are higher than in local labour markets with smaller populations of immigrants. This is after controlling for the other characteristics of local labour markets which might be responsible for spatial wage differentials. The message of this study is clear: immigration on the whole has a positive economic effect in this context.

Ethnic Identity and Language

Studies of ethnicity and integration based on census data are compromised because of the disclosure control measures that constrain the availability of data to a limited number of ethnic groups. The ethnic groups defined by the Office of National Statistics (ONS), such as Black African or Other Asian, often fail to reveal the diversity of structure and experiences associated with specific minority populations from different parts of the world. In Chapter 9, *Lavinia Mitton* and *Peter Aspinall* focus their attention on the Black African diaspora in the UK. They use a range of data sources including Labour Force Surveys from 2003, 2006 and 2007 and data extracted from the Individual Controlled Access Microdata Sample (CAMS), which is a more detailed version of the 2001 Individual Sample of Anonymised

Records (SAR) file and which has to be accessed at ONS in a safe setting. Mitton and Aspinall produce a profile of the Black African population according to country of birth and demonstrate the diversity that exists not only in the size and demographic structure of its sub-populations but also in terms of family, household and religious characteristics. They also use data from other survey sources to investigate expressions of national and ethnic identity amongst those from different parts of Africa and they show that some groups, like the Kenyans, feel more British than others, such as the Somalis. In terms of language indicators, it is the Somalis who are the least integrated of all Black Africans whereas Zimbabweans and Nigerians face only slight language barriers. Recent work on Somalis in Sheffield (Valentine and Sporton, 2008) points to the need for policies to support young Somalis to integrate into the UK that enable them to retain and develop a strong sense of their own cultural identity and heritage whilst supporting them to integrate and access education, jobs and services.

Ethnicity and Health

Researchers and policy makers have been interested for several decades in health disparities between racial or ethnic groups with debates, often contentious, about whether observed differences in health disparities are explained by genetic or social differences (Braun, 2002). There is certainly no doubt that health disparities do occur between ethnic groups in western countries as indicated by data from the 2001 Census on the proportions of ethnic populations with limiting long-term illness (LLTI) in England. Figure 1.6 presents LLTI rates for four broad age groups ranked according to the percentage of the ethnic population with LLTI aged 65 and over. It shows that the highest age-specific rates of illness occur amongst Asians over the age of 50 and the lowest rates are experienced by the Chinese. Black Caribbean, Other Black and Mixed White-Black Caribbean also have relatively high rates of LLTI in the retirement (50–64) age range. Whilst half of the national aggregate population aged 65 and over and a quarter of those aged 5–64 have a LLTI, less than 10% of those aged 16–49 and 4% of those aged 0–15 are recorded as having a LLTI. Amongst the ethnic groups at younger ages, it is the Other Black, Mixed White-Black Caribbean and Pakistani ethnic groups that have the highest illness rates and the Chinese have significantly lower rates than the other groups.

Two chapters in this book explore different aspects of the relationship between ethnicity and health in more detail. Firstly, in Chapter 10, *Vanessa Higgins* and *Angela Dale* use data from the 2001 Health Survey for England (HSE) to consider the variations by ethnic group in levels of obesity and physical activity. The prevalence of obesity is increasing globally, with nearly half a billion of the world's population now considered to be overweight or obese and it is often hypothesised that the obesity epidemic is related both to dietary factors and to an increasingly sedentary lifestyle. Higgins and Dale show that whilst there are disparities by ethnic

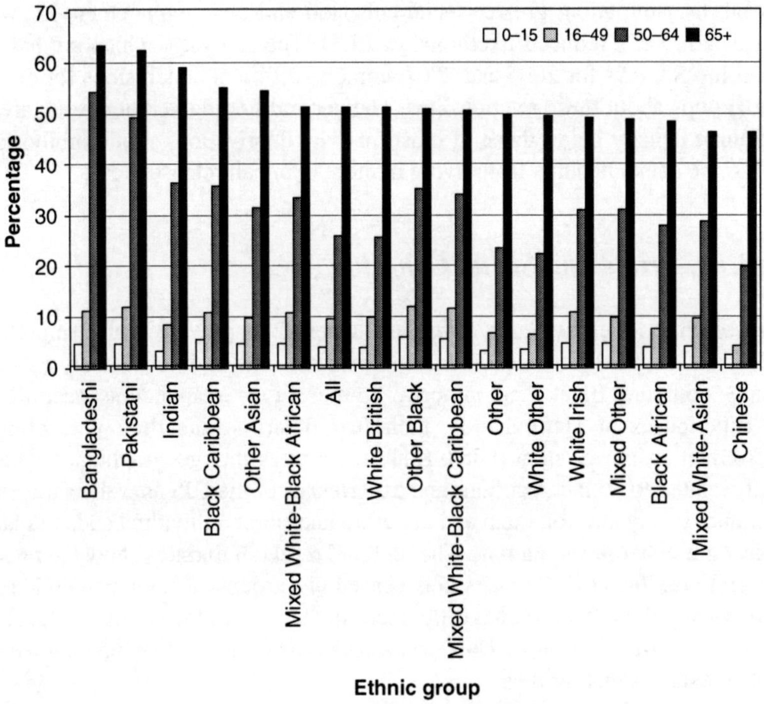

Fig. 1.6 Limiting long-term illness rates by ethnicity and broad age group, 2001 (Source: 2001 Census Standard Table 107)

group for those aged 16 and over, there are also major differences between males and females in both levels of obesity and physical activity. However, the relatively low levels of obesity in the Chinese population of England, consistent with the low LLTI shown for this group in Fig. 1.6 is not explained by particularly high levels of physical activity.

Whilst all ethnic minority populations contain individuals and families whose wealth enables them to choose to live in more affluent housing and neighbourhoods, the residential neighbourhoods of ethnic minority groups are usually more likely to be deprived, with poor quality housing and low quality facilities and services. It is logical to expect poorer health outcomes for those who live in more deprived areas, yet the paradox is that, on certain health measures, ethnic minorities living in areas of higher ethnic density do better than those living in areas of lower ethnic density and lower levels of multiple deprivation. This conundrum, known as the ethnic density effect, is the focus of Chapter 11 by *Mai Stafford, Laia Bécares* and *James Nazroo*. They explore different indicators of ethnic density and investigate whether ethnic density, measured as either co-ethnic density, overall ethnic minority density or perceived ethnic density, is associated with lower likelihood of racial discrimination, greater social cohesion and civic engagement as well as better health, i.e. a reduced likelihood of LLTI. The analyses, which are based on Citizenship Surveys for 2005 and 2007, come to different conclusions for different ethnic groups about these relationships. The general finding is that despite areas of high ethnic density being those of most material deprivation, ethnic minorities do derive some social benefits from living in more ethnically dense areas.

Ethnicity, Crime and Social Cohesion

The research reported by *Paula Kautt* in Chapter 12 employs British Crime Survey (BCS) data from 2001 to 2007 with multivariate and multilevel analyses to statistically compare Black and minority ethnic survey respondents according to their experiences of victimization, their fear of crime and their perceptions of the Criminal Justice System (CJS). Kautt recognises that geographical location is directly related to both perceptions and experiences of the CJS as well as the impact that ethnicity may have on them and therefore takes both individual and area factors into account in her investigations. The reported research findings show the presence of several significant differences between ethnic groups in their perceptions and experiences of the CJS as well as differences in the various factors that influence the responses of different groups. Thus, what works for White British may not work for Black or Asian British groups.

Data from the BCS are also used by *Joanna Taylor, Liz Twigg* and *John Mohan*, in Chapter 13 to investigate the links between ethnic heterogeneity and perceptions of social cohesion. Recent debates in the literature have suggested that increased diversity within western societies is associated with lower levels of social cohesion but, to date, there have been few studies which explore these issues for small geographical areas in the UK. The research presented in Chapter 13 explores this terrain by exploiting the rich resources available in the BCS which, as well as seeking information about people's experiences of crime, also poses a number of questions concerning unfavourable aspects of quality of life such as anti-social behaviour and reduced collective efficacy. The researchers have linked the BCS results to a number of external datasets in order to generate measures of neighbourhood diversity and socio-economic deprivation and then used multilevel modelling to determine the relative importance of various area characteristics in the explanation of perceptions of anti-social behaviour and low levels of collective efficacy. Particular attention is paid to unpacking the exact size of the effect of neighbourhood ethnic diversity, as opposed to neighbourhood disadvantage, on these perceptions of quality of life and the conclusions challenge the view that the impacts of heterogeneity are negative and that this causes ethnically diverse neighbourhood residents to 'hunker down' or, in the words of Stephen (Putnam, 2007, pp. 150–151), to *withdraw even from close friends, to expect the worst from their community and its leaders, to volunteer less, give less to charity and work on community projects less often, to register to vote less, to agitate for social reform more but have less faith they can actually make a difference, and to huddle unhappily in front of the television.* The modelling results indicate that, after allowing for socio-economic characteristics of both individuals and areas, ethnic diversity does not appear to make any difference to people's perceptions of the quality of life in the neighbourhoods where they live.

Ethnic Population Projection

The last chapter in the book reports on the progress that has been made by *Paul Norman, Phil Rees, Pia Wohland* and *Peter Boden*, in constructing a population projection model that generates projections of the future ethnic group populations of the UK at local authority level. This research team has developed new methods for estimating the components of demographic change for each of 16 ethnic groups (as used in the 2001 Census) for historical periods using a range of secondary data sources. The example estimates of ethnic age-specific fertility rates in 2001 demonstrate the different fertility behaviour of ethnic groups in Leeds compared with Bradford after a decade in which estimated total fertility

Table 1.2 Main data sets used in forthcoming chapters

Chapters	Author(s)	Data sources
2	Finney	Census 1991, 2001, CAMS; components of population change estimates
3	Sabater	Census 1991, 2001
4	Dubuc and Haskey	Census 2001; Labour Force Survey (LFS)
5	Feng, Boyle, van Ham and Raab	ONS Longitudinal Study (LS)
6	Stillwell and Hussain	2001 Census Standard and Commissioned Tables
7	Simon	2001 Census Commissioned Table
8	Shapira	Annual Population Survey 2006
9	Mitton and Aspinall	Labour Force Survey (LFS) Q3 2003, Q2 2005, Q3 2006 and Q4 2007; Census 2001, CAMS; Citizenship Survey, 2007; National Survey of Sexual Attitudes and Lifestyles II, 2000–2001 (NATSAL II); Millennium Cohort Study, 2006
10	Higgins and Dale	Health Survey for England (HSE) 2007; focus groups
11	Stafford, Becares and Nazroo	2001 Census; Citizenship Survey, 2005 and 2007
12	Kautt	British Crime Survey 2001–2006; 2001 Census
13	Taylor, Twigg and Mohan	British Crime Survey (BCS) 2006–2007; 2001 Census; Index of Deprivation (2007); Rural and Urban Classification 2001
14	Rees, Norman, Wohland, and Boden	1991 and 2001 Census Areas Statistics, samples of Anonymised Records and Commissioned Tables; Labour Force Survey (LFS); vital statistics; mid-year population estimates; Total International Migration (TIM) statistics; National Insurance (NINo) registrations; GP registrations

rates have also been changing. Similarly, there are intriguing variations between local authorities in life expectancies at birth between ethnic groups which will feed into the projections together with the estimates and internal and international migration derived from administrative and survey data sets. Furthermore, the model incorporates a mechanism for estimating the future number of children born to parents of different ethnic groups, an increasingly important proportion of the non-White population. This is a pioneering project but the final results – the projections themselves – will be of immense interest to national and regional organisations as well as local authorities whose current understanding of the ethnic complexion of the population is limited to what the 2001 Census has provided.

Secondary Data Sources

The preceding section indicates how the studies presented in this book report novel empirical findings that address some of the current debates on ethnicity and integration in the UK. They also represent a unique overview of how secondary data sets are being used to answer research questions on ethnic minorities using a range of quantitative analytical techniques. The contents of the book therefore reflect the fundamental aim of the *Understanding Population Trends and Processes* initiative: to conduct analysis on secondary data sources using quantitative methods rather than to collect primary data and employ qualitative methods. We conclude the chapter with a summary of the data sets that have been used by the authors of each chapter (Table 1.2), highlighting the continued importance of the population census, but also demonstrating the usefulness of a number of surveys.

References

Alba, R.D. and Nee, V. (2003) *Remaking the American Mainstream: Assimilation and the New Immigration*, Harvard University Press, Cambridge.

Braun, L. (2002) Race, ethnicity and health. Can genetics explain disparities? *Perspectives in Biology and Medicine*, 45(2): 159–174.

Brewer, C. and Suchan, T. (2001) *Mapping Census 2000: The geography of US diversity, Census Special Reports Series CENSR/01-1*. US Census Bureau, US Government Printing Office, Washington, DC.

Bulmer, M. (1996) The ethnic group question in the 1991 census of population in Coleman, D. and Salt, J. (eds.), *Ethnicity in the 1991 Census. Volume 1. Demographic Characteristics of the Ethnic Minority Populations*, Office of National Statistics, HMSO, London, pp. xi–xxix.

Cho, L.J., Retherford, R.D. and Choe, M.K. (1986) *The Own-Children Method of Fertility Estimation*, University of Hawaii Press, Honolulu.

Coleman, D. and Salt, J. (eds.) (1996) *Ethnicity in the 1991 Census, Volume 1: Demographic Characteristics of the Ethnic Minority Populations*, Office for National Statistics, London.

Duncan, O.B. and Duncan, B. (1955) A methodological analysis of segregation indexes, *American Sociological Review*, 20: 210–217.

Dwyer, C. and Bressey, C. (eds.) (2008) *New Geographies of Race and Racism*, Ashgate, Aldershot.

Farley, R., Steeh, C., Krysan, M., Jackson, T. and Reeves, K. (1994) Stereotypes and segregation: Neighborhoods in the Detroit area, *American Journal of Sociology*, 100: 750–780.

Finney, N. and Simpson, L. (2007) *Internal Migration and Ethnic Groups: Evidence for the UK from the 2001 Census* (CCSR Working Paper 2007-04), CCSR, University of Manchester, Manchester.

Finney, N. and Simpson, L. (2009) *Sleepwalking to Segregation? Challenging Myths About Race and Migration*, The Policy Press, Bristol.

Galster, G.C. (1990) White flight from racially integrated neighborhoods in the 1970s: The Cleveland experience, *Urban Studies*, 27: 385–399.

Gans, H. (1992, April) Second generation decline: Scenarios for the economic and ethnic futures of the post-1965 American immigrants, *Ethnic and Racial Studies*, 15: 173–191.

Glazer, N. and Moynihan, D.P. (1963) *Beyond the Melting Pot: The Negroes, Puerto Ricans, Jews, Italians, and Irish of New York City*, MIT Press, Cambridge.

Goering, J.M. (1978) Neighborhood tipping and racial transition, *Journal of the American Institute of Planners*, 44: 68–78.

Gorard, S. (2000) *Education and Social Justice*, University of Wales Press, Cardiff.

Gordon, M.M. (1964) *Assimilation in American Life: The Role of Race, Religion, and National Origins*, Oxford University Press, New York.

Hansen, K., Hawkes, D. and Joshi, H. (2009) The timing of motherhood, mothers' employment and child outcomes in Stillwell, J., Coast, E. and Kneale, D. (eds.), *Fertility, Living Arrangements, Care and Mobility, Understanding Population Trends and Processes*, Vol. 1, Springer, Dordrecht, pp. 59–80.

Hargreaves, A.G. (1995) *Immigration, Race and Ethnicity in Contemporary France*, Routledge, London.

Hatton, T.J. (2005) Explaining trends in UK immigration, *Journal of Population Economics*, 18(4): 719–740.

Hussain, S. and Stillwell, J. (2008) *Internal Migration of Ethnic Groups in England and Wales by Age and District Type* (Working Paper 08/03), School of Geography, University of Leeds, Leeds.

Jackson, P. (1987) *Race and Racism: Essays in Social Geography*, Allen and Unwin, London.

Johnston, R., Burgess, S., Wilson, D. and Harris, R. (2006) School and residential segregation: An analysis of variation across England's local education authorities, *Regional Studies*, 40(9): 973–990.

Johnston, R., Forrest, J. and Poulsen, M. (2002) Are there ethnic enclaves/ghettos in English cities? *Urban Studies*, 39(4): 591–618.

Johnston, R., Poulsen, M.F. and Forrest, J. (2005) On the measurement and meaning of residential segregation: A response to Simpson, *Urban Studies*, 42(7): 1221–1227.

Karn, V. (1997) *Ethnicity in the 1991 Census, Volume 4: Employment, Education and Housing Among the Ethnic Minority Populations of Britain*, Office for National Statistics, London.

Krysan, M. (2002) Whites who say they'd flee: Who are they and why would they leave? *Demography*, 39(4): 675–696.

Lee, B.A. and Wood, P.B. (1991) Is neighbourhood racial succession place-specific? *Demography*, 28(1): 21–40.

Li, Y. and Heath, A. (2009) Struggling onto the ladder; climbing the rungs: Employment and class positions of minority ethnic groups in Britain in Stillwell, J., Norman, P., Thomas, C. and Surridge, P. (eds.), *Spatial and Social Disparities Understanding Population Trends and Processes*, Vol. 2, Springer, Dordrecht.

Massey, D.S. and Denton, N.A. (1988) The dimensions of residential segregation, *Social Forces*, 67: 281–315.

Mateos, P. (2007) A review of name-based ethnicity classification methods and their potential in population studies, *Population Space and Place*, 13(4): 243–263.

ONS Census Advisory Group (2008) *2011 Census Questionnaire Content, AG(08)12*, ONS, London.

Peach, C. (ed.) (1996a) *Ethnicity in the 1991 Census, Volume 2: The Ethnic Minority Populations of Great Britain*, Office for National Statistics, London.

Peach, C. (1996b) Does Britain have ghettos? *Transactions of the Institute of British Geographers*, 22(1): 216–235.

Peach, C. (2007) *Slippery Segregation: Discovering or Manufacturing Ghettos?* (Working Paper), University of Manchester Institute for Social Change, Manchester.

Peach, C., Robinson, V. and Smith, S. (1981) *Ethnic Segregation in Cities*, Croom Helm, London.

Portes, A., Fernández-Kelly, P. and Haller, W. (2005) Segmented assimilation on the ground: The new second generation in early adulthood, *Ethnic and Racial Studies*, 28: 1000–1040.

Portes, A. and Zhou, M. (1993) The new second generation: Segmented assimilation and its variants, *The Annals of the American Academy of Political and Social Science*, 530: 74–96.

Poulsen, M. (2005, August 31–September 2) *The "new geography" of ethnicity in Britain?* Unpublished paper presented to the annual conference of the Institute of British Geographers and the Royal Geographical Society, London.

Poulsen, M. and Johnston, R. (2006) Ethnic residential segregation in England: Getting the right message across, *Environment and Planning A*, 38(12): 2195–2199.

Poulsen, M., Johnston, R. and Forrest, J. (2001) Intraurban ethnic enclaves: Introducing a knowledge-based classification method, *Environment and Planning A*, 33(11): 2071–2082.

Poulsen, M., Johnston, R. and Forrest, J. (2009) *Using Local Statistics to Portray Ethnic Residential Segregation in London* (CMPO Working Paper Series No. 09/213), Centre for Market and Public Organisation, University of Bristol, Bristol.

Putnam, R. (2007) E Pluribus Unum: Diversity and community in the twenty-first century. The 2006 Johan Skytte Prize Lecture, *Scandinavian Political Studies*, 305(2): 137–174.

Rankin, J. and Bhopal, R. (1999) Current census categories are not a good match for identity, *British Medical Journal*, 318(7199): 1696.

Ratcliffe, P. (ed.) (1996) *Ethnicity in the 1991 Census, Volume 3: Social Geography and Ethnicity in Britain: Geographical Spread, Spatial Concentration and Internal Migration*, Office for National Statistics, London.

Sabater, A. and Simpson, L. (2009) Enhancing the population census: A time series for sub-national areas with age, sex and ethnic group dimensions in England and Wales, 1991–2001, *Journal of Ethnic and Migration Studies*, 35(9): 1461–1477.

Salt, J., Latham, A. and Dobson, J. (2009) *On the Move? Labour Migration in Times of Recession. What Can We Learn from the Past?* (Policy Network Paper), Policy Network, London.

Simpson, L. (2004) Statistics of racial segregation: Measures, evidence and policy, *Urban Studies*, 41(3): 661–681.

Simpson, L. (2007) Ghettos of the mind: The empirical behaviour of indices of segregation and diversity, *Journal of the Royal Statistical Society: Series A (Statistics in Society)*, 170: 405–424.

Simpson, R. (2009) Delayed childbearing and childlessness in Stillwell, J., Coast, E. and Kneale, D. (eds.), *Fertility, Living Arrangements, Care and Mobility, Understanding Population Trends and Processes*, Vol. 1, Springer, Dordrecht, pp. 23–40.

Smallwood, S. and Chamberlain, J. (2005) Replacement fertility: What has it been and what does it mean? *Population Trends*, 119: 16–27.

Smith, S. and Ratcliffe, A. (2009) Women's education and childbearing: A growing divide in Stillwell, J., Coast, E. and Kneale, D. (eds.), *Fertility, Living Arrangements, Care and Mobility, Understanding Population Trends and Processes*, Vol. 1, Springer, Dordrecht, pp. 41–58.

Stafford, M., Bécares, L. and Nazroo, J. (2009) Objective and perceived ethnic density and health: Findings from a United Kingdom general population survey, *American Journal of Epidemiology*, 170(4): 484–493.

Stillwell, J., Coast, E. and Kneale, D. (eds.) (2009) *Fertility, Living Arrangements, Care and Mobility, Understanding Population Trends and Processes*, Vol. 1, Springer, Dordrecht.

Stillwell, J. and Hussain, S. (2010) Exploring the ethnic dimension of internal migration in Great Britain using migration effectiveness and spatial connectivity, *Journal of Ethnic and Migration Studies*, Forthcoming.

Summers, D. (2009, January 30) Brown stands by British jobs for British workers remark, *The Guardian*.
UK Statistics Authority (2009) *Migration Statistics: The Way Ahead* Report 4, UKSA, London.
Valentine, G. and Sporton, D. (2008) Developing identity: Somali children in Sheffield, *The Yorkshire and Humber Regional Review*, 18(2): 11–12.
Vertovec, S. (2006) *The Emergence of Super-Diversity in Britain* (Working Paper), COMPAS, University of Oxford, Oxford.
Vickers, D., Rees, P. and Birkin, M. (2003) *A New Classification of UK Local Authorities Using 2001 Census Key Statistics* (Working Paper 03/3), School of Geography, University of Leeds, Leeds.
Whitehead, T. (2009, August 28) Baby boom Britain, *The Daily Telegraph*, 1.
Yorkshire and Humber Regional Migration Partnership (2009) *Finding Sanctuary, Enriching Yorkshire and Humber – The Regional Integration Strategy for Refugees and Asylum Seekers 2009–2011*, YHRMP, Leeds.
Zubrinsky, C.L. (2000) Neighborhood racial composition preferences: Evidence from a multiethnic metropolis, *Social Problems*, 47: 379–407.

Chapter 2
Ethnic Group Population Change and Integration: A Demographic Perspective on Ethnic Geographies

Nissa Finney

Introduction

The changing ethnic composition of Britain's neighbourhoods has attracted considerable public policy attention in the first decade of the twenty-first century. Urban disturbances in several British towns in the summer of 2001, and terrorist attacks in the USA in September of the same year, ushered in a new paradigm of ethnic relations policy that replaced strategies of multiculturalism that had characterised the British approach in the 1990s (Kalra and Kapoor, 2009; Kundnani, 2007; Robinson, 2005). Concern shifted from meeting the needs of diverse groups to preventing 'parallel lives' along ethnic or religious lines through strategies of community cohesion (Cantle, 2001; CoIC, 2007). An important dimension of the new approach was the emphasis on place-based community and concern with physical separation or residential segregation. The concern was that residential separation would reduce mixing and lead to poorer inter-ethnic understanding and greater inter-ethnic conflict. In many ways, the ideas informing the community cohesion agenda harked back to theories of straight-line assimilation (Alba and Nee, 1997) – that social integration of minorities is directly and linearly linked to residential integration.

At the same time, observations were made about the continued clustering of minority ethnic populations which was interpreted as separation of ethnic groups; a flight of the White majority and retreat of the minority groups. The discourses of flight, retreat and parallel lives quickly became ingrained in policy circles, despite evidence of similar housing experiences and aspirations of majority and minority populations (Harries et al., 2008; Phillips, 2006), increasing inter-ethnic understanding (Ford, 2008) and decreasing residential segregation (Simpson, 2007). Moral panic and myths about race, migration and segregation characterised policy and public debates (Finney and Simpson, 2009a).

N. Finney (✉)
School of Social Sciences, The Cathie Marsh Centre for Census and Survey Research (CCSR), The University of Manchester, Manchester M13 9PL, UK
e-mail: Nissa.Finney@manchester.ac.uk

J. Stillwell, M. van Ham (eds.), *Ethnicity and Integration*, Understanding Population Trends and Processes 3, DOI 10.1007/978-90-481-9103-1_2,

The discourses of retreat and conflict have been challenged by research on the demographics of ethnic group population change which has sought to understand the processes underlying local population dynamics. Simpson et al. (2008) suggested a demographic explanation of population change: a sequence of clustering and dispersal of immigrant-origin populations as these populations mature in their age structure and pass through demographic events of the life course. Finney and Simpson (2009b) investigated these hypotheses for districts in Britain and found clustering of minority populations due mainly to natural growth, an in situ excess of births over deaths, not unexpected given the young age structures of ethnic minority populations. Simultaneously, Britain's minority groups are migrating from the areas in which they are most concentrated to elsewhere in Britain and this is evident in the 1990s and 2000s, at district and ward scales (Simpson and Finney, 2009; Simon, 2010; Stillwell and Hussain, 2010).

The defining characteristic of a demographic approach is the decomposition of population change (for a specified area and time period) into four component processes: people being born, people dying, people migrating into the area and people migrating out of the area. This is what demographers know as the demographic balancing equation. It has been argued that the meaning of residential patterns of ethnic groups in Britain, and the meaning of changes in those patterns, requires an understanding of how the components of population change act together (Finney and Simpson, 2009b; Simpson et al., 2008). Furthermore, demographic differences between ethnic groups in Britain, particularly in their age structures as a result of the timing of the main waves of immigration, mean that the dynamics of population change may differ between ethnic groups.

This chapter builds on this emerging body of work about the demographics of neighbourhood ethnic group population change. It contributes to the debate in several ways: by introducing original ward level estimates of demographic components of population change which overcome deficiencies of existing data sources; by analysing population change at the ward scale, a smaller geographical level than has previously been investigated; and by introducing age into the analyses. The chapter demonstrates that ward level population change is a result of in situ natural growth plus dispersal through migration. It shows how ethnic group population dynamics vary by age thus demonstrating the importance of understanding demographic change across different stages of the life course, a point also made in relation to segregation in the following chapter by Sabater (2010). The evidence in this chapter reinforces the message that ethnic conflict or divergence cannot be assumed to explain, or be a result of, geographical patterns of ethnic group population change.

This introduction is followed by an outline of the data and definitions used in the chapter with a focus on the ward level estimates of components of population change. These components are then examined for England and Wales as a whole, followed by the example of neighbourhood population dynamics in the London ward of Southall Broadway in the 1990s. The next section presents an investigation of processes of population change in neighbourhoods of differing ethnic minority concentration, with population dynamics distinguished by ethnic group and age. The chapter concludes with a discussion of the key findings.

Measuring Neighbourhood Ethnic Group Population Change

In order to assess neighbourhood ethnic group population dynamics, measures are needed of the components of population change and the geographical areas of interest must be defined. This section describes the derivation of ward level components of change estimates which are the basis for the analysis in this chapter, and explains the categorisation of wards into groups representing minority ethnic concentration.

In the UK, there are limited data on the demographics of ethnic groups for small areas which explains our limited knowledge of the demographic dynamics of population change. Birth and death registrations do not record ethnic group and although migration data by ethnic group have been available in the census of 1991 and 2001, there are weaknesses too with these data. In particular, they measure migration only in the year prior to the census, give no measure of emigration, provide migration measures for broad ethnic groups only and do not allow analysis of migration by ethnic group and age simultaneously.

This study therefore produced estimates of the demographic components of population change. Well established demographic techniques were used to decompose population change over the inter-censal decade, 1991–2001, into estimates of births, deaths and net migration (Edmonston and Michalowski, 2004; Rowland, 2002). These techniques were developed for application to ethnic groups, small areas and the data available in the UK. The resultant dataset is particularly original in its estimation of the age structure of the net impact of migration over a decade with emigration included. The method has the advantage of being applicable at all geographical scales. A disadvantage of the method, however, is that it provides statistics of net migration; details of inflows, outflows, origins and destinations are lacking. This section provides a brief overview of the estimation procedures; for full technical details, see Simpson et al. (2008).

The demographic balancing equation, that population change is the sum of natural increase (births minus deaths) and net migration (arrivals minus departures), can be rearranged to express net migration as a residual: (arrivals–departures) = population change – (births–deaths). The components of population change estimates use this equation to calculate net migration as the part of population change which is not due to births or deaths (natural change). Population change is easily obtained from censuses and other population estimates in the UK. The challenge to estimate net migration during the period is thus reduced to measuring natural change and subtracting it from population change.

Vital statistics of recorded births and deaths are not available for ethnic groups in Britain as they are in some other countries (e.g. in the USA, Voss et al., 2004). However, estimates can be made by the survival method which deducts from the population an estimate of the number of people in each age-sex-ethnic-area category who survived over the defined period (1991–2001 in this case) to estimate deaths. Survival ratios from life tables can be applied from the starting population (forward survival) or the end point population (reverse survival) (Rowland, 2002). Fertility rates are used to estimate births.

An adaptation of the survival approach was used in this research, and applied to each ethnic group in each of the 8,797 electoral wards of England and Wales, for males and females and each single year of age. Wards in Britain on average have a population of 6,500. The estimation involved five stages that take into account differences between ethnic groups and localities. First, the number of births into each age cohort that will be aged between 0 and 9 at 2001 were estimated using child-woman ratios in 1991 and the number of children in 2001. Second, these births estimates were scaled so that when summed across ethnic groups they are consistent with official vital statistics data by ward, age and sex for the relevant year. Third, an initial estimation of the number of deaths was made using an average of the forward and reverse survival methods. Fourth, these deaths estimates were scaled so that when summed across ethnic groups they are consistent with total deaths from official vital statistics for each ward for the period 1991–2001. Fifth, final estimates of net migration were generated using the demographic balancing equation described above. This procedure gives an estimate of births, deaths and net migration for each ethnic group-ward-sex-age combination.

The success of this method depends partly upon the quality of the measure of population change. The research presented here used estimates produced by Sabater and Simpson (2009), which give populations for wards of England, Wales and Scotland by sex, single year of age and ethnic group for 1991 and 2001. Each estimate is based on census data but takes into account the problems of non-response, alteration to the enumeration of students, timing adjustment between census day and mid-year, changes to the ethnic group census categories and ward boundary changes (harmonisation of 1991 small areas to 2001 boundaries using proportional allocation based on geographical conversion tables). For the purposes of comparison over time, the population of published ethnic groups at each of the two time points have been aggregated to eight compatible categories: White, Caribbean, African, Indian, Pakistani, Bangladeshi, Chinese and Other, with the 2001 Mixed groups being included in the residual Other category. The first seven of these groups are the most coherent and stable classifications from 1991 to 2001 (Office for National Statistics, 2006; Simpson and Akinwale, 2007). The residual eighth category is used for completeness but is very diverse and of different composition in the 2 years.

There is much debate about the meaning of census ethnic group categories and their appropriateness for understanding diversity in the UK (Aspinall, 2000). The eight groups used in this chapter are defined by a combination of colour and national origin and are internally diverse. Most broadly, they can be seen to represent the main groups of immigrants who arrived in Britain after the Second World War, predominantly labour migrants from elsewhere in the Commonwealth (the Indian sub-continent and the Caribbean). These migrants have been followed by chain migration from the same origins, including migration of family members. The African and Chinese groups can be considered more diverse in terms of their immigrant streams; they comprise established immigrants and newer immigrants, particularly young adults migrating since the 1990s for work and study and, in the case of Africans, refugees. The ethnic categories used here can by no means be considered a representation of the essential character of a group of people. However, an understanding of their immigration history and resulting demographics is helpful in examining sub-national population change.

Electoral wards are the scale of analysis in this chapter, as described above. In Tables 2.5 and 2.6, they have been grouped into five categories based on their percentage of non-White (or ethnic minority) population. This division is such that each quintile of wards has the same non-White population but in differing concentrations (Table 2.1). Thus, there are a small number of wards in the 'highest non-White concentration' category compared to the 'lowest non-White concentration' category. On average, wards in England and Wales have 5.4% non-White population. The lowest minority concentration wards, of which there are 7,426, have, on average, 2.4% non-White population. The highest minority concentration wards, of which there are 101, have, on average 65.0% ethnic minority population, with a maximum of 87.7%. It is worth noting that even the wards with the highest ethnic minority population proportion are diverse in that they comprise a number of different ethnic groups. For the ethnic minority populations, wards of highest minority concentration are in London, such as in the districts of Brent, Harrow, Lambeth and Newham. Indians are also in high concentration in wards of Leicester; Pakistanis and Bangladeshis in Bradford; and Chinese in Birmingham and Manchester.

The areas of high minority concentration tend to be urban areas, very often close to urban centres. This is a result of the geographical patterns of initial settlement of immigrants to urban areas where affordable housing and work was available. At least two thirds of districts in the high and highest ethnic minority concentration categories are in London or principal provincial cities. In comparison, half of the districts in the lowest ethnic minority concentration category are remote, rural or mixed urban and rural. There is a significant Pearson correlation of 0.6 between districts classed by increasing minority concentration and districts classed by increasing urbanness (using the OPCS classification). It is important, therefore, when interpreting population change in relation to ethnic minority concentration, to consider the role of urban form and whether this offers an explanation as plausible, or more plausible, than ethnic minority concentration.

Table 2.1 White and minority composition of quintiles of non-White concentration for wards of England and Wales

Quintile of non-White concentration	2001 population		Percentage of population (mean for wards)		No. of wards
	White	Minorities	White	Minorities	
Lowest	36,736,420	922,508	97.6	2.4	7,426
Low	6,681,110	922,501	87.9	12.1	790
Medium	2,580,015	923,261	73.6	26.4	298
High	1,255,000	924,238	57.6	42.4	182
Highest	494,810	920,115	35.0	65.0	101

Drivers of Ethnic Group Population Change for England and Wales

We begin with the national picture of population change and an examination of the contributions of natural change and migration to the changing diversity of England and Wales in the 1990s. Table 2.2 gives the components of population change from 1991 to 2001 for England and Wales for eight ethnic groups. The first row, for the population as a whole, confirms a picture of population growth that results both from a net gain from migration and a net gain from excess births over deaths. Migration in this table is international migration, the balance of movements into and out of England and Wales including flows to and from Scotland and Northern Ireland. In relation to population size, natural growth is a greater contributor to population growth than net immigration. This is also the case for the White, Caribbean, Indian, Pakistani, Bangladeshi and Other groups. However, the relative size of the contributions of natural change and migration varies between ethnic groups. Over the decade natural change was responsible for population growth of around 20% for the African, Pakistani, Bangladeshi and Other groups compared with 0.06% for the White population whose rate of natural growth was lowest. A considerable range is also evident in the net international migration rates, from a loss of 7% of the Caribbean population through a small growth of 0.4% of the White population to population increase of 30% due to migration for the African population.

It is clear from Table 2.2, then, that each ethnic group has a different demographic story which is shaping its population change nationally and locally. The ethnic groups that have the largest proportions of immigrants – African, Chinese and Other – are growing rapidly both through the immigration itself and immigrants having children. The more established immigrant-origin groups – Indian, Pakistani and Bangladeshi – gain less through immigration and greatly through natural growth as the second generations reproduce. The youthful Caribbean population gains through births exceeding deaths but loses through emigration.

This demographic story cannot be fully understood without attention to age variation. Indeed, it is well established that migration varies through the life course, as does mortality. Figure 2.1 illustrates age variation in total net migration by presenting mean rates for wards of England and Wales for the inter-censal decade by ethnic group. With the exception perhaps of the Caribbean group, the age-migration profile of each ethnic group takes approximately the same shape, peaking in young adulthood from relative stability at other ages. The level of migration, however, varies considerably between ethnic groups with the White and South Asian groups having lower rates than the recent immigrant groups of African and Chinese origin, particularly in the young adult ages.

The pattern for the Caribbean group is interesting because it is exceptional. We have already seen that, on balance, Caribbeans are moving out of England and Wales. Figure 2.1 tells us that this out-migration is of people of family ages (aged under 20 and 30–45 in 2001) and retirement ages (aged 65 and over in 2001). It is possible to speculate that this emigration represents ‘return’ migration to the Caribbean.

Table 2.2 Components of population change for ethnic groups in wards of England and Wales, 1991–2001

	Population in 1991	Population in 2001	Births	Deaths	Natural change (births – deaths)	Net migration 1991–2001	Rate of natural change (%)	Rate of net migration (%)
Total	50, 748, 033	52, 359, 979	6, 470, 671	5, 552, 044	918, 627	693, 319	1.19	0.9
White	47, 429, 019	47, 747, 355	5, 460, 812	5, 415, 271	45, 541	272, 795	0.06	0.38
Caribbean	569, 621	572, 212	96, 703	31, 309	65, 393	−62, 802	7.64	−7.34
African	255, 336	494, 668	98, 667	7, 950	90, 717	148, 615	18.05	29.57
Indian	891, 827	1, 053, 302	178, 946	39, 719	139, 227	22, 247	9.82	1.57
Pakistani	494, 973	727, 726	192, 336	18, 621	173, 715	59, 039	20.23	6.87
Bangladeshi	176, 912	286, 693	88, 574	5, 911	82, 663	27, 118	25.81	8.47
Chinese	173, 184	233, 346	32, 726	6, 887	25, 839	34, 322	8.91	11.84
Other	757, 161	1, 244, 677	321, 907	26, 377	295, 530	191, 985	21.42	13.92

Source: Components of population change estimates. Rates use the mean of 1991 and 2001 populations as the denominator.

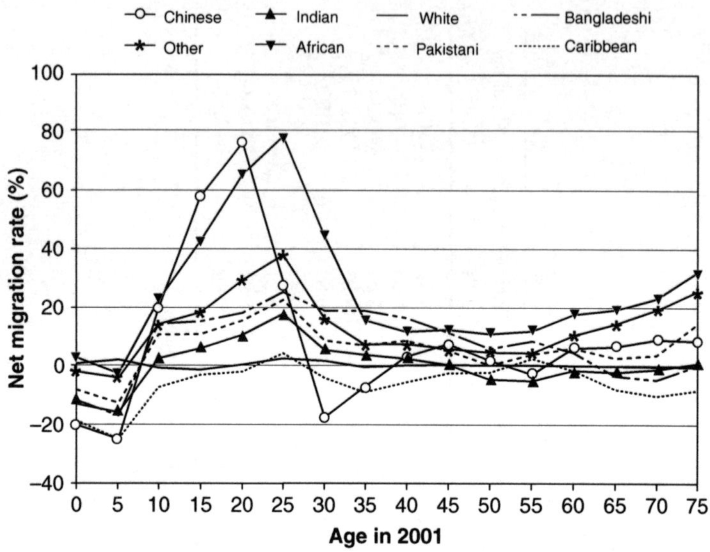

Fig. 2.1 Mean net migration (international and internal) rates for wards in England and Wales by age and ethnic group, 1991–2001 (Source: Components of population change estimates. Rates use the mean of 1991 and 2001 populations as the denominator)

Southall Broadway: An Illustration of Neighbourhood Ethnic Group Population Dynamics

At the national level demographic variation in population change of ethnic groups can be seen. However, the complexity of population change and the benefits of devising detailed demographic estimates of components of change are particularly evident when sub-national patterns are analysed. Here, neighbourhood population dynamics are illustrated with the example of the ward of Southall Broadway in the district of Ealing in west London. Southall Broadway has been chosen because it is the ward in Britain with the smallest proportion of White residents (12%). In the nineteenth and early twentieth centuries, the area was important as a transport link on the Great Western Railway, the primary road from Oxford to London and the Great Union Canal from Birmingham to London. This position led to the development of brick and ceramics industries, flour mills and chemical plants. Southall Broadway has a long history of migration from outside England, attracting Welsh migrants in the 1920s and 1930s and, from the 1950s, migrants from India who were employed in nearby industries including the rapidly expanding Heathrow airport. The largest cultural group is Indian Punjabis and this is reflected in the local facilities such that the area is colloquially known as ‘Little India’. 37% of the population is Sikh and a further 20% Muslim, Hindu and Christian respectively.

Tables 2.3 and 2.4 and Figs. 2.2 and 2.3 present ethnic group population dynamics for the decade 1991–2001 for the ward of Southall Broadway. Table 2.3 shows

Table 2.3 Components of population change for ethnic groups in the ward of Southall Broadway, 1991–2001

Ethnic group	Population 1991	1991 population (%)	Population 2001	2001 population (%)	Population change	Rate of population change (%)	Natural change	Net migration
White	1,481	9.9	1,651	12.2	170	10.8	−240	410
Caribbean	513	3.4	387	2.9	−126	−28.1	−27	−99
African	380	2.5	595	4.4	215	44.2	−8	223
Indian	9,670	64.6	7,211	53.4	−2,460	−29.1	−439	−2,020
Pakistani	1,744	11.6	1,480	11.0	−265	−16.4	−42	−223
Bangladeshi	63	0.4	84	0.6	21	28.8	−2	23
Chinese	6	0.0	40	0.3	34	145.3	−2	36
Other	1,123	7.5	2,050	15.2	927	58.4	−44	970
Total	14,981	100.0	13,497	100.0	−1,484		−804	−680

Source: Components of population change estimates. Rates use the mean of 1991 and 2001 populations as the denominator.

Table 2.4 Percentage of 2001 population of Southall Broadway ward in each age category for White, Indian and Pakistani

Age group	White	Indian	Pakistani
0–9	15.95	12.19	17.26
10–19	10.93	14.75	19.51
20–29	17.48	18.88	18.34
30–39	20.27	17.71	18.04
40–49	10.10	13.41	11.25
50–59	7.72	8.75	8.16
60–69	7.42	8.42	6.25
70–79	6.69	4.81	1.03
80 +	4.24	1.08	0.17

Source: Components of population change estimates.

the population change over the decade for each ethnic group and how that change is made up of natural change (the balance of births and deaths) and net migration (the balance of migration into and out of the ward). The natural change and net migration figures are also displayed in Fig. 2.2. Table 2.4 gives the age structure of the ward's 2001 White, Indian and Pakistani populations. The line graph presents net migration over the decade by ethnic group and age (Fig. 2.3).

In 1991, Southall Broadway's population of around 15,000 people was 65% Indian, 12% Pakistani, 10% White and around 13% of other ethnic groups. Over the 1990s, the ward lost population (around 1,500 people) and the balance of the ethnic groups shifted such that the diversity of the ward increased. By 2001, therefore, 53% of the population were Indian, 15% from Other ethnic groups (which includes the Mixed categories), 12% White and 11% Pakistani (Table 2.3). The ward's

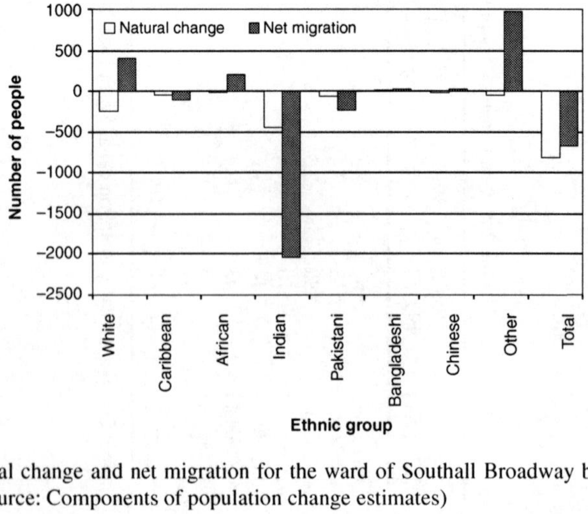

Fig. 2.2 Natural change and net migration for the ward of Southall Broadway by ethnic group, 1991–2001 (Source: Components of population change estimates)

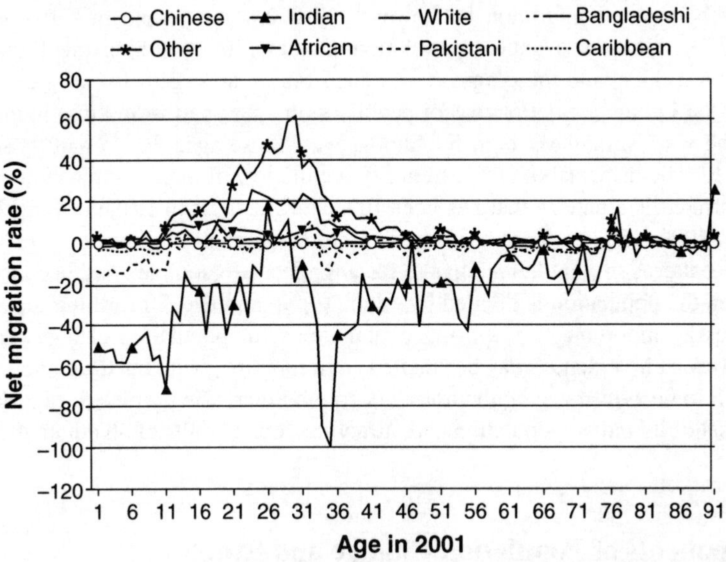

Fig. 2.3 Mean net migration (international and internal) rates for White, Indian and Pakistani ethnic groups for the ward of Southall Broadway by age, 1991–2001 (Source: Components of population change estimates. Rates use the mean of 1991 and 2001 populations as the denominator)

population is youthful as well as diverse; a quarter of the White and Indian and a third of the Pakistani population were under 20 years old in 2001. The White population is the most elderly in structure with 18% of White people in the ward over the age of 60 (compared with 14% of Indians and 7% of Pakistanis) (Table 2.4).

The White, African, Bangladeshi, Chinese and Other populations of Southall Broadway grew during the 1990s. Although each of these groups lost population through natural decrease, the loss was outweighed by gains of in-migrants, either from elsewhere in England and Wales or from other countries (Fig. 2.2). Migration gains were particularly high for the White, African and Other populations and, as Fig. 2.3 shows, were of people aged in their 20s and 30s. This suggests the ward is a destination for recent in-migrants and for young White, African and Other adults already residing in England and Wales wishing to relocate to western London.

Over the decade, there was a decrease in the Caribbean, Indian and Pakistani populations of Southall Broadway. This was a result of more people dying than being born in the ward and a result of more people leaving the ward (for destinations elsewhere in Britain or abroad) than arriving in it. Loss due to migration was particularly high for the Indian population representing over 80% of population loss for this group, at a rate of 24%. This pattern of out-migration of Indians and in-migration of other groups is consistent with theories of dispersal from residential co-ethnic concentrations and increased mixing as a result of migration.

The balance of migration is, however, different for people of different ages (Fig. 2.3). All groups gained population in their 20s including the Indian and Pakistani groups, and these ages represented the greatest gain for all groups. The loss of the Indian population was of people of all ages apart from those in their late 20s, and was particularly high for family ages, those aged 30–45 and those aged under 20. The dispersal of ethnic minority populations from areas in which they are concentrated is a pattern that has been found for districts in Britain (Simpson and Finney, 2009) and is evident here for the ward of Southall Broadway.

The patterns of population change for any place are complex and become more so when the population is divided by ethnic group and age. Unearthing these complexities is important in proposing explanations for population change. Southall Broadway, at first glance, may be labelled an immigrant ghetto but the demographics reveal it to be a diverse neighbourhood becoming increasingly mixed, experiencing dispersal of its Indian population and attracting young adults of all ethnic groups.

Components of Population Change and Ethnic Minority Concentration

The growth, or not, of concentrations of ethnic minority populations has been a central concern of community cohesion debates. Indeed, community cohesion strategies have sought to combat perceived problems of 'retreat' into ethnic enclaves. But does the evidence at the local level show movement towards co-ethnic concentrations or is there dispersal and increasing diversity, as in Southall Broadway? Table 2.5 presents components of population change for wards grouped according to their concentration of ethnic minority (non-White) population. Such a categorisation is useful because it enables assessment of in situ growth and dispersal, a theory that has been put forward to explain population change in minority concentrations defined at larger geographical scales (Simpson et al., 2008).

The net migration pattern of the White population represents movement away from wards of highest minority ethnic concentration and towards areas of lowest minority ethnic concentration. This is dispersal from minority concentrations reflecting the well documented processes of suburbanisation and counterurbanisation of the White population (Champion, 1989). Minorities taken as a whole are moving in the same direction: net migration is greatest to areas of lowest minority concentration and least to areas of highest minority concentration. Dispersal is also clear for the Indian and Chinese populations. The pattern for other groups is less evident. Pakistanis have highest migration to areas of lowest minority concentration; but second highest migration to areas of highest minority concentration. Bangladeshis have highest migration to wards of high and highest minority ethnic concentration. Caribbean population is lost from all categories of ward and especially so for wards of medium minority concentration. The African group is the only group for whom the lowest migration is to the wards of lowest ethnic minority concentration.

Table 2.5 Components of population change for wards grouped by minority ethnic concentration by ethnic group, (a) counts and (b) rates, 1991–2001

Quintile	White	Minorities	Caribbean	African	Indian	Pakistani	Bangladeshi	Chinese	Other
(a) Net migration									
Lowest	553,839	186,177	−387	14,090	23,794	26,642	7,499	17,525	97,013
Low	−24,151	93,880	−9,663	23,182	13,593	11,577	487	10,089	44,614
Medium	−54,075	43,220	−22,543	33,614	5,666	4,758	1,209	4,626	15,891
High	−111,871	54,737	−19,601	53,031	−6,260	3,171	7,760	1,986	14,650
Highest	−90,947	42,510	−10,609	24,699	−14,546	12,890	10,163	96	19,817
(a) Natural change									
Lowest	29,439	171,669	6,351	7,220	23,158	16,220	10,593	10,296	97,832
Low	35,832	174,159	12,823	12,852	30,889	34,013	12,102	6,086	65,392
Medium	719	178,024	17,021	25,149	24,199	35,073	15,702	4,804	56,075
High	−3,961	178,948	18,891	30,613	23,797	36,819	18,158	3,248	47,422
Highest	−16,489	170,287	10,308	14,882	37,184	51,590	26,108	1,405	28,810
(b) Net migration rate (%)									
Lowest	1.5	25.0	−0.6	35.2	16.2	43.6	24.4	20.5	30.8
Low	−0.4	11.9	−9.4	42.9	6.4	9.9	1.6	20.4	20.2
Medium	−2.1	5.3	−16.3	33.6	3.2	3.9	3.0	13.1	7.8
High	−8.5	6.8	−11.8	43.2	−3.9	2.5	15.5	8.7	9.3
Highest	−16.6	5.2	−10.8	42.3	−5.2	7.0	12.7	0.9	19.0
(b) Natural change rate (%)									
Lowest	0.1	23.1	9.8	18.1	15.8	26.5	34.4	12.0	31.1
Low	0.5	22.1	12.5	23.8	14.5	28.9	38.8	12.3	29.5
Medium	0.0	21.9	12.3	25.1	13.8	29.0	39.4	13.6	27.7
High	−0.3	22.2	11.3	25.0	15.0	28.8	36.3	14.2	30.0
Highest	−3.0	20.9	10.5	25.5	13.4	28.0	32.6	13.9	27.7

Source: Components of population change estimates. Rates use the mean of 1991 and 2001 populations as the denominator. Minorities are all non-White groups.

Natural change is positive in all ward types for all groups apart from for Whites in wards of high and highest minority concentration. For Whites, the patterns suggest suburbanisation of the reproductive population. For the Indian, Pakistani and Bangladeshi groups, natural growth is greatest in absolute terms in areas of highest ethnic minority concentration. For the Chinese group, natural change decreases as minority concentration increases, perhaps reflecting the more dispersed nature of the reproductive population with high proportions of urban populations being students.

The patterns described are largely confirmed by the rates of net migration and natural change which clarify the process of dispersal for Whites and minorities (Table 2.5b). For all minority groups apart from African, net migration rates are greatest for the wards of lowest ethnic minority concentration and these rates are high (up to 44% growth). The rate of natural population loss for Whites is greatest from areas of highest minority concentration; the rate of natural growth for minorities is high – around 20% – and varies little by category of ward. For individual minority groups, natural growth shows no clear patterns by concentration of minorities. Rates are no higher in wards of highest ethnic minority concentration than in other wards for any ethnic group.

Examination of components of population change for wards classified by ethnic concentration has revealed patterns of dispersal and confirmed the importance of natural growth of non-White populations in wards throughout England and Wales. However, the processes of natural change and migration are age specific: generally it is the elderly who die and those in their 20s and 30s who produce children; and young adults of each ethnic group are considerably more mobile than other age groups (Fig. 2.1; Finney, submitted). There are also different geographies of migration for different age groups (Finney and Champion, 2008; Plane and Jurjevich, 2009), with young adults tending to locate in urban areas whilst other ages migrate away from cities. Given that there is a high correlation between urbanness and ethnic minority concentration for wards in England and Wales it is important to consider migration patterns by age.

Table 2.6 presents net migration for wards classified by concentration of ethnic minority population (as in Table 2.5) for Whites and minorities, for young adults and people of other ages taken together. Migration as a component of population change is focused on here as this is the main driver of changing geographical patterns, particularly for young adults who are the most mobile age group. Net migration from the components of change estimates has been decomposed into internal migration and international migration in the final two columns of Table 2.6. This decomposition should be read as indicative because of discrepancies in the three measures of migration used in the table.

The table reveals two important findings. First, the pattern of dispersal/suburbanisation which has been seen for the White and minority populations as a whole is evident for children and older adults but not for young adults. Second, there is not a clear pattern of international migration contributing to the growth of minority populations in areas in which they are concentrated more than other areas and for young adults both White and minority, immigration is greatest to the areas of least ethnic minority concentration.

Table 2.6 Migration for neighbourhoods grouped by minority ethnic concentration by ethnic group and age, 1991–2001

	Total migration		Migration within Britain		International migration (indicative estimate)	
Quintile	White	Minorities	White	Minorities	White	Minorities
Young adults						
Lowest	−65,914	5,883	−73,300	−2,467	7,400	8,400
Low	34,527	7,220	29,733	1,900	4,800	5,300
Medium	25,755	6,787	21,733	833	4,000	6,000
High	10,541	5,255	8,300	1,667	2,200	3,600
Highest	3,258	4,119	13,533	−1,933	−10,300	6,000
Non young adult						
Lowest	121,298	12,735	76,767	6,567	44,500	6,200
Low	−36,942	2,168	−13,967	4,200	−23,000	−2,000
Medium	−31,162	−2,465	−15,767	−1,433	−15,400	−1,000
High	−21,728	219	−31,867	−1,100	10,100	1,300
Highest	−12,353	132	−15,167	−8,233	2,800	8,400

Sources: For Total Migration: Components of change estimates, 1991–2001 divided by ten to approximate a yearly figure. Based on wards of England and Wales. White is all Census White groups; Minorities are all others (see Simpson and Akinwale, 2007). For Migration within Britain: 2001 Census CAMS, 2000–2001 scaled to 100% from figures for 3% sample. Based on districts of Britain. White is White British; Minorities are all non-White groups. Young adults are aged 18–29; non young adults are all other ages taken together. International migration has been estimated by subtracting migration within Britain from total migration and is only indicative of patterns due to the discrepancies in the total and internal migration measures as described above. Figures have therefore been rounded to the nearest 100.

The areas of lowest ethnic minority concentration, which can be alternatively seen as the most White areas and also the most rural areas, overall lost White young adults, gained Whites of other ages and gained minorities of all ages due to migration. This was a result of young adults, White and minority, moving from the lowest minority concentration neighbourhoods to elsewhere in Britain whilst those areas gained young adults, both White and minority, from abroad. At the same time, the lowest minority concentration areas gained Whites and Minorities of ages under 18 and over 29 as a result of migration from elsewhere in Britain (suburbanisation) and from abroad.

Highest minority concentration areas gained White and minority young adults. For Whites, this was a result of net in-migration from elsewhere in Britain (internal urbanisation) and net emigration. For minorities this was a result of net out-migration to elsewhere in Britain together with net immigration. For non young adult ages, areas of highest minority concentration lost Whites and gained minorities. This resulted from out-migration of Whites and minorities to elsewhere in Britain and net gain of whites and minorities from abroad.

Conclusions

This chapter has used original estimates of components of population change by ethnic group and age for wards in England and Wales to examine processes of sub-national ethnic group population change from a demographic perspective. England and Wales's changing ethnic geography in the 1990s is a result of local dynamics of natural change and migration which together paint a picture of minority concentrations growing through in situ natural growth and becoming increasingly diverse through dispersal and suburbanisation of existing residents and arrival of newcomers through young adult urbanisation and immigration. The general patterns are made up of considerable variation between places and ethnic groups. The evidence in this chapter reinforces the message from studies of larger geographical scales (Finney and Simpson, 2009b; Simpson et al., 2008) that ethnic conflict or divergence cannot be assumed to explain, or be a result of, geographical patterns of ethnic group population change.

Nationally, natural change is contributing more to population growth than immigration, especially for immigrant origin groups who have younger age structures than the long-term White population, and are thus a more reproductive population. Immigration is an important component of population growth for those ethnic groups with a recent immigration history (African and Chinese particularly). The immigration of young adults of these and other ethnic groups has implications for future natural growth, should the migrants settle and build families in Britain. Caribbean emigration from England and Wales is an exception and the phenomenon, perhaps reflecting 'return' migration of families and older adults to the Caribbean, warrants further investigation.

The patterns of population change for any place are complex and become more so when the population is divided by ethnic group and age. Unearthing these complexities is important for proposing explanations for population change. Southall Broadway, at first glance, may be labelled an immigrant ghetto but the demographics reveal it to be a diverse neighbourhood becoming increasingly mixed, experiencing dispersal of its Indian population and attracting young adults of all ethnic groups. Even the neighbourhoods of highest concentration of an ethnic group are becoming more mixed through processes that need not be seen as ethnically specific: dispersal within London to outer neighbourhoods such as Southall Broadway and counterurbanisation, particularly of families, from the capital (Stillwell and Hussain, 2010).

There is movement of both Whites and minority groups from areas of ethnic minority concentration, a process of dispersal and suburbanisation that is creating greater ethnic mixing. Net migration rates are greatest for wards of lowest ethnic minority concentration for each ethnic group. Of the minority groups, dispersal is particularly evident for the Indian and Chinese groups who are known to be the most socially upwardly mobile of the immigrant origin groups. This raises the question of whether other minority groups are restricted in their residential mobility by financial and other barriers, particularly given research that shows similarities in housing aspirations across ethnic groups (Harries et al., 2008; Phillips, 2006). The African group does not exhibit dispersal from minority concentrations perhaps reflecting the tendency for this recent immigrant group to locate in urban centres.

For minority groups there appears to be little relationship between ethnic concentration of an area and natural change. Rates of natural growth are high for minority groups – around 20% – regardless of the ethnic minority concentration of the wards in which they live. For Whites, deaths outweigh births in concentrations of minority population (urban centres). Whites are reproducing in the most White areas indicating suburbanisation of the reproductive White population.

The direction of migration in relation to areas of differing minority concentration is not consistent for all ages. The pattern of dispersal/suburbanisation which has been seen for the White and minority populations as a whole is evident for children and older adults but not for young adults. This is the case both for Whites and minorities. It is likely that the explanations are not related with ethnicity but rather life stage and the tendency of young adults to move to urban centres for study and employment opportunities (Mulder, 1993; Finney and Champion, 2008; Plane and Jurjevich, 2009; Finney, submitted).

Finally, this chapter has hinted at interesting dynamics of internal and international migration. Although theories of chain migration suggest immigrants will predominantly target previous settlement areas there is not a clear pattern of international migration contributing to the growth of minority populations in areas in which they are concentrated more than other areas. Indeed, for young adults both White and minority, immigration is greatest to the areas of least ethnic minority concentration.

Future work can take from this chapter the importance of considering all components of population change and examining processes of change for young adults separately from other age groups. A lifecourse approach would be particularly valuable in this regard. It is necessary to improve our understanding of the combined contributions of internal and international migration to local population change, and the relationship between these two forms of migration, and between them and natural change. Explaining patterns of population change would benefit from focus on the experiences of specific ethnic groups in their particular demographic, geographic and immigration contexts, including investigation of their motivations and migration decision making. Developing this body of work in this way will help us to challenge further claims of ethnic retreat and assess whether ethnic residential patterns should be a focus of research and policy at all.

Acknowledgements I am grateful to Ludi Simpson and Angela Dale for their invaluable guidance and to the Economic and Social Research Council for Fellowship funding (Grant RES-163-27-0011). I am privileged to have been part of the UPTAP programme and I thank the co-ordinator, John Stillwell, and all those involved for their support.

References

Alba, R. and Nee, V. (1997) Rethinking assimilation theory for a new era of immigration, *International Migration Review*, 31(4): 826–874.

Aspinall, P. (2000) The challenges of measuring the ethno-cultural diversity of Britain in the new millennium, *Politics and Policy*, 28(1): 109–118.

Cantle, T. (2001) *Community Cohesion: A Report of the Independent Review Team*, Home Office, London.

Champion, A.G. (ed.) (1989) *Counterurbanisation. The Changing Pace and Nature of Population Deconcentration*, Arnold, London.

Commission on Integration and Cohesion (CoIC) (2007) *Our Shared Future.* http://collections.europarchive.org/tna/20080726153624/http://www.integrationandcohesion.org.uk/Our_final_report.aspx

Edmonston, B. and Michalowski, M. (2004) International migration in Siegel, J. and Swanson, D. (eds.), *The Methods and Materials of Demography*, Elsevier, London, pp. 455–492.

Finney, N. and Champion, T. (2008) *Labour Markets, Skills and Talents: Residential Migration.* Working Paper for the Manchester Independent Economic Review, Manchester.

Finney, N. and Simpson, L. (2009a) *Sleepwalking to Segregation? Challenging Myths About Race and Migration*, Policy Press, Bristol.

Finney, N. and Simpson, L. (2009b) Population dynamics: The roles of natural change and migration in producing the ethnic mosaic, *Journal of Ethnic and Migration Studies*, 35(9): 1479–1496.

Finney, N. (submitted) Life stage explanations of ethnic differences in internal migration of young adults in Britain.

Ford, R. (2008) Is racial prejudice declining in Britain? *British Journal of Sociology*, 59: 609–636.

Harries, B., Richardson, L. and Soteri-Proctor, A. (2008) *Housing Aspirations of White and Second Generation South Asian British Women*, Joseph Rowntree Foundation, New York, NY.

Kalra, V.S. and Kapoor, N. (2009) Interrogating segregation, integration and the community cohesion agenda, *Journal of Ethnic and Migration Studies*, 35(9): 1397–1415.

Kundnani, A. (2007) Integrationism: The politics of anti-Muslim racism, *Race and Class*, 48(40): 24–44.

Mulder, C.H. (1993) *Migration Dynamics: A Life Course Approach.* Thesis Publishers, Amsterdam.

Office for National Statistics (2006) *A Guide to Comparing 1991 and 2001 Census Ethnic Group Data*, Office for National Statistics, Titchfield.

Phillips, D. (2006) Parallel lives? Challenging discourses of British Muslim self-segregation, *Environment and Planning D*, 24(1): 25–40.

Plane, D.A. and Jurjevich, J.R. (2009) Ties that no longer bind? The patterns and repercussions of age-articulated migration, *The Professional Geographer*, 61(1): 4–20.

Robinson, D. (2005) The search for community cohesion: Key themes and dominant concepts of the public policy agenda, *Urban Studies*, 42(8): 1411–1428.

Rowland, D. (2002) *Demographic Methods and Concepts*, Oxford University Press, Oxford.

Sabater, A. (2010) Ethnic residential segregation over time and age cohorts in England and Wales, 1991–2001 in Stillwell, J. and van Ham, M. (eds.), *Ethnicity and Integration Understanding Population Trends and Processes*, Vol. 3, Springer, Dordrecht, pp. 133–151.

Sabater, A. and Simpson, L. (2009) Correcting the census: A consistent time series of ethnic group, age, sex for small areas in England and Wales, 1991–2001, *Journal of Ethnic and Migration Studies*, 35(9): 1461–1478.

Simon, A. (2010) Do ethnic groups migrate towards areas of high concentration of their own group within England and Wales? in Stillwell, J. and van Ham, M. (eds.), *Ethnicity and Integration Understanding Population Trends and Processes*, Vol. 3, Springer, Dordercht.

Simpson, L. (2007) Ghettos of the mind: The empirical behaviour of indices of segregation and diversity, *Journal of the Royal Statistical Society A*, 170(2): 405–424.

Simpson, L. and Akinwale, B. (2007) Quantifying stability and change in ethnic group, *Journal of Official Statistics*, 23(2): 185–208.

Simpson, L. and Finney, N. (2009) Spatial patterns of internal migration: Evidence for ethnic groups in Britain, *Population, Space and Place*, 15: 37–56.

Simpson, L., Finney, N. and Lomax, S. (2008) *Components of Population Change: An Indirect Method for Estimating Births, Deaths and Net Migration for Age, Sex, Ethnic Group and Sub-regional Areas of Britain, 1991–2001* (CCSR Working Paper 2008-03), University of Manchester, Manchester.

Simpson, L., Gavalas, V. and Finney, N. (2008) Population dynamics in ethnically diverse towns: The long-term implications of immigration, *Urban Studies*, 45(1): 163–184.

Stillwell, J. and Hussain, S. (2010) Ethnic internal migration in England and Wales: Spatial analysis using a district classification framework in Stillwell, J. and van Ham, M. (eds.), *Ethnicity and Integration Understanding Population Trends and Processes*, Vol. 3, Springer, Dordrecht, pp. 105–132.

Voss, P., McNive, S., Hammer, R., Johnson, K. and Fuguitt, G. (2004) *County-Specific Net Migration by Five Year Age Groups, Hispanic Origin, Race and Sex, 1990–2000*, University of Wisconsin, Madison, WI.

Chapter 3
Ethnic Residential Segregation Change in England and Wales

Albert Sabater

Introduction

Since the landmark publication by Ernest Burgess (1928) on residential segregation in American cities, the study of the separation of groups in different contexts and at different scales has been a key aspect of the analysis of urban landscapes. Many segregation measures have been proposed following publication of the seminal paper on indices by Duncan and Duncan (1955), including a detailed examination of their properties and interrelationships by Massey and Denton (1988). The conceptual framework within which residential segregation is analysed is generally based on the idea that high levels of segregation are problematic, because this implies that a subgroup of the population is isolated from opportunities, resources and amenities (Kaplan and Holloway, 1998; Logan, 1978; Massey et al., 1987). Such correlation between segregation and socio-economic well-being has also become an issue of public debate in Europe, generally associated with the African American model of inner city segregation (Fortuijn et al., 1998).

In Britain, segregation is a topic in which policy makers have become increasingly interested. This has occurred partly as a consequence of disturbances in English towns in 2001 which resulted in the implementation of community cohesion plans in each local authority (Cantle, 2001). It is also a result of the bombings of the London Underground in 2005 which sparked an emotive debate on whether ethnic minority communities were living 'parallel lives' (Phillips, 2006). More recently, the attention has been focused on cities such as Leicester and Birmingham which could become Britain's first minority White cities within a decade (Herbert, 2007). There is, however, a growing body of research which suggests that the view of increasing segregation and the threat of ghettos is not supported by evidence, despite both the unfavourable economic position of ethnic minorities and the evidence of discrimination towards them (Dorling and Rees, 2003; Peach, 1996a, 1998; Phillips, 1998; Simpson, 2004, 2007).

A. Sabater (✉)
Centre d'Estudis Demogràfics, Universitat Autònoma de Barcelona, Edifici E7, Bellaterra (Barcelona), 08193, Spain
e-mail: asabater@ced.uab.es

J. Stillwell, M. van Ham (eds.), *Ethnicity and Integration*, Understanding Population Trends and Processes 3, DOI 10.1007/978-90-481-9103-1_3,

Although ethnicity data from successive censuses are often used to compare population change, new research has shown that such comparisons can be misleading if inconsistencies between censuses such as changes in the population definition, changes in the treatment of non-response, changes in ethnic group classification and age standard outputs and changes in geographical boundaries are not allowed for (Sabater and Simpson, 2009). The aim of this chapter is twofold. First, it provides more insight on the impact of changing definitions, quality of data and changes in geographical units on the values of segregation. Second, the research aims to contribute to fill the gap in knowledge about residential segregation over age cohorts. In summary, the purpose of this chapter is to address four questions which deserve more investigation following previous studies:

- To what extent does the analysis that corrects for the incompleteness of the census change the values of segregation indices?
- What is the degree to which changes in census boundaries can alter the interpretation of variation in segregation indices?
- Is segregation greater at some life stages (represented by age cohorts) than at others?
- To what extent does the pattern of segregation over age cohorts differ between ethnic groups?

Data and Measures

Enhancing the Population Census

Although the 1991 and 2001 Censuses in Great Britain have measured the principal variables to compare populations over time and space, such comparisons are subject to four types of bias that make comparisons of populations over time difficult (Sabater and Simpson, 2009; Simpson et al., 1997). These biases relate to:

- the population definition, which defines who is a resident, and has changed between the 1991 and 2001 Censuses;
- the treatment of non-response which was different in 1991 and 2001 and varied between ethnic groups, areas and ages;
- key classifications, which changed between 1991 and 2001, including ethnic group and age in standard outputs; and
- geographical boundaries used for standard census outputs, which changed after local government reviews during the 1990s.

Since these aspects are likely to affect the empirical behaviour of indices of segregation, the sources of data used in this chapter are both the 1991 and 2001 Censuses and complete mid-1991 and mid-2001 population estimates (Sabater, 2008).[1] Since harmonised data for the same years by ethnic group for postcode sectors in Scotland are not available, these sub-national areas have not been included in the analysis. In order to examine the outcomes of the indices of segregation, seven ethnic groups are used to make more suitable comparisons between 1991 and 2001: White, Black Caribbean, Black African, Indian, Pakistani, Bangladeshi and Chinese. The use of this seven-category classification therefore reflects those ethnic groups for whom self-definition is most constant over time (Bosveld et al., 2006; Simpson and Akinwale, 2007).

Two Common Measures

Many measures have been formulated in an attempt to indicate the degree of segregation, with the term 'index wars' reflecting a hostile debate about what is the most effective way to measure segregation (Peach, 1996a). For analysis reported here, only two distinct measures are used to review the level and direction of change in two dimensions of spatial variation: *evenness* and *exposure*. Evenness is measured with the traditional index of dissimilarity (Duncan and Duncan, 1955) and indicates how evenly distributed one ethnic group is geographically compared to the rest of the population (Massey and Denton, 1988). The index of dissimilarity (*ID*) is conceived to measure an unequal geographical spread, and it is often interpreted as an indicator of the proportion of one group's population who would have to move to be distributed across areas in the same way as the rest of the population. The formula to calculate *ID* is defined as:

$$ID = 0.5 \times \sum_i \left| \frac{N_{gi}}{N_{g\bullet}} - \frac{N_{\bar{g}i}}{N_{\bar{g}\bullet}} \right| \tag{3.1}$$

where N_{gi} refers to the population of ethnic group g in locality i; $\bar{g}$ refers to the rest of the population; and the summation over an index is represented by the dot symbol. The same equation can be used to compare the spread of any two groups by superseding the second term in the formulae with the area's proportion of a second group h. Generally, *ID* is expressed as a percentage with index values between 0 and 100. Values between 0 and 30 indicate low segregation, values between 31 and 60 indicate moderate segregation, and values between 61 and 100 indicate high levels of segregation (Massey and Denton, 1993, p. 20).

Exposure is measured by the index of isolation (the P^* measure) and is used to indicate the average local concentration of an ethnic group (Lieberson, 1963). The

[1] Census data as published from Table S06 (1991) and Table CAST03 (2001) across wards and districts have been employed. Complete population estimates have been used for the same years and areas (available at http://www.ccsr.ac.uk/research/PopulationEstimates.htm).

P^* index is also conceived as an indicator of the probability that members of each ethnic group will meet with members of their own group and can be expressed as:

$$P^* = \sum_i \left(\frac{N_{gi}}{N_{g\bullet}}\right)\left(\frac{N_{gi}}{N_{\bullet i}}\right) \tag{3.2}$$

The interpretation of this index is also straightforward when expressed as a percentage. If the index is close to 0, it indicates that the average local concentration of the group being studied is very low. In contrast, if the index values are close to 100, this highlights a high level of concentration, thus meaning that all members of the group are in areas where no other groups live.

Population Change and Index Values Over Time

Population Change

Figure 3.1 demonstrates that using complete mid-1991 and mid-2001 population estimates makes a difference to the sub-national comparison of population change of ethnic groups over time. This illustrates that using census output for England and Wales can lead to misleading figures on population change by ethnic group. For this purpose, a Universal Data Map (Durham et al., 2006) is used to show the total impact of adjusting data from each census for a consistent treatment of students,

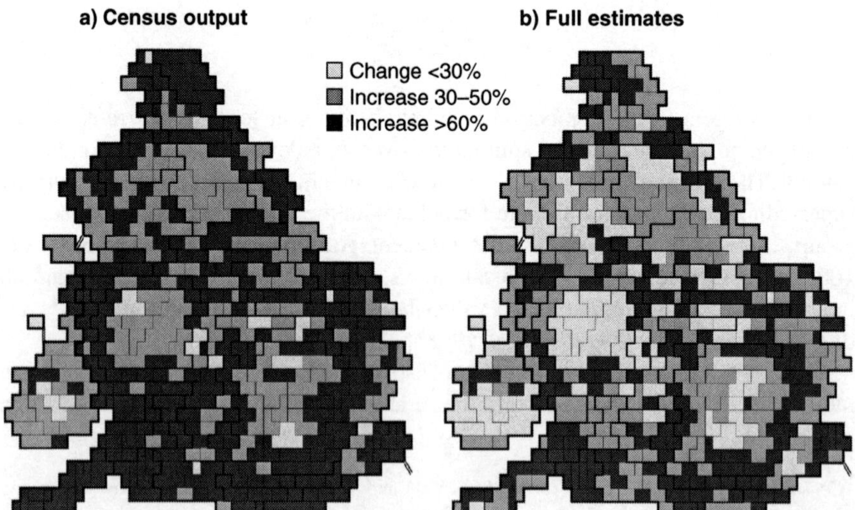

Fig. 3.1 Percentage population change between 1991 and 2001 for non-White groups for 2001 districts in England and Wales (Source: 1991 and 2001 Censuses)

non-response and the move from census date to mid-year. The cartogram showing census output is adjusted so that 1991 data refer to 2001 district boundaries.

The results for both the census and the complete population estimates display a widespread population growth of the non-White groups in districts across England and Wales. Many districts experience a growth in the total non-White populations of over 60%, with three districts only showing a decrease – due to the withdrawal of USA armed forces during the 1990s (Suffolk Coastal, Cherwell, and Forest Heath). The greater population growth experienced outside the urban centres of London, West Midlands and Yorkshire highlights the spreading out of cultural diversity beyond the main cosmopolitan areas. Although the census and the complete population estimates show these two trends of minority population growth and spreading diversity, the detail of the maps reveals that the census output is misleading on both counts. First, there are many more areas of slower population change indicated on the map of complete population estimates in Fig. 3.1 because of the better capture of non-response within the 2001 Census. As a consequence, the unadjusted census overestimates increases in the non-White population. Second, the overestimation of non-White population growth is mainly in the urban areas where the census undercount is greatest, thus making the spreading of diversity understated by the census. The impact of undercount can be very significant amongst young male adults with a recent history of immigration. For example, young male adults in 1991 from ethnic groups such as the Black Caribbean, Black African, Black Other and Bangladeshi groups experience percentage adjustments of more than 40% nationally. The largest adjustments in 2001 are also found among males in their twenties and early thirties of the same ethnic groups, with an increase over the published census population of about 10% nationally (Sabater and Simpson, 2009; Simpson et al., 1997).

These results highlight that some comparisons between censuses are misleading if inconsistencies between censuses are not allowed for. Analyses of population change over time and space in England and Wales with complete mid-1991 and mid-2001 population estimates imply that the introduction of adjustments is needed (Sabater, 2008). This chapter evaluates the effect of using complete mid-year estimates on the values of segregation. The review of the marginal changes provides a clearer picture of the extent to which the analysis of segregation over time is affected by changing definitions, quality of data and changes in geographical units.

National Index Values Over Time

The last two censuses allow a comparison of residential segregation over time. However, an essential part of this research is to show the marginal changes in indices of segregation caused by using 1991 and 2001 Census output directly as published. For this purpose, complete mid-year estimates for the same years are employed, which incorporate adjustments to make more suitable comparisons over time. Table 3.1 displays the values of the selected indices calculated across wards of England and Wales in 1991 and 2001 using these two sources of data. The first dimension, evenness, which is represented by the *ID*, shows how each ethnic group

Table 3.1 Residential segregation of ethnic groups across wards in England and Wales, 1991–2001

		Census			Complete estimates	
Index	Group	1991	1991/2001[a]	2001	1991	2001
Evenness						
ID	White	61.4	60.9	58.8	60.5	57.3
	Black Caribbean	68.9	68.6	67.1	68.0	65.7
	Black African	71.1	70.7	70.6	69.6	69.4
	Indian	65.3	64.8	62.1	64.2	60.9
	Pakistani	75.1	74.5	71.8	74.2	69.7
	Bangladeshi	74.2	73.1	71.7	72.7	67.9
	Chinese	42.2	41.0	42.0	42.5	37.5
Exposure						
*P**	White	95.3	95.3	93.5	94.9	93.3
	Black Caribbean	7.6	7.4	7.3	7.9	7.1
	Black African	4.3	4.2	8.2	4.6	8.0
	Indian	15.6	14.7	15.5	15.5	15.2
	Pakistani	13.9	13.4	17.4	14.0	16.8
	Bangladeshi	10.9	10.3	13.7	10.9	13.2
	Chinese	0.8	0.8	1.2	0.9	1.1

[a] 1991 Census data with 2001 boundaries.
Sources: 1991 and 2001 Censuses and mid-1991 and mid-2001 complete estimates.

in England and Wales has become more evenly distributed between 1991 and 2001 with both census output and complete mid-year estimates. Although ethnic minority groups only represent 9% of the total population in England and Wales in 2001, their geographical distribution is far from even as observed since 1991 with the release of census data with an ethnic group dimension (Owen, 1992; Peach, 1996a). The higher values of *ID* for non-White groups simply indicate this pattern of distribution with ethnic minority groups more concentrated in particular areas, with the largest values of unevenness among groups whose history of immigration to the UK is most recent, such as the Pakistani, Bangladeshi and Black African groups.

Whilst the direction of change in the geographical spread of ethnic groups is similar with both sources of data, the level of change is significantly higher when complete mid-year estimates are used. The results suggest that the average clustering has decreased over the decade by 2–5% points, with the largest percentage changes evident when complete mid-year estimates are used. This would indicate that, overall, the introduction of adjustments that take into account changing definitions, quality of data and changes in geographical units have contributed to a reduction of *ID* values for each ethnic group. The decrease on the index values of *ID* using complete estimates would be in line with the results on population change of ethnic minority groups shown in Fig. 3.1. Thus, the spreading of diversity beyond the main cosmopolitan areas is under-stated by the census mainly as a result of the overestimation of non-White groups in big urban concentrations. This suggests that the better capture of non-response with the complete population estimates adds to the minority groups and to the rest of the population with the same geographical pattern, thus increasing the similarity of each ethnic group with the rest of the population.

The second dimension, exposure, largely reflects the national composition of ethnic groups across wards in England and Wales. The values of P^* for both 1991 and 2001 display how the White group is by far the most exposed compared with the rest of the population followed by South Asian minority groups. However, the values of P^* between 1991 and 2001 for the White group illustrate that the index of isolation has decreased over the decade. In contrast, P^* values show an increase of exposure for those groups such as the Black African, Pakistani and Bangladeshi groups whose population growth has been in full operation during the decade. The values of P^* for both census counts and the complete population estimates also give evidence that all ethnic minority groups are living in wards in which they form a small percentage of the ward's population. For example, none of the ethnic minority groups reaches a value of 20%, thus indicating that the proportion of a given ethnicity living in high local concentrations is generally low. The index values are greatest for the three South Asian groups (Indian, Pakistani and Bangladeshi) with a local concentration in 2001 that ranges between 13 and 17%, thus implying that, on average, the groups with most exposure to others live in areas where more than 80% of the population are from other groups. These results highlight that there are differences in the extent to which the local average concentration of ethnic groups is changing. As expected, the fastest growing minorities, the Pakistani and Bangladeshi groups, show the largest increase in the index values of exposure between 1991 and 2001.

Finally, Table 3.1 also shows how decreases in *ID* and P^* are recorded after converting the same census data from 1991 to 2001 wards for all ethnic groups, thus indicating that the harmonisation of boundaries de-emphasises segregation. This would be consistent with the reduction in the number of wards between the 2 years from 9,509 to 8,850, with average population size increasing from 5,247 to 5,880 respectively.

Index Values for Selected Districts Over Time

Since index values can be highly sensitive where groups are small (Voas and Williamson, 2000), it is generally more important to focus the attention on those areas with large groups and where ethnic minority groups represent a substantial percentage of the total population (Peach, 1996a). Table 3.2 displays the same index values in six urban areas where the non-White population forms a significant percentage of the total population. As seen earlier on, the analysis over time indicates that the use of complete population estimates that correct for the census shortcomings change the value of segregation indices. The use of census output already indicates that the majority of groups have become more spread out geographically in these districts, a tendency that becomes more pronounced with the use of complete estimates, with the only exception being the Chinese group, whose distribution

Table 3.2 Residential segregation of ethnic groups across wards in selected districts, 1991–2001

Index	Group	District	Census			Complete estimates	
			1991	1991/2001[a]	2001	1991	2001
Evenness							
ID	White	All districts	61.4	60.9	58.8	60.5	57.3
	Black Caribbean	Croydon	38.2	37.8	38.5	38.1	37.9
	Black African	Southwark	28.9	26.5	25.6	26.1	25.1
	Indian	Leicester	54.8	48.4	51.4	53.1	51.4
	Pakistani	Bradford	60.3	60.3	59.8	59.9	59.4
	Bangladeshi	Birmingham	67.0	67.2	63.3	65.4	61.0
	Chinese	Manchester	27.7	27.6	32.5	27.7	30.6
Exposure							
*P**	White	All districts	95.3	95.3	93.5	94.9	93.3
	Black Caribbean	Croydon	8.2	8.1	12.7	8.8	12.5
	Black African	Southwark	11.3	10.7	10.3	11.5	10.1
	Indian	Leicester	43.8	38.4	44.4	42.9	44.3
	Pakistani	Bradford	31.0	31.0	38.9	31.3	38.6
	Bangladeshi	Birmingham	6.3	6.3	7.8	6.3	7.4
	Chinese	Manchester	1.2	1.2	2.6	1.6	2.4

[a] 1991 Census data with 2001 boundaries.
Sources: 1991 and 2001 Censuses and mid-1991 and mid-2001 complete estimates.

appears to be less uniform over the decade, a characteristic that follows the particularly strong urban pattern of this group in Manchester. These results constitute an example on how ethnic groups can be distributed so that they are overrepresented in some areas and underrepresented in others (Massey and Denton, 1988). As a consequence, clusters are likely to remain and create a residential 'mosaic' rather than a residential 'melting pot' (Peach, 1996a).

As expected, the analyses of P^* for 1991 and 2001 show how the composition of ethnic groups across wards in these districts is different compared to the national composition. P^* values are generally greater in these areas than nationally, thus suggesting the greater significance of each group in the selected districts. The results indicate that on average the majority of ethnic minorities lived in areas with more people of their own group than they did in 2001 and, therefore, their likelihood of meeting someone of their own group across wards in these districts increased between 1991 and 2001. Although these results are expected to change after significant streams of immigration, it is also considered that the growth of ethnic minority populations with a relatively young age structure such as the Black Caribbean, Indian, Pakistani, Bangladeshi and Other populations occurs more through natural growth than immigration between 1991 and 2001 (Finney and Simpson, 2009).

Similarly the effect of re-warding over time on the index values is also shown on Table 3.2. The results clearly display how the effect of such boundary changes can be particularly misleading. For example, in Leicester the use of 2001 ward boundaries leads to a reduction of the index values of *ID* and P^* for the Indian group by 6%. Therefore, the results reveal that unless a consistent geographical approach with time series is taken (e.g. wards as defined in 2001), it is difficult to know whether changing trends are taking place or whether observed changes are simply an artefact of a boundary change.

Index Values Across Life Stages

Exploring Variations by Age Cohorts

Whilst a fair amount is known about residential segregation, research assessing changes over age cohorts is just starting to get under way. Here, the degree of ethnic residential segregation among various age cohorts is reported with the index of dissimilarity as a way to examine the extent to which residential segregation varies at some life stages and whether the life pattern of segregation differs between ethnic groups. For this purpose the complete mid-1991 and mid-2001 population estimates are used for eight different age cohorts across wards in England and Wales as well as for selected districts. Since age carries with it culturally defined behavioural norms, it is used to trace regularities associated with processes and events across the life course (Courgeau, 1985) such as that on migration (Rogers et al., 1978). Within this context, index values of the resident population aged 0–6 in 1991 are compared with index values for those aged 10–16 in 2001. Similarly, those aged 7–16 in 1991 are compared with the equivalent for those aged 17–26 ten years later. Consequently, the results for these groups will allow us to illustrate changes in the level of segregation for a first age segment focused on preparation and education. Similarly, the index values are analysed by taking into consideration other age segments such as those related to family building and work, and retirement.

Index Values by Age Cohorts Nationally and for Selected Districts

Figure 3.2 displays the index values of *ID* by age cohorts across wards in England and Wales and for selected districts in 1991 and 2001. The graphs clearly indicate how the level of unevenness for each age cohort in 1991 and 10 years later is generally higher among ethnic groups other than White, with the exception of the Chinese group, whose geographical distribution appears to be more widely dispersed than the other ethnic groups. The common view is that for Chinese, *links to restaurants and takeaways catering for the total population would produce such a degree of dispersal of small pockets of population* (Peach, 1996a, p. 224).

The change in evenness across wards show a reduction of the index values of *ID* for the majority of age cohorts, thus indicating that all groups and age cohorts have become more evenly distributed between 1991 and 2001. The analysis also

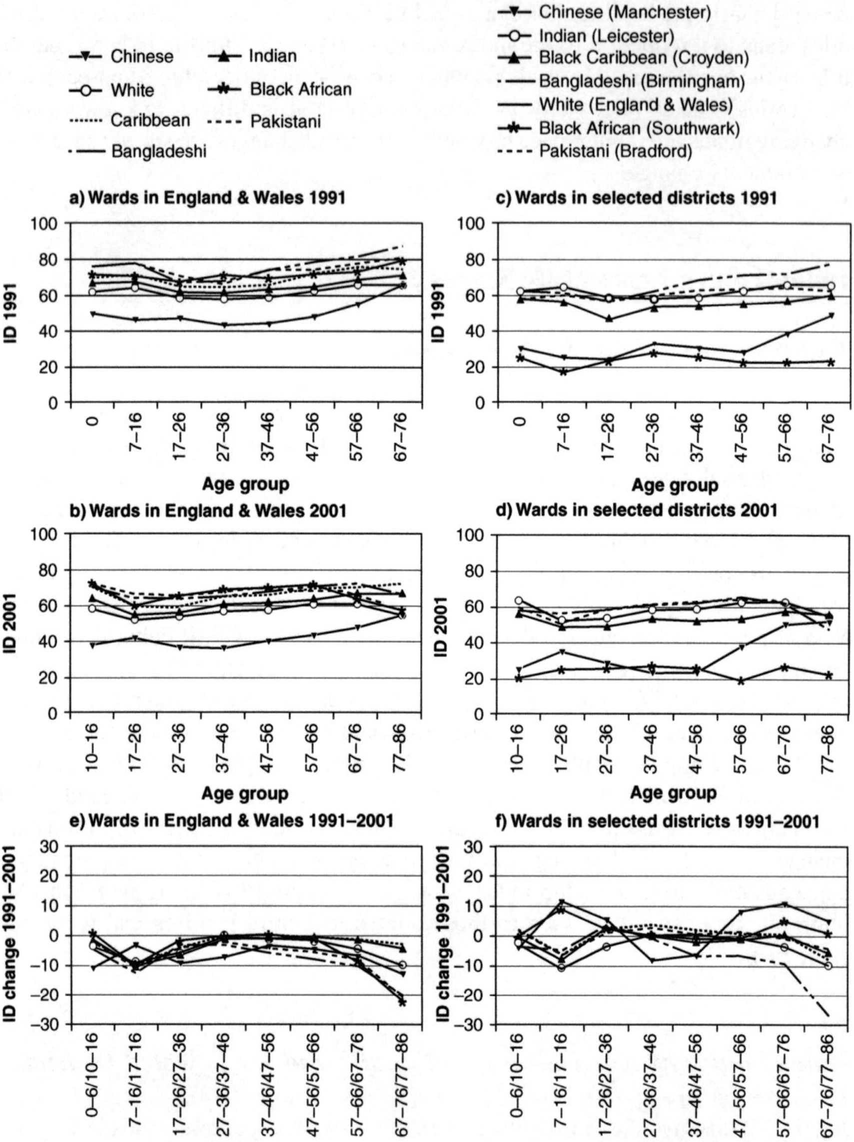

Fig. 3.2 Residential segregation of ethnic groups by age cohorts across wards in England and Wales and for selected districts, 1991–2001 (Source: Mid-1991 and mid-2001 complete estimates)

reveals a very similar pattern of change in evenness between ethnic groups across age cohorts. Whilst the youngest group (which refers to children living with their parents) and adult ages display similar changes in evenness during the decade, a significant decrease in unevenness is found among young adults. During the early adulthood phase, represented by the age cohort 7–16 in 1991 and 10 years later, it becomes apparent that a shift in the residential distribution between schoolchildren and young adult ages (some of them university students) results in much lower levels of segregation. Whilst this explanation seems to be applicable to all groups, an exception is found with the Chinese group, whose unevenness has increased from low levels, most likely due to the impact of international migration of overseas students to UK universities.

During the middle adulthood phase, represented by the age cohorts 17–26, 27–36, 37–46 in 1991 and 10 years later, the change in the index values of *ID* is reduced, with some groups, including the White group, becoming less evenly distributed. The concentration of interplays between demand and supply in jobs and housing in metropolitan areas would explain the greater unevenness for these age cohorts. However, the human capital of each group and particularly the impact of social networks is also likely to explain the relative differences between groups in the middle aged phase. The decline in the proportion of late middle ages in the total population of big cities would then be defining the dividing line between *the places to leave and the places to head for* (Dorling and Thomas, 2004, p. 28). From this perspective, those who can afford to will move from big urban concentrations to less urban environments, thus reflecting the extended process of suburbanisation from cities to mixed urban areas (Champion, 1996).

Finally, during the late adulthood phase and post-retirement age, represented by the age cohorts 47–56, 57–66 and 67–76 in 1991 and 10 years later, an increase in evenness is observed. These results substantiate the idea that the elderly are more likely to leave than to move to the big cities (Fokkema et al.,1996), thus highlighting a possible negative balance of migration of elderly people in dense urban areas which contributes to the suburbanisation process, particularly of the White group. However, not much should be made of the changes from older age cohorts of ethnic minority groups because these are likely to be affected by a significant number of neighbourhoods with small numbers of ethnic groups.[2]

The analysis of ethnic residential segregation by age cohorts for selected districts is displayed as a way to examine whether the regularities observed nationally are also reproduced in some urban areas. Generally, the results unveil similar changes on the index values of *ID* by age cohorts, although local areas are clearly more affected by the transfers of minority members as a result of population movement to areas where they are under-represented and *vice versa*. For example, the index values of *ID* for those in the early adulthood phase, represented by the age cohort 7–16 in 1991 and 10 years later are similar in appearance with the results obtained nationally for England and Wales. Whilst it replicates the patterns of greater evenness

[2]The inclusion of small populations in the complete estimates that are more evenly spread than in the census due to the random rounding of 1s and 2s to 0s and 3s (ONS, 2006) is likely to decrease the index values of *ID*. In the complete estimates, 0s and 3s tend to become smoothed to values between 0 and 3. Although this might be a more realistic picture than the lack of 1s and 2s in the census, the truth cannot be known, thus adding approximation to all analysis, particularly for small areas as discussed by Stillwell and Duke-Williams (2007).

for these ages for the majority of groups, some groups such as the Black African in Southwark and the Chinese in Manchester appear to be less evenly distributed over the decade, thus highlighting the likely impact of international migration and in-migration of members of these two groups to neighbourhoods where they are already overrepresented.

During the middle adulthood phase, an increase in unevenness is noticed for all ethnic minority groups, particularly for the age cohort 17–26 and 10 years later. The influence of the population momentum due to the young age structure of ethnic minorities is likely to generate population growth in local areas which also experience the transfer of net migration. Such population dynamic features combined with the geographically specific labour demands and the pressure on the housing market in urban areas are generally considered the key explanations for the promotion of clusters (Simpson et al., 2008).

Finally, the index values of *ID* point out again a tendency to be lower during the late adulthood phase and post-retirement age. As mentioned earlier, these results are likely to hold true for some groups more than others. Although the pace of population ageing is an ongoing process for all groups, only the White group and some long-established minority groups such as the Indian and the Black Caribbean may be worth the analysis due to their significance in numbers. Nonetheless, one may also speculate about the gains in unevenness of some groups such as that of the Chinese group, which is probably affected by international migration of elderly Chinese who have settled within the frame of family reunification, and the characteristic movement of the Chinese group from mixed urban areas to densely populated cities (Finney and Simpson, 2009).

Conclusions

This chapter has shown that, despite the growth of ethnic minorities between 1991 and 2001 in England and Wales (Champion, 2005; Rees and Butt, 2004; Sabater, 2008; Simpson, 2004), ethnic residential segregation has reduced for all groups over time and age cohorts. Four key findings emerge from the empirical analysis in this chapter:

First, the analysis that corrects for the census' incompleteness demonstrates that, overall, the use of complete mid-year estimates is likely to change the value of segregation indices. Although the outcome of less residential segregation over time has been validated with both the last two censuses and complete mid-1991 and mid-2001 population estimates, the latter has provided evidence of greater differences in reducing residential segregation over time. In other words, ethnic groups appear to be even more evenly spread across localities when complete estimates are employed. The analysis suggests that the population in inner-city areas in which the highest concentrations of ethnic groups were found in 1991 has become more evenly distributed despite the growth in situ of ethnic groups. This finding is consistent with the evidence of spreading diversity suggested by the analysis of population change after taking into account non-response not included in the census output. Similarly, this idea of dispersal of ethnic minorities to outer-city areas is also supported by other research (Hussain and Stillwell, 2008; Johnston et al., 2002; Salt and Rees, 2006; Simpson et al., 2008).

Second, the analysis using consistent census boundaries over time shows that the interpretation of change in segregation indices can be altered and misleading when data directly from census output are used. The results highlight that what initially looks like an increase in segregation can turn out to be purely artefactual, reflecting solely ward boundary changes between 1991 and 2001. Within this context, since in the UK electoral wards are frequently changed in order to ensure electoral equality, the use of a consistent time series appears to be fundamental in order not to confound trends in residential segregation with boundary changes. The analysis indicate that after converting census data from 1991 to 2001 wards, a decrease in residential segregation is observed for all groups, with alterations on the index values that can be greater than the impact of changes over time. Although the redrawing of electoral boundaries is increasingly subject to the residential mosaic of ethnic groups, it is still unclear as to the extent to which the variable ethnicity may be more or less relevant to the Boundary Committees that redraw electoral boundaries so as to reflect community identity (Chisholm and Dench, 2005).

Third, the analysis across age cohorts demonstrates how residential segregation is greater at some life stages, particularly during the middle adulthood phase, which is interpreted as a result of the concentration of ethnic groups in their middle ages in predominantly urban areas, thus manifesting the demographic consequences of relatively recent and past immigration streams. Contrarily, the index values for younger and post-retirement ages suggest that segregation is much lower during these life stages. Two particularly interesting results are noted: the decrease in segregation over the period for young adults (ages 17–26) and the different experience of the Chinese ethnic group. Since the segregation indices do not describe the various factors which contribute to local population change such as migration patterns, the analysis of ethnic residential segregation may be improved by taking into account population movement at different life-stages. Within this context, further research is needed to assess the extent to which de-segregation for young adults is an age effect linked to migration to urban areas for work or study; and the extent to which it may be a cohort effect, reflecting the beginnings of an 'integrated generation'.

Finally, the analysis across age cohorts has also revealed that the pattern of segregation over the life course does not differ significantly between ethnic groups. Despite the differences between individual ethnic groups in the level of segregation, a similar pattern of segregation over the life course is found. These results are especially relevant as they clearly display that depending on the life stage reached, the level of measured segregation can differ greatly regardless of ethnicity. What this may be suggesting is that the residential pattern of ethnic groups measured by the indices is not simply a consequence of residential segregation but rather an interrelated aspect of different life stages. Therefore, it is assumed that the occurrence of different events which can be related to the family life cycle and work affect the outcomes in the measured segregation, which in turn are influenced by socio-spatial inequalities in education, employment and housing. Considering the demography of immigration, residential segregation is expected to change after significant streams of immigration. For ethnic groups in their early years of immigration, segregation is likely to increase for a while as there is a tendency for new immigrants to settle initially in ethnic concentration areas where kinship ties are strong. Therefore, the index values reflect the settlement pattern of international migration around the family, cultural and religious support given by social networks. However, when families begin to move elsewhere the index values are likely to change in different directions as a result of the movement away from original settlement areas. Just as in the case of previous migrants moving out from areas of concentration, this general direction can be easily related in appearance to those following Irish and Jewish immigration to Britain (Peach, 1996b). However, this is clearly a process that is equally explained by the different periods of settlement and dispersal trajectories of each group. Those ethnic groups with the most recent history of immigration to England and Wales, the Black African, Pakistani and Bangladeshi groups, show the highest level of residential concentration as a result of their clustering in towns and cities, where old private housing is more readily available and employment markets and services such as education are more accessible (Musterd, 2003; Simpson, 2004).

Acknowledgements The author is grateful to Ludi Simpson and David Voas for their constructive and useful comments on this chapter. The research reported has been supported by an ESRC Post-doctoral Fellowship (PTA-163-27-0002) commissioned under the Understanding Population Trends and Processes (UPTAP) programme. Census data are Crown copyright. The complete mid-1991 and mid-2001 population estimates are census-based and have been prepared by members of the Cathie Marsh Centre for Census and Survey Research (CCSR) at the University of Manchester.

References

Bosveld, K., Connolly, H. and Rendall, M. (2006) *A Guide to Comparing 1991 and 2001 Census Ethnic Group Data*, Office for National Statistics, London, available online at http://www.statistics.gov.uk/articles/nojournal/GuideV9.pdf

Burgess, E. (1928) Residential segregation in American cities, *Annals of the American Academy of Political and Social Science*, 14: 105–115.

Cantle, T. (2001) *Community Cohesion: A Report of the Independent Review Team*, Home Office, London.

Champion, A. (1996) Internal migration and ethnicity in Britain in Ratcliffe, P. (ed.), *Ethnicity in the 1991 Census*, Vol. 3, HMSO, London, pp. 135–173.

Champion, A. (2005) Population movement within the UK in Chappell, R. (ed.), *Focus on People and Migration*, Palgrave Macmillan, Basingstoke, pp. 92–114.

Chisholm, M. and Dench, G. (2005) *Community Identity: Literature Review and Analysis for Periodic Electoral Reviews*, Electoral Commission, London.

Courgeau, D. (1985) Interaction between spatial mobility, family and career life-cycle: A French survey, *European Sociological Review*, 1(2): 139–162.

Dorling, D. and Rees, P. (2003) Anation still dividing: The British census and social polarisation, 1971–2001, *Environment and Planning A*, 35(7): 1287–1313.

Dorling, D. and Thomas, B. (2004) *People and Places: A 2001 Census Atlas of the UK*, The Policy Press, Bristol.

Duncan, O.B. and Duncan, B. (1955) A methodological analysis of segregation indexes, *American Sociological Review*, 20: 210–217.

Durham, H., Dorling, D. and Rees, P. (2006) An online census atlas for everyone, *Area*, 38: 336–341.

Finney, N. and Simpson, L. (2009) Internal migration and ethnic groups: Evidence for Britain from the 2001 census, *Population, Space and Place*, 14(2): 63–83.

Finney, N. and Simpson, L. (2009) Population dynamics: The roles of natural change and migration in producing the ethnic mosaic, *Journal of Ethnic and Migration Studies*, 35(9): 1479–1496.

Fokkema, T., Gierveld, J. and Nijkamp, P. (1996) Big cities, big problems: Reason for the elderly to move? *Urban Studies*, 33(2): 353–377.

Fortuijn, J.D., Musterd, S. and Ostendorf, W. (1998) International migration and ethnic segregation: Impacts on urban areas, *Urban Studies*, 35: 367–370.

Herbert, I. (2007) Leicester to be the first city where white people are minority, *The Independent*, September 11. Available online at http://www.independent.co.uk/news/uk/this-britain/leicester-to-be-first-city-where-white-people-are-minority-401968.html

Hussain, S. and Stillwell, J. (2008) *Internal Migration of Ethnic Groups in England and Wales by Age and District Type* (Working Paper 08/3), School of Geography, University of Leeds, Leeds.

Johnston, R., Forrest, J. and Poulsen, M. (2002) Are there ethnic enclaves/ghettos in English cities? *Urban Studies*, 39(4): 591–618.

Kaplan, D. and Holloway, S. (1998) *Segregation in Cities*, Association of American Geographers, Washington, DC.

Lieberson, S. (1963) *Ethnic Patterns in American Cities*, The Free Press of Glencoe, New York, NY.

Logan, J. (1978) Growth, politics and the stratification of places, *American Journal of Sociology*, 184: 404–416.

Massey, D., Condran, G. and Denton, N. (1987) The effects of residential segregation on black social and economic well-being, *Social Forces*, 66: 29–56.

Massey, D. and Denton, N. (1988) The dimensions of residential segregation, *Social Forces*, 67: 281–315.

Massey, D. and Denton, N. (1993) *American Apartheid*, Harvard University Press, Cambridge.

Musterd, S. (2003) Segregation and integration: A contested relationship, *Journal of Ethnic and Migration Studies*, 29(4): 623–641.

ONS (2006) *2001 Census Disclosure Control*. Office for National Statistics. Available online at http://www.statistics.gov.uk/census2001/pdfs/ag0106.pdf

Owen, D. (1992) *Ethnic Minorities in Great Britain: Settlement Patterns, National Ethnic Minority Data Archive* (1991 Census Statistical Paper No. 1), Centre for Research in Ethnic Relations, University of Warwick, Coventry.

Peach, C. (1996a) Does Britain have ghettos? *Transactions, Institute of British Geographers*, 21(1): 216–235.

Peach, C. (1996b) Black Caribbeans: Gender and geography, ethnicity in the 1991 census in Peach, C. (ed.), *Ethnicity*, Vol. 2, Stationary Office, London.

Peach, C. (1998) South Asian and Caribbean ethnic minority housing choice in Britain, *Urban Studies*, 35(10): 1657–1680.

Phillips, D. (1998) Black minority ethnic concentration, segregation and dispersal in Britain, *Urban Studies*, 35(10): 1681–1702.

Phillips, D. (2006) Parallel lives? Challenging discourses of British Muslim self-segregation, *Environment and Planning D: Society and Space*, 24(1): 25–40.

Rees, P. and Butt, F. (2004) Ethnic change and diversity in England, 1981–2001, *Area*, 36(2): 174–186.

Rogers, A., Raquillet, R. and Castro, L.J. (1978) Model migration schedules and their applications, *Environment and Planning A*, 10(5): 475–502.

Sabater, A. (2008) *Estimation of Ethnic Groups in Sub-national Areas for Analysis of Population Change, England and Wales, 1991–2001*. PhD thesis, Cathie Marsh Centre for Census and Survey Research, University of Manchester, Manchester.

Sabater, A. and Simpson, L. (2009) Enhancing the population census: A time series for subnational areas with age, sex and ethnic group dimensions in England and Wales, 1991–2001, *Journal of Ethnic and Migration Studies*, 35(9): 1461–1478.

Salt, J. and Rees, P. (2006) *Globalisation, Population Mobility and Impact of Migration on Population. Public Policy Seminar Series*, Economic and Social Research Council (ESRC), Swindon.

Simpson, L. (2004) Statistics of racial segregation: Measures, evidence and policy, *Urban Studies*, 41(3): 661–681.

Simpson, L. (2007) Ghettos of the mind: The empirical behaviour of indices of segregation and diversity, *Journal of the Royal Statistical Society Series A*, 170(2): 405–424.

Simpson, L. and Akinwale, B. (2007) Quantifying stability and change in ethnic group, *Journal of Official Statistics*, 23(2): 185–208.

Simpson, L., Cossey, R. and Diamond, I. (1997) 1991 Population estimates for areas smaller than districts, *Population Trends*, 90: 31–39.

Simpson, L., Gavalas, V. and Finney, N. (2008) Population dynamics in ethnically diverse towns: The long-term implications of immigration, *Urban Studies*, 45(1): 163–183.

Stillwell, J. and Duke-Williams, O. (2007) Understanding the 2001 census interaction data: The impact of small cell adjustment and problems of comparison with 1991, *Journal of the Royal Statistical Society Series A*, 170(2): 1–21.

Voas, D. and Williamson, P. (2000) The scale of dissimilarity: Concepts, measurement and an application to socio-economic variation across England and Wales, *Transactions Institute of British Geographers*, 25: 465–481.

Chapter 4
Ethnicity and Fertility in the United Kingdom

Sylvie Dubuc and John Haskey

Introduction

Post-Second World War immigration has greatly impacted on the ethnic composition of the UK population. After the Second World War, a number of historical phenomena contributed to the rise of immigration from New Commonwealth countries – the decolonisation processes and post-colonial sequelae (including Indian partition, 'Africanisation' of Uganda and Kenya and post-colonial poverty), while post-war reconstruction and economic recovery in Britain created job opportunities. Caribbean immigrants – then called West Indians – arrived mostly in the 1950s and 1960s. Despite some early work immigration by women up to the early 1960s (Byron, 1998), the peak years of migration, the overall proportion of men among immigrants was higher than that of women (Foner, 2009). At the same time, migrants from the Indian sub-continent arrived, mainly men and on a temporary basis (Ballard, 1990; Brown, 2006; Peach, 1996).

The demand for labour had slowed dramatically by the late 1960s; after the adoption of restrictive immigration laws in 1962, when workers had to choose between returning to their place of origin (with the risk of not been allowed to come back to the UK) or settling in the UK. Many chose to settle and, in the late 1960s, the migration of dependants from the Caribbean and India – mainly children and women joining their husbands – dominated the immigration flow into Britain. Since then, the Afro-Caribbean population has essentially grown through the increase in the number of UK-born Caribbeans. A part – and sometimes a major part – of the ethnic minority groups is now made up of the settled immigrants' successive generation(s), born in the UK (Mitton and Aspinall, 2010).

The Indian community grew further with the arrival of Indian immigrant families from East Africa forced to leave their African country of settlement in the 1970s as a result of the post-colonial 'Africanisation' movement (caused by insecurity and expulsions). These 'twice migrants', mainly from Gujarat, had

S. Dubuc (✉)
Department of Social Policy and Social Work, University of Oxford, Oxford OX1 2ER, UK
e-mail: sylvie.dubuc@socres.ox.ac.uk

J. Stillwell, M. van Ham (eds.), *Ethnicity and Integration*, Understanding Population Trends and Processes 3, DOI 10.1007/978-90-481-9103-1_4,

established themselves in the East African British Colony where they formed the middle class and were generally relatively highly educated and wealthier than Indian-born immigrants to the UK (Brown, 2006).

Family reunions started later for the Pakistani and even more recently for the Bangladeshi communities, as strongly suggested by data from the Home Office (Berrington, 1996). The Bangladeshis and the Black Africans were the fastest growing groups in the 1980s (Jones, 1993). Immigration of Black Africans has increased in the last decades (Daley, 1996; Mitton and Aspinall, 2009, 2010) and, as a result, the non UK-born Black African population still forms a large part of this ethnic group. The same consideration also applies to the Chinese population in the UK. In recent years, immigrants to the UK have come from increasingly diverse countries of origin, largely augmenting the ethnic group 'Others' (Vertovec, 2007). In the most recent years of the early twenty-first century, the ethnic and cultural diversity of the population of the UK has been further diversified by immigration flows from the European Union's newest members (Vertovec, 2007).

The ethnic and cultural composition of British society has become very diverse, as is illustrated in Table 4.1. This raises a number of questions and concerns from civil society and policy makers on issues such as: ethnic and racial discrimination; the challenges faced by new settlers to adapt to their new environment; and British society's capacity to adjust to an increasing cultural diversity. These concerns have also translated into a questioning of whether projections of the different ethnic minority populations should be made to provide an informed debate on future prospects (Haskey, 2002).

It should be noted that different nomenclatures were used to refer to the visible immigrant populations during the 1960s and 1970s – such as coloured immigrants or Commonwealth immigrants – and debate during that period concentrated upon 'race' and 'racial minorities'. However, in recent decades, the different concept of

Table 4.1 Ethnic composition of the UK population, 2001

Ethnic group	Population	Percentage of total UK population
White British	50,366,497	85.7
White Irish	691,232	1.2
White other	3,096,169	5.3
All mixed	677,117	1.2
Indian	1,053,411	1.8
Pakistani	747,285	1.3
Bangladeshi	500,000	0.8
Other Asian	247,644	0.4
Black Caribbean	565,876	1.0
Black African	485,277	0.8
Black other	97,585	0.2
Chinese	247,403	0.4
Other	230,615	0.4

Source: Census (2001).

ethnicity gained ground. Recognising the issues associated with ethnic diversity, the need to monitor population changes, and address multi-cultural challenges, an ethnic group question was planned for the 1981 Census. In the circumstances, it proved impractical to implement a question on an individual's ethnicity, but a subsequently revised and tested ethnic question was successfully included in the following census, in 1991. Although the 1981 Census failed to include an ethnic group question, such a question had been first introduced into the 1979 Labour Force Survey (LFS) – and, with additional questions such as 'Year of entry into the UK' – has provided, and continues to provide, some valuable series estimates (Haskey, 1997). The 1979 LFS ethnic group question was modified in 1981 and revised again in 1991 to accord with the census ethnic group questions. The ethnic categories[1] were further revised in the 2001 Census, and also used in the 2001 LFS. Technical details on capturing and coding ethnic group in the LFS since 1992 have been published (Haskey, 1996).

Ethnicity encapsulates cultural background and specific characteristics shared by individuals, which reflect and promote the sub-population's identity (e.g. ancestry, cultural heritage, language, nationality, territory of origin, religion and other shared characteristics). What constitutes an ethnic group has been, and remains, subject to much discussion (for example, see Aspinall, 2000; Ballard, 1996; Berthoud et al., 1997; Bulmer, 1996; Coleman and Salt, 1996; Haskey, 1997; Modood, 2005; Solomos and Back, 1996). A recent study in Canada comparing responses from the same individuals to the ethnic question asked in the 2001 Census and the question differently formulated in a survey in 2002, found that responses did not match in about a quarter of the cases, showing that question wording in surveys influences ethnic responses (Boyd and Shida, 2009).

Ethnic categories in British census and surveys are mainly based on physical appearance ('race', skin colour), country or region of (ancestral) origin and language, those characteristics being generally closely linked. Some groups benefit from a relatively more specific identity than others (e.g. Indian, Pakistani and Bangladeshi groups compared with Black African or White Other groups – the latter being separately identified since 2001). However, some ethnic groups, the 'Indian' category for instance, could be broken down still further into language, place of origin and religious sub-groups (Peach, 1996). There is no objective criteria that would allow a strict definition of ethnicity since ethnicity is self-defined and self-assigned by those surveyed, thus with the necessary constraint of predefined categories, and an individual's ethnic group may vary over time (Haskey, 2002). For instance, a study by Simpson and Akinwale (2007) using ONS Longitudinal Survey data in which they traced individuals from the 1991 to the 2001 Census has shown that many individuals, mostly from the Black Caribbean and Black African groups, changed their self-defined ethnicity, largely availing themselves of the new ethnic

[1] With the growing proportion of UK-born descendants of immigrants, the country of birth has become an increasingly inaccurate proxy for analysing the ethnic composition of the population of the UK.

categories in the 2001 Census ('Black Other'; 'Mixed White and Black Caribbean'; and 'Mixed White and Black African' groups). Similarly, the introduction of the category 'White Other' has offered a more subtle picture of the White population since 2001, despite its heterogeneity and large internal cultural diversity.

With regard to estimating the present and future ethnic composition of the UK, it is useful, when analysing ethnic data, to consider the limitations of predefined categories and how respondents classify themselves. The exercise is complicated if the analysis of time series involves a change in classification, although the facility offered by the ONS Longitudinal Study to compare individuals' own ethnicity according to both 1991 and 2001 Census classifications assists in this task. The present and future ethnic composition of the UK population depends mostly on net migration and fertility by ethnicity. In this chapter, we investigate the fertility of ethnic groups based on the 2001 Census ethnic categorisation. The change in ethnic group classification, mentioned above, highlights the difficulties of capturing an evolving social construct. An example is the 2001 Census classification's acknowledgement of ethnic minority respondents' wish to identify themselves as 'British' – by providing the categories 'Black or Black British' and 'Asian or Asian British'.

In the UK, a number of studies have demonstrated fertility differentials by ethnic group, generally based on the 1991 Census ethnic categories, some including published estimates up to 2001 (Coleman and Dubuc, 2010), and some questioning the 'converging trends' hypothesis. Fertility variability across ethnic groups suggests that fertility behaviour is driven by cultural and/or social characteristics that are ethnic-specific – and potentially influenced by the reproductive behaviours exhibited in the country of origin of the first generation settled in the UK. Therefore, three major factors could lead to fertility convergence: (i) a homogenisation of fertility behaviour worldwide; and/or (ii) a decreasing impact of the (ancestral) place of origin in influencing attitudes toward childbearing and ideal family size among ethnic minority populations in the UK; and/or (iii) structural (socio-economic) integration. Immigrants originating from countries where reproductive behaviour differs significantly from the host country are thought to maintain fertility rates resembling those of their country of birth, presumably more or less depending on their duration of settlement in the country of immigration, and especially their place of upbringing. According to the 'converging trends' hypothesis, the prevalence of the cultural model of the country of origin is expected to play a lesser role in influencing the fertility behaviour of the second generation and the influence of society on the upbringing of the children of immigrants is expected to have a bearing on their reproductive behaviour. Fertility of the second generation, and successive generations, should therefore converge to the UK average. Unless a relatively large number of immigrants feed the growth of a particular ethnic group, the proportion of UK-born minority ethnic population is expected to increase and drive fertility of the corresponding ethnic group closer to the UK average. However, it may be argued that cultural diversity is one among other factors influencing reproductive behaviour and socio-economic differences across ethnic groups may explain, at least in part, the inter-group differences in fertility observed. Fertility convergence may therefore be curbed by the persistence of socio-economic differences across ethnic groups.

This chapter aims to assess the likelihood and potential for fertility convergence across ethnic groups. Studying demographic characteristics by ethnic group is not only useful in describing the UK population's current composition, but also in understanding the influences on how it might evolve in the future. However, there are some important gaps in the demographic data needed for these tasks, and a recent review of the considerations and requirements involved in making fertility assumptions for population projections by ethnic group appraised all the data sources for analysing ethnic fertility, including census, the Labour Force Survey (LFS), Hospital Episode Statistics, the General Household Survey and Longitudinal Study data (Sporton and White, 2002).

In this chapter we describe and use the Labour Force Survey Own Child Method and recent refinements introduced to produce improved fertility estimates for ethnic sub-populations and present up-to-date fertility estimates for 1987–2006. The results are discussed in terms of the convergence hypothesis, potential causes of fertility variability across groups and future fertility expectations.

Methods of Estimating Ethnic Fertility

LFS-Own Child Method to Estimate Age-Specific Fertility Rates

Fertility estimates by ethnic group produced in the UK are generally based on indirect methods, since the legal births registration system does not record the ethnicity of the mother or indeed that of the child or father. Conventional calculations of age-specific fertility rates (ASFRs) are usually based on birth registration numbers divided by the mid-year estimated number of women of fertile age, and by mother's age:

$$\text{ASFR}(x) = \text{Number of births to women aged } x/\text{Number of women aged } x \quad (4.1)$$

and total period fertility rates (TFR) are readily derived from ASFRs:

$$\text{TFR} = \text{Sum of ASFR}(x) \times \text{ age-group of } x \text{ (e.g. } \times 1 \text{ if single year, } \times 5 \text{ if five year group)} \quad (4.2)$$

Because birth registrations are not available by ethnic group, indirect methods have been used instead to estimate ethnic births. Census data have been extensively used to produce child-women ratios as the census currently constitutes the best source for deriving fertility rates by ethnic group at regional and local geographical levels (see, for example, Large et al., 2006; Rees, 2008; Rees et al., 2008). Recently, hospital records have improved with respect to ethnicity information (Moser et al., 2008)[2] and offer a promising data source for future ethnic fertility estimation. The

[2]In 2005, 89% of births in England and Wales were recorded with an ethnicity according to a study by Moser et al. (2008).

LFS provides a useful source to derive annual ethnic group fertility estimates at a national level. The LFS is a (quarterly) annual cross-sectional household survey providing extensive information on household individuals, including age, sex, ethnicity and many other individual characteristics. The LFS now has a panel design, but, for demographic applications, is mostly used cross-sectionally. The use of LFS data together with the 'Own-Children Method' (OCM) was first proposed in the UK by Berthoud (2001) to analyse teenage births to ethnic minority women and further applied by Coleman and Smith (2005) to produce national fertility rates from 1965 to 2001 by ethnic group. A crude form of OCM was earlier used to make rough estimates of the annual growth rates of each of the different ethnic minority populations (Haskey, 1992).

The OCM of fertility estimation (Cho et al., 1986; UN and NRC, 1983) is a reverse-survival technique for estimating age-specific fertility rates using census or cross-sectional household survey data. The technique has been designed to enable the derivation of fertility estimates in countries where vital registration is unreliable, but relatively more accurate census or household survey data exist (Cho et al., 1986). In the absence of vital statistics by ethnicity of the mother, this technique has been applied in the UK using LFS data (3rd quarter annually) and has subsequently proven to be a valid approach to estimating UK national inter-censal ASFRs and TFRs by ethnic group. Estimates of national TFRs produced using LFS data by the OCM are very close to those using ONS vital registration data (Fig. 4.1).

Whilst the general trend in TFR for all women in the UK over the last 46 years obtained using the LFS-OCM is in line with the available official data from the ONS (vital registration), note that the data for the most recent years are more uncertain as they are based on smaller numbers. For instance, the 2006 TFR value is based on the sole 2006 survey data. In contrast, for 2001, TFRs are derived from six sets of survey data pooled together.

Another strength of the method is the use of a *single* data source for estimating the numbers of both the births and the women at risk of childbearing, limiting the bias which can occur through bringing together data from two different sources.

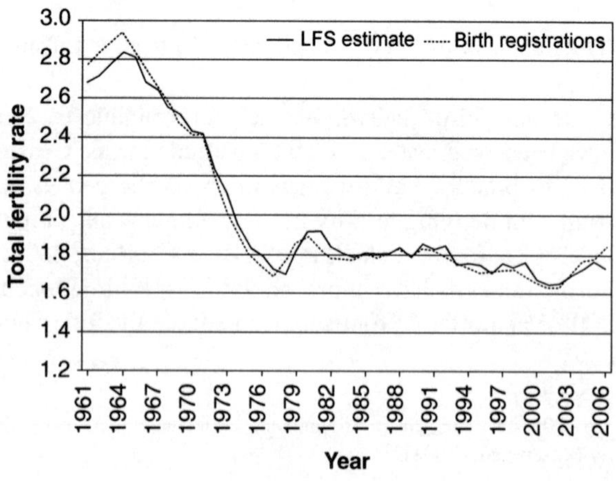

Fig. 4.1 Total fertility from OCM from LFS compared with ONS registration statistics, 1961–2006 (Source: Coleman and Dubuc, 2010. Note: Household units were used to produce the LFS data in Fig. 4.1. Family units were unavailable up to the 1990s)

A limitation of the LFS data is its sample size (despite being relatively large for most other purposes) when it comes to studying small groups. However, by aggregating LFS data over several years (2001–2006), it is possible to produce reliable inter-censal estimates even for relatively small minority ethnic groups. The number of women aged 15–49 years old over the period 1988–2006 by ethnic group was as follows: 2,336,617 White British; 124,704 White Other; 53,368 Indian; 33,108 Pakistani; 31,879 Black Caribbean and Other Black, Black African; 17,027 Mixed; 16,821 Other Asian; 14,261 Other; 11,840 Chinese; and 11,164 Bangladeshi women.

LFS-OCM, a Reverse Survival Technique for Inter-Censal Fertility

The OCM makes use of basic household records (from censuses or surveys) – which provide information on the age and sex of individuals resident within the household – to estimate the number of children by their age, and the age of their mother at the time of the survey, as well as the number of women at risk of childbearing by age. This information allows the derivation of ASFRs. Because the OCM matches children to their mother within the household, using the relationship between household members, it carries the advantage, over simple reverse-survival techniques, of avoiding – or at least minimising – the risk of selecting children who are not related to any woman in the household.

This matching procedure has been automated (EasWesPop Program) and made available by the East West Center (Honolulu, Hawaii). The program allows, within each household surveyed, children aged 0–14 to be matched to women aged 15–60 years old according to their stated relationship. This matching is performed in order to retro-construct the births to women of childbearing age, by age of the mother up to 14 years before the survey, based on their respective ages at the time of the survey. For instance, if in 2005 a child 14 years old was identified together with his/her 35 year old mother, the woman would be estimated to have had a birth when aged 21 in 1991. The estimated annual numbers of births by age of the mother are then divided by the 'appropriate' numbers of women to compute ASFRs in 2005 and over the previous 14 years.

Retro-constructing births based on children who are older at the time of the survey brings the further advantage of minimising the well known and documented problem of undercounted babies and infants in censuses and surveys (e.g. Hattersley and Creeser, 1995; NIRSA, 2001; ONS, 2001). Another strength of the method derives from matching children to women of a particular ethnic group without restricting the ethnic denomination of the children, since the matching procedure is based solely on the relationship between household members. Therefore the calculations more accurately reflect the fertility of women of mixed origin than, for instance, the corresponding estimates based on child-women ratios (CWR), which require both the mother and child to have the same designated ethnic group. In the UK, the Mixed population is generally young and rapidly growing, while their parents are usually *not* of Mixed ethnic group. Therefore, ratios of 'Mixed children' to 'Mixed women' (CWRs) greatly overestimate the fertility of Mixed ethnic group women. OCM estimates should also be more accurate for the fertility rates of women of other ethnic groups where Mixed children will be counted.

The OCM can only link children living in the same household as their mother. Because most of the children under the age of 15 stay with their mother in the event of their parents' separation (Berthoud, 2001; Murphy and Berrington, 1993), the possible underestimation of fertility through this restriction remains low. Furthermore, this potential underestimation may be partly compensated by a risk of overestimation of fertility in the cases where women are living with their step-children; both factors are likely to be marginal, however. Two other sources of possible underestimation of fertility – involving (i) the procedure of matching children to their mother at the household level, and (ii) the inability to take death rates into account – have been recognised (Berthoud, 2001). These aspects are considered below (for further detail on the method see Berthoud, 2001). An extensive description of the LFS-Own-children method presented here and its assessment is developed in Dubuc (2009).

OCM Refinements Correcting for Fertility Under-Estimation

Two methodological refinements, using family units and mortality retro-correction, were applied to enhance the accuracy of the fertility estimates produced here. More than one nuclear family may live within a household. In the LFS, each individual is characterised by a household serial number and his/her relation to the head of household. Since 1992, a family unit codification, and the recording of the relationship of family members to the head of family unit, have been introduced. This information was utilised in the OCM approach and the differences in TFR estimates using family units instead of household relationships (which had not been complete, since not all possible pairs of relationships had been collected) were tested. The program used for the matching procedure is sophisticated enough to recognise relationships between members of different nuclear families within the same household – such as cohabitation between parent(s); child and grandchild both present, or a sibling of the head of household also living in the household, for example. The difficulty in matching children to mothers increases within increasing complexity of household composition, since the coding of relationships is not endlessly exhaustive and the child-mother relationship may not possibly be deduced from the relationship of each one to the head of household, especially in the case of unrelated, or distantly related family members (Dubuc, 2009).

The number of births in the years prior to the survey (reverse-survived) was corrected for mortality occurring between the birth of the child and their age at the time of the survey. A similar retro-correction was applied to the number of women. Research on health inequality by ethnicity suggests that death rate patterns are likely to differ across ethnic groups. Recently, Rees and Wohland (2008) have proposed a method to estimate mortality by ethnic groups using illness ratios. In 2008, the ONS began publishing some statistics on infant mortality by ethnicity in England and Wales suggesting differences across ethnic groups, with particularly higher death

Table 4.2 TFR of main ethnic groups before and after refinement

Ethnic group	Difference in the TFR (2000–2006)[a] (%)
White British	1.35
White Other	1.70
Black Caribbean	1.51
Black African	2.76
Indian	1.09
Pakistani	2.67
Bangladeshi	1.90
Chinese	1.74

[a]The difference recorded after refinement using family unit and retro-mortality correction compared to calculations based on household unit and without mortality correction.
Source: Authors' estimates based on LFS.

rates amongst Pakistani and Black Caribbean infants. Since death statistics have never been available by ethnic group, the same mortality pattern has been assumed for all groups for the last 20 years. The UK population death rates by age and sex between 1976 and 2006 provided by ONS (Table D9552) were used, and, for children from 0 to 14 years old, the average male/female annual death rate (deaths per 1,000) was calculated using a sex-ratio of 105. The average sex-ratio calculations come from (ONS, 2008; Table 4.1) and birth registration data (Dubuc and Coleman, 2007).

These refinements increased the overall 2000–2006 TFR by 1.6%. The difference made by incorporating the retro-correction for mortality was small (variation of TFR= 0.37%) as corrections in the numerator and the denominator partly compensate (Equation 4.2) and probably also because mortality of both children and women of childbearing age is rare in the UK. This results in a very marginal impact of change in mortality on the OCM estimates (Dubuc, 2009). Interestingly, underestimation varies across ethnic groups (Table 4.2), fluctuating between 1 and 2.7%, with underestimation being largest for the Pakistani and Black African groups. This variation, introduced by the use of family unit to match the children to their mother, may suggest a relatively larger prevalence of more complex households for some groups (e.g. Pakistani and Black African). The implementation of the family unit matching and retro-correction for mortality, both correcting for small under-estimation, should increase the precision of the estimates, for the reasons given above.

Variations in the Quantum and Tempo of Childbearing by Ethnic Group

Fertility Trends by Ethnicity

As expected, over the period 1987–2006, the TFRs for White British women, the major ethnic group (Fig. 4.2) fit well with the general trend for all women (Fig. 4.1),

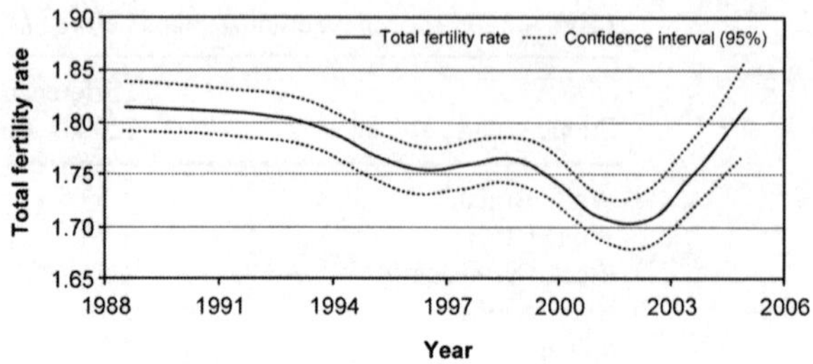

Fig. 4.2 Trend in 3-year average TFR of the White British women, 1987–2006 (Source: Authors' estimates based on LFS)

including a continuous rise in the four most recent years. Figure 4.3 shows the trends in TFR for the ethnic minority groups in the UK (Other White, Indian, Pakistani, Black Caribbean, Black African, Bangladeshi, Chinese, Mixed, Asian others and Others) over the same period using longer time intervals to allow trend estimates for smaller ethnic minority groups. Note that, due to very small numbers, the category 'Black Other' was merged with the closest group, 'Black Caribbean', to monitor the trend in fertility. The average TFR of 'Black Other' women for the overall period (1987–2006) was about 1.8, and scarcely affects the level of fertility of the Black Caribbean group when added. Over the period 1987–2006, Mixed: White and Black-Caribbean women accounted for just over one third of the total Mixed ethnic

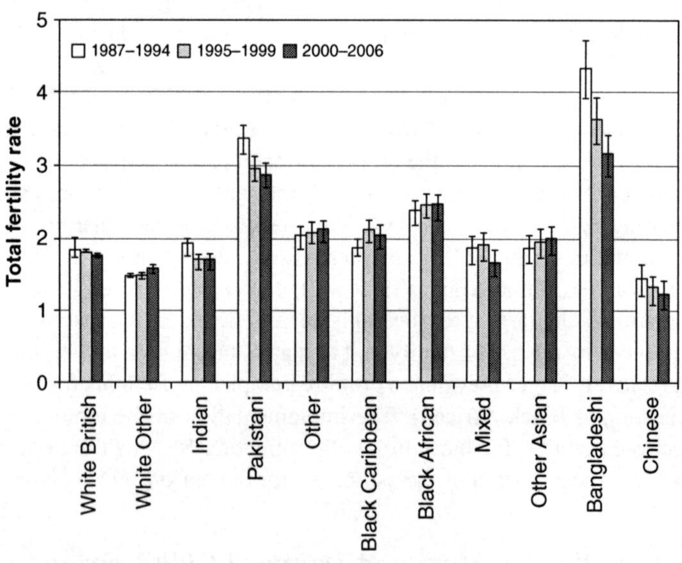

Fig. 4.3 Trend in TFR by main ethnic group, 1987–2006. Ethnic categories are sorted by decreasing frequency of the number of women aged 15–49 in 2006 LFS, third quarter (White British are 86.6%, White Other 5.3%, Indian 1.7%, Pakistani and Other 1.2%, other groups are about 0.5% and below of the sum of women with an ethnic group. Ethnicity was not stated for 6.2% of women) (Source: Authors' estimates based on LFS)

Table 4.3 Decreasing standard deviation of TFR by ethnic group

Period	Mean	Standard deviation	Coefficient of variation	Sample size
1987–1994	2.12	0.753	0.355	1,023,267
1995–1999	2.09	0.575	0.276	889,623
2000–2006	2.00	0.487	0.243	763,295

Source: Authors' estimates based on LFS.

group women; Mixed: White and Asian, and 'Other Mixed' accounted for a quarter each, and the remaining Mixed women were Mixed: White and Black African. Since about one half of the Mixed population was still below 16 years old in 2001, the number of mixed origin adult women was especially small. Therefore just one set of estimates was made for the Mixed ethnic group – for all the Mixed groups taken together. The TFR for the Mixed ethnic group women was close to that for White British.

The rise in the Black African and Black Caribbean TFRs in the 1990s has not been continued in recent years (Fig. 4.3). The most notable decreasing trends in TFRs are those for the Bangladeshi and Pakistani groups; although they started from a very high level, they fell to a level still comparatively high – around 2.8 children per woman – in 2000–2006, when the TFR for White British women was below 1.8. The TFR for Indian women has fallen below that for White British women, while the previously very low fertility of the White Other has since risen slightly. Taken together, there is less variability in the level of the TFRs across ethnic groups in recent years compared with that in the 1990s, as illustrated by the decreasing coefficient of variation of TFR by ethnic group over the three periods studied (Table 4.3).

Women's Age at Childbearing, Patterns and Changes

Not only the level of fertility but also the timing of childbearing varies across groups. Figure 4.4 shows the diversity in the tempo (and quantum) of childbearing across ethnic groups. White Other, the Chinese and Other Asian women tend to have their children later, on average, than the other groups. The age pattern at childbearing of Black Caribbean women and Mixed women (Fig. 4.4a) is distinctive from others, showing a relatively high birth rate for young women aged under 25, as well as for women in their late 30 s and older, but a relatively low birth rate amongst women in their late 20 s, compared with the age profiles for women of other ethnic groups. This suggests the co-existence of at least two distinct social sub-categories within these ethnic groups (See discussion below regarding late/delayed childbearing).

Interestingly, Fig. 4.4b shows the diversity of age patterns of childbearing between the different ethnic groups comprising the Asian population. The quantum and tempo of childbearing of Indian women is the closest to that of White British women, albeit with lower birth rates amongst young Indian women aged under 25.

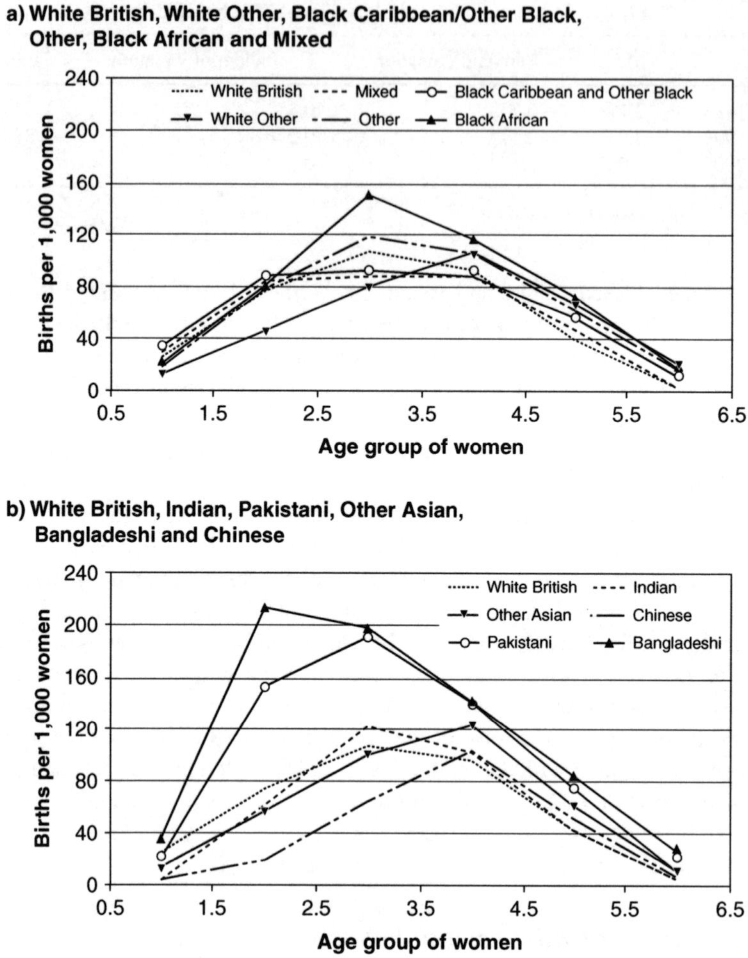

Fig. 4.4 Variation in the timing of childbearing (Source: Authors' estimates based on LFS)

Pakistani and Bangladeshi women have more children and record younger ages at childbearing than other Asian population women (and all other ethnic groups). This phenomenon may be related to the remarkably low level of women working, the lowest of all ethnic groups (Lindley et al., 2004). In contrast, the Chinese and 'Other Asian' women tend to have their children later in their child-bearing years.

A delay in childbearing, possibly associated with women's increased involvement in higher education and paid work, has been observed in recent years in the UK (ONS, 2005). Figure 4.5 shows the change in the age pattern at childbearing over time for White Other, Indian, and Pakistani women (the larger minority groups), compared with that for White British women. Postponement of childbearing is more or less pronounced depending on the women's ethnicity. White British women have

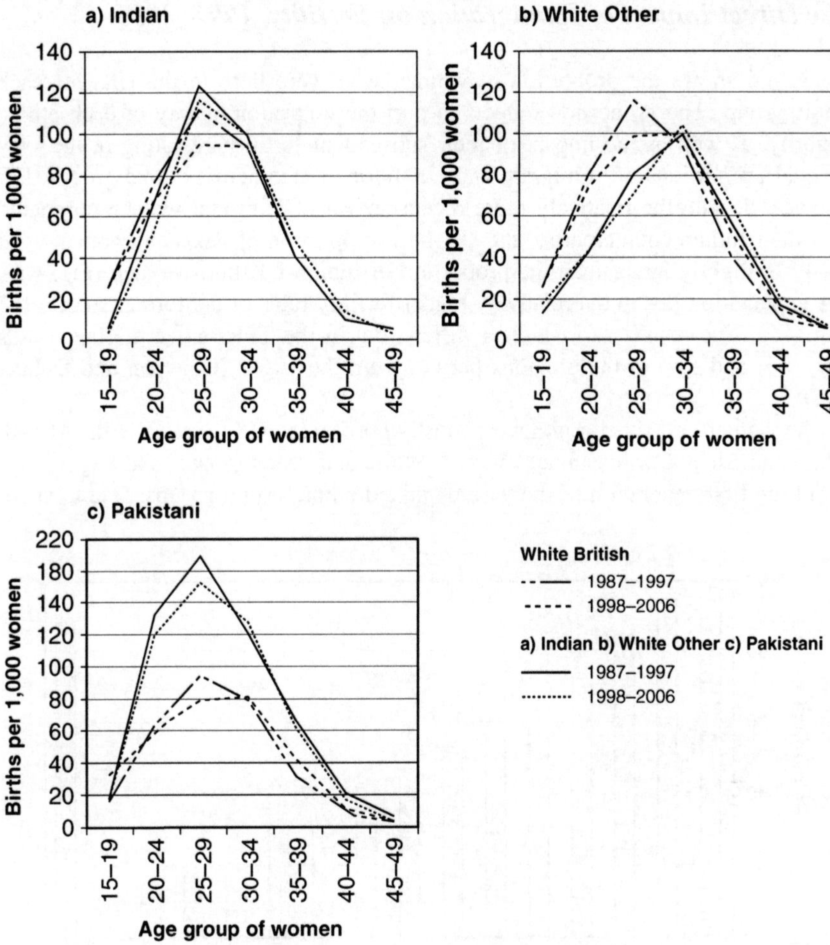

Fig. 4.5 Change in the ASFRs, 1987–2006, White British, White Other, Indian and Pakistani (Source: Authors' estimates based on LFS)

continuously delayed childbearing since the late 1980s, tending to have fewer children in their 20 s and more children later. Indian women also show signs of delayed childbearing in the recent period. Postponement appears even more pronounced for White Other women for whom the average age at childbearing was already older than that of White British women in the late 1980s and early 1990s. In contrast, there appears little evidence for delayed childbearing amongst Pakistani women, for whom fertility decline occurred in every age-group. However, in more recent years, the reduction in the number of children per 1,000 women has been more pronounced at younger ages than at older ages in women's child-bearing years. This may be a consequence of delayed childbearing for some Pakistani women combined with a reduction in the average number of children born.

The Direct Impact of Immigration on Fertility, 1997–2006

Figure 4.6 shows the proportion of women who were born in the UK, for each ethnic group. The proportion reflects in part the migration history of each ethnic minority, as well as the impact of their subsequent fertility, resulting in the very unequal proportions of immigrant and UK-born women across ethnic groups. For instance, despite the relatively more recent arrival of Pakistani women compared with their Indian counterparts,[3] the UK-born proportion of Pakistani women aged 15–49 is slightly larger than the proportion of Indian UK-born women (Fig. 4.6). The explanation lies in the relatively higher fertility rates of the former since 1987 (Fig. 4.3). The results show a clear differential in the TFRs since the late 1980s (Fig. 4.3) and also in the previous period, from the 1960s (Coleman and Dubuc, 2010).

The women of Mixed origin were mostly born in the UK, especially the Mixed: White and Black Caribbean, and Mixed: White and Asian groups, and largely represent the first generation of the various mixed ethnic origin groups. Due to small

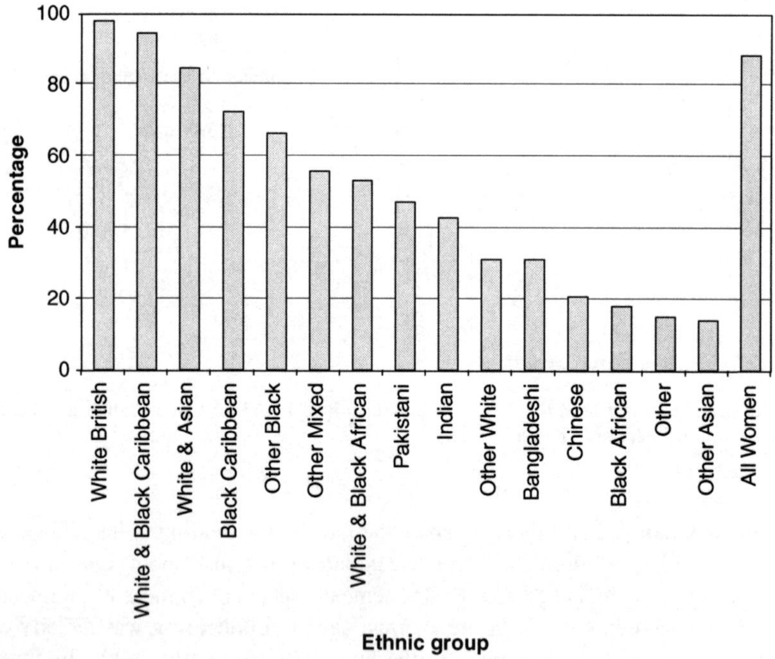

Fig. 4.6 Women aged 15–49: proportion of UK-born by ethnicity, 2002–2006 (Source: LFS data, third quarter 2002–2006)

---

[3]In recent years, the immigration of Indian students appears to have increased significantly, however (Vertovec, 2007).

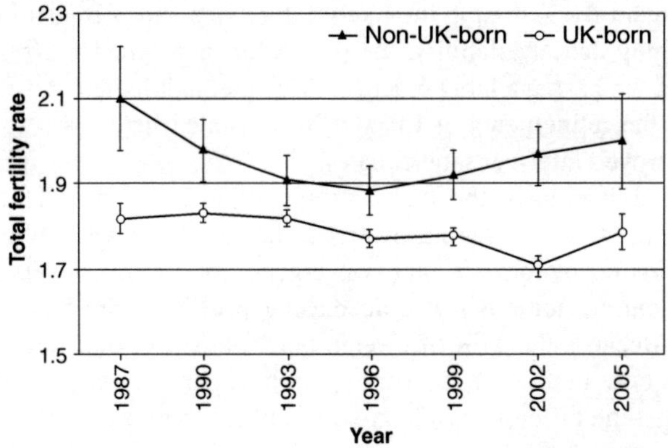

Fig. 4.7 Trend in the TFR of UK-born and foreign-born women in the UK, 1987–2006 (Source: LFS data, third quarter 2000–2006)

sample numbers, a comparison of the TFRs between the UK-born and the foreign-born sub-populations of each ethnic group was not possible. However, the trend in the TFRs for all women, by their country of birth – UK or non-UK – (Fig. 4.7) shows the contribution of immigrant women (meaning first generation in the UK) to the TFR of the UK population. Immigrant women mainly belong to one or other of the different ethnic minorities (about 82% of non UK-born women aged 15–49 in 2002–2006 were not White British).

Comparing Figs. 4.2 and 4.7, it appears that the fertility of White British women (Fig. 4.2) closely matches the trend in the TFR of UK-born women (Fig. 4.7). The trend in the TFRs of the native and foreign-born population (Fig. 4.7) also shows that the general fertility decline recorded in the 1990s and early 2000s would have been more pronounced without the contribution of births to foreign-born women. However, the general rise in the TFR since 2002 (Dunnell, 2007) appears to be jointly due to increases in the fertility of both the immigrant and the UK-born women (Fig. 4.7).

Overall, the TFR of immigrant women has always been higher than that of UK-born women. Therefore, ceteris paribus, the reduction in the proportion of foreign-born women amongst each ethnic minority group – which should occur in the case of stable net migration flows – may be expected to lower the overall TFR in the near future.

Conclusions

Producing fertility estimates by ethnic group is the necessary first step to understanding how the factor of ethnicity contributes to overall fertility behaviour. The analysis shows some distinct differences in the quantum and tempo of childbearing across ethnic groups. Inter-ethnic variability in fertility varies over time, and fertility estimates therefore need updating regularly. Monitoring these changes is a major requirement for assessing the likely future size and composition of the population. Changing data availability, the search for more precise estimates, and the desire to adopt the best available practice, drive methodological developments, just as employing the refinements of LFS-OCM presented here was the incentive for producing improved inter-censal estimates.

Since the publication of the first fertility estimates by main ethnic group (up to 2001), the question of converging trends has been a major subject of debate. Results support the hypothesis that convergence of fertility levels across ethnic groups has occurred, although at a decreasing pace over the more recent period (2001–2006). Because the TFR of foreign-born women is, on average, higher than that of women born in the UK, the varying proportions of immigrant (foreign-born) women amongst the different ethnic groups is likely to give rise to some variability in their TFRs – which may decrease in the future, if net migration remains stable. However, it remains unclear whether full convergence will occur or whether variability will persist between ethnic groups. For instance, a large majority of Black Caribbean women were born in the UK but over the last 20 years this ethnic group has consistently recorded a higher TFR than that of both the total UK and White British women.

Furthermore, if the fertility of foreign-born women as a whole appears relatively high, it may mask differences across ethnic groups. The especially low and declining fertility of the Chinese is associated with a very high proportion of foreign-born Chinese (Fig. 4.6). This observation may reflect the particular profile of Chinese immigrant women, notably the rise in migration of students and highly skilled workers from South East Asia since the 1980s (Cheng, 1996). The relatively older average age at childbearing of this group, often associated with higher education and professional ambitions, is in line with this migration trend. Different social profiles and characteristics are likely to impact on the quantum and tempo of childbearing of each ethnic group. Generally, it is important to remember that differences in level and timing of childbearing between ethnic groups are not necessarily due to ethnicity per se but also due to different migration histories, age compositions, and social and socio-economic profiles.

The results suggest that childbearing has been delayed amongst ethnic minority women in the recent period (1998–2006). This change in the timing of childbearing is likely to be associated with women's involvement in higher education and paid employment. Indeed, Lindley et al. (2006) found an increase in the percentage of women in paid work during the period 2000–2003, compared with the earlier period 1992–1995, for Black African, Indian, Pakistani/Bangladeshi and White women – which especially benefited those with a higher education for the latter. This is concomitant with the decrease in fertility of women in their 20 s observed in each of the four major groups – the White British, White Other, Indian and Pakistani (Fig. 4.5). The forthcoming 2011 Census should provide valuable data to analyse further the relationship between women's employment status and childbearing behaviour.

Making fertility assumptions for the future remains a challenge – and a better understanding of the factors influencing the variability in fertility behaviour will help in this task. Further, because ethnicity is a social construct, difficulties arise when trying to project the population by ethnic group based on estimated future fertility trends by women's ethnic group. Evaluating ethnic affiliation of a child based on his/her mother's ethnic self-identification is especially challenging because a child may develop a personal ethnic identification different from his/her mother. It might be a marginal issue when both parents are of the same ethnic group, but not completely negligible as noted by Sporton and White (2002). For example, children of Black Caribbean parents may classify themselves as Black British instead of Black Caribbean. Consequently, when applying fertility rates to estimate the future size and composition of the population, the number of children likely to classify themselves as a different ethnicity from that of their mother should be *pro rata* redistributed to the group(s) to which they assign themselves. In the case of Mixed unions, the difficulty is exacerbated (Sporton and White, 2002), and the growing importance of the different Mixed categories of the ethnic minority population will further challenge the way fertility trends are used in projection models. Consequently, monitoring the ethnic self-identification of respondents in the census, the LFS and possibly other surveys, and comparing it with their parent's declared ethnicity will provide important background information for projection models, as well as a reflection on the dynamic nature of ethnicity.

Acknowledgements This work was supported by the Economic and Social Research Council, Grant RES-163-25-0049 and the authors are thankful to David Coleman for his collaboration.

References

Aspinall, P. (2000) The challenges of measuring the ethno-cultural diversity of Britain in the new millennium, *Policy and Politics*, 28(1): 109–118.

Ballard, R. (1990) Migration and kinship: The differential effect of marriage rules on the processes of Punjabi migration to Britain in Clarke, C., Peach, C. and Vertovek, S. (eds.), *South Asians Overseas: Contexts and Communities*, Cambridge University Press, Cambridge, pp. 219–249.

Ballard, R. (1996) Negotiating race and ethnicity: Exploring the implications of the 1991 census, *Patterns of Prejudice*, 30(3): 3–33.

Berthoud, R. (2001) Teenage births to ethnic minority women, *Population Trends*, 104: 12–17.

Berthoud, R., Modood, T. and Smith, P. (1997) *Ethnic Minorities in Britain, the Fourth National Survey of Ethnic Minorities in Britain*, Policy Studies Institute, London.

Berrington, A. (1996) Marriage patterns and inter-ethnic unions in Coleman, D. and Salt, J. (eds.), *Ethnicity in the 1991 Census: Demographic Characteristics of the Ethnic Minority Populations*, HMSO, London, pp. 178–212.

Brown, J.M. (2006) *Global South Asians. Introducing the Modern Diaspora*, Cambridge University Press, Cambridge.

Boyd, M. and Shida, N. (2009) Unstable ethnicities: Impacts of question wording and respondent characteristics, Paper presented at the annual meeting of Population Association of America, 29 April–2 May, Detroit, paa2009.princeton.edu/abstractViewer.aspx?submissionId=90638

Bulmer, M. (1996) The ethnic group question in the 1991 Census of population in Coleman, D. and Salt, J. (eds.), *Ethnicity in the 1991 Census of Population, Volume 1: Demographic Characteristics of the Ethnic Minority Populations*, HMSO, London.

Byron, M. (1998) Migration, work and gender: The case of post-war labour migration from the Caribbean to Britain in Chamberlain, M. (ed.), *Caribbean Migration: Globalised Identities*, Routledge, London, pp. 217–231.

Cheng, Y. (1996) The Chinese: Upwardly mobile in Peach, C. (ed.), *Ethnicity in the 1991 Census, Volume 2: The Ethnic Minority Populations of Great Britain*, HMSO, London, pp. 161–180.

Cho, L.-J., Retherford, R.D. and Choe, M.K. (1986) *The Own-Children Method of Fertility Estimation*, University of Hawaii Press for the Population Institute, East-West Center, Honolulu.

Coleman, D. and Dubuc, S. (2010) The fertility of ethnic minority populations in the United Kingdom, 1971–2006, *Population Studies*, 64(1).

Coleman, D.A. and Smith, M.D. (2005) *The Projection of Ethnic Minority Populations: Problems and Data Needs* (Background Paper No 2), Oxford Centre for Population Research, Oxford, http://www.spsw.ox.ac.uk/oxpop/publications%20files/WP13.pdf

Coleman, D. and Salt, J. (1996) *Ethnicity in the 1991 Census of Population, Volume 1: Demographic Characteristics of the Ethnic Minority Populations*, HMSO, London.

Daley, P. (1996) Black-Africans: Students who stayed in Peach, C. (ed.), *Ethnicity in the 1991 Census, Volume 2: The Ethnic Minority Populations of Great Britain*, HMSO, London, pp. 44–65.

Dubuc, S. (2009) Application of the own-children method for estimating fertility of women by ethnic groups in the UK, *Journal of Population Research*, 26(3): 207–225.

Dunnell, K. (2007) The changing demographic picture of the UK. National statistician's annual article on the population, *Population Trends*, 130: 9–21.

Foner, N. (2009) Gender and migration: West Indians in comparative perspective, *International Migration*, 47(1): 3–30.

Haskey, J. (1992) Demographic characteristics of the ethnic minority populations of Great Britain in Bittles, A.H. and Roberts, D.F. (eds.), *Minority Populations: Genetics, Demography and Health*. Proceedings of the 27th annual symposium of the Galton Institute, Macmillan, London, pp. 182–207.

Haskey, J. (1996) The ethnic minority populations of Great Britain: Their estimated sizes and age profiles, *Population Trends*, 84: 33–39.

Haskey, J. (1997) Population review: (8) The ethnic minority and overseas-born populations of Great Britain, *Population Trends*, 88: 13–30.

Haskey, J. (2002) Projections of the population by ethnic group: A sufficiently interesting or a definitely necessary exercise to undertake? in Haskey, J. (ed.), *Population Projections by Ethnic Group: A Feasibility Study* (Studies in Medical and Population Subjects No. 67, TSO), HMSO, London, pp. xxi–xxxii.

Hattersley, L. and Creeser, R. (1995) *The Longitudinal Study, 1971–1991: History, Organisation and Quality of Data*, Appendix XIV. Office of Population Censuses and Surveys (LS Series No. 7), London, pp. 354–357, http://www.celsius.lshtm.ac.uk/publications/lsvol.html

Jones, T. (1993) *Britain's Ethnic Minorities: An Analysis of the Labour Force Survey*, Policy Studies Institute, London.

Large, P., Gosh, K. and Fry, R. (2006) *Population Estimates by Ethnic Group* (Methodology Paper), Office for National Statistics, London.

Lindley, J., Dale, A. and Dex, S. (2004, April) Ethnic differences in women's demographic, family characteristics and economic activity profiles, 1992 to 2002, *Labour Market Trends*, 115: 153–165.

Lindley, J., Dale, A. and Dex, S. (2006) Ethnic differences in women's employment: The changing role of qualifications, *Oxford Economic Papers*, 58: 351–378.

Mitton, L. and Aspinall, P. (2009) Black African in Britain: Integration or segregation? Presentation at the UPTAP workshop, 24 March, University of Leeds, http://www.uptap.net/wordpress/wp-content/uploads/2009/04/lavinia-mitton-presentation.pdf

Mitton, L. and Aspinall, P. (2010) Black Africans in England: A diversity of integration experiences in Stillwell, J. and van Ham, M. (eds.), *Ethnicity and Integration Understanding Population Trends and Processes*, Vol. 3, Springer, Dordrecht, pp. 179–202.

Moser, K., Stanfield, K.M. and Leon, D.A. (2008) Birthweight and gestational age by ethnic group, England and Wales 2005: Introducing new data on births, *Health Statistics Quarterly*, 39: 22–31.

Murphy, M. and Berrington, A. (1993) Constructing parity progression ratios from household survey data in Ni Bhrolchain, M. (ed.), *New Perspectives on Fertility in Britain*, HMSO, London, pp. 17–32.

NISRA (Northern Ireland Statistics and Research Agency) (2001) *Counting Everyone in – the Big Challenge* (Census 2001 Factsheet 4). Accessed 19 January, 2009, http://www.geog.leeds.ac.uk/projects/migrants/Presentations/StakeholderMeeting_18December_4P-4.pdf

ONS (2001) *One Number Census Quality Assurance Information: Quality Assurance Themes* (Census 2001). Accessed at http://www.statistics.gov.uk/census2001/pdfs/babies-ethnic-pop.pdf

ONS (2005) *For the First Time Women in Early 30s Have Higher Fertility Rates than Women in Late 20s, Birth Statistics 2004* (Series FM1 no. 33). Accessed at www.statistics.gov.uk/statbase/Product.asp?vlnk=5768

ONS (2008) *Table 1.4, Population Trends, 134*. Available at http://www.statistics.gov.uk/STATBASE/ssdataset.asp?vlnk=9543

Peach, G.C.K. (ed.) (1996) *Ethnicity in the 1991 Census, Volume 2: The Ethnic Minority Populations of Great Britain*, HMSO, London.

Rees, P. (2008) What happens when international migrants settle? Projections of ethnic groups in United Kingdom regions in Raymer, J. and Willekens, F. (eds.), *International Migration in Europe: Data, Models and Assessment*, Wiley, London, pp. 329–358.

Rees, P., Norman, P., Wohland, P. and Boden, P. (2008) *Estimating Fertility by Ethnic Group, Ethnic Group Population Trends and Projections for UK Local Areas*. Presentation to a Stakeholder Meeting, 18 December, City Hall, London.

Rees, P. and Wohland, P. (2008) *Estimates of Ethnic Mortality in the UK* (Working Paper 08/04), School of Geography, University of Leeds, Leeds, Accessed 12 January, 2009, http://www.geog.leeds.ac.uk/wpapers/08-04.pdf

Simpson, L. and Akinwale, B. (2007) Quantifying stability and change in ethnic groups, *Journal of Official Statistics*, 23(2): 185–208.

Solomos, J. and Back, L. (1996) *Racism and Society*, Macmillan, London.

Sporton, D. and White, P.E. (2002) Fertility in Haskey, J. (ed.), *Population Projections by Ethnic Group, a Feasibility Study* (Studies in Medical and Population Subjects No. 67, TSO), HMSO, London, pp. 81–92.

United Nations and National Research Council (1983) *Manual X: Indirect Techniques for Demographic Estimation* (Population Studies, No. 81; ST/ESA/SER.A/81.), United Nations, New York, NY.

Vertovec, S. (2007) The emergence of super-diversity in Britain, *Ethnic and Racial Studies*, 30(6): 1024–1054.

Chapter 5
Neighbourhood Ethnic Mix and the Formation of Mixed-Ethnic Unions in Britain

Zhiqiang Feng, Paul Boyle, Maarten van Ham and Gillian Raab

Introduction

Numerous geographical studies over the last few decades have explored ethnic segregation (e.g. Burgess et al., 2005; Johnson et al., 2005; Peach, 1996; Simpson, 2004). Most have used cross-sectional data to determine how geographically segregated different ethnic minority groups are, while a few have also explored how these patterns have changed over time for different groups (Sabater, 2010). At the heart of these studies is the notion of ethnic mixing in different places, with the implicit assumption that less segregated places include a mix of households from different ethnic groups. None of these studies explore ethnic mixing *within households* and the contextual factors that might influence this (Wright et al., 2003). In a world where ethnic homogamy is the rule rather than exception, mixed-ethnic unions demonstrate the breakdown of ethnic barriers and are indicative of the degree of ethnic embeddedness, a particularly sensitive political issue at the current time. The persistent segregation and exclusion of ethnic minorities has caused tensions between minority and majority populations, despite the apparent efforts made by successive British governments to promote racial equality and 'integration'.

Against this background, it is reassuring to find that over the past several decades, the number of mixed-ethnic unions has increased substantially, although admittedly from a small base (Coleman, 2004). The 1% census sample from the Office for National Statistics (ONS) Longitudinal Study (LS) reveals that there has been a 65% increase in the total number of mixed-ethnic unions between 1991 and 2001 in England and Wales. Such unions have profound effects on the ethnic composition of the population, especially in the creation of new minority groups of mixed origin. It is estimated that nearly a million people report themselves as having a mixed-ethnic identity in Britain today (CRE, 2006).

Z. Feng (✉)
School of Geography and Geosciences/Longitudinal Studies Centre – Scotland (LSCS), University of St Andrews, Fife KY16 9AL, Scotland, UK
e-mail: zf2@st-andrews.ac.uk

J. Stillwell, M. van Ham (eds.), *Ethnicity and Integration*, Understanding Population Trends and Processes 3, DOI 10.1007/978-90-481-9103-1_5,

The geographical study of mixed-ethnic couples is not new, although most of this research has been conducted in the US (Peach, 1980; Wong, 1999). Building on a long history of research on residential segregation, this research explores how mixed-ethnic couples contribute to changing ethnic geographies. For example, Holloway et al. (2005) in the US examined the factors which increased the likelihood of mixed-ethnicity households living in predominantly White neighbourhoods. Their cross-sectional study found that mixed-ethnic households were more likely to live in mixed neighbourhoods than single ethnic households but it is impossible from this research to determine whether couples of this type were more likely to form in such neighbourhoods, or whether selective mobility occurred as these couples sought out residential neighbourhoods which they found more suitable. To explore these issues in detail requires longitudinal data.

A limited amount of research has also examined mixed-ethnic unions in the UK, mainly using cross-sectional data from the 1991 Census 1% Household Samples of Anonymised Records (SAR) or from the UK Labour Force Surveys (LFS) (e.g. Ballard, 1997; Berrington, 1996; Coleman, 1985, 2004; Data Management and Analysis Group Update, 2005; Holdsworth and Dale, 1997; Johnston et al., 2006; Muttarak, 2004). The 1994 Fourth National Survey of Ethnic Minorities has also been used to a limited extent to investigate mixed-ethnic unions (Muttarak, 2003). Most of these studies focused on basic patterns and trends in the growth of mixed-ethnic unions. A notable exception is Muttarak's (2004) study which investigated the socio-economic determinants of mixed-unions using LFS data. However, none of these studies used longitudinal data to explore the geography of the formation of mixed-ethnic couples. This study uses data from the Longitudinal Study (LS) for England and Wales and is the first UK study to examine the influence of geographical context on the formation of mixed-ethnic unions. By using longitudinal data, we are able to establish whether living in a mixed-ethnic neighbourhood makes it more likely for people to end up in mixed-ethnic unions.

Theoretical Background

The formation of unions is the result of preferences with regard to partner characteristics and the opportunity structure of available partners. In general, people prefer partners who are similar to them in demographic, social, economic and cultural characteristics – so called marital homogamy. Assimilationist theories (Gordon, 1964) argue that immigrants often possess distinct cultural traits and socio-economic status from members of the host society and that these may hinder interactions between immigrants and the host group. The process of assimilation starts with acculturation, proceeds through structural assimilation and is regarded as completed when the ethnicity of immigrants is no longer a notable characteristic to themselves and to members of the host society. According to this perspective, the most 'assimilated' members of minority groups will be more likely to partner members from majority groups. The observation that many mixed-ethnic unions involve ethnic minorities with higher levels of education or qualifications, and the observation that second and later generation ethnic minorities experience higher rates of mixed-ethnic unions appear to support such theories (Hwang et al., 1997; Muttarak, 2004).

Blau (1977) and colleagues (Blau et al., 1982) claim that inter-group relations depend not only on willingness among members of different groups to interact, but also on the opportunities to do so. Although assimilation or integration may enhance the willingness to interact, inter-ethnic relations cannot take place unless opportunities for interactions exist. People spend most of their lives in local and functional places such as neighbourhoods, schools, workplaces and leisure places. The opportunity for inter-ethnic relationships is thus determined by attributes of local marriage markets such as the size of the minority group, the availability of potential partners in the minority group, the availability of potential partners in the majority group, and the social and spatial proximity between minority and majority groups.

Although endogamous relationships are most common, exogamous relationships can be beneficial for those involved. Status exchange theories assert that a lower status majority group member is more likely to partner a minority group member if the latter has a higher socio-economic status (White and Sassler, 2000). According to some economics-based explanations, this kind of status exchange helps both partners maximize their complementary benefits; both parties benefit from the utility functions of their significant other. This hypothesis is supported by studies of mixed marriage between Black and White people in the US (Kalmijn, 1993; Schoen and Wooldredge, 1989), but no support was found in studies of mixed marriages between Asians and Whites (Fu, 2006; Shoen and Thomas, 1989).

Spatial proximity between ethnic groups increases the probability of intermarriage (Blau, 1977; Bossard, 1932; Cready and Saenz, 1997; Morgan, 1981). Contemporary geographical theories have highlighted the mutual constitutivity of the social and the spatial (Delaney, 2002). Places are not simply reflective of social relations but are regarded as influential in constituting and reinforcing social relations. On the one hand, residential segregation along ethnic lines hampers the opportunities of meeting people from different ethnic groups. The concentration of a minority group within a neighbourhood also tends to reinforce the sense of belonging to the group and thus potentially reduces the propensity for exogamy. On the other hand, proximity breeds familiarity, recognition of commonality and the eventual disappearance of race as a meaningful social category (Delaney, 2002). As a consequence, we expect that the formation of mixed-ethnic partnerships will be influenced by these contextual factors (Lievens, 1998).

Thus, we assume that contact between ethnic groups within mixed ethnic neighbourhoods will break down prejudice (Ihlanfeldt and Scafidi, 2002). Ellison and Powers (1994) found that interracial contact, especially if it occurs early in life, leads to a greater likelihood that African Americans and Whites will have close interracial friendships as adults. Sigelman et al. (1996) found similar results in Detroit, showing that early interracial contact in schools was particularly associated with more interracial contact as adults. Emerson et al. (2002) confirm the role of early interracial contact, relating it to more racially diverse social and friendship circles later in life, including an increased probability of attendance at multiracial religious congregations and interracial marriages.

Some argue that residential proximity has become less important in explaining the growth of mixed-ethnic unions as the local neighbourhood is only one space in which contacts may be made (Houston et al., 2005). In one of the few studies to address the issue of where couples meet, Bozon and Heran (1989) found that the importance of the neighbourhood reduced steadily in twentieth century France; by the 1980s only 5% of all couples stated that they met locally. Kalmijn and Flap (2001) also reported that less than 10% of Dutch couples ever shared a neighbourhood environment. Ellis et al. (2006) showed that mixed-ethnic households consistently had a high propensity of living in neighbourhoods with low concentrations of the ethnic group of the ethnic minority partner. They concluded that this was because mixed-ethnic households choose to live in such neighbourhoods, dwelling less on the fact that neighbourhoods also influence the probability of forming mixed-ethnic unions.

Here we explore whether ethnic concentration in a neighbourhood setting influences whether people engage in mixed-ethnic partnerships. Intuitively, we might expect that living in a mixed-ethnic neighbourhood may increase the likelihood of such couple formation, although the literature review above suggests that those living in neighbourhoods with a low concentration of their own ethnic group may be more likely to out-partner. Specifically, we explore the likelihood that minority ethnic individuals choose a White partner in different geographical contexts.

Data and Methods

This study has used data from the Office for National Statistics Longitudinal Study (ONS-LS), which is a nationally representative 1% sample of the England and Wales population including approximately 500,000 people. The study began in the 1970s and links information from the 1971, 1981, 1991 and 2001 Censuses. The sample was updated through intercensal births, deaths, immigrations, embarkations and re-entries. In addition to census data, information is linked from cancer registrations, births to sample mothers and enlistments from the Armed Forces. The study was designed as a continuous, multi-cohort study with samples drawn from subsequent censuses using the same selection criteria. Information on the household members of ONS-LS members is also included in the data, although the records for these individuals are not linked through time. In addition to the individual-level micro data, the ONS-LS contain some variables from the censuses which capture the characteristics of the small areas in which each sample member lived. As the data are geocoded, it is possible to attach additional geographical variables – such as the mixed-ethnic neighbourhood indicators developed in this study – to individual ONS-LS members.

We focus on data from the 1991 and 2001 Censuses, as information on ethnicity was not captured in 1971 and 1981. Unfortunately, the ethnicity questions in the 1991 and 2001 Censuses were different. The 2001 Census question on ethnicity was changed to capture the rise in the number of people who reported 'mixed-ethnicity'. For consistency across 1991 and 2001 and following previous studies (Bradford,

Table 5.1 1991 and 2001 ethnicity definitions

Ethnic group	1991	2001
White	White	British Irish Other white
Black	Black-Caribbean Black-African Black other Black and White	Black-Caribbean Black-African Other Black White and Black-Caribbean White and Black-African
South Asian	Indian Pakistani Bangladeshi	Indian Pakistani Bangladeshi
Other Asian	Chinese Other Asian	Chinese Other Asian
Other	Other ethnic group: non-mixed origin Other ethnic group: mixed origin	White and Asian Other mixed Other ethnic group

Source: ONS-LS.

2006; Platt et al., 2005) we identified five broad ethnic groups: White, Black, South Asian, Other Asian, and Other (Table 5.1). However, in our analyses we excluded the Other group which is a small, heterogeneous group.

Between 1991 and 2001 a small number of individuals changed the way they recorded their ethnicity. This was most common among mixed-ethnic and Black groups. In the analysis of the pattern of mixed-ethnic unions we used the ethnicity variables for 1991 and 2001 separately for each sample as some of the 1991 members were not followed in 2001 due to attrition. In the analysis of the formation of mixed-ethnic unions, we used the 2001 variable to establish the ethnicity for each LS member. In the 2001 Census, 2.9% of responses to the ethnicity question were imputed, falling to 2.1% among LS members who were linked between 1991 and 2001. Imputation appears to be more common among those belonging to minority groups. Unfortunately, the imputation is not very reliable (Platt et al., 2005) and we therefore dropped LS members with imputed ethnicity.

We included both married and cohabiting couples of mixed-ethnic origin in our definition of mixed-ethnic unions (see also Berrington, 1996; Coleman, 2004; Liang and Ito, 1999; Model and Fisher, 2002; Muttarak, 2004; Wong, 1999). Cohabitation is of increasing importance and failure to include cohabiting couples would underestimate the number of mixed-ethnic unions. Furthermore, because mixed-ethnic unions are relatively rare, including cohabiting couples also boosts our sample size and enhances the statistical power of our models.

The literature suggests that the ethnic mix of people's residential context influences the probability of forming a mixed-ethnic union. The scale at which people's residential contexts should be measured is debatable (van Ham and Feijten, 2008). With regard to union formation, people meet potential partners, for example, at school, in the workplace and at leisure places and these can stretch from the direct surroundings of the home to the neighbourhood, to whole cities and larger regions. Together, these meeting places form the local marriage market area. In this study, we measure marriage markets at two spatial levels: local government districts and wards. On average, local government districts contain populations of around 120,000 (regional marriage market area) while wards contain populations of around 6,000 (neighbourhoods or local marriage market area). For each of these spatial levels we calculated the ethnic mix of the population.

We classified ethnic marriage market areas (districts) and neighbourhoods (wards) in England and Wales into three types based on the concentration of ethnic minorities in these areas: lowest concentrated, medium concentrated and highest concentrated. This classification is ethnic group specific, based on the percentage of that group in an area. Say for Black people, the classification was based on the percentage of the Black population in districts and wards. Cut-off points were then chosen so that Black population was distributed approximately equally across neighbourhood types. The minimum and maximum percentages of each ethnic minority group, the number of areas in each category, and the total White and minority ethnic populations are listed in Table 5.2 for districts and in Table 5.3 for wards.

Rather than focusing on either district or ward level measurements of ethnic concentration, we used a combination of the two spatial scales. Someone might live in an ethnically homogeneous ward, but within an ethnically diverse district, or the other way around. To examine the combined effect of district and ward level ethnic concentrations, we therefore constructed a variable with nine area types, based on the cross tabulation of the three district level types and the three ward level types. It is not surprising that types of districts and types of wards are correlated. As a result,

Table 5.2 Classification of 1991 districts by level of ethnic mix

Concentration	Minimum (%)	Maximum (%)	Number of districts	White population	Non-White population
	Black	Black			Black
Lowest	0	4.2	378	42,121,368	295,717
Medium	4.3	11.2	18	3,779,845	313,654
Highest	11.3	22.0	7	1,036,649	274,796
	South Asian	South Asian			South Asian
Lowest	0	5.7	368	40,447,744	486,528
Medium	5.8	13.5	25	5,081,356	564,006
Highest	13.6	24.7	10	1,408,762	396,549
	Other Asian	Other Asian			Other Asian
Lowest	0	0.7	335	36,454,024	113,639
Medium	0.8	2.4	51	8,023,667	113,123
Highest	2.5	4.6	17	2,460,169	112,449

Source: 1991 Census SAS.

Table 5.3 Classification of 1991 wards by level of ethnic mix

Concentration	Minimum (%)	Maximum (%)	Number of wards	White population	Non-White population
	Black	Black			Black
Lowest	0	5.1	9,027	43,730,252	293,723
Medium	5.2	15.3	348	2,393,667	294,933
Highest	15.4	46.6	134	814,534	291,692
	South Asian	South Asian			South Asian
Lowest	0	8.2	9,070	43,884,131	481,595
Medium	8.3	27.4	340	2,502,201	481,898
Highest	27.5	78.7	99	552,121	479,766
	Other Asian	Other Asian			Other Asian
Lowest	0	0.9	8,360	39,313,936	111,695
Medium	1.0	2.7	845	5,769,979	111,926
Highest	2.8	12.2	304	1,854,538	111,430

Source: 1991 Census SAS.

there were very few highest concentrated wards in the lowest concentrated districts and lowest concentrated wards within highest concentrated districts. We had to combine some categories together. So, medium concentrated and highest concentrated wards were combined within lowest concentrated districts into a single category, and lowest concentrated and medium concentrated wards were combined with highest concentrated districts. This left us with seven, rather than nine, categories in total.

We used a combination of descriptive and modelling methods to explore ethnic out-partnering with members of the white population. Initially, we compare the percentages involved by demographic and socio-economic status. We then extend this to estimate the likelihood of out-partnering in a multi-variate model, using multinomial logit regression. The dependent variable was the partnership status in 2001: in co-ethnic unions (0), in mixed-ethnic unions (1), and remaining single (2). These models produced two sets of coefficients, separately predicting the propensity of forming a mixed-ethnic union in comparison to forming a co-ethnic union and predicting the propensity of remaining single compared to being in a co-ethnic union. Our focus is the formation of mixed-ethnic unions with White partners as mixed-ethnic unions between different minority groups are rare. Thus we only present and discuss the results which compare mixed-ethnic unions between a minority and a White partner with co-ethnic unions. This is equivalent to considering a logistic regression for those forming unions, with the outcome being whether the union is a mixed union compared to a co-ethnic union.

Patterns of Mixed-Ethnic Unions

It is useful to provide first a general picture of mixed-ethnic unions in England and Wales. This analysis is based on ethnic minority LS members aged 16 and over and in a partnership in 1991 and 2001 respectively. Table 5.4 shows the distribution

Table 5.4 Percentage of ethnic minority LS members by gender and ethnicity of partners, 2001

		Partner			
Ethnic group	Gender	Same group	White	Other minority	Total
Black	Male	65.7	31.1	3.1	3,521
	Female	72.6	24.9	2.4	3,188
South Asian	Male	93.3	4.8	1.7	12,103
	Female	93.8	3.3	2.8	12,042
Other Asian	Male	70.5	14.2	15.1	2,215
	Female	71.0	20.1	8.7	2,199

Source: ONS LS, Authors' calculations.

of minority men and women by ethnicity of their partner in 2001. The majority of men and women live with a partner from their own ethnic group. Black men are the most likely to be in a mixed ethnic union; 31% of Black men have a White female partner. Black women also have a high out-partnering rate; 25% of Black women have a White male partner. Both South Asian men and women have very low rates of exogamous partnerships with Whites (4.8 and 3.3%). Other Asian men and women have exogamous partnering rates in between the other two groups. Just over 14% of the Other Asian men have a White partner and over 20% of Other Asian women have a White partner. The gender disparity in the propensity of out-partnering (Black and South Asian men are more likely than women to partner with a White person, while for Other Asians women are more likely to choose a White partner than men) is a consistent finding over the last two decades (Berrington, 1996; Coleman, 2004; Muttarak, 2004).

Mixed-ethnic unions not involving a White partner are more rare. Other Asians are the most likely to partner with someone from another (non-White) ethnic minority group (15.1% of men and 8.7% of women). The low rates of partnerships involving members from two different ethnic minority groups are not surprising given the relatively small sizes of these groups and their geographical distributions (Berrington, 1996).

The out-partnering rates of ethnic minority groups vary with age (Table 5.5). In general, the rate of exogamous partnerships between ethnic minority group members and White partners is highest among young people, suggesting that they are more open to mixed relationships than older generations. The only exception is for South Asian men where there is no evidence of any trend with age due to the small numbers with White partners.

Mixed ethnic partnerships are more likely among those who cohabit than among those who are married (Table 5.6). For cohabiting men in all three ethnic minority groups the mixed-ethnic union rate is over 40%. Among married men, the rates of mixed ethnic unions range from 4 to 25%. The situation is similar for women. Berrington (1996) suggested that people who choose to cohabit may hold less traditional marriage views and are also more likely to choose a partner from a different ethnic group. In addition, cohabitation might be easier than

Table 5.5 Percentage of ethnic minority LS members living with a White partner by gender and age, 2001

		Black		South Asian		Other Asian	
		%	Total	%	Total	%	Total
Men	16–34	44.5	761	4.7	2,919	14.9	387
	35–59	29.7	2, 041	4.6	6,832	14.2	1,477
	60+	19.1	777	5.1	2,481	12.2	385
Women	16–35	30.9	1, 010	3.8	4,123	21.4	602
	35–59	24.1	1, 804	3.2	6,762	19.9	1, 400
	60+	10.6	440	1.9	1,278	16.6	216

Source: ONS LS, Authors' calculations.

marriage because in some marriage traditions parents have to grant permission for the partnership.

Assimilation theory suggests that ethnic minorities with higher socio-economic positions are generally better assimilated in their host society and thus more likely to form partnerships with the White group than those in lower socio-economic groups. Tables 5.7 and 5.8 present the percentages of ethnic minority men and women in mixed-ethnic unions by social class and by educational qualifications. As expected, for South Asian men and Other Asian men, those in the higher social classes are the most likely to be in a mixed-ethnic union. Surprisingly, for Black men, the lower social classes are the most likely to be in a mixed-ethnic union. The results for women are very similar to those for men, although Other Asian women in all social classes are almost twice as likely to be in a mixed-ethnic union than Other Asian men. Low rates of mixed-ethnic unions are found among those whose social class is unknown.

Asians and Other Asian men and women with higher levels of education are the most likely to select partners from different ethnic groups. However, the pattern for Blacks is different where men with degrees are less likely to out-partner and there is no evidence of a difference by education for women. Different ethnic groups experience different stages or patterns of assimilation (Muttarak, 2004), and it may be that

Table 5.6 Percentage of ethnic minority LS members living with a White partner by gender and union type, 2001

		Black		South Asian		Other Asian	
		%	Total	%	Total	%	Total
Men	Married	25.9	2, 868	3.9	11, 966	12.3	2, 125
	Cohabiting	49.8	711	43.6	266	44.4	124
Women	Married	21.6	2, 694	2.7	11, 942	17.8	2, 070
	Cohabiting	38.2	560	35.7	221	50.7	148

Source: ONS LS, Authors' calculations.

Table 5.7 Percentage of ethnic minorities living with a White partner by gender and social class, 2001

	Black		South Asian		Other Asian	
	%	Total	%	Total	%	Total
Men						
Professional/managerial	32.8	996	9.6	3,233	21.9	831
Skilled non-manual	34.2	333	4.8	1,166	12.4	275
Skilled manual	33.0	812	3.0	2,997	9.4	489
Partly skilled/Unskilled	36.2	641	2.1	2,412	7.9	229
Not stated	19.4	797	3.3	2,424	8.4	425
Women						
Professional/managerial	30.1	943	10.7	1,761	38.7	569
Skilled non-manual	29.5	701	5.7	1,921	22.6	514
Skilled manual	25.4	173	1.5	456	6.7	150
Partly skilled/Unskilled	25.6	559	1.3	2,234	12.6	309
Not stated	13.3	878	1.2	5,791	8.7	676

Source: ONS LS, Authors' calculations.

Black people are better integrated into mainstream society across the educational and social class spectrum.

Figure 5.1 shows the change in the percentage of mixed-ethnic unions between 1991 and 2001 by ethnic group and gender. The general pattern is one of growth, apart from Other Asian women where there seems to be a small drop in the percentage of mixed-ethnic unions with a White partner (from 32 to 29%). The largest increase in mixed-ethnic unions is observed for South Asian women (although the overall rate remains low) and for Other Asian men.

Table 5.8 Percentage of economically active ethnic minorities living with a White partner by gender and educational qualification, 2001

	Black		South Asian		Other Asian	
	%	Total	%	Total	%	Total
Men						
No qualification	34.1	1,925	2.9	7,609	9.4	1,111
Sub degree	31.3	556	6.5	1,302	13.5	288
Degree	24.2	993	8.9	3,061	20.8	813
Women						
No qualification	24.3	1,817	1.8	8,924	11.2	1,222
Sub degree	26.1	410	4.0	1,012	22.5	258
Degree	24.6	984	9.2	2,133	34.1	715

Source: ONS LS, Authors' calculations.

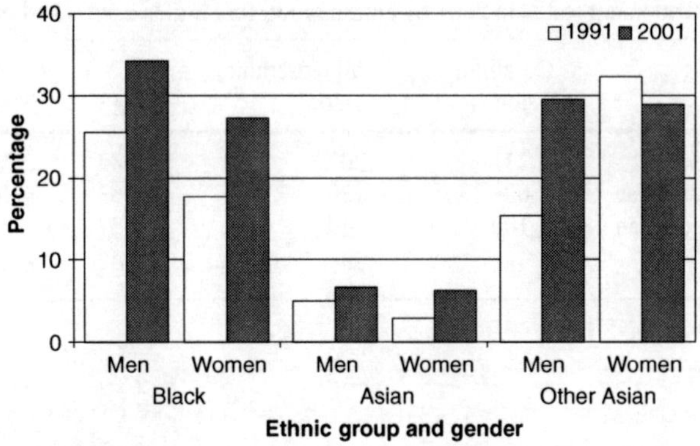

Fig. 5.1 Percentage of ethnic minorities living with a white partner in 1991 and 2001 (Source: ONS LS, Authors' calculations)

Formation of Mixed-Ethnic Unions

The Sample Descriptions

So far we have presented cross-sectional data on mixed-ethnic unions for 1991 and 2001. In the remainder of this chapter we focus on the formation of mixed ethnic unions between 1991 and 2001. We investigate which individual characteristics measured in 1991 are associated with ending up in a mixed-ethnic union and we focus particularly on the role of the neighbourhood ethnic concentration in union formation. The sample includes single people who were aged 6 and over in 1991 and who were also captured in the 2001 Census. The sample includes a total of 7,136 people: 2,422 Blacks, 4,017 South Asians, and 697 Other Asians (Table 5.9). By 2001, about 25% of the 1991 singles ended up living with a partner from either the same ethnic group or the White group. Single South Asians were the most likely to form a partnership with almost one third of them entering marriage or cohabitation between 1991 and 2001. In contrast, Black singles were the least likely to enter a partnership with only 18% being married or cohabiting in 2001. Of all those who lived with a partner in 2001, 48% of Blacks, 11% of South Asians, and 42% of Other Asians had chosen a White partner. The proportions are much higher than the prevalence rate, which shows that people who were in the UK for a relatively long period of time (in this case, at least between 1991 and 2001) were more likely to partner with someone from the majority group.

In addition to the geographical variables we included a range of individual control variables expected to be related to the likelihood of out-partnering (Table 5.10). For LS members who were under 16, or under 21 and in full-time education, the social class and educational qualifications of the head of household were used as proxies.

Table 5.11 gives the percentage of ethnic minorities in mixed-ethnic unions in 2001 by ethnic group and 1991 neighbourhood type (both at ward and district

Table 5.9 Partnership status in 2001 by ethnic group for singles aged 6 and over in 1991

	Co-ethnic union	Mixed-ethnic union	Single	Total
Black	231	207	1,984	2,422
South Asian	1,034	120	2,863	4,017
Other Asian	100	70	527	697
Total	1,365	397	5,374	7,136

Source: ONS LS.

level). As indicated earlier, we have defined three types of neighbourhoods: ethnically lowest concentrated neighbourhoods, medium concentrated neighbourhoods and highest concentrated neighbourhoods. We created separate neighbourhood measures for each ethnic group. Table 5.11 shows that for all three ethnic groups, those in lowest concentrated neighbourhoods in 1991 had the highest probability of forming a partnership with a White person by 2001. Those originating in areas

Table 5.10 Characteristics in 1991 of LS members single in 1991

		Black	South Asian	Other Asian
Gender	Male	43.8	49.4	51.4
	Female	56.2	50.6	48.6
Age 1991	6–14	34.9	51.8	40.6
	15–34	47.2	40.7	44.8
	35 and over	17.9	7.4	14.6
Country of birth	Born in UK	74.7	67.4	54.8
	Born outside UK	25.3	32.6	45.2
Qualification[a]	No qualification	93.0	92.4	82.8
	Degree and above	7.0	7.6	17.2
Social class[a]	Professional & managerial	20.7	19.9	30.7
	Skilled non-manual	21.7	13.8	18.5
	Skilled Manual	14.7	19.4	20.1
	Partly skilled & unskilled	21.0	23.2	10.9
	Not Stated	21.9	23.7	19.8
Housing tenure	Owned	49.7	81.0	71.3
	Social renting	44.1	13.9	17.9
	Private renting	6.2	5.1	10.8
Region	North	6.5	11.5	7.7
	Yorkshire & East Anglia	6.4	11.8	7.2
	Midlands	18.6	27.6	12.5
	South	12.1	12.7	19.2
	London	55.1	35.6	50.1
	Wales	1.4	0.9	3.3

[a]Head of household data used for those under 21 in full-time education.
Source: ONS LS.

Table 5.11 Percentage in mixed-ethnic unions in 2001 of LS members who were single in 1991 and in a partnership in 2001 by ethnic group and 1991 area type

	Black		South Asian		Other Asian	
	%	Total	%	Total	%	Total
Marriage market area (district)						
Lowest concentrated	65.4	211	16.1	311	54.8	73
Medium concentrated	36.2	138	12.5	368	27.9	61
Highest concentrated	29.3	99	7.8	489	42.5	40
Neighbourhood type (ward)						
Lowest concentrated	64.2	201	20.1	338	51.9	79
Medium concentrated	40.3	139	10.3	388	37.8	45
Highest concentrated	29.6	108	5.9	442	32.0	50

Source: ONS LS.

with a relatively high concentration of their own group were the least likely to out-partner. The only exception to this pattern is Other Asians where the numbers are too small to provide reliable evidence.

Modelling Results

We present separate models for each ethnic group in Table 5.12. For each group we model the probability that a single person in 1991 forms a mixed-ethnic union with a White person or remains single by 2001, compared to the base category who are in co-ethnic unions. Note, again, that for brevity we only present the model parameters for the mixed-ethnic category. We include a combined district level and ward level measurement of ethnic concentration.

As expected, those born outside the UK were less likely to live with a White partner for all three ethnic groups. For Blacks, the modelling shows higher rates at younger ages and no significant difference in rates by social class. For South Asians, social class was a very important determinant of out-partnering showing a highly significant gradient over the categories. For South Asians in the multivariate model, the group with the highest out-partnering rate is the oldest group, but this is relative to the rate expected from other characteristics of this group, especially born outside the UK, where the expectation of out-partnering may be low. For Other Asians, women were more likely than men to choose a White partner, which is different from Black or South Asian women who were no different from Black or South Asian men. Other Asians in skilled manual occupations were more likely to be partnered with a White person, but this must be interpreted in the light of the relatively small numbers in this group. None of the housing tenure, educational qualifications or region categories is significant for any of the three ethnic groups, after adjustment for other factors.

Table 5.12 Odds ratios of forming a mixed-ethnic union compared to a co-ethnic union between 1991 and 2001 by ethnic group, results from multinomial logistic regression

	Black (N=438)		South Asian (N=1,154)		Other Asian (N=170)	
	Odds ratio		Odds ratio		Odds ratio	
Category	Estimate	95% CI	Estimate	95% CI	Estimate	95% CI
Gender						
Female	1.24	0.83–1.86	0.91	0.62–1.34	1.98**	1.00–3.89
Male (base)	1		1		1	
Age 1991						
35 and over	0.58	0.23–1.48	8.92***	3.56–22.33	4.78***	1.47–15.58
15–34 (base)	1		1		1	
6–14	2.43**	1.15–5.11	0.40***	0.21–0.79	1.72	0.55–5.38
Country of Birth						
Born outside UK	0.31***	0.16–0.57	0.59**	0.39–0.90	0.38**	0.17–0.83
Born in UK (base)	1		1		1	
Qualification					1	
Degree and above	0.66	0.31–1.43	0.82	0.44–1.52	1.31	0.50–3.41
None (base)	1		1		1	
Social Class						
I & II	1.15	0.60–2.20	3.29***	1.66–6.51	2.00	0.50–8.02
III NM	0.76	0.41–1.39	2.34**	1.19–4.59	0.94	0.27–3.26
III M	0.89	0.48–1.67	1.83*	0.88–3.79	4.24**	1.11–16.25
Not Stated	0.87	0.45–1.68	1.05	0.51–2.17	1.14	0.30–4.37
IV & V (base)	1		1		1	
Housing tenure						
Social renting	1.35	0.86–2.10	0.94	0.51–1.75	1.32	0.48–3.62
Private renting	1.28	0.61–2.65	1.39	0.66–2.93	0.74	0.27–2.01
Owned (base)	1		1		1	

Table 5.12 (continued)

Category	Black (N=438)		South Asian (N=1,154)		Other Asian (N=170)	
	Odds ratio		Odds ratio		Odds ratio	
	Estimate	95% CI	Estimate	95% CI	Estimate	95% CI
Region						
Yorkshire & EA	0.90	0.32–2.58	0.64	0.29–1.42	0.57	0.11–2.92
Midlands	0.66	0.29–1.50	0.69	0.34–1.39	0.48	0.10–2.30
South	1.84	0.73–4.62	1.10	0.55–2.21	1.19	0.29–4.90
London	0.59	0.26–1.34	0.96	0.51–1.83	0.60	0.10–3.47
Wales	4.72	0.49–45.15	0.41	0.04–3.68	6.75	0.50–91.93
North (base)	1		1		1	
District & Ward						
Lowest concentrated & Moderately/Highest concentrated	0.77	0.36–1.67	0.47**	0.23–0.98	1.19	0.21–6.77
Medium concentrated & Lowest concentrated	0.65	0.27–1.56	0.91	0.48–1.73	0.32	0.07–1.47
Medium concentrated & Medium concentrated	0.39***	0.20–0.75	0.47**	0.25–0.87	0.84	0.26–2.75
Medium concentrated & Highest concentrated	0.48	0.19–1.21	0.19***	0.08–0.45	0.36	0.07–1.80
Highest concentrated & Least/Moderately concentrated	0.52	0.14–1.91	0.55*	0.26–1.13	0.88	0.15–5.04
Highest concentrated & Highest concentrated	0.35***	0.16–0.77	0.41***	0.21–0.79	0.96	0.19–4.76
Lowest concentrated & Lowest concentrated (base)	1		1		1	

* $p<0.10$; ** $p<0.05$; *** $p<0.01$.

The ethnic mix of neighbourhood is important for Black and South Asian ethnic groups. This was true for both district and ward level when each was included in the model without the other (data not shown). The absence of a relationship with the ethnic mix of the neighbourhood for the Other Asian group, which was also found when each was considered alone, may relate to the small numbers in this group.

To further illustrate the impact of neighbourhoods on the propensity of choosing a White partner we calculated probabilities of forming mixed-ethnic couples by ethnic group and neighbourhood type (Fig. 5.2). In the calculations, all variables except those measuring mixed partnerships were set to the reference category. As a result the probabilities are for individuals who were male, aged 15–34, born in the UK, with no higher qualifications, in social class IV or V, living in owner occupied houses and in North England.

From Fig. 5.2 we can see that Black men or South Asian men who lived in districts with a medium or highest concentration of their own group in 1991 were less likely to choose White people as partners than those living in districts with the lowest concentration of their own group. People living in highest concentrated areas in 1991 were least likely to out-partner by 2001. This confirms what we find from Table 5.11. It is not very clear from Fig. 5.2 what the trend is at the ward level but

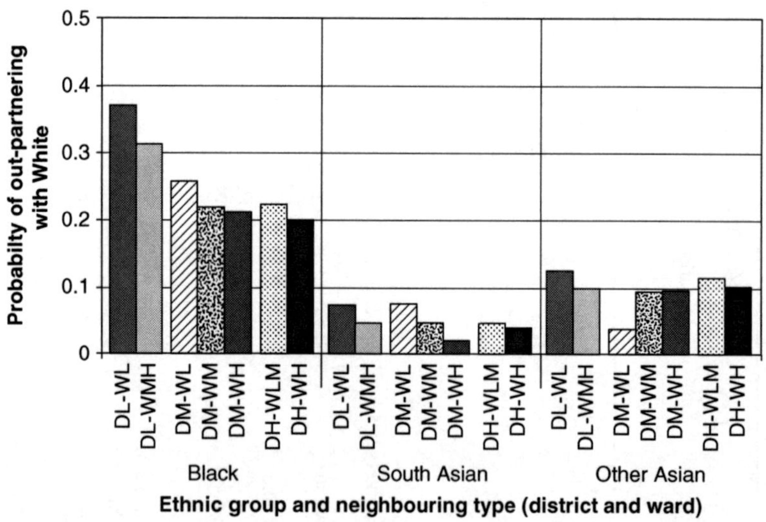

Fig. 5.2 Probability of forming a mixed ethnic union in 2001 by ethnic group and 1991 district and ward type. Note: The probability is for male, aged 15–34, born in the UK, with no higher qualifications, in social class IV or V, living in owner occupied houses and in North England. DL-WL: lowest concentrated district and lowest concentrated ward; DL-WMH: lowest concentrated district and medium concentrated or highest concentrated ward; DM-WL: medium concentrated district and lowest concentrated ward; DM-WM: medium concentrated district and medium concentrated ward; DM-WH: medium concentrated district and highest concentrated ward; DH-WLM: highest concentrated district and lowest concentrated or medium concentrated ward; DH-WH: highest concentrated district and highest concentrated ward

the model which includes ward level concentration categories (not shown here) indicates the same trend as those at the district level, again confirming the descriptive results in Table 5.11.

For all three ethnic groups, within the same type of districts, the probability of out-partnering declines along with the increase in concentration of their own group at the ward level (Fig. 5.2). This shows that ethnic concentration at the ward level has an effect independent from that at the district level. The only exception is that Other Asians show a different trend across different wards within medium concentrated districts. Again, partly due to their small numbers, the difference between propensities among Other Asian singles across different types of areas is not significant.

For Blacks, the variation in the probability of out-partnering is more associated with the ethnic mix at the district level than with that at the ward level: the differences between probabilities of different district types are larger than that across ward types. It can be concluded that districts are more relevant than wards in influencing formation of mixed-ethnic unions for Blacks. In contrast, for South Asians, the variation in probability of out-partnering is more associated with the ward level ethnic mix than the district level ethnic mix. Thus, it can be concluded that wards exhibit more influence than districts in formation of mixed-ethnic unions for South Asians. The pattern is not so clear for Other Asians but, overall, the districts look to have more influence, although it is not significant.

Conclusions

Previous studies of geographical segregation have largely ignored mixed-ethnic households. From the few studies conducted in the US, it has been found that the geography of mixed-ethnic households is different from that of co-ethnic households. For example, mixed-ethnic couples in Los Angeles were found to be more likely to live in mixed neighbourhoods (Ellis et al., 2006) and this was argued to relate to residential decision making. In fact, mixed-ethnic households may choose to live in such locations, but they may also be more likely to form there and it is not possible to tease out the relative importance of these different processes using cross-sectional data.

In this chapter we made use of longitudinal data, which allowed us to explore whether spatial proximity influences the likelihood of out-partnering. Specifically, we examined whether minority ethnic people who live in less ethnically concentrated areas were more likely to form a partnership with a White person than those in more ethnically concentrated areas. If this is true then the observed pattern by Ellis et al. (2006) should be at least partly attributed to the process of the formation of mixed-ethnic unions rather than purely attributed to a subsequent migration process.

We used data from the ONS-LS, which is a nationally representative sample of the population in England and Wales and estimated the likelihood of out-partnering with a White person for three ethnic groups, Black, South Asian, and Other Asian, across different types of geographical area, controlling for individual variables. We used two methods of classifying geographical areas based on districts and wards, the former relating more to the broader marriage market area and the latter to the local neighbourhood. To explore the neighbourhood effects at the different scales, we also derived the combined neighbourhood types, which is the interaction between districts and wards. The combined neighbourhood type allows us to explore the relative importance of two geographical levels within the same modelling framework. Another benefit is that from the segregation perspective, a ward which is highly concentrated with a minority group within a White dominant district can be regarded as highly segregated compared to a ward which is highly concentrated but within a highest concentrated district.

Both districts and wards are relevant as people develop their social networks, and relationships not only in their immediate neighbourhoods but also in workplaces, schools and local leisure centres. As wards are more approximations of immediate neighbourhoods where people interact through daily activities like going to school and shopping, districts are more proxies of working or other social networking experiences. The levels of concentration at both district and ward level were found to be significant predictors for mixed-ethnic unions among Blacks and South Asians, but not among Other Asians who are smaller in number and are much less geographically segregated that the other ethnic minority groups. Blacks and South Asians who lived in lowest concentrated areas had increased chances of choosing a White partner.

The negative association between the propensity of out-partnering and the concentration of the minority group is in line with a small number of previous studies (Hwang et al., 1994, 1997; Livens, 1998; Muttarak, 2004), although these were based on measures calculated for much larger geographical areas. Thus, those ethnic minorities living in areas with high concentrations of their own group have a greater chance of meeting potential partners from their own group. Larger concentrations of a minority group may also enforce the identity of the group and discourage exogamous relationships. In contrast, in areas with a low concentration of a particular minority group the opportunities for meeting a partner from their own group is constrained, elevating the probability of developing a relationship with someone from the majority white group. For those under 16 from minority groups in 1991 being surrounded by a white majority in their daily life affects their partnership choice when they become adults.

The results from this study lend support to the theory that segregation hinders the formation of mixed-ethnic unions. A concentrated ward within a lowest concentrated district is more segregated than a lowest concentrated ward within the same type of district and the likelihood of forming a partnership with a White person among Blacks and South Asians who lived in the first type of areas is lower than for those who lived in the second type of area.

Most studies of geographical influences on mixed ethnic unions have used cross sectional data and have often been based on ecological relationships between out-partnering and segregation measures (Kalmijn, 1998). Our study is the first to use longitudinal data integrating individual and geographical variables to examine how the geographical context influences the likelihoods of out-partnering. Our study suggests although importance of spatial proximity may have declined in affecting partnership choice among ethnic minorities (Kalmijn and Flap, 2001), it is still a significant factor which should not be ignored.

Acknowledgements This research is funded by the ESRC under the Understanding Population Trends and Processes (UPTAP) programme (Award Ref: RES-1563-25-0045). The permission of the Office for National Statistics to use the Longitudinal Study is gratefully acknowledged, as is the help provided by Julian Buxton of the Centre for Longitudinal Study Information & User Support (CeLSIUS). CeLSIUS is supported by the ESRC Census of Population Programme (Award Ref: RES-348-25-0004). The data from ONS which is Crown copyright and reproduced with the permission of the controller of HMSO and Queen's Printer for Scotland. This work uses research datasets which may not exactly reproduce National Statistics aggregates. The authors alone are responsible for the interpretation of the data.

References

Ballard, R. (1997) Negotiating race and ethnicity: Exploring the implications of the 1991 Census, *Patterns of Prejudice*, 30: 3–33.

Berrington, A. (1996) Marriage patterns and inter-ethnic unions in Coleman, D. and Salt, J. (eds.), *Ethnicity in the 1991 Census: Demographic Characteristics of the Ethnic Minority Populations*, HMSO, London, pp. 178–212.

Blau, P.M. (1977) *Inequality and Heterogeneity*, The Free Press, New York, NY.

Blau, P.M., Blum, T.C. and Schwartz, J.E. (1982) Heterogeneity and intermarriage, *American Sociological Review*, 47: 45–62.

Bossard, J.H. (1932) Residential propinquity as a factor in marriage selection, *American Journal of Sociology*, 38: 219–224.

Bozon, M. and Heran, F. (1989) Finding a spouse: A survey of how French couples meet, *Population*, 44: 91–121.

Bradford, P. (2006, May) *Who Are the Mixed-Ethnic Group?* Office for National Statistics, London.

Burgess, S., Wilson, D. and Lupton, R. (2005) Parallel lives? Ethnic segregation in the playground and the neighbourhood, *Urban Studies*, 42: 1027–1056.

Coleman, D. (1985) Ethnic intermarriage in Great Britain, *Population Trends*, 40: 4–10.

Coleman, D. (2004) Partner choice and the growth of ethnic minority populations, *Bevolking en Gezin*, 33: 7–34.

Commission for Racial Equality (CRE) UK (2006) *Integration, Multiculturalism and the CRE.* http://www.cre.gov.uk/diversity/integration/index.html

Cready, C.M. and Saenz, R. (1997) The nonmetro/metro context of racial/ethnic outmarriage: Some differences between African Americans and Mexican Americans, *Rural Sociology*, 62: 335–362.

Data Management and Analysis Group Update (2005) *Inter-Ethnic Unions*, DMAG, London.

Delaney, D. (2002) The space that race makes, *The Professional Geographer*, 54: 6–14.

Ellis, M., Wright, R. and Parks, V. (2006) The immigrant household and spatial assimilation: Partnership, nativity, and neighbourhood location, *Urban Geography*, 27: 1–19.

Ellison, C.G. and Powers, D.A. (1994) The contact hypothesis and racial attitudes among black Americans, *Social Science Quarterly*, 75: 385–400.

Emerson, M.O., Kimbro, R.T. and Yancey, G. (2002) Contact theory extended: The effects of prior racial contact on current social ties, *Social Science Quarterly*, 83: 745–761.

Fu, X.N. (2006) Impact of socioeconomic status on inter-racial mate selection and divorce, *Social Science Journal*, 43(2): 239–258.

Gordon, M.M. (1964) *Assimilation in American Life*, Oxford University Press, New York, NY.

Holdsworth, C. and Dale, A. (1997) Issues in the analysis of ethnicity in the 1991 British census, *Ethnic and Racial Studies*, 20: 160–180.

Holloway, S.R., Ellis, M., Wright, R. and Hudson, M. (2005) Partnering 'out' and fitting in: Residential segregation and the neighbourhood contexts of mixed-race households, *Population, Space and Place*, 11: 299–324.

Houston, S., Wright, R., Ellis, M., Holloway, S. and Hudson, M. (2005) Places of possibilities: Where mixed-race partners meet? *Progress in Human Geography*, 29: 700–717.

Hwang, S.S., Saenz, R. and Aguirre, B.E. (1994) Structural and individual determinants of outmarriage among Chinese, Filipino, and Japanese Americans in California, *Sociological Inquiry*, 64: 396–414.

Hwang, S.S., Saenz, R. and Aguirre, B.E. (1997) Structural and assimilationist explanations of Asian American intermarriage, *Journal of Marriage and the Family*, 59: 758–772.

Ihlanfeldt, K.R. and Scafidi, B.P. (2002) The Neighbourhood contact hypothesis: Evidence from the multicity study of urban inequality, *Urban Studies*, 39: 619–641.

Johnson, R., Poulsen, M. and Forrest, J. (2005) On the measurement and meaning of residential segregation: A response to Simpson, *Urban Studies*, 42: 1221–1227.

Johnston, R., Poulsen, M. and Forrest, J. (2006) Ethnic residential segregation and assimilation in British towns and cities: A comparison of those claiming single and dual ethnic identities, *Migration Letters*, 3: 11–30.

Kalmijn, M. (1993) Trends in black/white intermarriage, *Social Forces*, 72: 119–146.

Kalmijn, M. (1998) Intermarriage and homogamy: Causes, patterns, trends, *Annual Review of Sociology*, 24: 395–421.

Kalmijn, M. and Flap, H. (2001) Assortative meeting and mating: Unintended consequences of organized settings for partner choices, *Social Forces*, 79(4): 1289–1312.

Liang, Z. and Ito, N. (1999) Intermarriage of Asian Americans in the New York City region: Contemporary patterns and future prospects, *International Migration Review*, 33(4): 876–900.

Lievens, J. (1998) Interethnic marriages: Bringing in the context through multilevel modelling, *European Journal of Population*, 14: 117–155.

Model, S. and Fisher, G. (2002) Unions between Blacks and Whites: England and the US compared, *Ethnic and Racial Studies*, 25: 728–754.

Morgan, B. (1981) A contribution to the debate on homogamy, propinquity, and segregation, *Journal of Marriage and the Family*, 43: 909–921.

Muttarak, R. (2003) *Who Intermarries in Britain?* MSc thesis, Department of Sociology, University of Oxford, Oxford.

Muttarak, R. (2004) Marital assimilation: Interethnic marriage in Britain, population and society: Issues, research, policy. Paper presented at the 12th biennial conference of Australian Population Association, 15–17 September 2004, Canberra, Australia.

Peach, C. (1980) Ethnic segregation and intermarriage, *Annals of the Association of American Geographers*, 70: 371–381.

Peach, C. (1996) Does Britain have ghettos? *Transactions of the Institute of British Geographers*, 21: 216–235.

Platt, L., Simpson, L. and Akinwale, B. (2005) Stability and change in ethnic groups in England and Wales, *Population Trends*, 121: 35–45.

Sabater, A. (2010) Ethnic residential segregation over time and age cohorts in England and Wales, 1991–2001 in Stillwell, J. and van Ham, M. (eds.), *Ethnicity and Integration, Understanding Population Trends and Processes*, Vol. 3, Springer, Dordrecht, pp. 47–62.

Schoen, R. and Thomas, B. (1989) Intergroup marriage in Hawaii, 1969–1971 and 1979–1981, *Sociological Perspectives*, 32(3): 65–82.

Schoen, R. and Wooldredge, J. (1989) Marriage choices in North Carolina and Virginia, 1969–71 and 1979–81, *Journal of Marriage and Family*, 51: 465–481.

Sigelman, L., Bledsoe, T., Welch, S. and Combs, M.W. (1996) Making contact? Black-White social interaction in an urban setting, *American Journal Sociology*, 101: 1306–1332.

Simpson, L. (2004) Statistics of racial segregation: Measures, evidence and policy, *Urban Studies*, 41: 661–681.

White, M.J. and Sassler, S. (2000) Judging not only by color: Ethnicity, nativity, and neighbourhood attainment, *Social Science Quarterly*, 81: 997–1013.

Wong, D. (1999) A geographical analysis of multiethnic households in the United States, *International Journal of Population Geography*, 5: 31–48.

Wright, R., Houston, S., Ellis, M., Holloway, S. and Hudson, M. (2003) Crossing racial lines: Geographies of mixed-race partnering and multiraciality in the United States, *Progress in Human Geography*, 27: 457–474.

van Ham, M. and Feijten, P.M. (2008) Who wants to leave the neighbourhood? The effect of being different from the neighbourhood population on wishes to move, *Environment and Planning A*, 40 (5): 1151–1170.

Chapter 6
Ethnic Internal Migration in England and Wales: Spatial Analysis Using a District Classification Framework

John Stillwell and Serena Hussain

Introduction

People move home for a range of different reasons and migration intensity is well known to fluctuate with stage in life course (Champion et al., 1998; Rogers and Castro, 1981). Age is a selective influence on migration rather than a causal driver (Stillwell, 2008). Children's migration propensity declines up to school-leaving age in the UK. Eighteen year olds move more than younger teenagers because they transfer into higher education, whereas highest propensities are found in the early 20s when young adults leave home or university for work reasons or to cohabit/marry. In most countries, the decline in migration with older working age levels out around retirement age and may increase in older old age as the need for institutional or family support becomes more necessary. In comparison with age, sex is much less differentiating in its influence on migration whilst the roles of different socio-economic characteristics tend to vary as socio-economic conditions change over time.

The research questions that we address in this chapter are whether there are distinctive variations in the propensities to migrate that are observed for different ethnic groups, whether these propensities vary similarly by age, and whether differences are apparent in the patterns of migration between different types of districts in England and Wales. The focus of the chapter is on internal migration in England and Wales taking place in the 12 months before the 2001 Census. In contrast to popular press coverage of immigration in recent years, relatively little attention has been paid to internal migration in the twenty-first century despite its importance as the key phenomenon responsible for population redistribution.

We begin with a short and selective review of geographical literature on ethnic population concentration and the characteristics of internal migration by ethnic group and by age. The data sets and spatial units used in the analyses are then described before turning attention to an examination of aggregate and age-specific

J. Stillwell (✉)
School of Geography, University of Leeds, Leeds LS2 9JT, UK
e-mail: j.c.h.stillwell@leeds.ac.uk

J. Stillwell, M. van Ham (eds.), *Ethnicity and Integration*, Understanding Population Trends and Processes 3, DOI 10.1007/978-90-481-9103-1_6,

ethnic migration propensities at the national level. Spatial analysis is reported in the subsequent sections that use the district classification framework developed by Vickers et al. (2003) to summarise the flows that occurred between and within districts in England and Wales. Particular attention is paid to net migration balances and rates for seven ethnic groups within the top tier (four 'families' of districts) and the more detailed third tier (23 'classes' of districts) of the Vickers et al. classification with variations in net migration by age and ethnicity between families also being presented. The chapter finishes with some concluding comments.

Context

Ethnic Population Concentration

Whilst the spatial concentration of ethnic minority populations in many cities and towns across Britain is indisputable (Champion, 2005; Johnston et al., 2002; Kyambi, 2005; Rees and Butt, 2004; Simpson, 2004; Stillwell and Hussain, 2008), there is much debate about the extent to which non-White groups are geographically polarised within these cities and whether these communities are becoming increasingly segregated as ethnic populations grow through natural increase and immigration. The debate, which focused in the 1990s on the question of whether or not ghettos had become a feature of British cities (Peach, 1996) has been catapulted into the public arena in the twenty-first century as a result of local and global events including the 2001 riots in Bradford, Oldham and Leeds, the bombings of the Twin Towers in 2001 and the London Underground in 2005. Dramatic events such as these have fuelled concerns about the level of integration experienced by ethnic minorities and whether it is a result of residential self-segregation that ethnic groups view themselves as being separate and distinct communities with inhabitants living 'parallel lives' (Phillips, 2006). As a result of the perceived negative impact of ethnic segregation, policy makers have become increasingly interested in ethnic geographies and community cohesion (Stillwell and Phillips, 2006; Simpson, 2007). Fears and predications of increasing segregation and ghettoisation have been accentuated by reports of Leicester and Birmingham becoming Britain's first minority White cities by 2019 and 2024 respectively (Gaines, 2007; Herbert, 2007). Negative press connotations have been associated with these academic reports of emerging plurality (Finney and Simpson, 2008) where no racial or ethnic group makes up the majority of the overall city population.

A number of studies question claims of increasing segregation. Peach and Rossiter (1996) and Simpson (2006) have presented evidence that ethnic ghettos do not exist in Britain. Research by Johnston et al. (2002) on ethnic enclaves indicates that Asians are the most spatially concentrated among minority ethnic groups and Bangladeshis demonstrate the highest level of residential concentration amongst Asians yet the overwhelming majority of Whites reside in areas where they form 80% or more of the local population. This results in an asymmetrical pattern of concentration, in that the majority of non-White ethnic groups live in areas where the White population are still the majority, whereas White groups generally live in predominately White residential areas. Therefore, even where non-White groups do cluster they tend to live in relatively mixed areas. Simpson (2004) argues that Bradford in the north or England, with its significant Asian population, is not becoming increasing ethnically polarised despite influences of natural change such as high fertility rates and continued migration in the form of overseas marriages and kinship networks. In fact, in a later study, Simpson found from his analysis of the 1991 and 2001 Census data using the indices of segregation and diversity, that there was more mixing through a natural process of growth of ethnic minorities and a greater evenness of population distribution (Simpson, 2006). For the most part, debates about segregated communities are fraught with moral panics and insufficient contextualisation. As Simpson states, *social policy for localities is better informed by a sociological and historical understanding of class, housing, employment and educational dynamics of neighbourhood and residential change. At the same time, the racially motivated barriers to movement and integration need to be dismantled and the structural causes of sustained poor inner city neighbourhoods addressed* (Simpson, 2004, p. 677). The recent volume by Finney and Simpson (2009) challenges the view that race and migration are the real threat to an integrated society, proposing instead that diversity and mobility are expected and benign.

The Impact of Immigration on Settled Communities

Ethnic minority populations in Britain are increasing in size and this is primarily due to natural change propelled by higher fertility rates and higher proportions of young people with minority communities. However, whilst demographic processes are likely to be important drivers of ethnic expansion and concentration, immigration from overseas of both White and non-White ethnic groups must be considered also. There has been interest in the US about the impact immigration has on internal migration of the indigenous majority. One strand of this work centres on Frey's theory of 'demographic balkanisation' which essentially creates spatial segmentation by ethnic group as a result of immigration and internal migration (Frey, 1996). In this view, increased immigration and settlement of non-White populations are prompting intolerant White communities to leave such areas resulting in a process dubbed 'White flight', investigated back in the 1960s in American cities by Tauber and Tauber (1965).

Ellis and Wright (1998), however, argue that immigrants settle in areas which have already been seen as less desirable and abandoned by White communities whose exit therefore creates vacant housing opportunities to be taken up by immigrants. Such pull/push factor theories are long established within the discourse on ethnic minorities and housing in the UK as well as in the USA. Historical accounts of settlement of immigrant populations demonstrate how discriminatory housing markets and modest financial means resulted in ethnic minority communities settling for housing in neighbourhoods which had been left behind and which no-one else wanted. Communities began to be established within such areas as a result of chain migration and a tightening of immigration laws, which meant that wives and children of immigrant workers, who had previously remained within the country of origin, were prompted to join their spouses. An example of such a study in Britain is that by Robinson (1993) who demonstrated how the geographical distribution of ethnic groups migrating at different periods in time was strongly related to change in economic pulls such as available employment and the existence of social and kin networks.

The 2001 Census has shown us that in comparison with approximately 6 million internal migrants during the count period, there were only 400,000 immigrants, 70% of whom were classified as White (Stillwell and Duke-Williams, 2005). Of the remaining 30% non-White immigrants, only 5–6% were Black and South Asian individuals. In addition, 456,700 people were shown to have migrated in the year before the 2001 Census but did not provide origin details. It is not possible to determine exactly what proportion of these migrants came from overseas, although it is possible to identify their ethnicity. Four out of five of those with no previous address listed were White, 5.5% were Black, 5.2% were Pakistani and Other South Asian, 2.6% were Indian and 2.5% were of Mixed ethnicity. Stillwell and Duke-Williams (2005) conducted analysis to look at linkages between immigration and White internal out-migration from areas gaining immigrants. They conclude that *those areas that have relatively high rates of immigration do also tend to have relatively high rates of net out-migration and rates of net migration loss falls as immigration rates decline. However, there are a number of districts that do not conform to this pattern and this suggests the need for a closer look at the types and locations of the areas concerned* (Stillwell and Duke-Williams, 2005, p. 27).

Internal Migration and Dispersal

A number of studies have looked at the propensities and patterns of internal migration of ethnic minorities in Britain in the last three decades. Using the 1987 Labour Force Survey (LFS), for example, Owen and Green (1992) found that non-White groups had higher rates for internal migration than Whites with the rate for Bangladeshis (22.5%) being over twice the rate for Whites (10.5%). Unpublished data from the Longitudinal Study (LS) was used by Robinson (1992) to identify the level and direction of inter-regional migration of Britain's Afro-Caribbean and Asian populations between 1971 and 1981. Analyses of 1991 Census data have been undertaken by Rees and Duke-Williams (1995), Rees and Phillips (1996), Champion (1996) and Owen (1997). Rees and Phillips, for example, report Chinese and Black Africans as being twice as mobile as Indians, Black Caribbeans and Pakistanis, whilst Owen reported that Chinese and other groups were most likely to move longer distances and South Asians least likely to move between districts. Champion's spatial analysis showed the greatest net losses of ethnic minorities were experienced in Greater London, West Yorkshire, West Midlands and Lancashire – all areas with significant ethnic minority populations to start with. The largest net gains were found in a diagonal strip of counties from Suffolk to Dorset (Champion, 1996, p. 172). This demonstrates that ethnic minority communities follow migration trends of the population as a whole in moving away from urban to less urban and even rural areas. Rees and Duke-Williams (1995) suggest that ethnic minority groups migrate to outer areas of cities where there are already concentrations of ethnic minority groups. They found that with London, Whites were leaving boroughs in Outer London and ethnic minorities were leaving Inner London boroughs and moving towards Outer London. It was found that Indians of all groups were experiencing this type of migration to the greatest extent and were leading migration from London and other large cities to non-metropolitan areas.

A number of studies of ethnic migration data have emerged since the results of the 2001 Census were released (such as Champion, 2005; Finney and Simpson, 2008; Simpson, 2004; Stillwell and Duke-Williams, 2005; Stillwell and Hussain, 2008, 2010; Stillwell and Phillips, 2006; Stillwell et al., 2008, Simon, 2010; Simpson and Finney, 2009; Stillwell, 2010) which have provided overviews and analyses of ethnic migration propensities, patterns and differences in distance migrated between ethnic groups. The ethnic variations in migration propensities have been confirmed using both micro (e.g. Samples of Anonymised Records, SAR) and aggregate data (Special Migration Statistics, SMS) and evidence has been presented to show movements away from areas of ethnic population concentration. Whilst work by the authors has demonstrated the processes of decentralisation from inner to outer boroughs in London, for example, this chapter aims to summarise the migration taking place across the whole of England and Wales at district level using data commissioned from ONS and described in the next section.

Data Sources and Spatial Units

Migration Data

Migration may be defined in various ways but the two most common forms of data measure changes of residence either as 'transitions' or as 'moves/events' (Stillwell et al., 2010). Transition data are collected in the national population census which asks respondents for their usual address on census day (29 April in the case of 2001) and 1 year prior to then. It is therefore possible to identify migrants by comparing addresses at these points in time. The data used in this chapter relate to migration that occurred between April 2000 and 2001 and exclude return or multiple moves over the period as well as migrants who were born and/or died during the course of the year (Bell et al., 2002). Despite exclusions such as these, the census is virtually the only source providing reliable and comprehensive data on migration by ethnic group. The data that we use are for seven ethnic groups that have been defined by the Office of National Statistics (ONS) and used to categorise migration flows at level 1 (district) in the Special Migration Statistics (SMS Table 3). The ethnic groups are defined as aggregations of the 16 groups used in the Key Statistics (Table 6.1).

Table 6.1 Ethnic groups defined in the 2001 Census

Ethnic group defined in key statistics	Ethnic group defined in special migration statistics (Level 1)	Abbreviation used in chapter
White British; White Irish; Other White	White	White
Indian	Indian	Indian
Pakistani; Bangladeshi; Other Asian	Pakistani and Other South Asian	POSA
Chinese	Chinese	Chinese
Caribbean; African; Other black	Caribbean, African, Black British and Black Other	Black
White and Black Caribbean; White and Black African; White and Asian; Other mixed	Mixed	Mixed
Other	Other	Other

Whilst data from the 2001 SMS are available by ethnic group disaggregated by sex at the district scale, there is no simultaneous cross-classification by age. Given the importance of age as a selective influence on migration, we requested a commissioned table from ONS (Table CO711) based on a set of age bands that reflect stages in the life course: children aged 0–15 who tend to migrate with their parents; teenagers aged 16–19 whose age range captures the movement away from home of those into their first independent living arrangement, including those moving to higher education; young adults aged 20–24 likely to be moving on from university into work as well as those moving between jobs or leaving the parental home for the first time; those in their late 20s (25–29) also likely to be driven by economic forces or the desire to get onto the housing ladder; those aged 30–44 who are more likely to be moving to residential space more suitable for families; the 45–59 age group which involves more mature migrants of working age who may be looking to downsize their homes after their children have moved away; and the final 60+ age group which contains a mixture of migrants including those moving for retirement reasons as well as those in elderly age groups seeking to be nearer to service facilities or family members.

Whilst these broad age bands are aligned with life course stages, they have also been determined through negotiation with ONS so as to minimize the effect of the small cell adjustment methodology (SCAM) applied to all 'cell' counts of data produced from the raw 2001 Census records for statistical disclosure reasons so that they do not contravene confidentiality legislation. In practical terms, it is understood that ONS have applied a methodology of adjusting all cell counts of 1 or 2 to values of 0 or 3, the impact of which has been reported by Stillwell and Duke-Williams (2006). Commissioned Table CO711 is therefore a table of counts of migrants between districts of England and Wales for seven ethnic groups and seven age groups which have been adjusted for SCAM. The cells representing the overall total flow between districts in Table CO711 are consistent with an aggregation of the component flows disaggregated by ethnic group and age. However, the total flows in England and Wales are not exactly the same as flows derived from the SMS and extracted using the Web-based Interface to Census Interaction Data (WICID) (Stillwell and Duke-Williams, 2003). In total, due to adjustment, there are approximately 2,000 fewer migrants in the SMS table than in the commissioned table. In most cases the differences are a relatively small percentage of the gross flows. We accept that a classification of ethnicity that lumps all White and Black people into single groups, and which aggregates Other South Asians with Pakistanis into one group, is far from ideal when there are likely to be significant differences between the groups comprising these classes. This, however, is the burden imposed by the restrictions of disclosure control.

Standard Table (ST101) was the source for corresponding populations at risk (PAR) used to compute migration rates for each age-specific ethnic group. This standard table provides data for eleven ethnic categories and 22 age group cohorts, so aggregation was required to derive PAR corresponding with the 49 age-specific ethnic groups used in the analysis.

Spatial Units

The data counts in Table CO711 were supplied by ONS for migration flows between 376 local authority districts in England and Wales including 33 London boroughs, 36 metropolitan districts, 68 unitary authorities and 239 other local authorities. In principle, the full matrix contains $367 \times 367 \times 7 \times 7$ or nearly 66 million cells, although many of these would contain zero flows. The magnitude of the analysis task at district scale is considerable and it is for this reason that we have decided to summarize flows by adopting a national area classification which places each district into a group according to key characteristics of the people who live in each area. By clustering districts in this way, a simplification of the original data can be achieved and patterns and relationships are easier to identify. Previous studies have used classifications such as 'rural and urban' or 'metropolitan and non-metropolitan' to identify trends in migration (Champion, 1989, 2006; Fielding, 1992). The classification of districts developed by Vickers et al. (2003) using 2001 Census Key Statistics assigns each district in the UK to each of three levels of classification depending on its socioeconomic, demographic or geographic characteristics. It does not incorporate any migration variables directly and so provides an appropriate framework.

The Vickers et al. classification involves three tiers of district classification: 'family', 'group' and 'class'. For the purposes of the analysis reported here, only the family and class levels have been used since the intermediate level does not add greatly to the insights gained from the other two levels. As depicted in Fig. 6.1, the districts are clustered into four 'families' which contain 23 'classes'. Although the ONS also has a similar national area classification at district level, the methodology and rationale for the selection of variables and clustering techniques used by Vickers et al. are more comprehensive and transparent. The four families

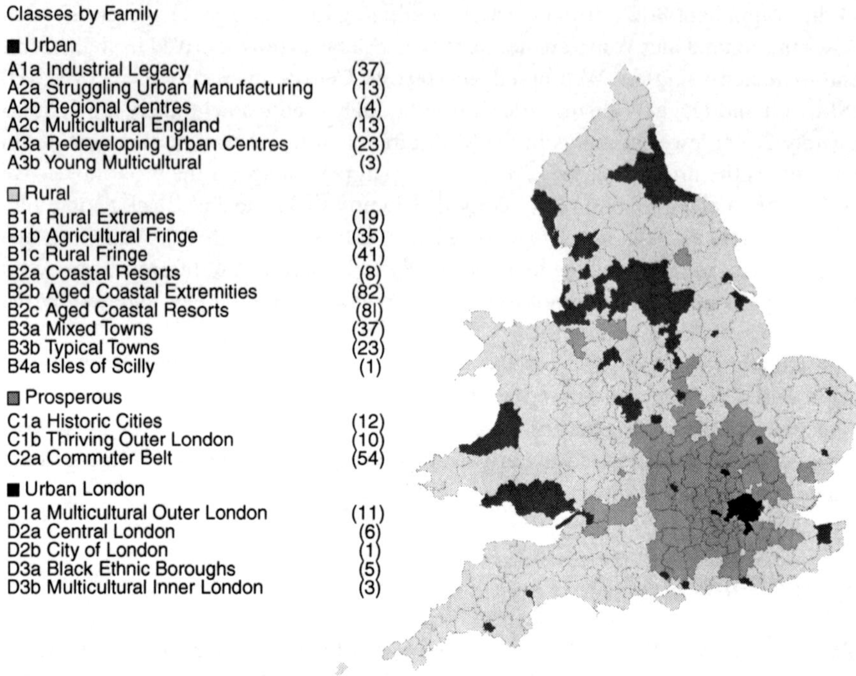

Fig. 6.1 Family tier (with classes) of the 2001 district classification in England and Wales

are ‘Urban London’ which includes five classes (Multicultural Outer London, Central London, City of London, Black Ethnic Boroughs, Multicultural Inner London); ‘Urban’ which includes six classes (Industrial legacy, Struggling Urban Manufacturing, Regional Centres, Multicultural England, Redeveloping Urban Centres, Young Multicultural); ‘Prosperous’ which includes three classes (Historic Cities, Thriving Outer London, Commuter Belt); and ‘Rural’ which includes eight classes (Rural Extremes, Agricultural Fringe, Rural Fringe, Coastal Resorts, Aged Coastal Extremities, Aged Coastal Resorts, Mixed Towns, Typical Towns, Isles of Scilly).

Ethnic Diversity and Migration Propensity

Due to a labour shortage at the end of the Second World War, migrant workers were recruited from the New Commonwealth to take up residence and employment in Britain. This eventually resulted in a significant ethnic minority presence, growing from 74,000 people in 1951 to 4.6 million in 2001 (Owen, 2006). The largest flows of immigrant workers took place over the decades of the 1950s, 1960s and 1970s. However, since the mid-1990s, net immigration to the UK has increased again to approximately 200,000 per annum with immigrants originating from across the world rather than overwhelmingly from New Commonwealth countries (Salt, 2005). The majority of post-war migrant workers found themselves in the most disadvantaged jobs which were essentially positions the indigenous population had refused to take. As a result of continued disadvantage and discrimination in the labour and housing markets, subsequent generations of British-born non-White populations still remain in similar positions to their predecessors, although different ethnic minority communities do appear to have differing levels of disadvantage and social and economic trajectories (Modood et al., 1996). In the following section, we explore the ethnic mix and age structure of the population and its migrant component.

Ethnic Mix

In terms of population size, the 2001 Census data show that the White population of England and Wales remains by far the most predominant group with non-White groups combining to constitute only 8.7% of the total population. Table 6.2 shows the population counts and migrant numbers ranked by population size. The Pakistani and Other South Asian (POSA) category makes up the largest minority group followed by Black, Indian and Mixed. The Chinese and Other groups contribute less than half a percentage each of the total population of England and Wales. Almost 5.5 million individuals moved usual residence during 2000–2001, 90.4% of whom were White. Half the non-White migrants were classified in the Black and POSA groups with Chinese and Other groups accounting for just over 6% in each case and migrants of Indian and of Mixed ethnicity being responsible for 19 and 18% respectively of total non-White internal migration.

The crude migration intensities shown in Fig. 6.2, computed using end-of-period populations and displayed in order of population size, indicate that it is the Asians (Indians in particular) that have lower rates of migration than Whites but that Whites

Table 6.2 Ethnic composition of population and migrants, England and Wales, 2001

Ethnic group	Population count	Percentage of total	Percentage of non-White	Migrant count	Percentage of total	Percentage of non-White
White	47,520,866	91.31	–	4,965,187	90.39	–
POSA	1,236,929	2.38	27.36	126,373	2.30	23.95
Black	1,139,575	2.19	25.21	138,000	2.51	26.15
Indian	1,036,807	1.99	22.93	101,234	1.84	19.19
Mixed	661,036	1.27	14.62	94,548	1.72	17.92
Chinese	226,950	0.44	5.02	33,340	0.61	6.32
Other	219,754	0.42	4.86	34,139	0.62	6.47
Total	52,041,917	100.00	100.00	5,492,821	100.00	100.00

Source: 2001 Census Standard Table ST101 and Commissioned Table CO711.

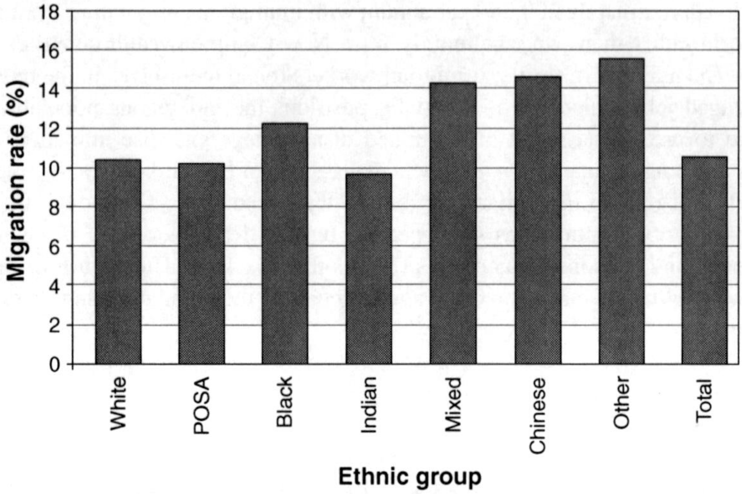

Fig. 6.2 Crude internal migration rates by ethnic group, England and Wales, 2000–2001 (Source: Computed from 2001 Census Standard Table ST101 and Census Commissioned Table CO711)

are less likely to migrate than each of the remaining ethnic groups and crude intensities for the Mixed, Chinese and Other groups are all over 14% compared with the overall rate of just over 10%.

Age Structure

One prominent difference between ethnic groups in 2001 is that of the age structure of their populations (Table 6.3). White people are older on average than people from non-White ethnic groups. Half of those of Mixed ethnic parentage are under the age of 15 compared with a third of POSA populations, 26% of Black populations, 19% of White and Other groups and 18% of Chinese. The proportion of people in the three age groups between 16 and 29 are higher in each case for all ethnic minorities than for Whites. In the cohorts aged 30–44 in 2001, Black and Other groups are 10% higher than the White and national average. The shares for groups with highest proportions of young people, namely Mixed and POSA, are much smaller than the shares for Whites after age 40. As a result of their length of settlement in this country, Blacks and Indians both have over 10% of their populations aged 60 or over in 2001. If the POSA group was disaggregated, the Pakistanis would have a slightly higher proportion of people within this age cohort than Bangladeshis, reflecting their slightly longer period of settlement in Britain. The place of birth statistics in the 2001 Census show that much of the change in the minority populations has come about through natural increase rather than immigration. The young age structures of Pakistani, Bangladeshi and Indian communities are a result of second and subsequent generation families with British-born children. In contrast, around 22% of the

Table 6.3 Age profile of ethnic groups in England and Wales, 2001

Ethnic group	Percentage							
	0–15	16–19	20–24	25–29	30–44	45–59	60+	Total
White	19.20	4.68	5.73	6.39	22.33	19.58	22.09	100.0
Mixed	50.01	8.33	7.84	6.81	16.87	6.03	4.11	100.0
POSA	33.53	8.19	10.32	9.81	20.81	10.59	6.75	100.0
Black	25.97	6.04	6.79	7.75	32.05	11.28	10.12	100.0
Indian	22.89	6.94	8.88	9.20	25.21	16.67	10.21	100.0
Other	19.27	5.86	9.62	12.61	31.47	16.33	4.84	100.0
Chinese	18.33	9.36	13.39	9.73	25.43	15.92	7.84	100.0
All people	20.15	4.91	6.00	6.60	22.55	18.93	20.86	100.0

Source: Computed from 2001 Census Standard Table ST101.

national White population are aged 60+ in 2001, numbering almost 10.5 million people and more than the non-White population in its entirety.

Variations in propensities to migrate have been found to be significantly influenced by age and this is reflected in changes that occur during the life course (Champion et al., 1998). In a discussion of the 'laws' of migration, Tobler wrote *one of the most studied regularities is the age profile of migrants* (1995, p. 335). Champion (2005) and Dennett and Stillwell (2008) have shown using 2001 Census data, as have others using earlier data (Owen and Green, 1992; Warnes and Ford, 1995), that migration rates are high for young children and then decline until 16 before rising to a peak in the early 20s. Young adults at this age have the highest propensity to migrate across all age cohorts and this can be explained by moving to universities or to employment after school/college or to jobs after completing university. This is followed by a reduction in migration from the mid-20s to mid-30s associated with establishing families and early child rearing. Migration rates do not pick up again until well after retirement age in the 70s and 80s which can be associated with greater need for care and moving to be in close proximity to family members for the elderly. This is known as the life course theory which is influenced by key stages in people's lives rather than simply a result of biological age itself (Warnes, 1992). In terms of the absolute volume of migration flows taking place in England and Wales by age and ethnic group (Table 6.4), we observe that, amongst non-Whites, it is the POSA group that is most numerous in the child age range and the Black group has the most migrants in the student age range. The POSA group dominates again in the early adult ages but Blacks are more numerous in older ages, significantly so in middle working age (30–44).

When age-specific migration rates are computed (Fig. 6.3) with end-of-period populations at risk as denominators, the schedules tell a rather different story. Despite their relative magnitude, the Indian and POSA groups experience the lowest migration rates in almost all ages and the rate differentials are most noticeable at ages 16–19, 20–24 and 25–29. At age 20–24, the POSA rate is only about 17%,

Table 6.4 Migrant numbers by age and ethnic group

	White	Black	POSA	Indian	Mixed	Other	Chinese	Total
0–15	938,732	31,244	35,533	18,147	39,201	5,606	3,829	1,072,292
16–19	349,409	10,025	9,041	8,423	8,577	2,125	3,898	391,498
20–24	869,943	18,711	22,314	20,838	16,047	5,854	10,647	964,354
25–29	709,696	18,711	19,576	17,035	10,676	6,527	4,997	787,218
30–44	1,188,119	45,345	27,857	25,945	15,368	10,600	7,261	1,320,495
45–59	455,130	8,568	7,111	6,636	2,862	2,505	1,842	484,654
60+	398,115	5,115	4,059	3,844	1,320	629	779	413,861
Total	4,909,144	137,719	125,491	100,868	94,051	33,846	33,253	5,434, 372

Source: ONS Commissioned Table C0711.

less than half the rate of migration of the Chinese, the most mobile group at this age and at age 16–19 years also.

Although the difference between ethnic group migration intensities is most noticeable in the 20–24 age group, the gap between the rates for Asians and others is apparent for those in their late teens. POSA migrants aged 16–19 have only a marginally higher migration rate than those aged 0–15. Given the inclusion of students on the 2001 Census migration counts, we conclude that POSA migrants are less inclined to move away from home to study in higher education or in fact to leave

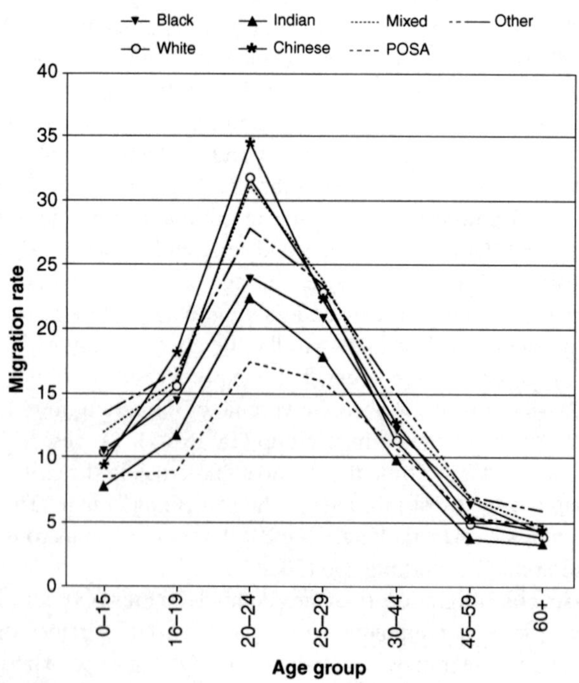

Fig. 6.3 National migration rates for ethnic groups by age, England and Wales, 2000–2001 (Source: Computed from 2001 Census Standard Table ST101 and Commissioned Table CO711)

home aged 20–24. Evidence from elsewhere (Johnston et al., 2005; Phillips et al., 2004) indicates that Bangladeshis have the highest levels of segregation amongst all ethnic groups.

Geographical Distribution of Ethnic Populations

As the primary pull factor for immigrants originating from the New Commonwealth was employment, the majority of early arrivals settled in urban industrial centres and large cities where jobs in manufacturing were largely based (Mason, 1995). Analysis of the 1991 Census showed that the majority of ethnic minority populations had remained concentrated in and around areas of original settlement. Greater London and the West Midlands were, in 1991, the main regions with the highest concentrations of ethnic minority communities (Owen, 1992; Rees and Phillips, 1996). The 2001 Census has also demonstrated that concentrations remain around the key areas of Greater London, the West Midlands, and Greater Manchester, West Yorkshire and the Leicester/Nottingham corridor in the East Midlands (Owen, 2006). Analysis of the 2001 Census data shows that within these localities, over a quarter of the population of Greater London and a fifth of the West Midlands belong to ethnic minorities. In terms of ethnic minority population shares across the country, half of all people of ethnic minorities reside in Greater London, with 20% living in Inner London. One eighth of all ethnic minorities reside in the West Midlands. In terms of ethnic breakdown, the largest percentage of Black communities can be found in Greater London, with over two thirds of these groups living there. The vast majority of the remaining Black communities can be found in the West Midlands and the South East. Over one third of all Asians live in Greater London. The second largest concentration of Asians is found in the West Midlands, followed by Lancashire, West Yorkshire and the East Midlands. At district level, the boroughs of Newham and Brent are home to the largest concentrations of ethnic minorities.

In terms of the Vickers et al. area classification at family level, Urban London has the largest proportion (35%) of non-White residents, of which the Black population contributes the largest number. Non-White ethnic minority residents constitute less than 10% in the other three families, with the POSA group being the largest non-White group in Urban areas. Approximately 5% of people in Prosperous areas and only 3% of those living in Rural areas are non-White. The percentages of each ethnic group that live in each of the four types of district family are shown in Fig. 6.4, illustrating the large proportion of Whites residing in Rural districts but also highlighting the concentration of over 60% of the Black population in Urban London and almost half the POSA population in provincial Urban districts, although these figures conceal significant differences between sub-groups; a higher proportion of Bangladeshis live in Urban London, for example. The Chinese and Mixed groups have similar proportions of people within each area type. They both have the largest proportions (of the non-White groups) living in Rural and Prosperous areas.

Further detail about the distribution of ethnic populations across England and Wales is revealed at the district 'class' level. Within the Urban London family, it is

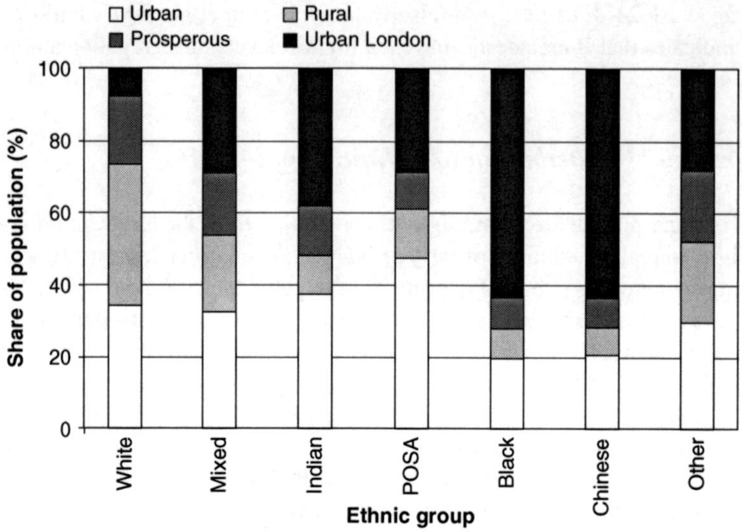

Fig. 6.4 Percentage shares of ethnic populations by family type, 2001 (Source: Computed from ONS Commissioned Table C0711)

unsurprising that Multicultural Inner London has the highest proportion of ethnic minority residents, with over 50% of all people living in this area type being of non-White ethnic groups. Over one third of Black Ethnic Boroughs and a quarter of Central London and the City of London are made up of non-White residents. The largest ethnic minority group in all three areas is Black. Over 30% of Multicultural Outer London is comprised of non-White groups although Indians and then Blacks make up the largest percentage of ethnic minority communities in this class. The class outside of London with the largest percentage of ethnic minority groups is, as expected, Multicultural England, with approximately 20% of residents being non-White. At the other end of the spectrum, the Rural class containing only one district, the Isles of Scilly, has the lowest proportion of non-White residents. Apart from its small mixed population, the Isles of Scilly has no counts of any other ethnic minorities in its population.

Internal Migration by Ethnic Group

Internal migration is the major contributing factor to population change *vis à vis* natural change due to differential fertility and mortality. Internal migration contributes not only to changes in the number of people but also to changes in the composition and structure of local populations, with implications for the physical environment but also the economic development of an area. Exploration of the changing compositions of ethnic minority populations is particularly relevant for issues of equal opportunities, service provision and social cohesion.

It is widely accepted that one of the most characteristic and persistent patterns of population redistribution through migration in Britain is that associated with the process of counterurbanisation with greater propensities for populations to migrate from metropolitan to non-metropolitan areas or to urban areas lower in the settlement hierarchy (Champion, 1989, 2005; Dennett and Stillwell, 2008). Champion (2005), Owen and Green (1992, p. 92), for example, refers to the *urban-rural shift (the movement of people from inner cities to the suburbs and more rural areas).* Moreover, other processes are continually occurring at an intra-city scale such as suburbanisation, gentrification, city centre living and residualisation which are causing new flows of migrants, while larger flows of 16–19 year olds are occurring into cities with big universities (Champion, 2005; Rees and Phillips, 1996). Movements motivated by employment opportunities in the young adult age groups also generate patterns of urbanisation that run counter to the processes of decentralisation that are more associated with middle and older age. In addition to age being an important selective influence on migration, there are also likely to be marked differences in distance of migration according to age and ethnicity (Champion, 2005; Finney and Simpson, 2008). In this instance, we consider flows within districts in the same family and between districts in different families by ethnic group.

Intra and Inter-district Shares

Figure 6.5 illustrates the percentages of all migration flows that take place within districts of the same family in 2000–2001, emphasising the urban focus of the non-White groups and the importance of Rural-Rural flows for Whites in relative terms. Almost 60% of White migration is either Urban-Urban or Rural-Rural, whereas

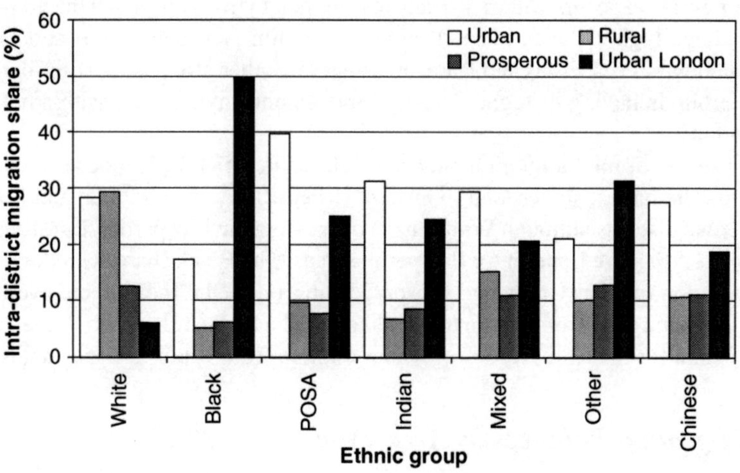

Fig. 6.5 Intra-district flows by family and ethnic group, 2000–2001 (Source: ONS Commissioned Table C0711)

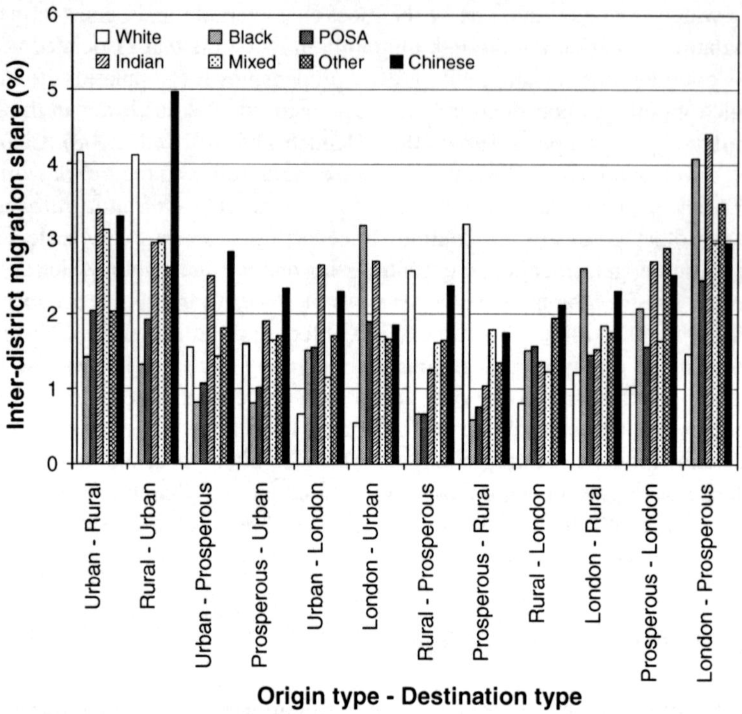

Fig. 6.6 Inter-district flows by family and ethnic group, 2000–2001 (Source: ONS Commissioned Table C0711)

50% of Black migration occurs within Urban London alone and almost 40% of POSA migration occurs within districts in provincial Urban areas. All the non-White groups have higher shares of total migration within provincial cities and London compared with Prosperous and Rural areas but the Other group is most similar to the Black group in having its highest share of movements taking place within boroughs of London.

The shares of total migration between districts in different families are shown in Fig. 6.6. The largest shares tend to involve Urban-Rural, Rural-Urban and London-Prosperous districts although Whites have over 3% in the Prosperous-Rural category and only 1.5% leave London for Prosperous areas. The Black share is predominantly from London to other Urban and Prosperous areas, like the Indians, but over 3% of Indians also migrate from Urban to Rural areas. The highest share of all inter-family flows is that for the Chinese, 5% of whom migrate from Rural to Urban areas.

Net Migration Balances by Area Type

Net migration balances provide a summary of the balances between the inflows and outflows for each ethnic group and Table 6.5 contains these calculations for both

Table 6.5 Net migration balances by ethnic group and area type, 2000–2001

Area		All	White	Indian	POSA	Chinese	Black	Mixed	Other
A	Urban	−2, 075	−4, 404	−979	216	242	2, 137	562	151
A1a	Industrial legacy	−2, 261	−1, 818	−289	−187	−161	−107	55	32
A2a	Struggling urban manufacturing	−8, 150	−8, 992	−449	119	25	1, 204	6	−69
A2b	Regional centres	3, 536	2, 708	367	143	238	27	−63	116
A2c	Multicultural England	−10, 694	−9, 921	−1, 030	−214	−13	390	−147	241
A3a	Redeveloping urban centres	15, 076	13, 005	406	413	285	415	594	−42
A3b	Young multicultural	424	614	16	−58	−132	−6	117	−127
B	Rural	54, 812	53, 033	384	105	−696	1, 445	905	−364
B1a	Rural extremes	1, 453	1, 476	−16	29	−33	14	−20	3
B1b	Agricultural fringe	14, 538	14, 709	−79	69	−345	68	250	−134
B1c	Rural fringe	15, 815	14, 859	387	37	−140	312	346	14
B2a	Coastal resorts	5, 904	6, 276	−65	57	−126	−57	2	−183
B2b	Ageing coastal extremities	12, 286	12, 206	−59	147	−104	38	61	−3
B2c	Ageing coastal resorts	7, 775	7, 812	−4	−8	−18	7	−26	12
B3a	Mixed urban	−2, 393	−2, 535	139	−462	75	237	188	−35
B3b	Typical towns	−566	−1, 770	81	236	−5	826	104	−38
C	Prosperous	−4, 001	−12, 316	2, 496	1, 084	517	3, 017	865	336
C1a	Historic cities	4, 925	3, 986	455	115	165	229	−59	34
C1b	Thriving outer London	−4, 086	−7, 713	949	730	163	1, 399	174	212
C2a	The commuter belt	−4, 840	−8, 589	1, 092	239	189	1, 389	750	90
D	Urban London	−48, 736	−36, 313	−1, 901	−1, 405	−63	−6, 599	−2, 332	−123
D1a	Multicultural outer London	−21, 730	−23, 958	−397	612	88	1, 901	−515	539
D2a&b	Central and city of London	−12, 576	−8, 605	106	−641	45	−2, 183	−828	−470
D3a	Black ethnic boroughs	−7, 726	−688	−310	−564	−217	−5, 095	−689	−163
D3b	Multicultural inner London	−6, 704	−3, 062	−1, 300	−812	21	−1, 222	−300	−29

Source: Computed from ONS Commissioned Table CO711.

families and their constituent classes from the Vickers et al. typology (column 2). In the top tier of the area hierarchy, Urban London is the family type that shows overwhelming losses of population through net migration; over 48,700 migrants left Urban London for the rest of England and Wales in 2000–2001 whereas the Rural family gained almost 55,000 migrants in net terms and is the only family to gain. The net losses from Urban and Prosperous areas are small in comparison. The pattern of net loss from Urban London is consistent across all ethnic groups as are net gains in Rural areas for all groups apart from the Chinese and Other, where losses are recorded. In both families, the balances are dominated by the net flows for Whites. In the case of non-London Urban, however, net losses of Indians as well as Whites are evident whereas the loss of Whites from Prosperous areas is significantly offset by gains in all the other ethnic groups, particularly Blacks and South Asians.

At the class level, interesting variations exist within families. Whilst all classes of Urban London lose through White net out-migration, Regional Centres, Redeveloping Urban Centres and Young Multicultural districts in provincial Urban areas all gain White net migrants. In Rural areas, Mixed Urban and Typical Towns also lose White migrants while Historic cities in Prosperous Britain gain Whites. In Urban London, it is not only Whites that are leaving Black Ethnic Boroughs and Multicultural Inner London; net migration losses are apparent for virtually all ethnic groups, whereas in Multicultural Outer London, net gains are recorded for all non-White groups except Indians and Mixed ethnicity migrants. Central and City of London gains Indians and Chinese through net migration but loses through net out-migration of other non-White groups, particularly Blacks. The processes of decentralisation of migration within Greater London are considered in more detail in Stillwell and Hussain (2010) and in Stillwell (2010).

As far as Urban England and Wales is concerned, the most significant balances in absolute terms are those of net gain by Blacks in Struggling Urban Manufacturing districts and net losses of Indians from Multicultural England. Apart from gains by Blacks and those of Mixed ethnicity, Multicultural England loses migrants in other non-White groups, whereas White gains in Young Multicultural districts are partially offset by net losses by those in the POSA, Chinese, Black and Other groups. In Rural areas, the balances of net migration are all relatively small, with the Chinese only gaining in Mixed Urban districts and Blacks only having net losses in Coastal Resorts. In contrast, absolute net migration balances for non-White ethnic groups in Prosperous areas are rather more significant. Whereas Whites are leaving Thriving Outer London and The Commuter Belt in net terms, these areas are gaining migrants from all non-White groups, particularly Blacks.

This is the reason for the relatively high rates of net migration gain for Prosperous areas that are shown in Fig. 6.7. Net migration gains, relative to population size, are most significant in Prosperous areas for all non-White groups, although the Black and Mixed groups also have positive net migration rates for Rural areas, whilst the Chinese and Other groups have negative net migration rates for this family of districts. Rates of Chinese net out-migration from London, however, are low compared with those of other groups, particularly the Mixed group.

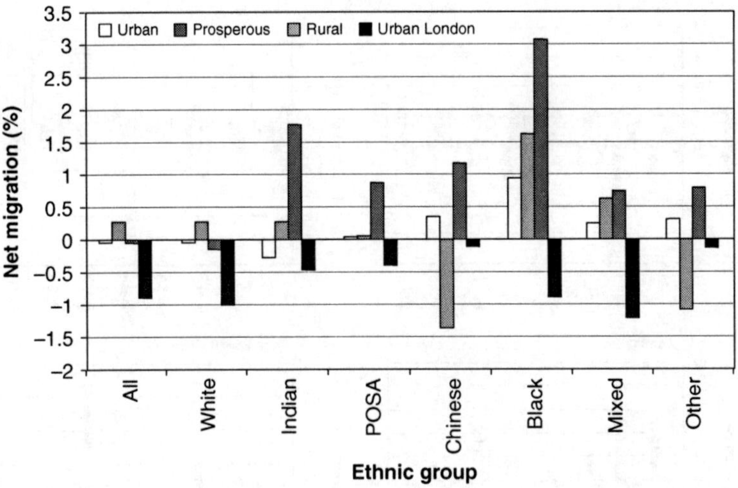

Fig. 6.7 Rates of net migration by ethnic group and family type, 2000–2001

Age Disaggregation

The ethnic net migration rates presented in Fig. 6.7 can be disaggregated by age to reveal more of the complexity of the interactions between districts in different family types, as illustrated in Fig. 6.8. In all age groups, the aggregate net rates are determined by the White ethnic groups because of their numerical dominance of the migration flows as well as the population denominators. However, there are some significant differences in the age-specific net migration rates between the ethnic groups, not least when we compare the first two graphs in Fig. 6.8, the net rates for 0–15 and 16–19 year olds.

Rates for the 0–15 age group in each ethnic group show some degree of conformity with net losses from Urban London, although these are dominated by high rates of net-outmigration for Whites of a similar magnitude to those in the parental age group, 30–44. Apart from children of Other ethnicity, all the remaining rates are positive for Rural and Prosperous areas, with highest rates in both these family types being associated with Blacks. In direct contrast, the ethnic rates of migration for the older teenagers are mostly negative for these two families whereas rates are mostly positive for Urban England and Wales. The Chinese group aged 16–19 experiences the highest rates of net loss from Rural areas yet have the highest rates of net gain in Urban areas and Urban London, whereas the rate of Black net in-migration to Prosperous parts is more than double that of the 0–15 age group. Other than the Chinese, London is not attractive in net migration rate terms to internal migrants from non-White ethnic groups, and the balance for Whites is zero – there are as many older White teenagers leaving Urban London as there are arriving.

The variations between ethnic groups in net migration rates are equally disparate for the two age groups of those in their 20s. London benefits hugely from high rates

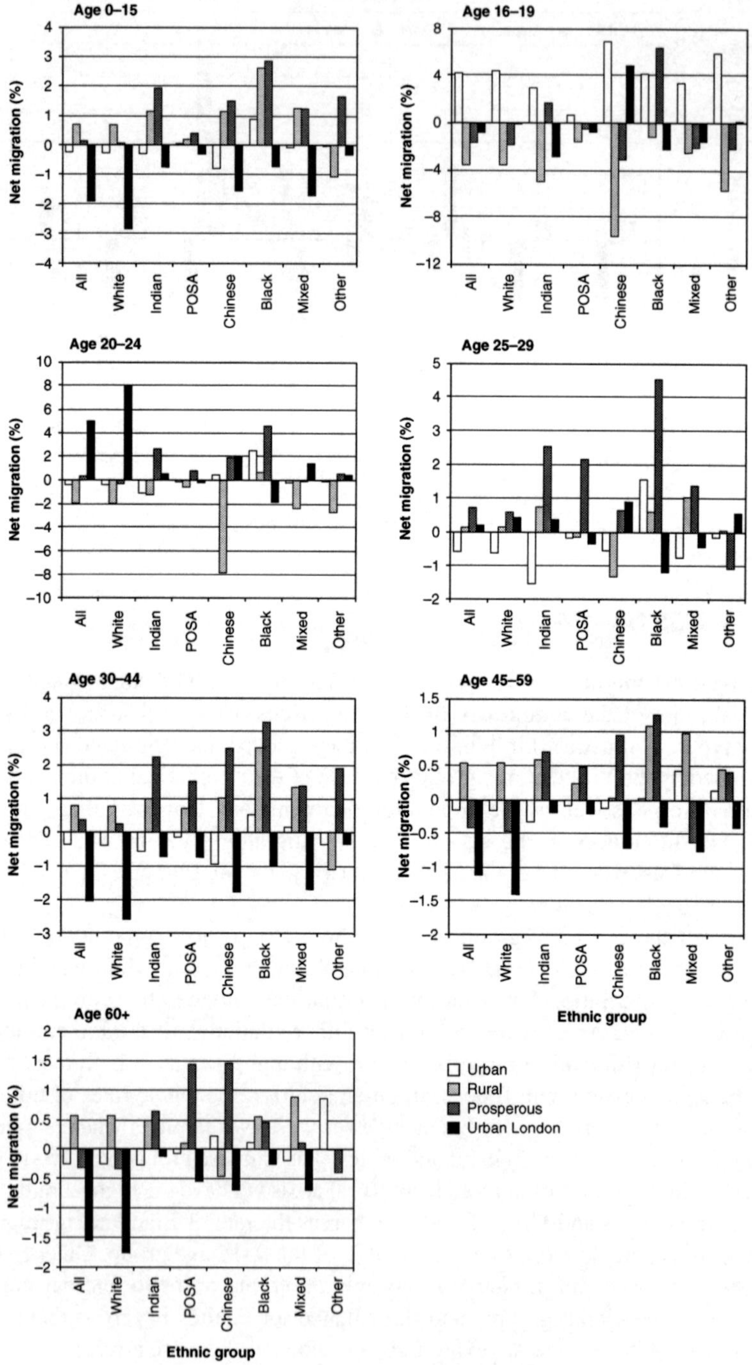

Fig. 6.8 Net migration rates by ethnic group, age group and family type, 2000–2001

of White net in-migration of those aged 20–24, partly reflecting the net inflow after graduation, but only marginally from those aged 25–29. The highest rates of net in-migration in the latter age group are of Blacks and Asians into Prosperous areas, with Urban areas having rates of net loss for all ethnic groups except Blacks. Ethnic group net migration rates for the two older working groups conform much more with those of the 0–15 age group, although rates of net gain or loss are lower in those aged 45–59. Negative rates of net migration in the oldest category, 60 and over, are for Whites from Urban London, although rates for this family type are negative across all ethnic groups. Positive net migration rates for this age group of migrants are highest for the POSA and the Chinese groups moving into Prosperous areas.

Figure 6.9 illustrates the variations in net migration rate between ethnic group by class of district. The graph juxtaposes histograms of net migration rates for 21 classes for each ethnic group, enabling some contrasting features to be identified,

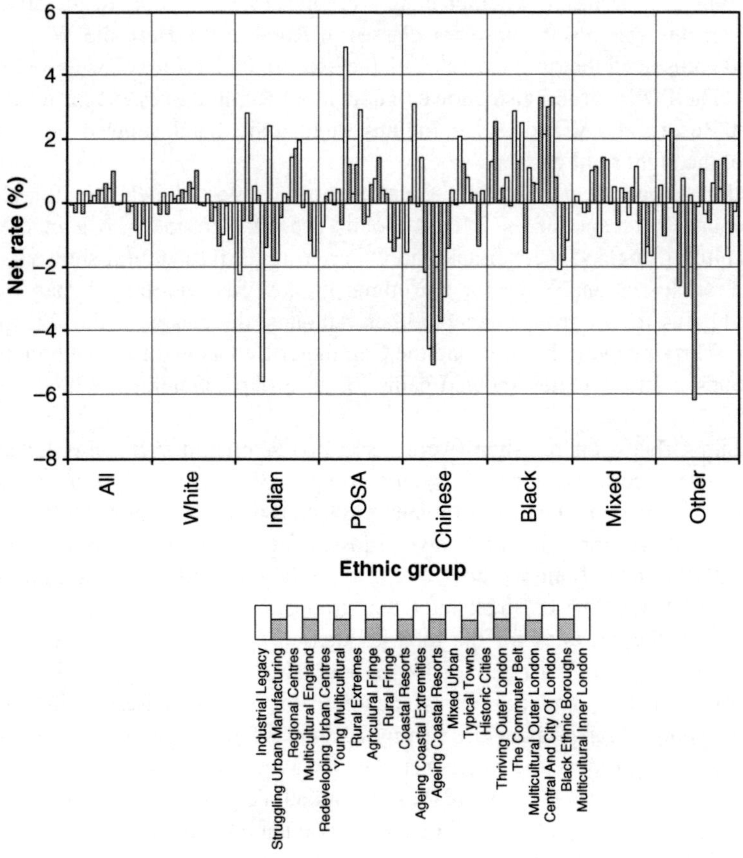

Fig. 6.9 Rates of net migration by ethnic group and class type, 2000–2001

such as the different spatial patterns of net rates for Indians compared with POSA, and the relatively high rates of net loss for Chinese from Rural classes compared with the gains in these classes by Blacks.

Table 6.6 presents the rates of net migration loss and gain for all migrants and each ethnic group that are higher than 1% in Fig. 6.9. Thus, Ageing Coastal Resorts are the only class of districts that gain at a rate over 1% for all migrants, whereas the City of London and Multicultural Inner London are the two classes of districts that lose at rates of over 1%. Across the spectrum of ethnic minorities, negative and positive net migration rates range between –5.6 and +4.9%. Analysis at the class level shows considerable diversity among ethnic groups in net migration rates and there is no clear pattern of losses and gains for any two groups. For example, Indian and POSA groups do not follow similar patterns of net rate gains or losses in a consistent enough way for general conclusions to be drawn about preferences among all South Asians.

There are similarities, however, between Indians and Whites in terms of net rate losses and gains within all the provincial Urban classes. Indians consistently mirrored Whites in terms of whether there were net losses or gains to the area type. However, this was not the case for classes of Rural areas. Here the White group showed gains in all the rural classes with the exception of Typical Towns and Mixed Urban. The POSA group also showed gains in all Rural classes except for Ageing Coastal Resorts and Mixed Urban. Indians, on the other hand, showed gains in only three of the eight rural classes.

Within Urban areas, Regional Centres showed rates of net gain for all ethnic minorities except for the Mixed group. The only groups who gained within Multicultural England were Black and Other. Young Multicultural showed a mixture of net losses and gains for the ethnic groups. Redeveloping Urban Centres showed gains for all groups except Other. Amongst the classes within Prosperous Britain, Thriving Outer London and the Commuter Belt gained for all ethnic minority groups. Historic Cities showed gains for all groups, including Whites, but not Mixed.

Within Urban London, there were losses for Whites in every class. The only class that showed losses for every ethnic group is Black Ethnic Boroughs. Central and City of London had gains of Indians and Chinese but losses for all other groups and Multicultural Inner London showed losses for all groups except for Chinese. Multicultural Outer London showed losses for Indians and the Mixed group and gains for POSA, Chinese, Black and Other groups.

Although the net rates for the total population fall within a 10% range, when broken down by age, net rates for losses and gains are much higher. This is as a result of a smaller population at risk denominator in some cases, whilst in other cases, it is due to high propensities to migrate among some age cohorts. As expected, 16–19 year olds produce the largest net rate increases and losses to different types of area. Regional Centres were popular among all ethnic groups aged 16–24, with net gains across all groups. Historic Cities was a popular class for 16–19 year olds with gains for all groups. Young Multicultural also gained for all migrants aged 16–19. Agricultural Fringe showed losses for all 16–19 year olds with the exception of the

Table 6.6 Class types with rates of net migration gain or loss >1% by ethnic group, 2000–2001

Ethnic group	Gain classes	Net rate (%)	Loss classes	Net rate (%)
All	Ageing coastal resorts	1.02	Multicultural inner London	–1.18
			City of London	–1.10
White	Ageing coastal resorts	1.04	Multicultural outer London	–1.35
			Multicultural inner London	–1.12
Indian	Regional centres	2.85	Rural extremes	–5.63
	Rural fringe	2.45	Industrial legacy	–2.26
	The commuter belt	2.00	Multicultural inner London	–1.66
	Thriving outer London	1.72	Black ethnic boroughs	–1.18
	Historic cities	1.45		
POSA	Rural extremes	4.92	Black ethnic boroughs	–1.51
	Ageing coastal extremities	2.93	City of London	–1.21
	Thriving outer London	1.44	Multicultural inner London	–1.09
	Coastal resorts	1.21		
	Agricultural fringe	1.20		
Black	Typical towns	3.32	City of London	–2.07
	The commuter belt	3.32	Black ethnic boroughs	–1.80
	Thriving outer London	3.05	Coastal resorts	–1.57
	Rural extremes	2.90	Multicultural inner London	–1.16
	Struggling urban Manuf	2.56		
	Rural fringe	2.54		
	Historic cities	2.18		
	Industrial legacy	1.33		
	Agricultural fringe	1.31		
	Ageing coastal extermities	1.13		
Chinese	Regional centres	3.12	Agricultural fringe	–5.09
	Historic cities	2.12	Rural extremes	–4.60
	The commuter belt	2.00	Coastal resorts	–3.73
	Thriving outer London	1.72	Ageing coastal Extremities	–2.94
	Redeveloping urban centres	1.44	Young multicultural	–2.17
			Rural fringe	–1.70
			Industrial legacy	–1.53
			Ageing coastal resorts	–1.43
			Black ethnic boroughs	–1.35
Mixed	Agricultural fringe	1.44	City of London	–1.89
	Rural fringe	1.39	Multicultural inner London	–1.64
	Young multicultural	1.15	Black ethnic boroughs	–1.36
	The commuter belt	1.14	Rural extremes	–1.04
	Redeveloping urban centres	1.05		
Other	Multicultural England	2.33	Coastal resorts	–6.23
	Regional centres	2.12	Agricultural fringe	–2.93
	Multicultural outer London	1.42	Young multicultural	–2.62
	Thriving outer London	1.31	City of London	–1.66
	Ageing coastal resorts	1.07	Struggling urban Manuf	–1.03

black group. Both Mixed Urban and Typical Towns showed losses for all 16–19 year olds, although the latter gained for all 25–44 year olds. All ethnic groups aged 20–29 experienced rates of gain within Thriving Outer London. Central and City of London was unpopular for all groups after the age of 30, as was Black Ethnic Boroughs after the age of 25. The Commuter Belt showed gains for all groups aged between 30 and 44 and Rural Fringe was a popular destination with gains for all groups from the age of 30 onwards.

Conclusions

This chapter has demonstrated that whilst aggregate flows of migration between and within districts in the year before the 2001 Census were dominated by flows of White migrants, with relatively coherent counterurbanisation patterns of net losses from large urban areas and net gains to Rural areas, the rates of migration for non-White ethnic groups vary in magnitude with Asians having relatively low rates compared with Whites and other ethnic minorities having relatively high rates, and with different groups having different spatial patterns of redistribution. It is the POSA group that has the lowest migration propensities and which has the highest proportion of migrants travelling over relatively shorter distances. Moreover, when the age dimension is added, we observe distinctive age-migration profiles for each ethnic group with POSA migrants on the one hand having propensities to move in the 16–19 age group that are no higher than for children aged 0–15, yet the Chinese on the other hand having rates that are more than double those of the POSA group. These differences in propensity are due to a range of different cultural, familial and socio-economic factors associated with each of the groups concerned which also partly determine the spatial pattern of out-migration and in-migration. A further exploration of these issues using additional data sources could add insight into understanding the low rates. Comparing proportions of students from these ethnic groups living in university halls of residence or all student households, for example, could provide an indication of whether these ethnic groups have a greater propensity to move away from home for study.

The complexity of the spatial patterns is difficult to understand effectively, especially if the spatial analysis involves the full matrix of flows between all the districts in England and Wales. The need to summarise spatial patterns is the reason why we have adopted an existing classification district system as an organising framework and in this chapter we have chosen to examine net migration taking place at two levels: between four families and 23 classes of district. The result is a series of findings about the intricacies of non-White when compared with White migration. Whilst all ethnic groups are leaving London in net migration terms, the Chinese and other groups are also leaving Rural areas; Whites and Indians are leaving Urban UK whereas these areas are gaining migrants from all the other ethnic minorities; and while Prosperous Britain has a negative net migration rate for Whites, the districts in this family gain overall from all non-White groups.

Vickers et al. identified five classes characterised by concentrations of ethnic minority groups, or as being particularly distinctive because of their ethnic minority populations: Black Ethnic Boroughs, Multicultural Inner London, Multicultural Outer London, Multicultural England and Young Multicultural. When the net flows for these areas are aggregated, all ethnic minority groups demonstrate greater net out-migration with the exception of those in the Other group. We conclude, therefore, that this is in keeping with the arguments regarding dispersal presented earlier in the chapter and that the use of the national district classification has been useful in providing further evidence that ethnic minority communities are moving away from areas with high concentrations of ethnic minorities rather than relocating to them. By definition, groups who do not have an established presence in a country tend not to be given political representation and recognition in the form of their own category within official data collection (Thernstrom, 2001). It could be argued that this is the case with the Other group, who were largely comprised of recent migrants to the United Kingdom. If this were true, in keeping with debates referred to earlier (Ellis and Wright, 1998), new migrants move to areas with the most assessible vacant housing, and these areas are often areas where there are established ethnic enclaves.

Further disaggregation by age group and by district class demonstrates the extent to which more aggregate flows conceal many differences in propensities and patterns of small sub-groups. This chapter has concentrated on net migration balances and rates, which themselves conceal information about the magnitude and patterns of outflows and inflows. Further work might usefully explore the gross flow components as well as the flows taking place within the families and classes using migration efficiencies, inflow/outflow ratios and rates of turnover and churn.

Acknowledgement The research reported in this chapter has been supported by an ESRC small research grant (RES-163-25-0028) commissioned under the Understanding Population Trends and Processes (UPTAP) programme.

References

Bell, M., Blake, M., Boyle, P., Duke-Williams, O., Rees, P. and Stillwell, J., et al. (2002) Cross-national comparison on internal migration: Issues and measures, *Journal of the Royal Statistical Society A*, 165(2): 1–30.

Champion, A.G. (1989) Internal migration and the changing distribution of population in Joshi, H. (ed.), *The Changing Population of Britain*, Blackwell, Padstow.

Champion, A.G. (1996) Internal migration and ethnicity in Britain in Ratcliffe, P. (ed.), *Ethnicity in the 1991 Census. Volume 3: Social Geography and Ethnicity in Britain: Geographical Spread, Spatial Concentration and Internal Migration*, HMSO, London, pp. 135–173.

Champion, A.G. (2005) Population movement within the UK in Chappell, R. (ed.), *Focus on People and Migration*, Palgrave Macmillan, Basingstoke, pp. 92–114.

Champion, A.G. (2006) *Demographic Trends in: Housing: Establishing the Evidence Base 2006*, RICS, London.

Champion, A.G., Fotheringham, A.S., Rees, P., Boyle, P. and Stillwell, J. (1998) *The Determinants of Migration Flows in England: A Review of Existing Data and Evidence*. Report for the Department of the Environment, Transport and the Regions, University of Newcastle upon Tyne, Newcastle.

Dennett, A. and Stillwell, J. (2008) *Internal Migration in Great Britain – A District Level Analysis Using 2001 Census Data* (Working Paper 07/08), School of Geography, University of Leeds, Leeds, p. 80.

Ellis, M. and Wright, R. (1998) The balkanisation metaphor in the analysis of US immigration, *Annals of the Association of American Geographers*, 88(4): 686–698.

Fielding, A. (1992) Migration and social mobility: South East England as an escalator region, *Regional Studies*, 26(1): 1–15.

Finney, N. and Simpson, L. (2008) Internal migration and ethnic groups: Evidence for Britain from the 2001 Census, *Population, Space and Place*, 14(2): 63–83.

Finney, N. and Simpson, L. (2009) *Sleepwalking to Segregation? Challenging Myths About Race and Migration*, The Policy Press, Bristol.

Frey, W. (1996) Immigration, domestic migration and demographic balkanisation in America: New evidence for the 1990s, *Population and Development Review*, 22(4): 741–763.

Gaines, S. (2007, September 11) Leicester heads for diversity milestone, *Society Guardian*.

Herbert, I. (2007, September 11) Leicester to be first city where white people are minority, *The Independent*.

Johnston, R., Forrest, J. and Poulsen, M. (2002) Are there ethnic enclaves/ghettos in English Cities? *Urban Studies*, 39(4): 591–618.

Johnston, R., Poulsen, M.F. and Forrest, J. (eds.) (2005) On the measurement and meaning of segregation: A response to Simpson. *Urban Studies*, 42, 1221–1227.

Kyambi, S. (2005) *Beyond Black and White, Mapping New Immigrant Communities*, Institute of Public Policy Research (IPPR), London.

Mason, D. (1995) *Race and Ethnicity in Modern Britain*, Oxford University Press, Oxford.

Modood, T., Berthoud, R., Lakey, J., Nazroo, J., Smith, P., Virdee, S., et al. (1996) *Ethnic Minorities in Britain: Diversity and Disadvantage*, Policy Studies Institute, London.

Owen, D. (1992) *Ethnic Minorities in Great Britain: Settlement Patterns, Centre for Research in Ethnic Relations*, University of Warwick, Kenilworth.

Owen, D. (2006) Demographic profiles and social cohesion of minority ethnic communities in England and Wales, Community, *Work and Family*, 9(3): 251–272.

Owen, D. and Green, A. (1992) Migration patterns and trends in Champion, A.G. and Fielding, A. (eds.), *Migration Processes and Patterns, Volume 1: Research Progress and Prospects*, Belhaven Press, London, pp. 17–38.

Peach, C. (1996) Does Britain have ghettoes? *Transactions, Institute of British Geographers NS*, 22: 216–235.

Peach, C. and Rossiter, D. (1996) Level and nature of spatial concentration and segregation of minority ethnic population in Great Britain, 1991 in Ratcliffe, P. (ed.), *Social Geography and Ethnicity in Britain: Geographical Spread, Spatial Concentration and Internal Migration*, HMSO, London, pp. 111–134.

Phillips, D. (2006) Parallel lives? Challenging discourses of British Muslim self-segregation, *Environment and Planning D: Society and Space*, 24(1): 25–40.

Phillips, D., Stillwell, J. and Burrage, A. (2004) Multicultural Leeds: Geographies of ethnic minorities and religious groups in Unsworth, R. and Stillwell, J. (eds.), *Twenty-First Century Leeds: Geographies of a Regional City*, Leeds University Press, Leeds, pp. 49–74.

Rees, P. and Butt, F. (2004) Ethnic change and diversity in England, 1981–2001, *Area*, 36(2): 174–186.

Rees, P. and Duke-Williams, O. (1995) The story of the British special migration statistics, *Scottish Geographical Magazine*, 111(1): 13–26.

Rees, P.H. and Phillips, D. (1996) Geographical spread, spatial concentration and internal migration in Ratcliffe, P. (ed.), *Ethnicity in the 1991 Census: Volume 3. Social Geography and Ethnicity in Britain: Geographical Spread, Spatial Concentration and Internal Migration*, Office for National Statistics, HMSO, London, pp. 23–109.

Robinson, V. (1992) Move on up: The mobility of Britain's Afro-Caribbean and Asian populations in Stillwell, J., Rees, P. and Boden, P. (eds.), *Migration Processes and Patterns, Volume 2: Population Redistribution in the United Kingdom*, Belhaven Press, London, pp. 271–291.

Robinson, V. (1993) Race, gender and internal migration within England and Wales, *Environment and Planning A*, 25: 1453–1465.

Rogers, A. and Castro, L.J. (1981) *Model Migration Schedules, RR-91-30*. International Institute for Applied Systems Analysis, Laxenburg.

Salt, J. (2005) *International Migration and the United Kingdom, 2004*. Report of the UK SOPEMI correspondent to the OECD, OECD, Paris.

Simon, A. (2010) Do ethnic groups migrate towards areas of high concentration of their own group within England and Wales? in Stillwell, J. and van Ham, M. (eds.), *Ethnicity and Integration Understanding Population Trends and Processes*, Vol. 3, Springer, Dordrecht, pp. 133–151.

Simpson, L. (2004) Statistics of racial segregation: Measures, evidence and policy, *Urban Studies*, 41(3): 661–681.

Simpson, L. (2006) *More mixing? More segregation*? Presentation at British Society for Population Studies Day Workshop on Migration and Multicultural Britain, London.

Simpson, L. (2007) Ghettos of the mind: The empirical behaviour of indices of segregation and diversity, *Journal of the Royal Statistical Society, Series A, Statistics in Society*, 170: 405–424.

Simpson, L. and Finney, N. (2009) Spatial patterns of internal migration: Evidence for ethnic groups in Britain, *Population, Space and Place*, 15: 37–56.

Stillwell, J. (2008) Inter-regional migration modeling: a review in Poot, J., Waldorf, B. and van Wissen, L. (eds.), *Migration and Human Capital*, Edward Elgar, Cheltenham, pp. 29–48.

Stillwell, J. (2010) Internal migration propensities and patterns of London's ethnic groups in Stillwell, J., Duke-Williams, O. and Dennett, A. (eds.), *Technologies for Migration and Commuting Analysis: Spatial Interaction Data Applications*, IGI Global, Hershey.

Stillwell, J. and Duke-Williams, O. (2003) A new web-based interface to GB Census of population origin-destination statistics, *Environment and Planning A*, 35(1): 113–132.

Stillwell, J. and Duke-Williams, O. (2005, 12–14 September) Ethnic distribution, immigration and internal migration in Britain: What evidence of linkage at the district scale? Paper presented at the British Society for Population Studies annual conference, University of Kent, Canterbury.

Stillwell, J. and Duke-Williams, O. (2006) Understanding the 2001 Census interaction data: The impact of small cell adjustment and problems of comparison with 1991, *Journal of the Royal Statistical Society Series A*, 170(2): 1–21.

Stillwell, J., Duke-Williams, O. and Dennett, A. (eds.) (2010) *Technologies for Migration and Commuting Analysis: Spatial Interaction Data Applications*, IGI Global, Hershey.

Stillwell, J. and Hussain, S. (2008) *Ethnic Group Migration Within Britain During 2000–01: A District Level Analysis* (Working Paper 08/2), School of Geography, University of Leeds, Leeds.

Stillwell, J. and Hussain, S. (2010) Exploring the ethnic dimension of internal migration in Great Britain using migration effectiveness and spatial connectivity, *Journal of Ethnic and Migration Studies*, Forthcoming.

Stillwell, J. and Phillips, D. (2006) Diversity and change: Understanding the ethnic geographies of Leeds, *Journal of Ethnic and Migration Studies*, 32(7): 1131–1152.

Stillwell, J., Hussain, S. and Norman, P. (2008) The internal migration propensities and net migration patterns of ethnic groups in Britain, *Migration Letters*, 5(2): 135–150.

Tauber, K.E. and Tauber, A.F. (1965) *Negroes in Cities: Residential Segregation and Neighborhood Change*, Atheneum, New York, NY.

Thernstrom, S. (2001) American ethnic statistics in Horowitz, D.L. and Noiriel, G. (eds.), *Immigrants in Two Democracies: French and American Experience*, New York University, New York, NY.

Tobler, W. (1995) Migration: Ravenstein, Thornthwaite, and beyond, *Urban Geography*, 16(4): 327–343.

Vickers, D., Rees, P. and Birkin, M. (2003) *A New Classification of UK Local Authorities Using 2001 Census Key Statistics* (Working Paper 03/5), School of Geography, University of Leeds, Leeds.

Warnes, A. (1992) Migration and the life course in Champion, A.G. and Fielding, F. (eds.), *Migration Processes and Patterns, Volume I: Research Progress and Prospects*, Belhaven, London, pp. 175–187.

Warnes, A.M. and Ford, R. (1995) Housing aspirations and migration late in life: Developments during the 1980s, *Papers in Regional Science*, 74: 361–387.

Chapter 7
Do Ethnic Groups Migrate Towards Areas of High Concentration of Their Own Group Within England and Wales?

Antonia Simon

Introduction

Ethnic segregation or clustering has often been perceived as a negative feature of migration in political and media arenas. It has been suggested that concentrations of minority ethnic groups, especially Asian Muslim groups, are likely to lead to racial tensions and hostility (Dustmann and Preston, 2001). Concerns have also been raised about how comfortably different ethnic groups will reside alongside each other. For example, in a speech to the Institute of Public Policy Research in 2004 about racial diversity within Britain, the then Home Secretary, David Blunkett MP, said: *There is evidence that the more diverse an area is in racial terms, the less likely its residents are to feel that they trust each other. This is an important argument and it is important that we examine it* (Blunkett, 2004).

Concentration has also been linked to segregation and social isolation. For example, in September 2005, Trevor Phillips, then chair of the Commission for Racial Equality, made a speech in Manchester in which he suggested that in Britain *we are sleepwalking our way to segregation.* What Phillips meant was that Britain's various ethnic groups were living apart from each other; *Increasingly, we live with our own kind. The most concentrated areas, what the social scientists call 'ghettos', aren't all poverty stricken and drug ridden. But they are places where more than two-thirds of the residents belong to a single ethnic group. Residential isolation is increasing for many minority groups, especially South Asians. Some minorities are moving into middle class, less ethnically concentrated areas, but what is left behind is hardening in its separateness* (Phillips, 2005). The speech generated an enormous response; many people disputed strongly the assertions Phillips made, including Simpson (2007), whilst others endorsed them. For example, Harriet Harman, Minister for Constitutional Affairs, was quoted as saying *We don't want to get into a situation*

A. Simon (✉)
Thomas Coram Research Unit, Institute of Education, University of London,
London WC1H 0AA, UK
e-mail: A.Simon@ioe.ac.uk

J. Stillwell, M. van Ham (eds.), *Ethnicity and Integration*, Understanding Population Trends and Processes 3, DOI 10.1007/978-90-481-9103-1_7,

like America – but if you look at the figures we are already looking like America (Guardian, 2005).

Clearly, understanding patterns of concentration and residential segregation, has been, and continues to be, important for considering Britain's current and possible future landscape in relation to ethnicity. This chapter presents evidence from a recently completed ESRC-funded research study (Simon, 2009) which set out to describe patterns of internal migration for a range of ethnic groups at the electoral ward level through a secondary analysis of 2001 Census data for England and Wales. This aim addressed the following research questions: Do people of different ethnic groups tend to move towards wards where their own ethnic group has a relatively high concentration? Or do people of different ethnic groups move away from wards where their own ethnic group has a relatively low concentration? In other words, are ethnic groups self-segregating? The chapter also provides an overview of the main theories and hypotheses concerning these trends both abroad and in Britain and debates some of the meanings and methods for measuring ethnic migration, concentration, segregation and settlement.

White Flight and White Avoidance

Residential segregation is often discussed in the context of a minority ethnic group residing separately from the majority ethnic group (e.g. White). In the US, for example, research on segregation has largely focused on the relation between the White majority ethnic group and African Americans. This research has been driven by two hypotheses – so-called 'White flight' – the tendency of White Americans to move out of areas when African Americans move in (Farley et al., 1994; Galster, 1990; Zubrinsky, 2000) – and 'White avoidance' – White Americans actively avoiding moving into areas where the concentration of African Americans is relatively high (Georing, 1978; Lee and Wood, 1991). Research evidence from the US exploring 'White flight' or 'White avoidance' has led to the identification of Black ghettos in America (e.g. Cutler et al., 1999), with the common interpretation being that residential segregation is motivated by racial prejudice. These interpretations have largely been developed from evidence about migration within certain US cities. For example, the Chicago School's 'invasion-succession' model (e.g. Hawley, 1950; McKenzie and Hawley, 1968), sought to determine the extent to which inflows of Black and other minority ethnic groups leads to the eventual change of an area's population from comprising predominately White people to more minority ethnic groups. In addition, the 1976 Detroit Area Survey and other such attitudinal surveys, have reported on the racial attitudes of White people and their tolerance for living near or next to Black people (e.g. Bobo and Zubrinsky, 1996; Clark, 1991; Farley, 1978). However, more recent research has identified that the out-migration of White people in the US is no longer simply related only to the presence of African Americans. This recent research suggests that segregation in the US and the flight of

White people is driven more by an increase in the minority ethnic population in general; comprising African Americans, Hispanics and Asians combined (Clark, 1992; Denton and Massey, 1991; Krysan, 2002; Zubrinsky and Bobo, 1996; Zubrinsky, 2000).

Hypotheses such as 'White flight' and 'White avoidance' reflect the significance being placed on spatial integration (where people of one group live relative to other groups) and on how well different groups integrate culturally and structurally into society. It is often assumed that spatial segregation leads to poor social integration. However, Finney and Simpson (2009) argue that *integration is not the opposite of segregation* and that *a degree of separateness is compatible with participation in work, education, housing and political processes* (p. 17). In addition, other recent research has questioned whether the objections by White people to living near to Black people are less likely to be motivated by racial tensions than by the desire to avoid local areas with characteristics that White people in America may associate with African American areas, such as high levels of crime and poverty (Crowder, 2000; Krysan, 2002). For example, Harris (2001) postulates what he calls the 'racial proxy hypothesis'; that in the US, White people leave Black areas because of the poverty within neighbourhoods with a high proportion of Black residents rather than for racial reasons per se. Keating (1994) also found that other neighbourhood factors may be more important than racial and ethnic considerations in shaping mobility decisions. In addition, Harris (1997) found that once individual and family-level characteristics had been taken into account, the racial composition of the local area had little effect on mobility decisions for White people. In keeping with this, Schuman and Bobo (1988) found that White people reported less resistance to the idea of remaining in integrated areas if residents of those areas were of the same or similar socioeconomic status to themselves. Similarly, Crowder (2000) points out the importance of housing tenure for shaping mobility decisions. He argues that *recent housing construction in a metropolitan area may increase mobility propensities by increasing the supply of relatively attractive housing options to serve as potential destinations and may enhance the ability of Whites to flee neighbourhoods with large minority populations* (p. 230). However, the lack of housing opportunities elsewhere may mean that White people are more likely to tolerate large minority populations in their local area.

Self-selected Segregation

Researchers are also debating whether migration is more likely to be motivated by the desire to live with one's 'own kind' (Clark, 1992). This is what has been referred to by some researchers as 'self-selected segregation' (e.g. Finney and Simpson, 2009; Simpson, 2007) and describes people choosing to live with others of the same cultural or ethnic group. In his 'spatial proximity model', Schelling (1969, 1971) hypothesised that it is the preference for own-group and other ethnic or racial combinations which drives people to choose to live in different neighbourhoods. Krysan (2002) describes this process as people being *drawn to neighbourhoods in which they share a cultural background with other residents, and so it is a 'pull' factor of neutral ethnocentrism that perpetuates segregation, not the 'push' factor of the presence of another group* (p. 680).

Analysing data collected from the 2002 Netherlands Housing Demand Survey, Van Ham and Feijten (2008) used the Schelling hypothesis as a basis for exploring whether people are less likely to have a wish to move when the characteristics of the population and the individual match, compared with the situation when these sets of characteristics differ. Their findings led them to conclude that *the desire to move out of one's neighbourhood seems to be shaped to some extent by one's attitudes towards one's neighbours* and that the evidence *supports the idea of voluntary segregation* (p. 1164). However, this is in contrast to evidence from Krysan's (2002) exploration of the individual-level attitudinal expressions of White flight using the Multi-City Study of Urban Inequality dataset on beliefs and attitudes of adults in metropolitan Atlanta, Boston, Detroit and Los Angeles. One of her key aims was to examine 'neutral ethnocentric reasons' for migration. In other words, she wanted to explore whether White people were motivated to move to areas with others of their 'own kind'. However, she found that only a *relatively small percentage .... 6% or 4%, respectively, said something like, 'Nothing in common with neighbors', 'Feel more drawn to people of my own race', and 'Not many of my own people around'* as reasons why White people moved into certain areas (p. 687). This leads her to conclude that *an entirely neutral ethnocentric interpretation of residential preferences is also unsupported by the data, given that only a small proportion of Whites explained their attitudes in terms that can be construed as cultural explanation ....at least in relation to integration with Blacks* (p. 692).

Compared with the US, British debates about residential segregation have tended to focus more on immigration and the resultant settlement patterns. British research has focused on the behaviour of the different minority ethnic populations, mapping the concentrations, dispersal and residential settlement of ethnic groups (e.g. Champion, 1996; Phillips, 1998; Ratcliffe, 1996) and the presence or absence of ghettos (e.g. Johnston et al., 2002; Peach, 1996; Poulsen, 2005). Ethnic changes and diversity have also been compared between the 2001 and earlier British censuses (e.g. Dorling and Rees, 2003; Rees and Butt, 2003; Sabater, 2010). This work has generally concluded that there was no evidence of ethnic ghettos in British cities. In addition, evidence has suggested that, rather than being motivated by racial tensions, the distribution or spread of ethnic groups is more likely to be explained by other area factors, such as the concept of counterurbanisation. Champion (1996) for example, has argued that internal migration in Britain has been characterised by a cascade of people from urban to suburban to rural areas. Recent research at the district level has shown that both White and non-White groups have experienced counterubanisation, particularly from London to other cities, mixed areas and rural areas and dispersal has occurred away from areas of greatest settlement (Finney and Simpson, 2007; Hussain and Stillwell, 2008). Finney and Simpson have argued this pattern of movement from urban to rural areas is *common to all ethnic groups*

(p. 17). However, it remains the case that relatively little is known about the internal migration of different ethnic groups within Britain, particularly in relation to concentration of own ethnic group and what the patterns are at the local level.

Using the 2001 Census to Explore Trends at the Electoral Ward Level

While previous research has provided some disconfirmation for assumptions that ethnic segregation is endemic in the UK, these analyses have largely focused on migration at the level of the local authority district. However, researchers have noted the dearth of ward-by-ward analyses examining the extent of self-selected segregation amongst a wide range of minority ethnic groups (Dorling and Rees, 2003; Finney and Simpson, 2007; Simpson, 2007), which they argue may capture local level movement better than analyses at the district level. Wards are electoral sub-divisions of districts. In England and Wales, the average ward contains approximately 5–6,000 people.

To answer the research questions posed in the introduction, a specially commissioned table from the 2001 Census was obtained from the Office for National Statistics (ONS). This table (CO355) specified information about internal migration within England and Wales at the electoral ward level. In the 2001 Census, respondents select their particular ethnic group from a list of 16 categories which are used as the basis for categories of ethnicity in other large-scale surveys. A guide to the collection and classification of ethnicity data (ONS, 2003) suggests that ethnic categories should be piloted and pre-tested so that the questions and the wording reflect, as accurately as possible, people's preferred descriptions of themselves. This guidance also recommends that categories of ethnicity are consistently described so that comparisons can be made between different large-scale datasets and that the categories must be developed to be sensitive enough to capture the increasing ethnic diversity within Britain due to inter-ethnic family formation and migration patterns.

The ONS guidance describes how ethnic categories have developed out of a combination of data, including country of birth which was, for many years, the only statistic regularly available but has *become increasingly less relevant when used on its own to specify ethnicity, as second and third generation children have been born since the main periods of migration* (ONS, 2003, p. 12). There are a number of other ways ethnicity could be derived. For example, from skin colour, which is still used to define White and Black groups but is *less suitable for distinguishing between different minority ethnic groups* (ONS, 2003, p. 13) and therefore unacceptable to some people. Ethnicity could also possibly be derived from racial groups which are used, for example, to define Chinese or Arab people and *have to an extent certain geographical connotations* (ONS, 2003, p. 14). In the commissioned data table, the number of ethnicity categories had to be restricted to the following eight because of the small cell sizes of some of the groups at the ward level: White-British, White-Irish, White-Other, Black, Indian, Pakistani and Bangladeshi, Mixed and Other ethnic group.

To measure migration, the 2001 Census asked each household to supply their current address, whether this was their usual address and whether it was their usual address 1 year ago. From this, ONS produce eight categories of migration (shown in Census Table S08), which capture population movement in the 12 months prior to the 2001 Census. The commissioned data table includes information about four of these categories, which together provide information about internal migration. These four categories count the number of people moving into (inflow) and out of (outflow) of approximately 9,000 wards within England and Wales. This commissioned data table shows the movement of people from the eight ethnic groups described above *between wards within the same district* (small inflow/outflow) and *between wards across districts* within England and Wales (large inflow/outflow).

Measuring Residential Segregation

Measuring residential segregation is not a straightforward process because the concept of segregation is complex, dynamic and multi-dimensional. For example, Finney and Simpson (2009) point to at least three aspects of segregation: spatial, cultural and structural segregation. They also note the importance currently being placed on 'spatial integration' for explaining what is happening locally, and how this differs. Consequently, there is no single measure for residential segregation; several indices have been developed to capture the different aspects of segregation and integration. The most widely used measure of residential segregation during the past 30 years has been the Index of Dissimilarity (ID), which is used as a demographic measure of the evenness with which two groups are distributed across a geographic area. Peach (1996) describes the ID as measuring the distribution of *two different populations over the same sub-set of residential areas (tracts, blocks, enumeration districts, wards etc.) of a city* (p. 218) with values of the index running from 0 (no segregation) to 100: a low score would indicate low segregation and a high score, high segregation. Another common measure for residential distribution is the Index of Segregation (IS) which is *used to designate the situation in which a group is measured against all other populations, minus itself*' (Peach, 1996, p. 218). Population evenness has also been measured with the Hoover Index of Population Concentration. This was introduced in 1941 by Edgar Hoover to *measure the evenness with which population was distributed among US states* and could be calculated for *small and large territorial units to show the scale at which concentration or dispersion occurs* (Long and Nucci, 1997, p. 431).

When considering how to measure segregation, it is very helpful to consider the comprehensive review by Massey and Denton which conceives residential segregation as a multidimensional phenomenon comprised of five dimensions of spatial variation (Massey and Denton, 1988):

- Evenness – which refers to the uneven spread or distribution of one social group relative to another group;
- exposure – which measures the extent to which social groups are in contact or exposed to another group, which Simpson (2007) argues *often refers to a high proportion of all groups other than White taken together but might equally refer to a specific group* (p. 408);
- clustering – which measures the extent to which areas inhabited by minority ethnic group members are joined to one another spatially, so that a high degree of clustering suggests that they are living side by side in an enclave and a low degree of clustering suggests that they are widely spread spatially;
- centralization – which measures the degree to which a group is located at the centre of an urban area; and
- concentration – which calculates how concentrated one group is by taking the average amount of physical space occupied by one group (e.g. Black people) relative to another group (e.g. White people) and compares this quantity to the ratio that would obtain if the first group were maximally concentrated and the second group were maximally dispersed.

These different measures of segregation were explored as possible methods for calculating inflow and outflow (Simon, submitted) because they each offer a means for describing how people live relative to one another and a method for calculating the distribution of different groups across the spatial landscape. However, they do not provide answers or possible reasons for why some groups may live in separate areas from other groups. These measures also do not capture the inflows and outflows of groups in relation to concentration of their own group. The most appropriate index currently available for calculating 'movement towards one's own group', and for measuring inflow and outflow, is Simpson's Index of Movement (2006). It defines net migration as the *out-migrants subtracted from in-migrants of a group towards the localities X where it is most prevalent as a proportion of its population in those areas* (p. 7). Simpson's methodology was adapted to provide separate measures of inflow and outflow in relation to concentration of own ethnic group for the study on which this chapter reports.

Patterns of Concentration and Movement in England and Wales

This section examines how concentration can be calculated and related to the movement of different ethnic groups within England and Wales using 2001 Census data.

Ward Level Concentrations of Ethnic Groups

To relate concentration to measures of movement requires a methodology for calculating concentration. However, as with residential segregation, there is no one single measure that is universally applied to measure concentration. For example, as described above, Massey and Denton (1988) referred to concentration as the relative space occupied by a minority group in a geographic area. According to this definition, if a group occupies even a small share of the total area, it is said to be residentially concentrated. However, Peach (1996) has argued that local area concentration should be calculated from the absolute percentage of a local area's population composed of a particular ethnic group. Peach (1996) also introduced the idea of an absolute threshold level for concentration, where the threshold is 30% or higher of the total local area population. However, Johnston et al. (2002) have since argued for the need to examine absolute concentrations in greater detail, at a range of different (e.g. 20, 30, 40, 80%) threshold levels (calculated on percentages of an area's population). This threshold analysis methodology allows an assessment to be made as to whether a group's members exceed a range of different thresholds in the local area.

In this chapter, for each ethnic group, concentration was calculated as the proportion of residents in a ward out of the total population (all ethnic groups combined). Concentration was therefore defined as a measure of the relative abundance of an ethnic group, not a measure of population density (Simon, submitted). Using this definition, the non-White group (made up of the census categories: Black, Indian, Pakistani and Bangladeshi, Mixed, Other) comprise approximately 9% of the total population in England and Wales. The Indian and Black ethnic groups make up the largest proportion of the non-White group at 2% each. While the White group (White-British, White-Irish White-Other) are relatively evenly spread throughout England and Wales, the non-White group, especially the Pakistani and Bangladeshi ethnic group, is more likely to be concentrated within specific areas of England and Wales. For example, this can be seen in the different distributions of population quintiles: for each ethnic group, the wards were grouped into quintiles such that each contained an equal number of people, approximately one-fifth of the group's population. Table 7.1 shows that the mean concentration in the bottom quintile for the White group, representing areas with the fewest White population, is approximately 75%, whereas the mean concentration in the top quintile for the White group, representing the area with the highest White population, is approximately 99%. In contrast, the mean concentration in the bottom quintile for the non-White group is

Table 7.1 Concentration of non-White and White groups in the bottom and top quintile groups, wards in England and Wales, 2001

Ethnic group	Mean concentration in lowest quintile (%)	Number of wards	Mean concentration in highest quintile (%)	Number of wards	Ratio highest/lowest
Non-White	1.88	7,549	65.49	99	34.8
White	74.69	1,214	99.33	2,694	1.3

Source: 2001 Census Commissioned Table CO355.

approximately 2% compared with approximately 65% in the top quintile. In addition, the highest concentrations of the non-White group are within 99 of the 8,796 wards within England and Wales, whereas the highest concentrations of the White group (of 99% and over) are within 2,694 wards within England and Wales. In other words, the White group have a much larger representation within wards in England and Wales than the non-White group relative to their own population.

A recent analysis by Finney and Simpson (2009) also shows that only eight wards in Britain (within the districts of Leicester, Bradford, Pendle, Ealing and Tower Hamlets) have a majority of one of the minority ethnic groups identified in the 2001 Census which they argue is *far from domination and is why no ghettos have been found in Britain* (p. 132). Their findings are similar to those in Table 7.1. They show that the highest proportion for a single minority group is 74%. Johnston et al. (2005) also provide evidence that while the majority of the non-White groups reside in areas where the White population are still the majority; the White people generally live in predominately White areas. All of these findings demonstrate much lower concentrations of minority ethnic groups within Britain than has been evidenced within some US cities. For example, Peach (1996) found that by 1950, over half of the Black population of Chicago was living in areas which were 100% Black.

In terms of differences between the minority ethnic groups in degrees of residential concentration, Johnston et al. (2005) have shown that the White-Irish ethnic group are the least concentrated, the Asian groups most concentrated (especially the Bangladeshis), with the Black groups occupying an intermediate position. Table 7.2 presents the concentration of individual ethnic groups in the bottom (lowest population) quintile and top (highest population) quintile analysed from the 2001 Census. It shows similar findings to those from Johnston et al. (2005). For example, the White-Irish are the ethnic group with the lowest mean concentration in the top quintile (at 5.06%) and the Pakistani and Bangladeshi ethnic group is the most highly concentrated minority group in the least number of wards (being concentrated in

Table 7.2 Concentration of the individual ethnic groups in bottom and top quintile groups, wards in England and Wales, 2001

Ethnic group	Mean concentration in lowest quintile (%)	Number of wards	Mean concentration in highest quintile (%)	Number of wards
Indian	0.37	7,862	39.95	44
Pakistani and Bangladeshi	0.29	8,197	50.59	27
Black	0.35	8,165	31.72	58
Mixed	0.45	5,828	4.62	235
White British	68.44	1,354	98.14	2, 209
White Irish	0.48	5,375	5.06	210
White other	0.92	5,270	17.80	148
Other ethnic group	0.33	6,842	8.90	129

Source: 2001 Census Commissioned Table CO355.

just 27 wards within England and Wales compared, for example, with 44 for the Indian ethnic group and 2,209 wards for White-British ethnic group).

The contrast between the White group and non-White group can clearly be evidenced by comparing Figs. 7.1 and 7.2 which show respectively the areas of England and Wales where the White-British ethnic group is concentrated and where the Pakistani and Bangladeshi ethnic group is most concentrated. The shaded categories in Figs. 7.1 and 7.2 are not based on the quintile groups used in the analysis reported in this paper (where each quintile represents one fifth of the group's population). For the White-British ethnic group, the map in Fig. 7.1 shows five shading categories based on equal counts of wards. However, for the map showing the concentration of the Pakistani and Bangladeshi group (Fig. 7.2), the five shading categories are based on natural breaks in the data (the five categories are not equal counts of wards or people in that group). The two maps could not be presented in the same way because the distribution of the Pakistani and Bangladeshi group is so different to that of the White-British group. For example, the White-British ethnic group is highly concentrated in most places within England and Wales, with slightly less concentration in the South East region. However, it should be noted that the difference between lowest and highest concentration for the White-British ethnic group is

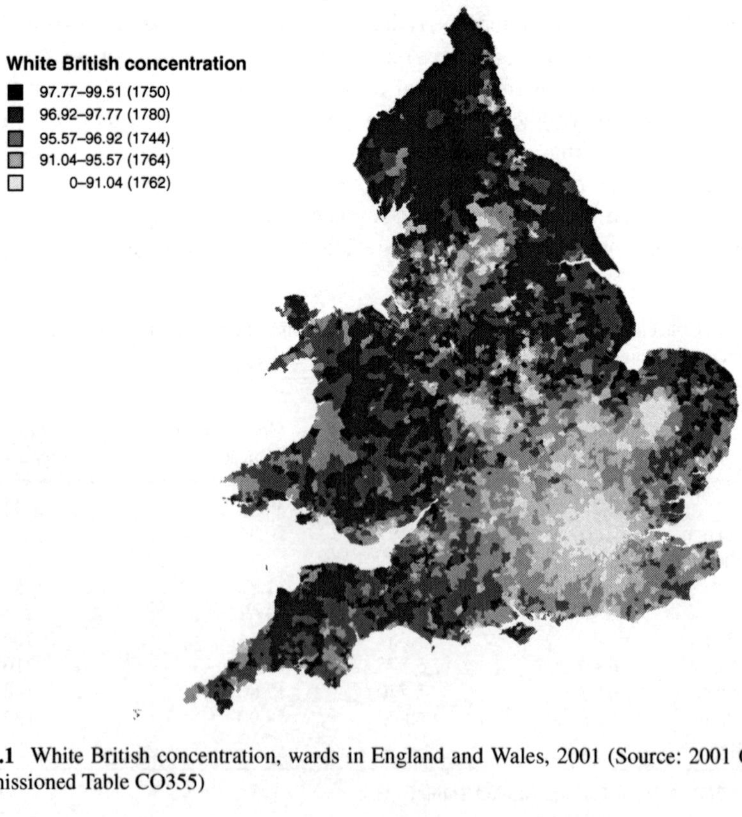

Fig. 7.1 White British concentration, wards in England and Wales, 2001 (Source: 2001 Census Commissioned Table CO355)

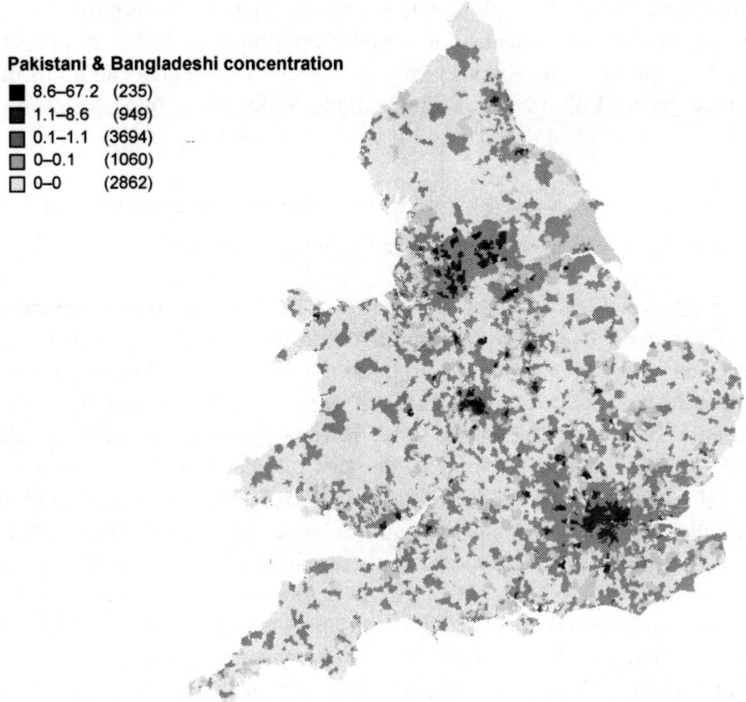

Fig. 7.2 Pakistani and Bangladeshi concentration, wards in England and Wales, 2001 (Source: 2001 Census Commissioned Table CO355)

comparatively small (Table 7.2 shows that the mean concentration for the White-British ethnic group is 68.4 in the lowest quintile and 98.1 in the highest quintile). In contrast, the map for the Pakistani and Bangladeshi ethnic group in Fig. 7.2 shows highest concentration in only a few areas of England and Wales, such as: Birmingham, Blackburn and Darwen, Bradford, Burnley, Derby, Luton, Manchester, Slough, Swindon, parts of London such as Tower Hamlets, Wolverhampton and Wycombe.

Movement Towards Areas of High Concentration of Own Ethnic Group

As discussed in the section above, while the White group is relatively evenly spread within Britain, minority ethnic groups, especially the Pakistani and Bangladeshi ethnic group, are concentrated within particular areas. It could be that areas of high concentration of minority ethnic groups are also locations likely to attract high inflows of people from the same ethnic group. If this were found to be true, it may provide evidence of self-segregation – of people choosing to live with others of the same ethnic group. To explore whether this is occurring, migration needs to be related to concentration. This can be done by counting the number of people from each of the ethnic groups who move towards or away from concentrations of their own ethnic group. Inflows within England and Wales are defined for each ethnic group as:

(Number of people who moved into wards within the same district + into wards located in another district/Total residents in the area) $\times$ 100

and a similar calculation is used for outflows. The net inflow rate (inflow minus outflow) was then related to concentration by sorting each ethnic group by the number of residents in the ward and then dividing into quintiles. The highest quintile contains areas with the largest numbers of that population. Dividing the population into quintiles allows an assessment to be made of movement towards populations of equal size and controls for the volatile rates associated with small or zero populations (Finney and Simpson, 2007). Figure 7.3 depicts the inflow, outflow and net migration rates for the highest quintile bands of concentration of the individual ethnic groups. In this chart, any figure above zero is a positive net inflow towards concentration of own ethnic group. A rate below zero indicates a net outflow from concentration of own ethnic group. Analysis of the rates in Fig. 7.3 reveals that minority ethnic groups are not moving towards concentrations of their own ethnic group. This pattern was particularly evident for the Indian, Pakistani

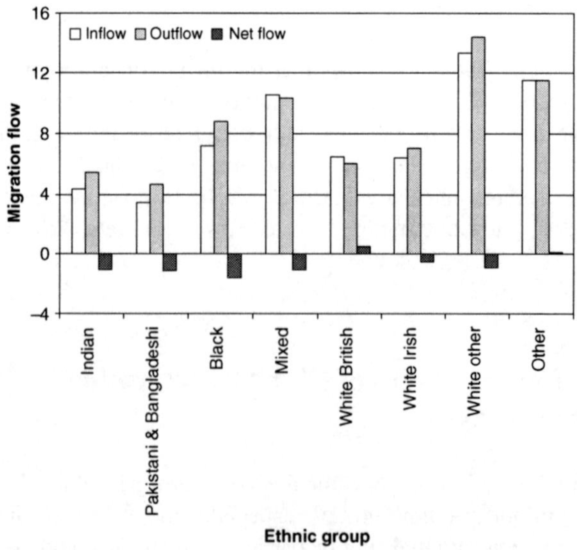

Fig. 7.3 Top quintiles of inflow, outflow and net migration rate for non-White and White groups relative to their own group in electoral wards in England and Wales, 2000–2001 (Source: 2001 Census Commissioned Table CO355)

and Bangladeshi, White-Irish and Black ethnic groups. In each case, the findings show a movement away from the areas in which their own ethnic group is most concentrated (there is greater outflow than inflow in wards with the highest concentration of their own ethnic group), resulting in a negative net-inflow into these areas. For example, for the Indian ethnic group, there is a decrease across the five quintiles from almost 13% inflow (12.85) in wards with the lowest concentration of the Indian ethnic group to almost 5% inflow towards wards with the highest concentration of the Indian ethnic group. Similarly, the Black ethnic group shows an inflow of almost 14% (13.86) into wards with the lowest concentration of the Black ethnic group compared with just over 7% (7.14) inflow towards wards with the highest concentration of the Black ethnic group.

Figure 7.3 also shows that, with the exception of the White-British group, these trends can also be evidenced for the combined White group. Table 7.3 shows the White group are more likely to migrate towards concentrations of their own group; the White group had a greater inflow than outflow into wards with the highest concentrations of White-British population, resulting in an overall positive net inflow.

In contrast, Table 7.3 shows that for the non-White group, there is greater outflow than inflow in wards with the highest non-White concentration (5.99% inflow compared with 7.15% outflow; –1.16% net) and greater inflow in wards with the lowest non-White concentration (11.88% inflow compared with 10.70% outflow; 1.18% net).

Regression analysis was carried out for this research (not shown) in order to ascertain whether the variation in inflow, outflow and net migration rates could be significantly explained by 'concentration' (Simon, submitted). The findings show that inflow and outflow rates are both related to concentration for nearly all the groups, so that the net effect of concentration is almost zero. Regression analysis was also conducted to examine the effect of concentration after controlling for some characteristics of the ward: rural-urban, housing tenure and employment, which were hypothesised to have an influence on internal migration (Simon, submitted).

Table 7.3 Quintiles of inflow, outflow and net-inflow for non-White and White groups relative to their own group in electoral wards in England and Wales, 2000–2001

		Migration 2000–2001 as percentage of 2001 population				
Group		Lowest concentration	Low concentration	Medium concentration	High concentration	Highest concentration
Non-White						
	Inflow	11.88	10.75	9.16	7.89	5.99
	Outflow	10.70	9.61	9.25	8.59	7.15
	Net	1.18	1.14	−0.09	−0.70	−1.16
White						
	Inflow	10.31	8.30	7.69	7.24	6.78
	Outflow	11.02	8.36	7.37	6.81	6.28
	Net	−0.71	−0.06	0.32	0.43	0.50

Source: 2001 Census Commissioned Table CO355.

Data on each of these factors were downloaded from publicly available sources and merged with the figures in the commissioned table. Taking one of these factors, the rural-urban characteristic of the ward, with the exception of the Pakistani and Bangladeshi ethnic group, most of the groups moved away from urban areas towards town and fringe areas or towards villages, hamlets and isolated dwellings. The rural-urban characteristic was also a better predictor of migration than concentration for all except the Pakistani and Bangladeshi ethnic group.

The Case of London

London, like many other world cities, is the destination for large numbers of foreign-born residents (Price and Benton-Short, 2007) and of all British cities it has the largest number of people born abroad – 6.35% of all people in the city (Kyambi, 2005). Recent evidence from the 2001 Census has shown that London's ethnic diversity is increasing (Finney and Simpson, 2009). This may make it a special case compared to the rest of England and Wales. Therefore, it may be helpful to analyse these internal migration trends for London separately from the rest of England and Wales. For example, Stillwell (2008) has shown from his analysis of overall net migration rates for wards in London, that London has its own internal dynamics which show large net losses of White people from inner London with *inner wards losing migrants to outer wards with the largest absolute losses occurring from the central boroughs* (p. 32). Figure 7.4 shows the inflow, outflow and net migration of the individual ethnic groups into London wards with the highest quintile bands

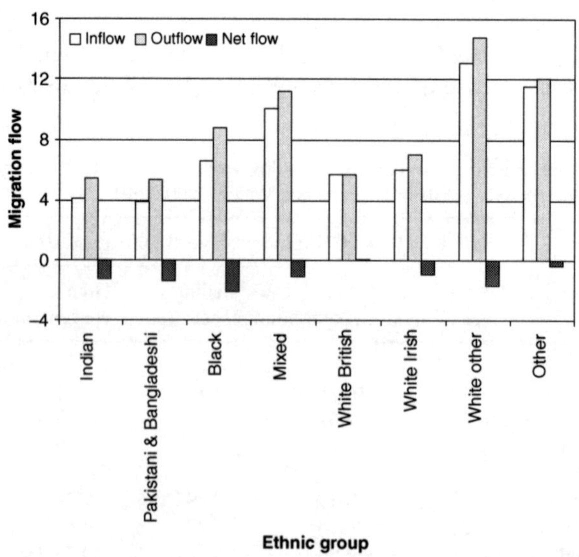

Fig. 7.4 Top quintile of migration rates for of non-White and White people in electoral wards in London, 2000–2001 (Source: 2001 Census Commissioned Table CO355)

Table 7.4 Migration by concentrations of non-White and White people in electoral wards in London, 2000–2001

Group		Migration 2000–2001 as percentage of 2001 population				
		Lowest concentration	Low concentration	Medium concentration	High concentration	Highest concentration
Non-White						
	Inflow	11.36	9.99	8.96	8.05	6.95
	Outflow	9.79	10.07	9.59	8.88	8.00
	Net	1.57	−0.07	−0.63	−0.83	−1.06
White						
	Inflow	10.83	11.06	9.38	6.74	5.69
	Outflow	11.90	11.70	9.92	6.95	5.73
	Net	−1.07	−0.64	−0.54	−0.21	−0.04

Source: 2001 Census Commissioned Table CO355.

of concentration of their own ethnic group. This includes movement between parts of London, but also to and from elsewhere in the UK. These figures show that the pattern of movement for all individual groups is actually very similar to the pattern discussed above for the whole of England and Wales. The pattern is for all ethnic groups to move away from London wards with high concentrations of their own ethnic group. For example, for the Indian ethnic group, the rate of outflow is greater (at 5.44%) than the inflow rate (of 4.07%) into wards with the highest concentration of the Indian population. Similarly, for the Black ethnic group, there is a greater rate of outflow (of 8.71%) than inflow (of 6.58%) into wards with the highest concentration of the Black population.

This pattern also holds for the combined non-White group, which shows a net outflow from London wards with the highest non-White population (Table 7.4: third row). However, unlike the pattern for England and Wales as a whole, the figures for the White group show a net outflow across the five quintiles of White concentration in London wards. In other words, there appears to be a trend for White people to move away from all London wards regardless of the concentration of the White group. Not surprisingly, given there is a tendency for them to move away from wards with high concentrations of their own ethnic groups, the pattern for the non-White group is to move towards wards within London with a high concentration of the White population.

Conclusions

This chapter has posed the question: Do ethnic groups migrate towards areas of high concentration of their own group within England and Wales? To answer this question, the chapter has discussed evidence which explored, through a secondary analysis of 2001 Census data, patterns of internal migration for a range of ethnic groups at the electoral ward level in relation to concentration. The findings from this research challenge some commonly held misconceptions that Britain is becoming increasingly ethnically segregated through people choosing to move to areas with more of their own ethnic group. Rather, they suggest that minority ethnic groups are more likely to migrate away from areas of highest concentration of their own ethnic group, with the consequence that many major cities are becoming more diverse.

To test the hypothesis of self-segregation, the research on which this chapter draws related concentration of own ethnic group to the internal migration of individual ethnic groups (Simon, submitted). There are two key findings from this research. Firstly, the findings show an outflow of people away from wards with the highest minority ethnic populations within England and Wales. For all ethnic groups, the outflow rate was greater than the inflow rate within wards with highest concentration of their own ethnic group; wards with lowest concentration of their own ethnic group had greater inflow than outflow rates. The only exception to this pattern was the White group who moved towards areas of high concentration of their own ethnic group. This is supported by recent analysis conducted by Finney and Simpson (2009), who found that *in almost every city with a sizeable inner area that has been the focus of immigration in the past 60 years, children of immigrants have on balance moved away from those areas, not to them or between them* (p. 136). Therefore, the research found no evidence of self-segregation for most ethnic groups within England and Wales. This is not to say that concentrations or clusters of some ethnic groups may not still be forming in certain areas of Britain but that this evidence indicates that internal migration, specifically movement towards one's own group, does not explain these patterns within England and Wales. Therefore other processes may better explain the current distributions of Britain's ethnic groups. One likely factor is the increase in natural growth (excess of births over deaths) for many of the minority ethnic groups. For example, Finney and Simpson (2009) have argued that most neighbourhoods have a growing minority population and that *the clustering of groups together is mainly a result of immigration and family-building* (p. 136). Using the city of Bradford as an example, they have shown that the number of minority births each year is greater than the number of minority immigrants. This explanation suggests that many of the minority ethnic groups with younger age distributions, such as the Pakistani and Bangladeshi ethnic group, will continue to grow within many British cities over the next decade or so.

Secondly, the findings reported in this chapter indicate that concentration has a limited utility for explaining why people move into or out of wards within England and Wales. For example, there is evidence that all groups, especially the White group, is migrating out of central areas of London. The research reported on here has shown that the movement is away from London wards of high concentration of their own group. This trend in London is particularly marked for the Black ethnic group. Similarly, the pattern for the whole of England and Wales shows that for all ethnic groups, with the exception of the White group, there has been a movement away from wards of high concentration of their own ethnic group. So, if concentration does not seem to be significantly related to patterns of migration, what other factors might be better predictors of these migration patterns? One socio-economic factor that has been discussed in this chapter, and which seems a better predictor than concentration, is the rural-urban characteristic of the ward. Stillwell (2008) shows, for example, that internal migration is occurring in a pattern from inner to outer London wards – indicating a process of suburbanization – and a pattern for movement from outer wards to areas outside Greater London – suggesting a process of counterurbanisation. Evidence from research reported in this chapter lends support to this idea, finding that for most ethnic groups, movement tends to be away from urban areas towards town and fringe areas or towards villages, hamlets and isolated dwellings (Simon, submitted). In addition, Finney and Simpson (2009) also conclude from their recent analysis that *Britain's minority ethnic residents tend to move out from existing settlement areas to neighbouring areas or suburbs* (p. 136).

Issues associated with residential segregation are high on the political and media agenda, with assumptions being made not only about the distribution of minority ethnic groups but also the motivations for why different groups reside in particular areas of the UK. The research reported in this chapter has described some important patterns of internal migration within England and Wales but has found no statistical evidence that inflow and outflow patterns are related to concentration of own ethnic group or that internal migration patterns within wards in England and Wales support the theory of self-segregation within England and Wales. This research could be usefully extended by conducting interviews with people of different ethnic groups, further to explore these patterns and to provide more insight into what motivates different groups to migrate within the UK.

Acknowledgements The author is very grateful to the ESRC for funding this research as part of its programme 'Understanding Population Trends and Processes' (UPTAP) grant reference RES-163-25-0036. The author would like to thank the editors of this book volume for their helpful comments on this chapter – particularly Professor John Stillwell, University of Leeds, for his encouragement and support in his role as director of the UPTAP programme. The author is also appreciative of the helpful advice on the quintile analysis given by Professor Ludi Simpson and Dr. Nissa Finney, both from the University of Manchester, and for all the support with the research on which this chapter reports from Charlie Owen and Professor Ann Phoenix, Thomas Coram Research Unit, Institute of Education.

References

Blunkett, D. (2004) *New Challenges for Race Equality and Community Cohesion in the 21st Century*. A speech by the Rt. Hon. David Blunkett MP, Home Secretary, to the Institute of Public Policy Research, 7th July 2004, http://www.ippr.org.uk/uploadedFiles/events/Blunkettspeech.pdf

Bobo, L. and Zubrinsky, C.L. (1996) Attitudes on residential integration: Perceived status differences, mere in-group preference, or racial prejudice? *Social Forces*, 74(3), 883–909.

Champion, T. (1996) Internal migration and ethnicity in Britain in Ratcliffe, P. (ed.), *Social Geography and Ethnicity in Britain: Geographical Spread, Spatial Concentration and Internal Migration* (Ethnicity in the 1991 Census), Vol. 3, HMSO, London, pp. 135–173.

Clark, W.A.V. (1991) Residential preferences and neighbourhood racial segregation. A test of the Schelling segregation model. *Demography*, 28, 1–19.

Clark, W.A.V. (1992) Residential preferences and residential choices in a multiethnic context. *Demography*, 29, 451–466.

Crowder, K. (2000) The racial context of White mobility: An individual-level assessment of the White-flight hypothesis. *Social Science Research*, 29, 223–257.

Cutler, D., Glaeser, E. and Vigdor, J. (1999) The rise and decline of the American ghettos. *Journal of Political Economy*, 107(3), 455–506.

Denton, N. and Massey, D. (1991) Patterns of neighborhood transition in a multi-ethnic world: US Metropolitan Areas, 1970–1980. *Demography*, 28, 41–63.

Dorling, D. and Rees, P. (2003) A nation still dividing: The British census and social polarisation, 1971–2001, *Environment and Planning A*, 35: 1287–1313.

Dustmann, C. and Preston, I. (2001) Attitudes to ethnic minorities, ethnic context and location decisions, *The Economic Journal*, 111(4): 353–373.

Farley, R. (1978) Chocolate city, vanilla suburbs: Will the trend toward racially separate communities continue? *Social Science Research*, 7: 319–344.

Farley, R., Steeh, C., Krysan, M., Jackson, T. and Reeves, K. (1994) Stereotypes and segregation: Neighborhoods in the Detroit area, *American Journal of Sociology*, 100: 750–780.

Finney, N. and Simpson, L. (2007) *Internal Migration and Ethnic Groups: Evidence for the UK from the 2001 Census* (CCSR Working Paper 2007-04), CCSR, University of Manchester, Manchester, www.ccsr.ac.uk/publications/working/2007-04.pdf

Finney, N. and Simpson, L. (2009) *'Sleepwalking to Segregation'? Challenging Myths About Race and Migration*, Policy Press, Bristol.

Galster, G.C. (1990) White flight from racially integrated neighborhoods in the 1970s: The Cleveland experience, *Urban Studies*, 27: 385–399.

Goering, J.M. (1978) Neighborhood tipping and racial transition, *Journal of the American Institute of Planners*, 44: 68–78.

Guardian (2005, September 19) Britain sleepwalking to segregation, *Guardian*.

Harris, D.R. (1997) *Race, class and social problems: Determinants of White residential mobility*. PhD dissertation, Northwestern University, Evanston.

Harris, D.R. (2001) Why are whites and blacks averse to black neighbors? *Social Science Research*, 30: 100–116.

Hawley, A.H. (1950) *Human Ecology: A Theory of Community Structure*, Ronald Press, New York.

Hussain, S. and Stillwell, J. (2008) *Internal Migration of Ethnic Groups in England and Wales by Age and District Type* (Working Paper 08/03), School of Geography, University of Leeds, Leeds.

Johnston, R., Forrest, J. and Poulsen, M.F. (2002) Are there ethnic enclaves/ghettos in English cities? *Urban Studies*, 39(4): 591–618.

Johnston, R., Poulsen, M.F. and Forrest, J. (eds.) (2005) On the measurement and meaning of segregation: A response to Simpson, *Urban Studies*, 42: 1221–1227.

Keating, W.D. (1994) *The Suburban Racial Dilemma: Housing and Neighbourhoods*, Temple University Press, Philadelphia, PA.

Krysan, M. (2002) Whites who say they'd flee: Who are they and why would they leave? *Demography*, 39(4): 675–696.

Kyambi, S. (2005) *Beyond Black and White Mapping New Immigrant Communities*, IPPR, London.

Lee, B.A. and Wood, P.B. (1991) Is neighbourhood racial succession place-specific? *Demography*, 28(1): 21–40.

Long, L. and Nucci, A. (1997) The Hoover index of population concentration: A correction and update, *Professional Geographer*, 49(4): 431–440.

Massey, D.S. and Denton, N.A. (1988) The dimensions of residential segregation, *Social Forces*, 67: 281–315.

McKenzie, R.D. and Hawley, A.H. (1968) *On Human Ecology; Selected Writings* (Edited and with an introduction by Amos H. Hawley), University of Chicago Press, Chicago, IL.

Office for National Statistics (2003) *Ethnic Group Statistics. A Guide for the Collection and Classification of Ethnicity Data*, HMSO, Newport, http://www.statistics.gov.uk/about/ethnic_group_statistics/

Peach, C. (1996) Does Britain have ghettos? *Transactions, Institute of British Geographers*, 21(1): 216–235.

Phillips, D. (1998) Black minority ethnic concentration, segregation and dispersal in Britain, *Urban Studies*, 35(10): 1681–1702.

Phillips, T. (2005, 22 September) *After 7/7: SLEEPWALKING to Segregation*, Speech given at the Manchester Council for Community Relations, Commission for Racial Equality, London.

Poulsen, M. (2005, 31 August) The new geography of ethnicity in Britain. Paper presented at the Royal Geographical Society annual conference, London.

Price, M. and Benton-Short, L. (2007) Immigrants and world cities: From the hyper-diverse to the bypassed. *Geojournal*, 68(2–3), 103–117.

Ratcliffe, P. (1996) Social geography and ethnicity: A theoretical, conceptual and substantive overview, in Ratcliffe, P. (ed.), *Social Geography and Ethnicity in Britain: Geographical Spread, Spatial Concentration and Internal Migration* (Ethnicity in the 1991 Census), Vol. 3, HMSO, London, pp. 135–173.

Rees, P. and Butt, F. (2003) Ethnic change and diversity in England, 1981–2001. *Area*, 36(2), 174–186.

Sabater, A. (2010) Ethnic residential segregation over time and age cohorts in England and Wales, 1991–2001 in Stillwell, J. and van Ham, M. (eds.), *Ethnicity and Integration Understanding Population Trends and Processes*, Vol. 3, Springer, Dordrecht, pp. 47–62.

Schelling, T.C. (1969) Models of segregation. *The American Economic Review*, 59, 488–493.

Schelling, T.C. (1971) Dynamic models of segregation. *Journal of Mathematical Sociology*, 1, 143–186.

Schuman, H. and Bobo, L. (1988) Survey-based experiments on White racial attitudes toward residential integration. *American Journal of Sociology*, 94, 273–299.

Simon, A. (2009) *Exploring the Movement of People from Different Ethnic Groups into or out of Wards with High or Low Density of Their own Ethnic Group* (ESRC End of Award Report, RES-163-25-0036), ESRC, Swindon.

Simpson, L. (2006) *Ghettos of the Mind: The Empirical Behaviour of Indices of Segregation and Diversity* (CCSR Working Paper 2006-06), CCSR, University of Manchester, Manchester.

Simpson, L. (2007) Ghettos of the mind: The empirical behaviour of indices of segregation and diversity. *Journal of the Royal Statistical Society A*, 107(2), 405–424.

Stillwell, J. (2008) *Internal migration of Britain's ethnic populations: Full research report, ESRC End of Award Report* (RES-163-25-0028), ESRC, Swindon.

Van Ham, M. and Feijten, P. (2008) Who wants to leave the neighbourhood? The effect of being different from the neighbourhood population on wishes to move. *Environment and Planning A*, 40, 1151–1170.

Zubrinsky, C.L. (2000) Neighborhood racial composition preferences: Evidence from a multiethnic metropolis. *Social Problems*, 47, 379–407.

Zubrinsky, C.L. and Bobo, L. (1996) Prismatic metropolis: Race and residential segregation in the city of the angels. *Social Science Research*, 25, 335–374.

Simon, A. (submitted) The migration of ethnic groups in relation to concentrations of their own ethnic group. *Journal of Ethnic and Migration Studies*.

Chapter 8
Understanding the Impact of Immigration on the Labour Market Outcomes of British Workers

Marina Shaginyan-Shapira

Introduction

The integration of immigrants into their new host society is by no means a one-directional process. Not only do immigrants need to adjust to their new host society, but also the receiving country needs to adjust in response, especially if the immigrant influx is large. Immigrants are believed to have a profound effect on the host country's labour market. It has been argued that a large influx of immigrant labour into the labour market will depress the wage levels of native workers and even of existing immigrant populations, especially if they have the same skill level as recent immigrants. New immigrants might push others out of some occupations and industries or out of the labour market altogether. However, most research on the effect of immigration on labour markets in various countries shows that immigrants have little if any negative impact on the wages and employment opportunities of native workers (Blanchflower et al., 2007; Borjas and Freeman, 1992; Cohen-Goldner and Paserman, 2004; Dustmann et al., 2005; Gilpin et al., 2006), with some research showing a positive labour market effect of immigration (Friedberg, 2001; Ottaviano and Peri, 2006).

Since the late 1990s, Britain has experienced a dramatic increase in the number of immigrants; with a further rise since 2004, when the Accession 8 (A8) countries of Eastern and Central Europe joined the European Union. At the same time, there was also growth of immigration to the UK from non-A8 countries, especially from the New Commonwealth. The recent immigration to the UK from the A8 countries has sparked a renewed interest in how an influx of immigrants from various national backgrounds and skill levels has impacted on the labour market opportunities and outcomes of various groups of workers in the host society (Blanchflower et al., 2007; Frijters et al., 2005; Manacorda et al., 2006).

Research on the labour market impact of immigration faces many methodological challenges and therefore the interpretation of current findings is complicated

M. Shaginyan-Shapira (✉)
Centre for Educational Sociology, Edinburgh University, Edinburgh EH8 8AQ, UK
e-mail: mshapira@staffmail.ed.ac.uk

J. Stillwell, M. van Ham (eds.), *Ethnicity and Integration*, Understanding Population Trends and Processes 3, DOI 10.1007/978-90-481-9103-1_8,

and most authors are very cautious in making their conclusions. The main reason for these difficulties is that the labour market outcomes of workers are determined by such a wide variety of factors that only after identifying and accounting for all these factors can one safely attribute the remaining differences in workers' labour market outcomes to spatial variations in the size of immigration populations. The objective of this research was to empirically evaluate contrasting theoretical frameworks of the impact of immigration on labour markets. We use the newly available Annual Population Survey (APS) data and various methodological tools for understanding the impact of immigration on the labour market. The main research question was whether or not there is a systematic relationship between the spatial concentrations of immigrant populations in Britain and the labour market outcomes of British workers? The following more specific research questions are addressed in this chapter:

- Are the spatial distributions of immigrants correlated with the labour market outcomes of various groups in Britain, in terms of their wages, employment and occupational opportunities?
- To what extent are differences in local labour market conditions affecting the relationship between the spatial distribution of immigrants and the labour market outcome of British workers?
- Are there differences in the effect of spatial concentrations of new and pre-2004 immigrants on labour market outcomes?

Theoretical Background

Classical Economic Theory

Most research on the effects of immigration on labour markets uses a classical economic theory approach which suggests that an influx of immigrant workers with particular skills causes a labour supply shock disrupting the local labour market equilibrium, resulting in a drop of wages for workers with similar skills. Immigrants may also displace native workers completely and force them out of the labour force (Borjas, 2003). Empirical studies from the US, Europe and Israel that investigate the above theoretical mechanisms are not conclusive. Some of these studies found a small positive effect of immigration while others reported a small negative effect of immigration. In any case, the size of the immigration effect is much smaller than can be expected based on classical economic theory assumptions. The variation in outcomes suggests that *the measured impact of immigration on … native workers fluctuates from study to study, but seems to cluster around zero* (Borjas, 2003, p. 1335).

Attempts to explain the absence of a significant negative impact of immigration on the host country's labour markets have produced a substantial literature in the UK and elsewhere. The main problem of the immigration labour market impact study, apparently, is to unravel the substitution and complementarity effects between immigrants and non-migrant workers. Frijters et al. (2005) demonstrate that immigrant job search is less successful than that of natives. Immigrants consequently do not effectively compete for jobs with natives; this partly explains why immigration has little impact on native employment. Similarly, Manacorda et al. (2006) find evidence that natives and immigrants in the UK, like elsewhere, are imperfect substitutes for native workers, which partly explains why the impact of immigration on the wages of the native-born population is small. There is also a more substantial criticism of the basic assumptions of quantitative research in this area and of elements of its methodology (Borjas, 2004). For example, there are implicit assumptions of a fixed quantity of jobs in the labour market that are not reflected in reality. The influx of migrants into the local labour market may boost development of both the service and manufacturing sectors and create new jobs and additional demand for manpower, including low-skilled and semi-skilled labour force positions (Sassen, 1988; Soja, 1989; Waldinger, 1999).

Current literature shows that it is more difficult to catch a negative labour market effect (if there is any) of immigration through macro-level quantitative studies because: (i) immigrants interact with non-migrant workers and can cause both occupational and residential mobility of the latter (Filler, 1992; Flug et al., 1994); (ii) immigrants are unevenly distributed through localities, industries and occupations, therefore estimates of their impact on the macro level are averaging round the zero level; and (iii) there is a problem of simultaneity when the case unobservable factors such as global economic conditions on the local labour market affect both the size and characteristics of immigrant populations and the labour market outcomes of non-migrant workers. However, while case studies of occupations and industries demonstrate a deleterious effect of immigration on resident workers (e.g. Waters, 1999), these case studies are suffering undoubtedly from a selection bias because they choose the very industries and occupations where a negative impact of immigration exists. Therefore, the only way to obtain robust estimates of the labour market effect of immigration is to develop further macro-level methodologies. Thus, one possibility is to instrument the potentially endogenous variables such as sizes of immigrant populations (Dustmann et al., 2005; Friedberg, 2001). Another direction of methodological development is to obtain a better understanding of how skills of migrants and non-migrants can be matched and to test how immigrants impact labour market outcomes of the resident population with a comparable level of skills. Borjas attempted this (2004, 2005) and found that, over time in the US, immigrants have much bigger negative effect on the wages of native workers with a comparable level of skills than had been estimated ever before. The alternative and new strategy employed in this research is to use multilevel regression modelling and include at the second, macro-level of the regression, the size of immigrant populations together with other characteristics of local labour markets (see the following section).

Opportunity Structure of the Labour Market and Spatial Inequality

The above criticism of the basic assumptions of classical economic heory introduces the idea that the opportunity structure of the labour market is not fixed; not only does it vary across local labour markets, but it also changes over time. Therefore, the conditions of local labour markets should be taken into account when the labour market impact of immigrants is considered. In recent decades, there has been a growing understanding that the labour market operates and is being regulated at the local and regional levels (Martin and Morrison, 2003). The spatial character of labour markets is determined by the fact that the majority of workers have local jobs and the majority of local jobs are held by local workers. Workers have to live within commuting distance from where they live (Cheshire et al., 2003).

Spatial differences in labour market opportunities are an important factor that may affect the labour market outcomes of workers across different labour markets. The opportunity structure of local labour markets has a particularly strong impact on labour market outcomes of low educated people, ethnic minorities and recent migrants, who generally have a limited commuting tolerance and therefore depend on local jobs (Van Ham, 2002; van Ham et al., 2001). Furthermore, one should take particular care to ensure that the relationship between the immigrant spatial concentrations and the labour market outcomes of workers does not result from the immigrant propensity of being concentrated spatially in labour markets with particular characteristics, for example, with a higher level of wages, or where job opportunities are mostly in low tech traditional industries. Such local labour market characteristics shape the socio-economic profiles of non-migrant workers. Therefore, some researchers choose to study the impact of immigrants on labour markets at the national instead of the local level (Borjas, 2001). Others use an instrumental variable approach and do not use the actual size of immigrant populations in the local labour markets but predict the size by means of other variables which in turn are not related to characteristics of local labour markets (Dustmann et al., 2005; Friedberg, 2001). In this study, we control for differences in labour market opportunities across local labour markets. The indicators of local labour market conditions we use include the employment rate, the degree of social inequality in the local labour market, and the degree of concentration of job opportunities in traditional industries such as building and manufacturing (Morrison and Berezovsky, 2003).

Ethnic Composition of Local Labour Markets and the Labour Market Impact of Immigrants

Finally, there is evidence that immigration has a varying effect on different groups of the host country population and that the labour market effect of immigration is different in labour markets with different degrees of segmentation or segregation. Most of this evidence comes from research conducted by sociologists rather than economists. This research has documented a large effect of immigration on the displacement of native workers and is informed mostly by the 'ethnic pluralism' approach (Lieberson, 1980) which implies that immigrants, as a rule, are entering local labour markets which are already ethnically diverse; this labour market impact of immigration is multi-directional rather than one-directional. This approach suggests that in contemporary multi-ethnic local labour markets, the position of new immigrants depends on the relative prestige of the latter among existing ethnic groups or, generalizing this further, among all low-status groups who are already present in the local labour market. Indeed, empirical findings from case studies and interviews of workers and employers confirm employer preferences to hire ethnic minorities who have a good reputation as workers. Thus, if immigrants are viewed as a poor substitute to even low-skilled native-born workers, and the latter are the preferable choice in the eyes of the local employers, an arrival of immigrants would be beneficial for local lower-status groups; immigrants would take less attractive jobs and contribute to the occupational mobility of the native born. However, if immigrants are perceived as better workers than the native groups, the former displace native-born ethnic minorities across whole industries (Waters, 1999). The ethnic pluralism approach also assigns importance to the relative size of the dominant ethnic group in the area – the smaller the latter is, then the more opportunities in higher-status occupations would be open to the local ethnic minorities/low-status groups once immigrants arrive and fill the least desirable positions in the labour market (Fossett et al., 1986; Shaginyan-Shapira, 2007; Tieda and Lii, 1987).

It is apparent that the multi-ethnic context of labour markets and the number and size of ethnic groups among the non-migrant population are very important factors in assessing the impact of immigration on the labour market. In summary, this research draws on classical economic theory, the geography of local labour markets and the sociological concepts of ethnic pluralism and ethnic queues, to explore how immigrant spatial concentration affects the labour market outcomes of workers.

Hypotheses

The following hypotheses were formulated on the basis of the theoretical background presented above:

H1: Immigrants have different impacts on different groups of the non-migrant population in Britain, and the direction and size of these impacts depends on the characteristics of immigrants, such as the period of their arrival, and the degree of correspondence between their skill level and the skill level of British-born workers. In particular, one might expect that pre-2004 immigration would negatively affect the labour market outcomes of low skilled British-born workers and British-born ethnic minorities, while 'new' immigrants, who are in general well educated, would affect negatively the labour market outcomes of people with a higher level of education.

H2: The nature of the labour market impact of immigrants depends, to a large extent, on the local labour market conditions. In particular, one may expect that accounting for the local labour market conditions will weaken the relationship between the spatial concentration of immigrants and the labour market outcomes of workers.

H3: The direction and the magnitude of the labour market impact of immigrants depends on the ethnic composition of the local labour market and the relative size of minority groups within it. In particular, the labour market impact of the spatial concentrations of pre-2004 immigrants would depend on the size of the British-born ethnic minority populations, while the labour market impact of the spatial concentrations of new immigrants would also depend on the size of the pre-2004 immigrant populations in local labour markets. Thus, in local labour markets where there exist large populations of British-born ethnic minorities, pre-2004 immigrants would have a smaller impact on the outcomes of the British population; similarly, in local labour markets where there exist large populations of pre-2004 immigrants, new immigrants would have a smaller impact on the outcomes of the British population compared with the impact in the local labour markets where the respective size of these populations is small.

Methodology

Research Design and Data

This research was designed to capture more accurately the effects of immigration on local labour markets. We have used 2006 Annual Population Survey[1] (APS) data. The APS (launched in 2004) was designed to provide reliable estimates at small area level at one time point. The 2006 APS[2] offers large and representative samples of at least 601 economically active individuals for 201 Unitary Authorities (UA)/Local Authority Districts (LAD), among which 180 UA/LAD with sufficiently large populations of immigrants were used in this study. The sample of individuals aged 16–65 was used in the study.

Although in most empirical studies, local labour markets are defined as travel-to-work areas (Reimer, 2003). In this study, we approximate the local labour markets by using UAs/LADs, with sufficiently large migrant populations. We did so because the immigrants and the socially and economically weaker populations which are expected to be affected most by immigration, tend to search for employment and work in proximity to their residences, ideally in the same localities of their residences (Mensah, 1995).

Labour market outcomes were measured in wages and in destination in the labour market (constructed through the socio-economic class variable), leading to the following two dependent variables: (i) natural logarithm of monthly wages of

[1]The APS comprises key variables from the Labour Force Survey (LFS), including education, employment and ethnicity.

[2]When this study began in 2007, the 2006 APS data provide the largest numbers for subpopulations of new immigrants arriving in Britain since 2004.

the employed population (excluding the self-employed); (ii) social classes I to III (managerial, professional and intermediate occupations), social classes V and VI (skilled manual and lower supervisory occupations), not having a social class (never worked/out of the labour force/long-term unemployed) and the reference category is social class VII (semi-skilled and unskilled manual occupations and short-term unemployed).

In terms of independent variables, at the level of individuals, the comparison groups are as follows: ethnicity (White British [reference group]), Immigrants, British-born ethnic minorities; religion (Christians [reference group], Muslims, Other religions); and the level of educational qualification (No or unknown qualification, below NVQ Level 2; NVQ Level 2, NVQ Level 3 [reference group], NVQ Level 4 and Level 5). Other variables are: marital status (single [reference group], married/cohabiting, widowed and divorced, separated); age (and age squared in the income regression); tenure in the UK for immigrants; gender (men [reference group]); and a series of control dummy variables in the regression model that predict labour market destinations as follows: student status; disability status; pensioner; single parent family; and number of children.

The contextual (local labour market) variable of main interest is the relative size of the immigrant population in the local labour market. Immigrants are not subdivided by their nationality or ethnic origin. Instead, all immigrants are subdivided into two broad groups: pre-2004 immigrants and 'new' or since-2004 immigrants. Rather than considering the corresponding proportions of pre-2004 and new immigrants in local labour markets, we have chosen to consider the proportion of the total immigrant population in the local labour market and then, additionally, to use the proportion of new immigrants in the total immigrant population. Such research design has certain advantages because it estimates the immigration impact whilst controlling for the size of the new immigrant population and, at the same time, it allows us to estimate not only the effect of the new immigration per se, but also to assess how the effect of the spatial concentration of new immigrants varies across local labour markets with different sizes of 'traditional' immigrant populations. The two following variables identify spatial concentrations of immigrants: (i) the percentage of the total economically active population in the UA/LAD who are not UK born and do not describe themselves as White British; and (ii) the relative size of the new immigrant population – the percentage of the migrant population in the UA/LAD who are 'new' migrants.

To resolve the problem of correlation between the size of the immigrant population and those particular characteristics of the local labour market which attract immigrants but also shape the socio-economic profiles of local workers, we account for contextual factors which shape the local labour market conditions (an example of such research design can be found in Shaginyan-Shapira, 2007). Local labour market conditions are made operational through using the following variables: the percentage of those in the total economically active population in the local labour market who are employed; the percentage of those in the total employed population who are employed in manufacturing jobs; the percentage of those in the total employed population who are employed in construction jobs; and the percentage of those in the total employed population who are employed in banking and finance. The degree of overall socio-economic well being in the locality is measured by (i) the percentage of those in the total employed population who are in socio-economic class I (according to the EGP classification); (ii) the percentage of those in the population aged 16–65 with the educational qualifications below NVQ Level 2; and (iii) the percentage of those in the total employed population who are employed in unskilled occupations. The variable that allowed us to identify the size of the British-born ethnic minority population was the percentage of those in the total economically active population in the UA/LAD who are British-born ethnic minorities.

Statistical Method

We use Hierarchical Linear Modelling (HLM) (Raudenbush and Bryk, 2002) which is appropriate for data with a clear hierarchical, nested structure (individuals within local labour markets). The general aim of HLM is to formulate and test hypotheses about how variables measured at the macro level affect the relationship between the independent and dependent variables oat the level of the individual. The individual level regression model provides (i) random intercepts to estimate how particular characteristics at the macro level affect average values of the dependent variables in each one of the macro-level units, and (ii) random slopes of particular independent variables which subdivide the population by sub-group so as to test whether all sub-groups in the particular macro-level unit are affected by the macro-level variables in a similar or different fashion.

We estimated multi-nomial multi-level regression models to predict the labour market destinations of the British population. We modelled random intercepts, and random slopes for the following individual-level independent variables: immigrant status; ethnicity; religion; and level of education. We also estimated linear multi-level regression to predict wages of the employed British population. The estimated models of income and of individual opportunities of being in the following labour market destinations, of economic inactivity, of being in higher status blue collar occupation (i.e. semi-skilled or lower supervisory occupations) and of being in white collar occupation (i.e. higher and lower managerial and professional and intermediate occupations) can be formally presented as follows:

$$Y_{ij} = (\gamma 00 + \sum_{j=1}^{j} \mu_{0j} + \sum_{j=1}^{J}\sum_{s=1}^{Sq} \gamma_{qk} Z_{sj}) + \sum_{j=1}^{J}\sum_{q=1}^{Q} \gamma_{q0} x_{qij} + \sum_{j=1}^{J}\sum_{q=1}^{Sq} \mu_{qj} x_{qij} + \sum_{j=1}^{J}\sum_{q=1}^{Q}\sum_{s=1}^{Sq} \gamma_{qs} z_{sj} x_{qij} \tag{8.1}$$

where $Y_{ij} = ln\ (wages)_{ij}$ in the income regression model and $Y_{ij} = Logit(E_k)_{ij}$ predicts the individual opportunities of being in particular labour market destinations where the subscript k indicates a particular labour market destination (k=1,2,3); subscripts i and j indicate individual i in locality j (j=1…J); X is a vector (length Q) of independent variables at the level of the individual ($x_{ijq}=\{x_{ij1}\ldots x_{ijQ}\}$); and z is a vector (length *S*) of independent variables at the level of the locality $(z_{js}=\{z_{j1}...z_{jS}\})$. The random intercept ($\gamma_{00}$) estimates the fixed effect of the intercept, μ_{oj} is the random intercept for the level two (localities) units and $\sum\gamma_{qs}z_{sj}$ estimates the level two covariates, i.e. the percentage of the all migrant population, the relative size of the new migrant population, the percentage of ethnic minorities, the percentage employed, the percentage employed in the manufacturing sector, the percentage employed in the construction sectors, the percentage employed in the banking and finance sector, and the degree of the overall socio-economic well-being of the locality measured as a percentage of the population in the socio-economic class I. The fourth term, $\sum\gamma_{q0}x_{qij}$, estimates individual level covariates (age, aged) squared, tenure in Britain for migrants, tenure squared, dummy variables for migrants, ethnic minorities, Muslims, religions other than Christian and Muslim, gender, being married, being ex-married, and a series of dummy variables for level of educational qualification in the regression that predicts the individual chances of being in a particular labour market destination.

It also includes the following control variables: number of children; a dummy variable for student status; a dummy variable for family status; a dummy variable for pensioner status; a dummy variable for disability status. Finally, the fifth term, $\mu_{qj}x_{qij}$, accounts for the random slopes of the level 1 variables, which it is assumed will vary between localities; and the sixth term, $\gamma_{qs}z_{sj}x_{qij}$, estimates the cross-level interactions between the locality-level variables and the following dummy variables: immigrant ethnic minority, Muslims and the five levels of educational qualifications (the slopes of the other independent variable are constrained to be constant across localities).

Results

Spatial Distributions of Immigrants in Britain

Figure 8.1 presents the composition of the population of immigrants in Britain by their national or ethnic origin and shows the differences in this composition that exist between immigrants who arrived in Britain before and since 2004. Eastern European immigrants, who used to be a small minority among the whole population of immigrants before 2004, make up more than a third of all migrants who arrived since 2004. Moreover, if only economically active post-2004 migrants are considered, the share of Eastern European immigrants among the latter is 40%. Other post-2004 migrants originate from three main sources – Africa, Western Europe and India.

Figures 8.2 and 8.3 show regional differences in percentage of immigrants in Britain. The highest percentage of immigrants (and British-born ethnic minorities) can be found in Inner and Outer London where they make up 35 and 27% of the total employed population aged 16–65 respectively, then in the West Midlands (14%), and in the South East, West Yorkshire, East Midlands and Great Manchester (where the immigrants make-up on average about 10% of the total population).

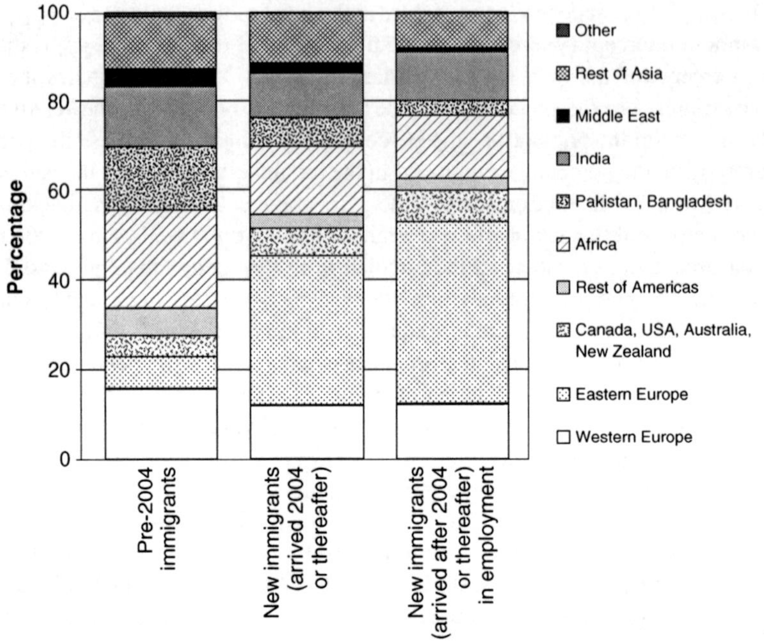

Fig. 8.1 National/ethnic origin of immigrants by period of arrival in Britain, 2006 (Source: APS 2006)

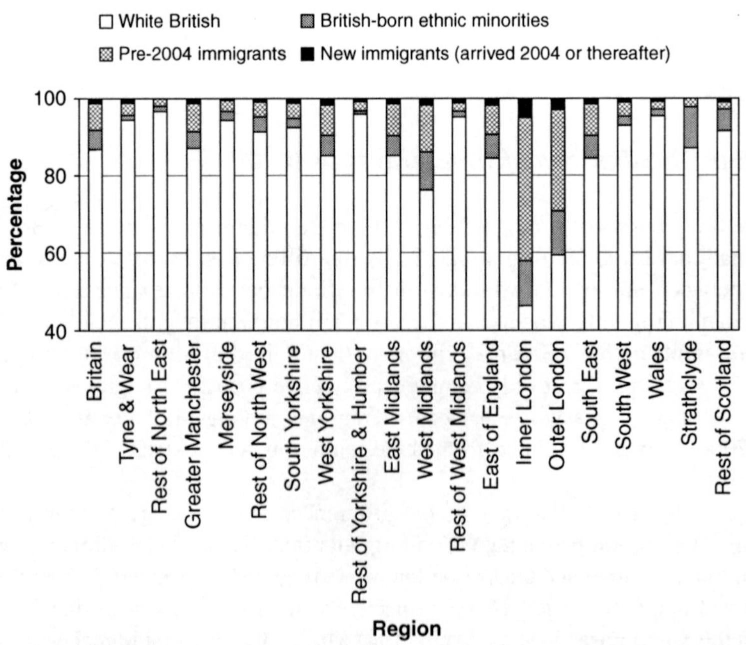

Fig. 8.2 Spatial distribution of the population of Britain by ethnicity, immigrant status and region, 2006 (Source: APS 2006)

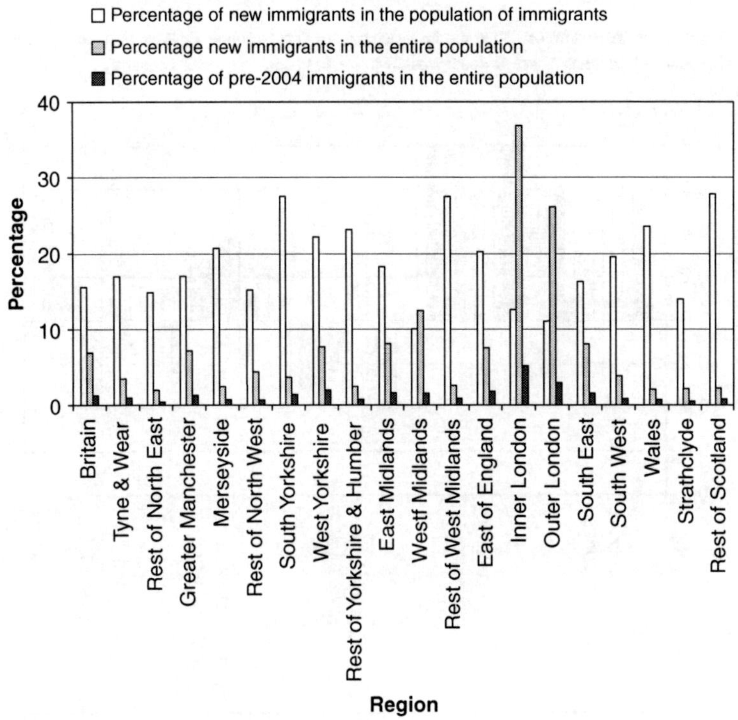

Fig. 8.3 Immigrant shares of total immigrant population in Britain, 2006 (Source: APS 2006)

Although the largest spatial concentrations of new immigrants coincide with the largest spatial concentration of the pre-2004 immigrants, the former are distributed more evenly throughout Britain than the latter, and therefore, have a relatively large representation in regions where spatial concentrations of pre-2004 immigrants are small. Thus, although the largest populations of new immigrants are found in such areas as Inner and Outer London and in the West Midlands (5 and 4% respectively of the total population in these regions), they make up only 10–12% of the whole population of immigrants in these areas. However, in other areas, such as Yorkshire, East Midlands, South Yorkshire, Wales and Scotland (excluding Strathclyde), where the size of the pre-2004 population of immigrants is relatively small, the size of the population of new immigrants is relatively large and makes up from 16 to 27% of all immigrants in the respective area.

Figures 8.4 and 8.5 present graphically the Pearson correlation coefficients between the spatial concentration of immigrants and the contextual characteristics of the regional labour markets.

Spatial concentrations of new immigrants have a positive, weak-to-moderate correlation with spatial concentrations of British-born ethnic minorities in seven out of eleven regions. In the Eastern region and in Scotland, the correlations are negative, whilst in Yorkshire and Humber and in Wales, the spatial concentrations of new

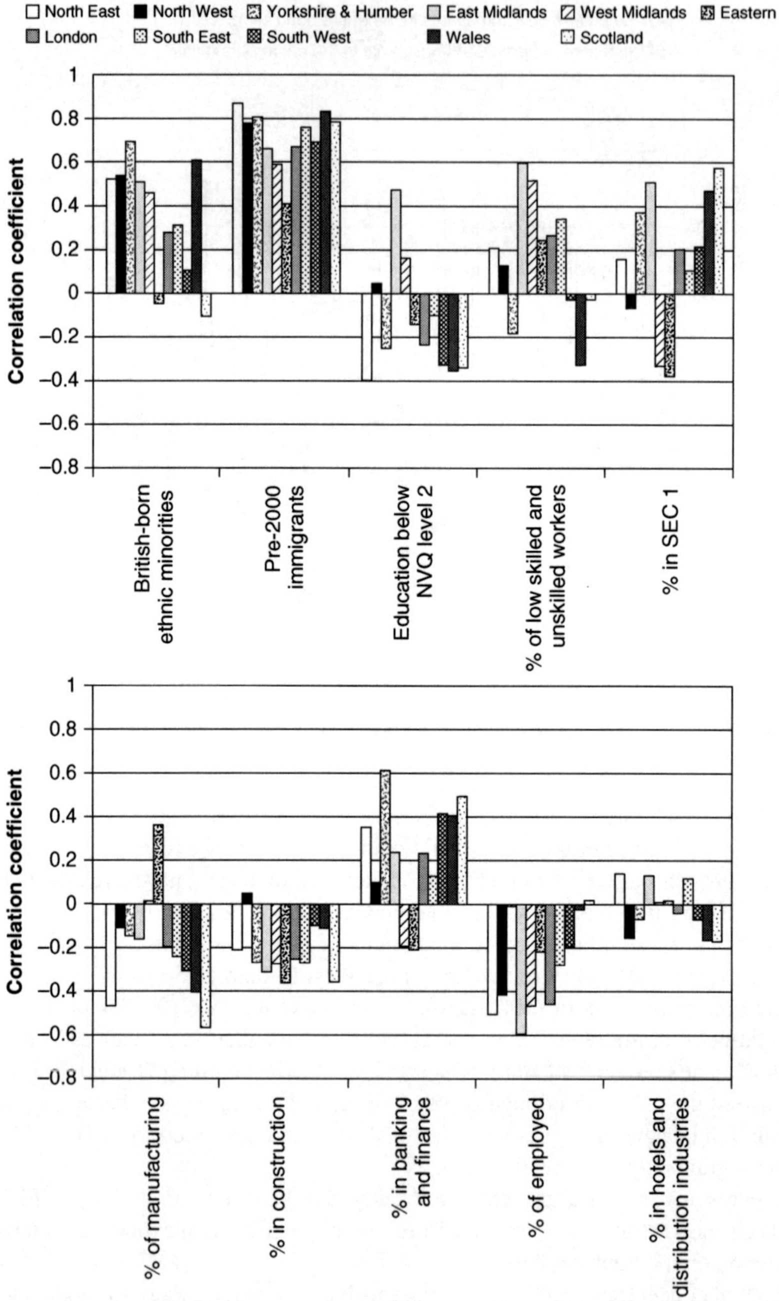

Fig. 8.4 Pearson correlations of spatial concentration on new (post-2004) immigrants with spatial concentration of pre-2004 immigrants, British-born ethnic minorities and various characteristics of local markets by region, 2006 (Source: APS 2006)

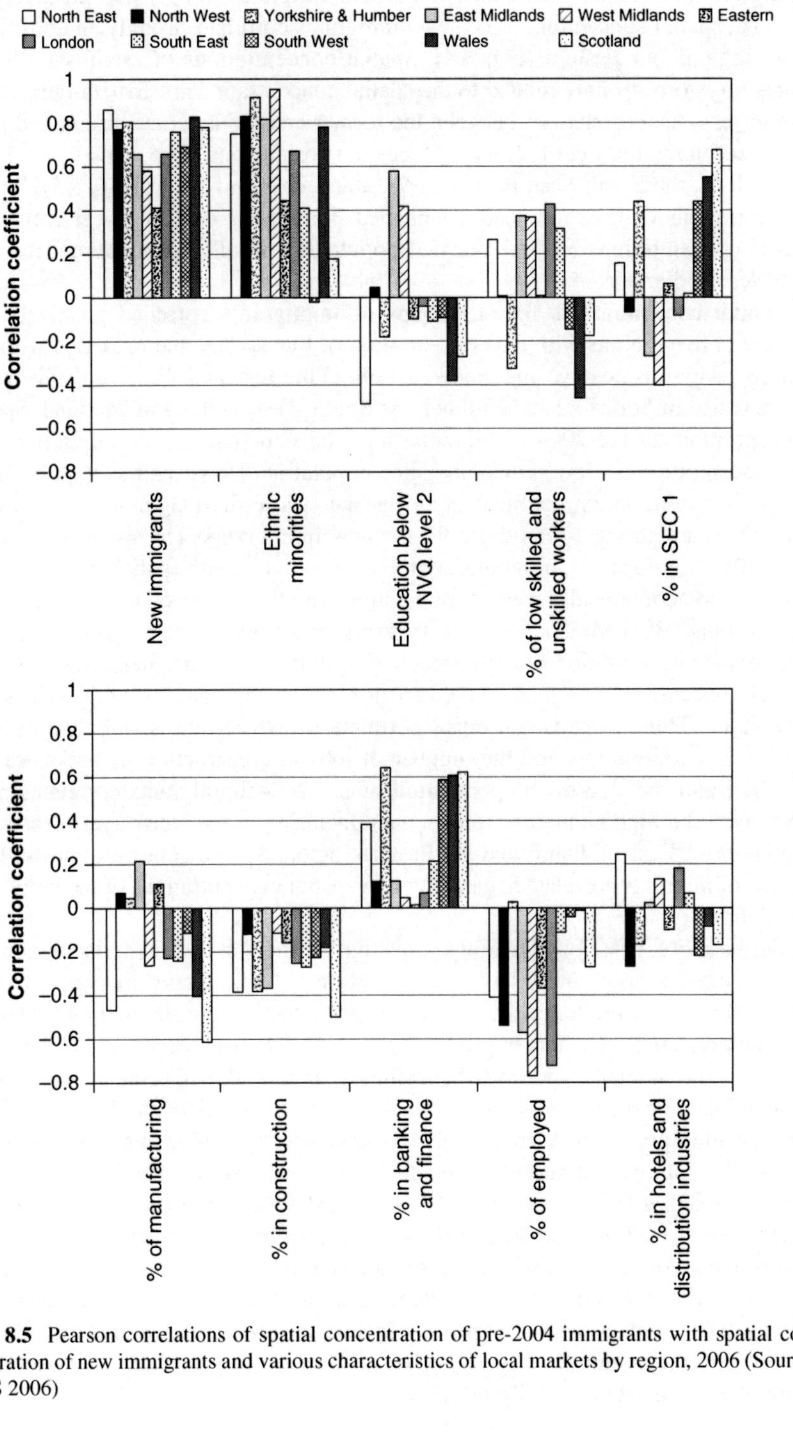

Fig. 8.5 Pearson correlations of spatial concentration of pre-2004 immigrants with spatial concentration of new immigrants and various characteristics of local markets by region, 2006 (Source: APS 2006)

immigrant and British-born ethnic minorities correlate strongly and positively. In contrast, spatial concentrations of new immigrants correlate strongly and positively in all regions but Eastern (Fig. 8.4). Spatial concentrations of established immigrants are more strongly related to the spatial concentrations of British-born ethnic minorities – the correlations between the former and the latter are strong and positive in seven regions out of eleven and they are positive and from weak-to-moderate in Scotland, the South East, the South West and Eastern regions (Fig. 8.5). Spatial concentrations of both new and established immigrants correlate negatively with spatial concentrations of less educated populations in all regions except the East and West Midlands.

Spatial concentrations for all groups of immigrants correlate positively and weakly in five regions with the concentration of low skilled and unskilled workers. The correlation is positive and moderate only in the East and West Midlands, while it is negative in Yorkshire and Humber, the South West, Wales and Scotland. Spatial concentrations of pre-2004 immigrants show the same patterns of correlation with the concentrations of low skilled/unskilled population. However, the magnitudes of the positive correlation coefficients are weaker while the magnitudes of negative correlation are stronger than those for the new immigrants. The spatial concentrations of both groups of immigrants are related positively with spatial concentrations of the socio-economically well-off population with the exception of the North West and East and West Midlands for all migrants, and London for pre-2004 migrants. The spatial concentration of both groups of migrants correlates negatively with the spatial concentration of jobs in construction and manufacturing with only a few exceptions. Thus, there is a positive correlation between the size of the population of new immigrants and the number of jobs in construction in Yorkshire and Humber; and the size of the population of pre-2004 immigrants correlates positively with the high number of jobs in manufacturing in the North West, Yorkshire and Humber, East Midlands and the Eastern region. Spatial concentrations of both groups of migrants correlate negatively with spatial concentrations of the employed population.

Furthermore, descriptive findings show that for the White-British population living in labour markets with large concentrations of immigrant populations (both pre-2004 and new immigrants), there is a more advantageous distribution of labour destinations, such as a larger proportion of white collar occupations (SEC I, II and III) and a smaller proportion of unskilled and semi-/skilled occupations (SEC V, VI and VII). For British-born ethnic minorities, larger populations of both pre-2004 and new immigrants are related to labour markets where ethnic minorities are more frequently employed in intermediate white collar occupations (SEC II); yet in such labour markets, ethnic minorities have a smaller share of self-employed workers and workers employed in semi-skilled/ skilled occupations, while they also have larger shares of economically inactive people and unskilled workers (Figs. 8.6 and 8.7).

Among the migrants themselves, larger spatial concentrations of migrants indicated labour markets where migrants had less unskilled and semi-skilled/skilled jobs, where they were more likely to be self-employed, yet where they were also more likely to be economically inactive.

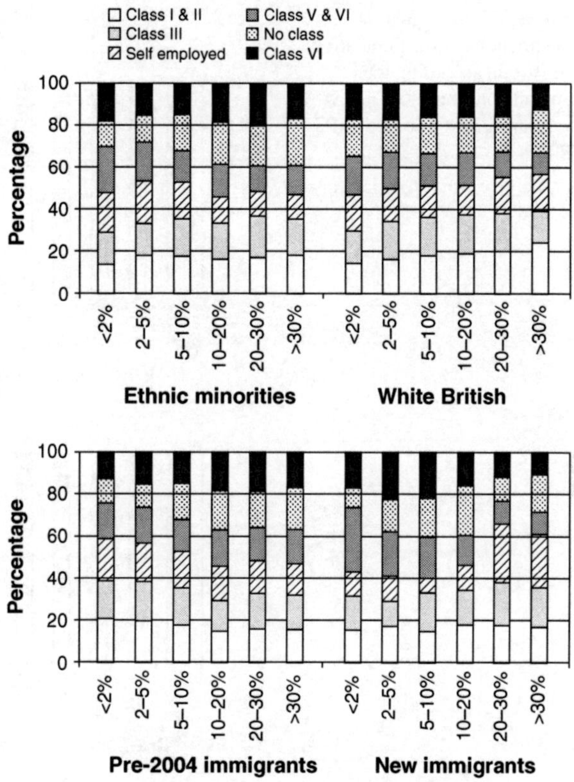

Fig. 8.6 Labour market destinations of the population in Britain according to the spatial concentration of pre-2004 immigrants, 2006 (Source: APS 2006)

So far, the findings show that associations between the spatial concentration of immigrants and the occupational outcomes of British population follow similar patterns both for concentrations of pre-2004 and new immigrants. Figure 8.8 confirms that the patterns of the relationship between the share of immigrant populations in local labour markets and the wages of British workers are also similar for both groups of immigrants. Indeed, wages of British-born Whites are higher in the labour markets with relatively larger immigrant populations and the wages are particularly high in labour markets where the relative size of the pre-2004 immigrant population reaches 20% or more, and where the relative size of new-immigrant populations reaches 5% or more of the total population in the local labour market. For the British-born ethnic minorities, the positive association between the relative size of immigrant populations and wages also exists but it is more modest than for the British-born Whites.

A resemblance between the patterns of association between the labour market outcomes of British workers and size of populations of both pre-2004 and new immigrants in labour markets, however, may merely reflect the fact that the largest concentrations of new immigrants coincide with the peaks of spatial concentration of pre-2004 immigrants (see Fig. 8.3 where the distributions of the populations of pre-2004 and new immigrants across regions are presented). Given this and

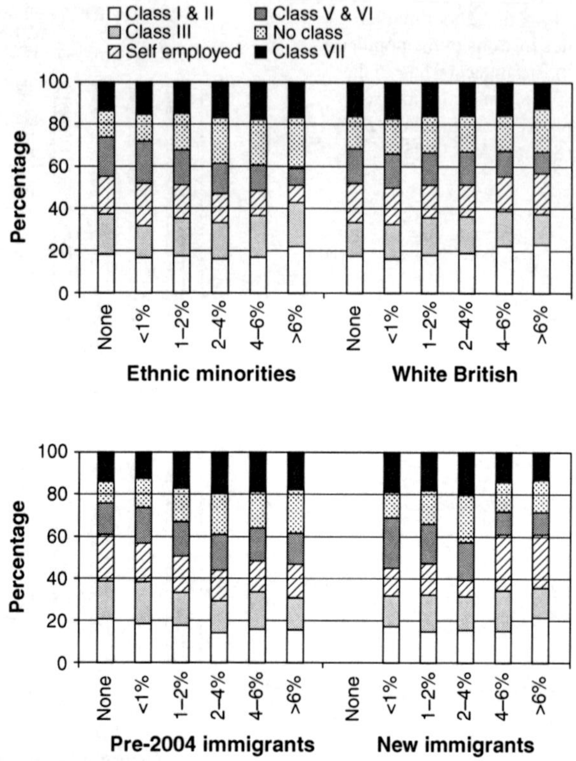

Fig. 8.7 Labour market destinations of the population in Britain according the spatial concentration of new migrants, 2006 (Source: APS 2006)

the fact that the relative size of the population of new immigrants is small in the total population, the association between the proportion of new immigrants in the total population and the labour market outcomes of British workers might mimic the association between the latter outcomes and the size of the population of pre-2004 immigrants, especially in regional or local labour markets with the largest spatial concentrations of pre-2004 immigrants. However, new immigrants are spread throughout Britain more evenly than pre-2004 immigrants and they have relatively large spatial concentrations also in regions where fewer pre-2004 immigrants live (Fig. 8.3). Therefore, a proportion of new immigrants in the population of immigrants in the regional/local labour market is more meaningfully related to the potential impact which new immigrants might have on the local labour market than the proportion of new immigrants in the total population of the regional/local labour market.

Indeed, data presented in Figs. 8.7 and 8.8 show that the pattern of relationships between the proportion of new immigrants in the population of all immigrants in a labour market and the labour market outcomes of British workers is different from the relationships between the latter outcomes and the size of the population of pre-2004 immigrants. Thus, an increase in the number of new immigrants in the population of all immigrants to 20% in the labour market is related to a 10% decrease in wages for the British-born ethnic groups; the latter increase is also associated

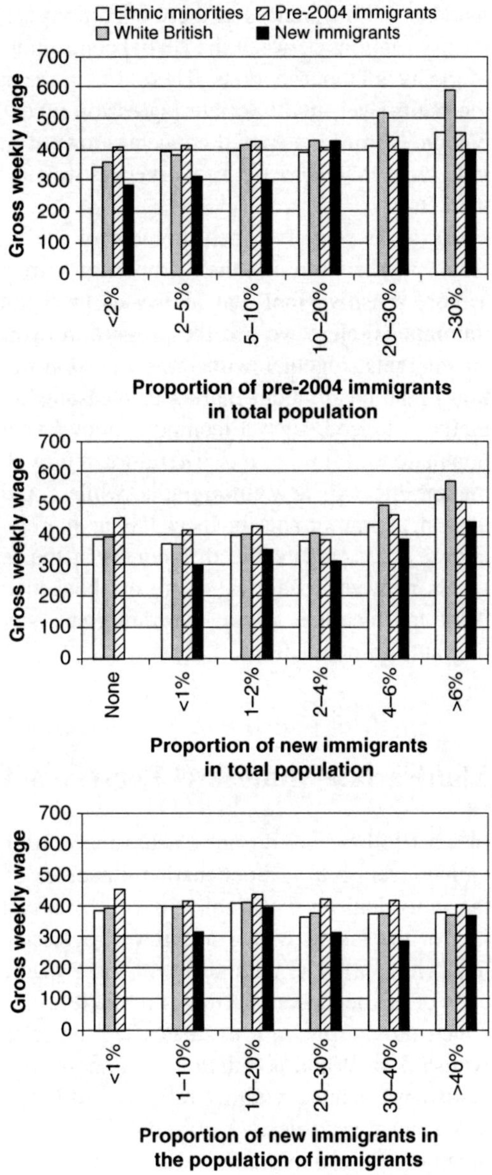

Fig. 8.8 Gross weekly wages of different groups of population according to the spatial concentration of immigrants, 2006 (Source: APS 2006)

with a slight decrease of the white collar occupation share among the British-born population, yet it is also associated with a decrease in the share of the economically inactive population, especially among the British-born ethnic minorities, and a corresponding increase in the share of semi-skilled and skilled workers.

However, the relationships described above between the spatial concentration of immigrants and the labour market outcomes of British workers account neither for the characteristics of individual workers, nor for the conditions of the local labour markets and differences in these conditions across Britain. Nor do they account for the associations between the spatial concentration of immigrants and the conditions of the local labour markets. Therefore, in the next section, we present the results of the multi-level, multi-variate regression modelling that predicts the labour market outcomes from the spatial concentrations of immigrants, while controlling for the individual characteristics of workers as well as for the characteristics of local labour markets.

As we expected, a measurement of the presence of new immigrants in local labour markets through their proportion in the population of all migrants provides a more sensitive tool that allows us to capture the labour market effect of new immigrants. Here we use the proportion of new immigrants in the population of all migrants, together with the proportion of all immigrants in the total population in the local labour market as measures of immigrant presence in local labour markets. Indeed, such a technique allows simultaneous control for the size of all populations of immigrants. Therefore, it provides us with net estimates of the labour market effect of new immigrants, while controlling for the size of the total population of immigrants in local labour markets. As a result, using this technique allows us to capture the differences in the labour market impact of new immigrants between localities where established migrants populations existed before 2004 and localities where the immigrants since 2004 formed the first significant migrant sub-populations.

Multivariate Multi-level Regression Results

In what follows we do not discuss the impact of variables measured on the individual level on the labour market outcomes of British population. Instead, we use the individual level variables as control variables and proceed with a consideration of the results of the multilevel regression modelling on local labour market level (level 2). The parameters of these macro-level variables were estimated for each of the dependent variables in the level 2 regressions (i) for random intercepts which provide us with estimates for the reference group of comparison, i.e. the British-born White population with an average level of educational qualifications, Christians or those without religious affiliation; and (ii) for the random slopes of independent variables, which subdivide the entire population into: British-born ethnic minorities; immigrants; religious minorities; and people with different levels of educational qualifications.

In Figs. 8.9 and 8.10, we present the outcomes of the multilevel modelling on the second level of the analysis, for the main macro-level variables of our interest, i.e. percentage of all immigrants in the local labour market and the percentage of new immigrants in the population of all migrants. Each estimated parameter is presented twice, that is before and after the variables which describe the opportunity structures of local labour markets and their ethnic compositions are introduced into the regression. The estimated parameters of the independent variables of main interest

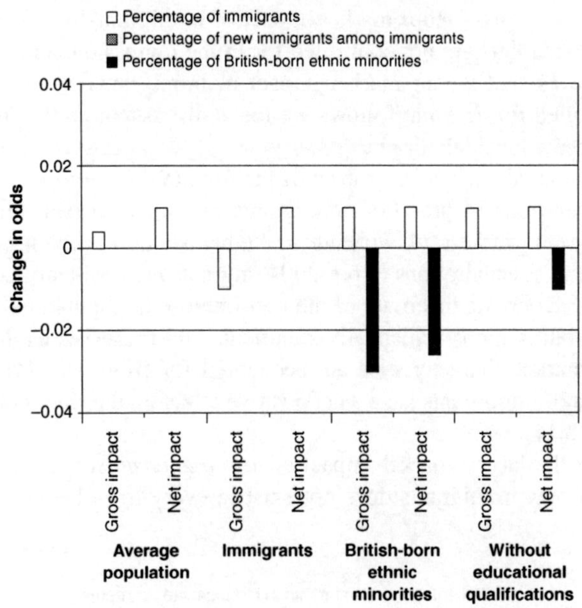

Fig. 8.9 Impact of 1% increase in the size of the immigrant population on the odds of economic activity versus the odds of unskilled jobs or short-term unemployment for different groups of the British population, 2006 (Source: APS 2006)

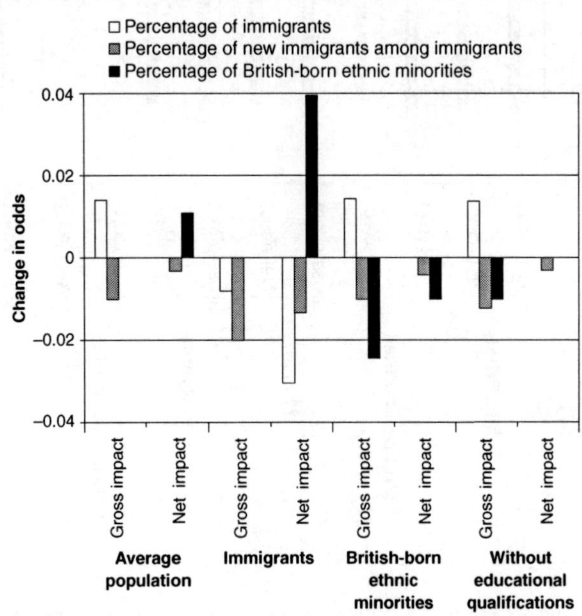

Fig. 8.10 Impact of 1% increase in the size of the immigrant population on the odds of higher status blue collar occupations versus the odds of unskilled jobs or short-term unemployment for different groups of the British population, 2006 (Source: APS 2006)

are referred to as 'gross labour market impact of immigrants' if the characteristics of local labour markets are not controlled for in the regression, and the parameters are referred to as 'net labour market impact of immigrants' if these characteristics are controlled for. In what follows we focus discussion on the 'net impact' of immigrants on the local labour markets.

In terms of the labour market impact of the *pre-2004 immigrants*, we found that spatial concentrations of pre-2004 immigrants are not related to the net chances of non-immigrant workers of working in higher status occupations (Fig. 8.10). However, spatial concentrations of pre-2004 migrants are positively associated with higher odds of economic inactivity of the non-immigrant population. This relationship weakens but remains statistically significant and preserves its direction when local labour market characteristics are accounted for (Fig. 8.9). Pre-2004 spatial concentrations of immigrants have a net positive effect on the wages of non-migrant workers (Fig. 8.11).

In terms of the labour market impact of *new immigrants*, we found that a negative effect of new immigrants does not exist in every local labour market with a

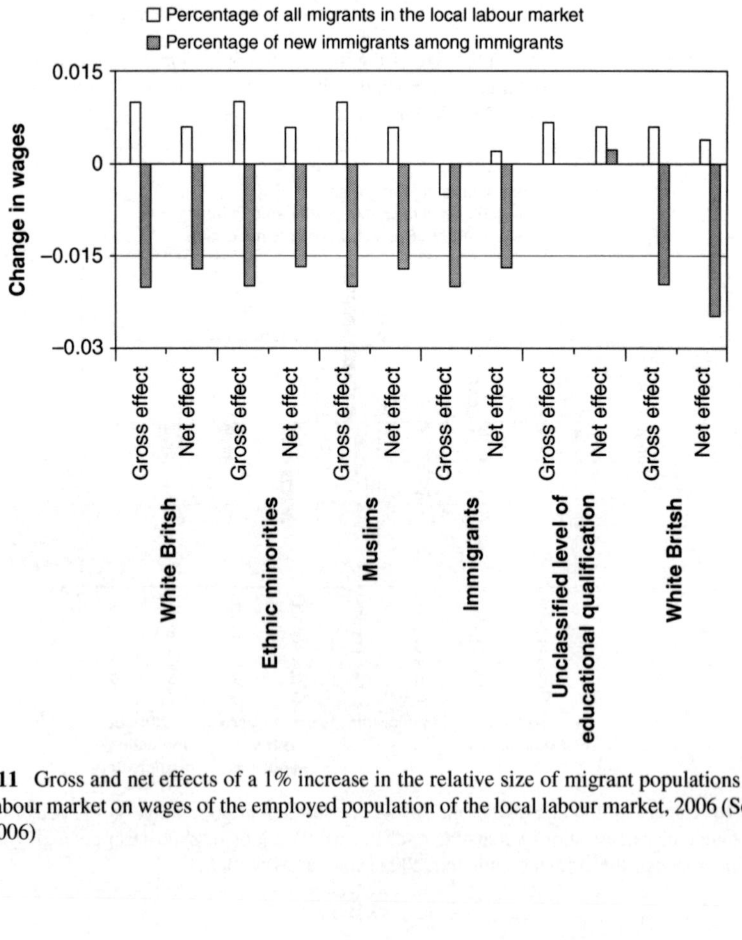

Fig. 8.11 Gross and net effects of a 1% increase in the relative size of migrant populations in the local labour market on wages of the employed population of the local labour market, 2006 (Source: APS 2006)

large population of new immigrants. The labour market impact of new immigrants depends on the size and composition of the immigrant population in local labour markets. The negative effect of the presence of new immigrants is felt by non-migrant workers only in those localities where immigrant populations were small before 2004 and thus where new immigrants make up a sizable proportion of the whole population of immigrants (Fig. 8.10). Thus, a higher proportion of new immigrants in the whole population of immigrants is negatively related to the odds of non-immigrant workers of working in white collar occupations. Accounting for the characteristics of the local labour markets does not cancel this relationship although it makes it weaker. In addition, a higher proportion of new immigrants in the whole population of immigrants is negatively related to wages of non-immigrant workers in white collar occupations. Accounting for the characteristics of the local labour markets does not cancel this relationship although it makes it weaker (Fig. 8.11).

When considering differences in the labour market impact of immigrants among sub-populations of the native-born in Britain, we found that immigrants have a similar effect on all groups of the non-migrant population except those with the highest level of educational qualifications. We did not find any evidence that British-born ethnic minorities or people with lower levels of education are affected by immigration in a more negative way than the White British population with an average level of education. However, wages of workers with the highest level of educational qualifications (NVQ level 5) are more negatively affected by the spatial concentrations of new immigrants in the localities which have small pre-2004 immigrant populations than the wages of people with other levels of educational qualifications. Furthermore, the spatial concentrations of pre-2004 immigrants are related positively, net of other characteristics of local labour markets, to wages of workers with the highest level of educational qualifications. However, this relationship is weaker than the relationship between the spatial concentrations of pre-2004 immigrants and the wages of workers with average or below average levels of educational qualifications.

What about the impact of the spatial concentrations of immigrants on immigrants themselves? We found that spatial concentration of immigrants has a stronger negative effect on the occupational opportunities of migrants themselves than on the non-migrant population. Thus, in local labour markets with large immigrant populations, immigrants are more likely to have unskilled jobs than work in higher status blue collar occupations or in white collar occupations, or have below-average levels of educational qualifications.

When looking at differences in the immigration labour market impact according to the ethnic composition of the local labour markets, we found that the ethnic composition of local labour markets does not mediate the relationship between spatial concentrations of immigrants and the labour market outcomes of non-migrant workers. Nor does accounting for the size of the ethnic minority population change the labour market effect of immigration.

On the relationship between the spatial concentration of British-born ethnic minorities and the labour market outcomes of different groups of British workers, we found that in localities with a high concentration of British ethnic minorities, both the White British population and especially the immigrants are more likely to work in white-collar occupations. Members of British-born ethnic minorities themselves are less likely to work in white-collar occupations in localities with a large presence of British-born ethnic minorities. For low skilled workers, a large presence of British-born ethnic minorities in the local labour market has a negative effect on their odds of higher status occupations.

Finally, concerning the relationship between the local labour market conditions and the immigration labour market impact, our findings show that local labour market characteristics are an important mediator between spatial concentrations of immigrants and the labour market outcomes of native workers. Controlling for the structure of local labour market characteristics changes the relationship between the size of immigrant populations and the labour market outcomes of the non-migrant population. Hence the impact of immigration on the labour market cannot be properly understood without first considering how the spatial differences in the labour market outcomes of individuals are related to spatial differences in the local labour market opportunity structure.

Conclusions

In this study we sought an answer to the question of whether or not spatial concentrations of immigrants have a negative impact on the employment outcomes of non-migrant workers in the British labour market, in terms of their odds of entry into employment, their odds of entry into more prestigious occupations and their wages. Multi-level, multi-nomial and linear regression analyses were conducted to explore whether variations across local labour markets in the employment outcomes of individuals were systematically related to the variations in the spatial concentration of immigrants, after accounting for variations in other characteristics of local labour markets that might be responsible for differences in labour market outcomes.

On the basis of the findings from this study it can be concluded that, overall, immigrants do not have a negative effect on the labour market outcomes (in term of wages and occupational attainment) of British workers. Moreover, in local labour markets where there exist larger higher spatial concentrations of immigrants, the wages of non-migrant workers are higher than in local labour markets with smaller populations of immigrants. The positive association between the spatial concentration of immigrants and the wages of non-migrant workers is net of other characteristics of local labour markets which might be responsible for the spatial wage differentials and indicates that immigrants on thea whole have a positive economic effect on British workers.

The evidence that the spatial concentration of immigrants is positively related with a higher level of economic inactivity of the non-migrant population, after accounting for other characteristics of local labour markets, may indicate that there is a possibility of competition between immigrants and native-born workers for low skilled occupations with a subsequent substitution of native workers by immigrants. However, alternative explanations are also possible. Thus, it might be the case that

British-born workers have more alternatives to low- paid employment and rely more on state benefits or personal savings than do the immigrants. It may also be the case that the migrants are taking jobs which are not wanted by the native-born population. In any case, only detailed case studies can confirm or reject the hypotheses about the competition between the immigrants and native workers.

Findings about the labour market impact of new (i.e. post-2004) immigrants deserve a separate discussion. Indeed, the findings show that the impact of new immigrants on the labour market outcomes of British workers is not different in a statistically significant way from the labour market impact of the established immigrants if new immigrants reside in local labour markets which already have large populations of immigrants who had arrived in Britain before 2004. However, in the local labour markets where, before 2004, the population of immigrants used to be very small, i.e. in the local labour markets where new immigrants make up a large proportion of the whole population of immigrants, the post-2004 immigrants have a negative effect on the labour market outcomes of the non-migrant population. Indeed, in such labour markets, a negative association exists between the spatial concentration of new immigrants and the wages of non-migrant workers; the latter also have a lower probability of working in white collar occupations.

In accord with our first hypothesis, immigrants have a different effect on different groups of workers. However, unlike our expectations, the results show that immigrants impact least favourably not on the least educated British-born workers and/or ethnic minorities, but on the most educated groups of non-migrant workers. Indeed, the findings show the group that is most negatively affected in terms of wages by new immigrants are those with the highest level of educational qualifications. Similarly, although the spatial concentration of established immigrants is positively related to the wages of non-migrant workers, the size of the positive effect is smallest for workers with the highest level of educational qualifications. Similarly, rather than competing with low educated workers for low-skilled occupations, new immigrants seem to affect the chances of workers to be working in white collar occupations. Nevertheless, these findings alone do not provide us with clear evidence of competition between new immigrants and native workers for white collar jobs; case studies of particular occupations are needed to confirm or reject the hypotheses about this competition.

Of course, a part of this association as well as other associations between the spatial concentration of immigrants and the labour market outcomes of workers results from spatial differences in the conditions of local labour markets, and disappears after these characteristics are being accounted for. This confirms our second hypothesis about the importance of local labour market conditions when the labour market impact of immigrants is considered. Indeed, findings from this research show that local labour market characteristics are an important mediator between the spatial concentrations of immigrants and the labour market outcomes of native workers. Controlling for the structure of local labour market characteristics changes the relationship between the size of immigrant populations and the labour market outcomes of non-migrant populations. Hence, the impact of immigration on the labour market impact cannot be properly understood without first considering how spatial differences in the labour market outcomes of individuals are related to spatial differences in the local labour market opportunity structure. These research findings show, however, that the reported association between spatial concentrations of immigrants and the labour market outcomes of non-migrant workers exist net of local labour market conditions.

The findings of this research support our third hypothesis only partially. Indeed, as we showed previously, ethnic composition of local labour markets in terms of the relative sizes of populations of new and established immigrants, has an important effect on the labour market outcomes of non-migrant workers. It might indicate that in local labour markets with relatively large immigrant populations before 2004, immigrants and non-immigrant workers had established a balance, with each group occupying particular occupational niches in these localities. The arrival of new immigrants after 2004 did not disturb this established balance as they entered existing labour market niches for immigrant workers. However, the situation may be quite different in those local labour markets where no significant immigrant population existed before 2004 – in these labour markets, new arrivals may compete for jobs with non-immigrants and negatively affect the labour market outcomes of the latter. However, contrary to our expectations, expressed in the third research hypothesis, the size of the ethnic minority population in the local labour market does not mediate between the spatial concentration of immigrants and the labour market outcomes of workers. The size of the ethnic minority population is important for the labour market outcomes of the ethnic minorities themselves, as well as other groups of workers, including immigrants. Indeed, a high percentage of British ethnic minorities positively affects the net odds of higher status occupations for the White British population and even more so for immigrants. However, for ethnic minorities themselves, as well as for low skilled workers, a large presence of British-born ethnic minorities in the local labour markets has a negative effect on their odds of higher status occupations.

How sure can one be in claiming these effects of immigration? In this research we extensively controlled for the opportunity structure and characteristics of populations of the local labour markets. The reported results are those which were found to be statistically significant after the differences in characteristics of local labour markets, where pre-2004 and new immigrants live were controlled for. Therefore, we believe that the reported effects of immigration are net of the other characteristics of local labour markets responsible for differences in the labour market outcomes of their populations. Additionally, in this research we tested the impact of the spatial concentration of immigrants both on wages and occupational opportunities and the evidence obtained is consistent and shows the same patterns of economic and occupational impact of immigrants. Therefore, we believe that despite the limitations and questions which remain open, this study considers the issue of the immigration impact on the labour market outcomes of British workers in a more comprehensive and systematic way than previous studies and offers additional insights on the important issue of the labour market consequences and impacts of immigration.

Acknowledgement This research was funded by an ESRC small grant (RES-163-25-0050).

References

Blanchflower, D., Saleheen, J. and Shadforth, C. (2007) *The Impact of the Recent Migration from Eastern Europe on the UK Economy*. Bank of England, available at http://www.bankofengland.co.uk/publications/speeches/2007/speech297.pdf

Borjas, J. (2001) *Does Immigration Grease the Wheels of the Labour Market?* Brookings Institution Press, Washington, DC, Brookings papers on Economic Activity, http://www.oecd.org/LongAbstract/0,2546,en_2649_34321_24741854_1_1_1_37435,00.html

Borjas, J. (2003) The labour market demand curve is downward sloping: Re-examining the impact of immigration on the labour market, *The Quarterly Journal of Economics*, 118(4): 1335–1374.

Borjas, J. (2004) *Increasing the Supply of Labour Through Immigration: Measuring the Impact on Native-Born Workers*, Centre for Immigration Studies, Washington, DC, http://www.cis.org.

Borjas, J. (2005, May) The labour market impact of high-skill immigration, *American Economic Review*, 95(2): 56–60.

Borjas, J. and Freeman, R.B. (eds.) (1992) *Immigration and the Work Force: Economic Consequences for the United States and Source Areas*, University of Chicago Press, Chicago, IL.

Cheshire, P., Monastiriotis, V. and Sheppard, S. (2003) Income inequality and residential segregation: Labour market sorting and demand for personal goods in Martin, R. and Morrison, P.S. (eds.), *Geographies of Labour Market Inequality*, Routledge, London.

Cohen-Goldner, S. and Paserman, D. (2004) *The Dynamic Impact of Immigration on Native's Labour Market Outcomes: Evidence from Israel* (IZA Working Paper 1315). Available at SSRN, http://ssrn.com/abstract=596962

Dustmann, C., Fabbri, F. and Preston, I. (2005) *The Impact of Immigration on the UK Labour Market* (CReAM Discussion Paper Series CDP No 01/05), Centre for Research and Analysis of Migration, Department of Economics, UCL, London.

Filer, R.K. (1992) The effect of immigrants arrival on migratory patterns of native workers in Borjas, J. and Freeman, R.B. (eds.), *Immigration and the Work Force: Economic Consequences for the United States and Source Areas*, University of Chicago Press, Chicago, IL.

Flug, K., Hercowitz, Z. and Levi, A. (1994) *A Small-Open Economy Analysis of Migration* (Working Paper 13), Foerder Institute for Economic Research, Tel Aviv.

Fossett, M.A., Galle, O.R. and Kelly, W.R. (1986) Racial occupational inequality, 1940–1980: National and regional trends, *American Sociological Review*, 51(3): 421–429.

Friedberg, R. (2001) The impact of mass migration on Israeli labour market, *The Quarterly Journal of Economics*, 16(4): 1347–1406.

Frijters, P., Shields, M.A. and Whitley-Price, S. (2005) Job-search of ethnic workers in the UK, *Economic Journal*, 115: F359–F376.

Gilpin, N., Henty, M., Lemos, S., Portes, J. and Bullen, C. (2006) *The Impact of Free Movement of Workers from Central and Eastern Europe on the UK Labour Market* (Working Paper No. 29), Department for Work and Pensions, London.

Lieberson, S. (1980) *A Piece of the Pie: Black and white Immigrants Since 1880*, University of California Press, Berkeley, CA.

Manacorda, M., Manning, A. and Wadsworth, J. (2006) *The Impact of Immigration on the Structure of Wages in Britain* (CEP Discussion Paper No. 754), Centre for Economic Performance, London School of Economics, London.

Martin, R. and Morrison, P.S. (2003) Thinking about the geographies of labour in Martin, R. and Morrison, P.S. (eds.), *Geographies of Labour Market Inequality*, Routledge, London.

Mensah, J. (1995) Journey to work and job search characteristics of the urban poor, *Transportation*, 22(1): 1–19.

Morrison, P.S. and Berezovsky, O. (2003) Labour market risk and the regions: Evidence from gross labour flows in Martin, R. and Morrison, P.S. (eds.), *Geographies of Labour Market Inequality*, Routledge, London.

Ottaviano, G.I.P. and Peri, G. (2006) *Rethinking the Gains from Immigration: Theory and Evidence from the US, Fondazione Eni Enrico Mattei* (Note di Lavoro 52.2006). Available at http://www.feem.it/NR/rdonlyres/D8689978-76C2-428D-A625-D0E49BBA81CE/2198/5206.pdf

Raudenbush, S.W. and Bryk, A.S. (2002) *Hierarchical Linear Models: Applications and Data Analysis Methods* (2nd ed.), Sage Publications, Thousand Oaks, CA.

Reimer, S. (2003) Employer strategies and the fragmentation of local employments: The case of contracting out local authority services in Martin, R. and Morrison, P.S. (eds.), *Geographies of Labour Market Inequality*, Routledge, London.

Sassen, S. (1988) *The Mobility of Labor and Capital*, Cambridge University Press, Cambridge.

Shaginyan-Shapira, M. (2007) *Ethnic Socio-Economic Inequality in an Immigrant Absorbing Society: Case of Israel*. Unpublished D. Phil. dissertation, University of Oxford, Oxford.

Soja, E.W. (1989) *Postmodern Geographies: The Reassertion of Space in Critical Social Theory*, Verso Press, London.

Tienda, M. and Lii, D. (1987) Minority concentration and ethnic inequality: Blacks, Hispanic and Asians compared, *American Journal of Sociology*, 93: 141–165.

van Ham, M. (2002) *Job Access, Workplace Mobility, and Occupational Achievement*, Eburon, Delft.

van Ham, M., Hooimeijer, P. and Mulder, C.H. (2001) Urban form and job access: Disparate realities in the Randstad, *Journal of Economic and Social Geography*, 92: 231–246.

Waldinger, R. (1999) Network, bureaucracy, and exclusion: Recruitment and selection in an immigrant metropolis in Bean, F. and Bell-Rose, S. (eds.), *Immigration and Opportunity: Race, Ethnicity and Employment in the United States*, Russell Sage Foundation, New York, NY.

Waters, M. (1999) West Indians and African Americans at work: Structural differences and cultural stereotypes in Bean, F. and Bell-Rose, S. (eds.), *Immigration and Opportunity: Race, Ethnicity and Employment in the United States*, Russell Sage Press, New York, NY, pp. 194–227.

Chapter 9
Black Africans in England: A Diversity of Integration Experiences

Lavinia Mitton and Peter Aspinall

Introduction

In 2001, people identifying as Black African made up around 0.9% of the total population of England out of a Black and Minority Ethnic (BME) population of 13% (National Statistics, 2009). This translates into around 476,000 people. Over the period 1993–2003, 10% of international immigrants originated in sub-Saharan Africa (Dustmann et al., 2003) forming the 'new African diaspora' (Koser, 2003).

Most of the discourse, policy and public understanding of migration and multiculturalism in Britain over the past 30 years has been based on the experience of Black Caribbean people who arrived between the 1950s and 1970s from Jamaica, Trinidad and other places in the Caribbean, and that of South Asian communities from India, Pakistan and Bangladesh. The experience of Black Africans as a distinct group from Black Caribbeans has not made nearly so much impact on public policy, even though Black African interview respondents have said that the umbrella term 'Afro-Caribbean' does not recognise important differences between Black people (Fimbo et al., 2001). However, the recognition of Black Africans by policy makers must change with the recent growth in this ethnic group. Further, there is enormous diversity within the Black African population (Aspinall and Chinouya, 2008; Elam and Chinouya, 2000; Elam et al., 2001). They come from over 40 different sub-Saharan countries of origin. There are hundreds of different ethnic and language groups, diverse religious practices and varied pre-migration lifestyles from nomadic farmers to city dwellers.

In addition, differing migration circumstances contribute to the diversity of the Black African migrant experience. The countries of origin of Black Africans reflect a wide range of political circumstances, from relative political stability to conflict-ridden anarchy. Many Black African people have entered the UK to study (UKvisas, 2008); on the other hand, many recent immigrants from Somalia and the Democratic

L. Mitton (✉)
School of Social Policy, Sociology and Social Research, University of Kent, Canterbury, CT2 7NF, Kent, UK
e-mail: L.Mitton@kent.ac.uk

J. Stillwell, M. van Ham (eds.), *Ethnicity and Integration*, Understanding Population Trends and Processes 3, DOI 10.1007/978-90-481-9103-1_9,

Republic (DR) of Congo have arrived through the asylum process (Home Office, 2008). The first and second generations, and men and women, have had varied experiences of the UK and different sets of identities have developed, as the data presented in this chapter illustrates.

There are conceptual issues around use of the category 'Black African' (Aspinall and Chinouya, 2008). For example, younger Black African people may not necessarily identify themselves as such (Elam et al., 2001). This chapter is about people who define themselves as Black African and focuses on people with roots in the UK or sub-Saharan Africa. The exception is Somalis reporting their ethnicity as 'Other', which we assumed to be Black African for our analysis, even though they might not self-define that way. This arises because those from Somalia may consider themselves to be Arab-African rather than Black African because of their religion and physical features (Elam et al., 2001). In addition, as in Harding and Balarajan's study (2000), a small proportion of those who reported themselves as Black Africans in our data were born in the Caribbean and had not identified with the 'Black Caribbean' option.

This chapter explores whether Black Africans from different countries of birth have different experiences of integration into British society through analysis of quantitative survey data. It focuses on England, which is where the overwhelming majority of Black Africans live. First, it outlines the changing pattern of Black African migration to Britain. Next, the age and gender composition of the population is outlined, followed by family and household structures. In the following sections, data are presented on three elements of integration: differing ethnic and national identities; use of the English language; and employment.

Although in theory identifying indicators of integration sounds simple, operationalising a definition is difficult, as the relevant data are often not available. Most definitions stress labour market participation as well as progress towards equality in employment and education. Indicators of integration have been put forward by Castles et al. (2002), the Council of Europe (1997), the Home Office (2004) and Ager and Strang (2004), for example. Any one of these indicators taken alone is not indicative of integration, which may take place differently in various sub-sectors. For instance, immigrants and refugees may find that they have access to the labour market but are excluded or disadvantaged in the welfare and education sectors. Often it is the interrelationship between indicators that is important and offers the greatest potential to deepen our understanding of integration experiences (Phillimore and Goodson, 2008). For example, inability to secure housing or poor health could impact on a refugee's ability to progress in other areas such as employment and education. On a practical level, integration processes are long-term by nature, making them hard to measure.

Relatively little attention has been paid to how migrants and refugees themselves feel about integration; refugees are often presented as rather passive recipients of interventions designed to integrate 'them' (Rutter et al., 2008). Ethnic minorities may attach different priorities to the integration indicators compared to the White majority. For example, while the host society may be concerned about unemployment and consequent welfare dependency, ethnic minorities themselves may focus on their lack of legal status and lack of access to services. Nevertheless, using indicators from several sources a picture can be built up, and we present here data on national identity, use of English and levels of employment.

Data Sources

This research analysed the 2001 English Census, the Labour Force Survey (LFS), Citizenship Survey (formerly known as the People, Families and Communities Study and Home Office Citizenship Survey), the National Survey of Sexual Attitudes and Lifestyles II, 2000–2001 (NATSAL II), and the Millennium Cohort Study.

The LFS is an ongoing quarterly sample survey of households living at private addresses in the UK. The survey seeks information on respondents' personal characteristics and their labour market status. Its purpose is to provide information on the UK labour market that can then be used to develop, manage, evaluate and report on labour market policies. The questionnaire design, sample selection and interviewing are carried out by the Office for National Statistics (ONS). It includes a variable on respondents' country of birth, which can be used to break down the Black African group into sub-groups. Each quarter's LFS sample of 60,000 households is made up of five 'waves', each of approximately 12,000 households. Each wave is interviewed in five successive quarters, such that in any one quarter, one wave will be receiving their first interview, one wave their second, and so on, with one wave receiving their fifth and final interview. As a result, there is an 80% overlap in the samples for successive quarters. The LFS is a complex sample survey design with stratification and clustering and requiring weighting, which we took into account in carrying out our analysis. Although the LFS has been used for ethnicity research (e.g. IPPR, 2007), our research also made use of the language variables available. We used pooled data from three quarters (two quarters for the language data) to obtain a sample size large enough for meaningful analysis of Black African ethnic sub-groups. Because each household is interviewed five times in consecutive quarters, we chose quarters in such a way as to avoid overlap in the sample. To increase the sample sizes, some of the countries with smaller samples were grouped.

We also used the 2007 Citizenship Survey, which has been carried out every other year since 2001 by Government departments. It collects a wide range of data, principally on the issues of community cohesion, community engagement, race and faith, volunteering and civil renewal in England and Wales. The dataset includes a total sample of 14,095 people aged 16 and over. This comprised a core sample of 9,336 people and a minority ethnic boost of 4,759. The Citizenship Survey is a complex sample survey design with stratification and clustering. On the other hand, the Millennium Cohort Study (MCS) is a birth cohort study focusing on children born in 2000 and 2001. The rationale for the study is that understanding the social conditions surrounding birth and early childhood is increasingly appreciated as fundamental to the study of the whole of the life course. The sample population for the study was drawn from all live births in the UK over 12 months from 1 September 2000 in England and Wales and 1 December 2000 in Scotland and Northern Ireland. The sample was selected from a random sample of electoral wards, disproportionately stratified to ensure adequate representation of all four UK countries, deprived areas and areas with high concentrations of Black and Asian families. The first sweep of data were collected when children were aged 9 months, and a second sweep when the children reached 3 years. The data used here were the third sweep, collected from early 2006 to early 2007 as the children were starting primary school.

The National Survey of Sexual Attitudes and Lifestyles II, 2000–2001 (NATSAL II) had as its main objectives to: provide a detailed understanding of patterns of sexual behaviour in Britain (including for example, numbers of sexual partners, frequency of different sexual practices, and gay (homosexual) experience); provide data for HIV/AIDS projections in Britain; assess whether there have been changes in behaviour since 1990–1991; and measure the prevalence of *chlamydia* infection via urine samples. A boost sample of people from four ethnic minority groups – Black Caribbean, Black African, Indian and Pakistani – was included. Unfortunately, the ethnic group variable in the dataset only gave 'Black', and so Black Africans could not be distinguished from Black Caribbeans. Black Africans were therefore identified as people whose ethnicity was given as 'Black' and who were born in Africa. Of course, a major limitation of the data is therefore that information on Black Africans born in the UK and the rest of the world could not be extracted. Nevertheless, the information on African languages spoken was quite detailed, and we were able to exploit that data.

All of these datasets suffer from a number of problems inherent in the data. The census may suffer from variation in participation rates according to country of birth. Census under-enumeration is highest among inner-city populations, irregular migrants, those with low literacy and those who do not speak English. Another problem is that all sources except the census are based on a sample and are therefore prone to sampling errors. These errors get larger as the sample size gets smaller. For these reasons, sample sizes are given to enable the reader to gauge the likely accuracy of the figures. There are also likely to be non-sampling errors, caused by potential respondents declining to take part in the survey or answering questions inaccurately. Unfortunately, survey response rates tend to be lower for minority groups. For these reasons, data should be treated as estimates rather than definitive figures. Nevertheless, the conclusion of our exploratory analysis of these data sources was that they can provide insights into the socio-economic circumstances of Black Africans.

Black African Immigration

An overwhelming proportion of adults are relatively recent migrants. According to the 2001 Census, over 80% of Black African adults were born outside the UK.

Table 9.1 clearly illustrates how many Black Africans have come to the UK in the last decade. Based on the 2001 Census and experimental statistics, it has been

Table 9.1 Country of birth of Black Africans by year of arrival in UK

Country of birth	2001–2005 (%)	1996–2000 (%)	1991–1995 (%)	1986–1990 (%)	1985 or earlier (%)	Total (%)	*Sample size (unweighted base)*
West Africa							
Nigeria	30.6	21.5	12.8	16.1	16.6	100	*537*
Ghana	33.4	15.2	10.4	12.4	26.9	100	*354*
Sierra Leone	26.3	20.6	17.7	13.6	19.1	100	*70*
Central Africa							
DR Congo	48.1	11.6	33.7	6.6		100	*50*
Other Central Africa[a]	60.6	24.1	7.4	5.4	2.4	100	*62*
East Africa							
Kenya	28.3	29.8	23.9	5.6	12.3	100	*81*
Northeastern Africa							
Somalia	42.4	35.8	13.7	7.1	1.0	100	*407*
Southern African							
Zimbabwe	58.8	27.0	7.7	1.2	4.3	100	*251*
Other Southern Africa[b]	58.9	16.6	8.2	2.9	12.8	100	*158*
Black African, born outside UK or sub-Saharan Africa	51.6	17.1	12.6	6.3	9.2	100	*207*

Sources: Labour Force Survey Q2 2005, Q3 2006 and Q4 2007, authors' calculations.
[a]Other Central Africa countries are: Angola, Burundi, Cameroon, Chad, Rwanda, Sao Tome and Principe, and Central African Republic.
[b]Other Southern African countries are: Botswana, Malawi, South Africa, Zambia, Lesotho, Swaziland, and Mauritius.

found that more than a third of the estimated growth of the Black African group in 2001–2003 was attributable to inflows of asylum seekers rather than natural growth (Large and Ghosh, 2006). As can be seen from Table 9.1, the most established Black African communities are from Sierra Leone, Nigeria and Ghana. However, the immigration pattern in Britain is changing from that set by the legacy of its colonial past. There has been an unprecedented increase in migrant flows from places which have no historical links with Britain, such as DR Congo.

Overall, according to the 2001 Census, migrants from Nigeria, Ghana, Somalia and Zimbabwe accounted for about 55% of Black African migrants residing in

Table 9.2 Country of birth of Black Africans in England, 2001

Country of birth	Percentage
Black African UK-born	32.7
West Africa	
Nigeria	16.4
Ghana	10.0
Sierra Leone	3.3
Other West Africa[a]	1.7
Central Africa	
DR Congo	2.0
Other Central Africa[b]	2.1
East Africa	
Uganda	3.2
Kenya	3.2
Other East Africa[c]	1.5
Northeastern Africa	
Somalia	7.9
Ethiopia	1.3
Eritrea	1.3
Sudan	1.1
Southern Africa	
Zimbabwe	3.6
South Africa	0.9
Zambia	1.0
Other Southern Africa[d]	1.0
Black African, born outside UK and sub-Saharan Africa	5.6

[a]In this table, as well as in all the tables based on the 2001 Census in this chapter, 'Other West Africa' refers to Benin, Burkina Faso, Cape Verde, Gambia, Guinea, Guinea-Bissau, Liberia, Mali, Mauritania, Niger, Senegal, Togo, Ivory Coast and Africa – West (unspecified).
[b]'Other Central Africa' refers to Angola, Burundi, Cameroon, Central African Republic, Chad, Equatorial Guinea, Gabon, Rwanda, and Sao Tome and Principe.
[c]'Other East Africa' refers to Tanzania and Africa – East (unspecified).
[d]'Other Southern Africa' refers to Botswana, Lesotho, Malawi, Mauritius, Mozambique, Namibia, and Swaziland.
Source: 2001 Census, CAMS © Crown copyright, authors' calculations.

England. However, Table 9.2, which shows the composition of the Black African population in the UK by country of birth, demonstrates that there is also a wide range of countries of birth of Black Africans. Changing admission policies and perceptions of these policies by potential migrants can strongly influence migration flows. It is possible that those seeking asylum now look for a wider selection of countries as some are perceived as easier to gain entry to (Okitikpi and Aymer, 2000). In addition, with increasing restrictions on entry to European countries, asylum seekers are becoming more dependent on human smugglers or traffickers, and have little choice of destination (Bloch, 2000). Family circumstances, cultural connections and the actions of a variety of institutions can produce scenarios in which there is no alternative to the actual destination arrived at (Day and White, 2002). In other words, those wanting to leave are forced to move to particular destinations.

The newest populations in Britain are from DR Congo, Zimbabwe and other countries in Central Africa and Southern Africa. Appreciation of the diversity of countries of birth of the Black African population is important for policy makers because people from different African countries face different barriers on arriving in the UK. As Koser (2003) argues, there should be a departure from the dominant African diaspora discourse, towards a plurality of African diasporas.

There can be widely differing characteristics even within groups of the same ethnic or national origin. For example, there are significant divisions of ethnicity, religion and region within Nigerians in the diaspora, so it is perhaps misleading to speak of the 'Nigerian community'. Styan found the relationship between London's Francophone populations to be tenuous at best (2003). Furthermore, rather than national identity, clanship is an active force for Somalis, although it is weaker among younger Somalis (Griffiths, 2000; Walters and Freda, 1999). Violence mirroring international conflicts, albeit infrequent, does occur within the Somali 'community' (Pillai et al., 2007). Clan dynamics have resulted in failings in representation, service provision and the funding provision of Somali community organisations (Hopkins, 2006). For example, some of Atubo and Batterbury's (2001) respondents were suspicious of the services offered by the local Somali advice centre as they felt that advice was biased and determined by clan membership.

Overall, the term 'ethnic minority' is a sweeping term embracing long-term migrants, the second and later generations, recently arrived migrants, and also people who initially settled in the UK as refugees. An assessment of the needs of different communities is required. For example, because of their different profile, new migrants present different challenges to public services than more established ethnic minority groups: the educational needs of migrant children may be different to those of second generation children. These observations underscore the point that simple ethnicity-focused approaches to understanding and engaging various minority communities in Britain, as taken in many models and policies within conventional multiculturalism, are inadequate and often inappropriate for dealing with migrants' needs or understanding their dynamics of inclusion or exclusion.

Demographic Characteristics

Age

Figure 9.1 shows the breakdown of Black Africans in England by age group. The age structure of the Black African population is youthful, as one would expect from a recent immigrant community, since it is often young adults of child-bearing age who leave their country. The Black African population in general is different from the White British population (Fig. 9.1) in there being fewer people over 45. The Black Africans born in the UK are concentrated in the under 16 years age bands. The proportion of older people is very low.

Current child migrants are predominantly from Somalia, Nigeria, Ghana, Kenya and regions outside the UK and sub-Saharan Africa. The age structure of the population from southern Africa is different in having a low proportion of child migrants, illustrating the dissimilar migratory profile of people from different African countries. This is linked to main periods of migration from each country, so the proportions over 45 are significantly lower for the relatively newer arrivals, especially those from DR Congo, Zambia, Somalia and Zimbabwe (Fig. 9.2).

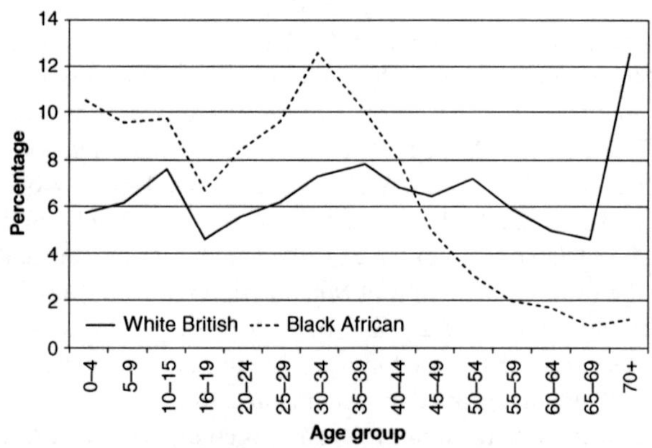

Fig. 9.1 Age group by ethnicity, White British and Black African, England (Source: 2001 Census, CAMS © Crown copyright, authors' calculations)

Gender

Women have different migration and integration experiences from men, facing differing social expectations from within their own community and from the host society (Spencer and Cooper, 2006). The patterns surrounding immigrants' country of origin, channels of migration, employment, legal status and rights tend to have highly gendered patterns. The migration experience can alter gender roles too:

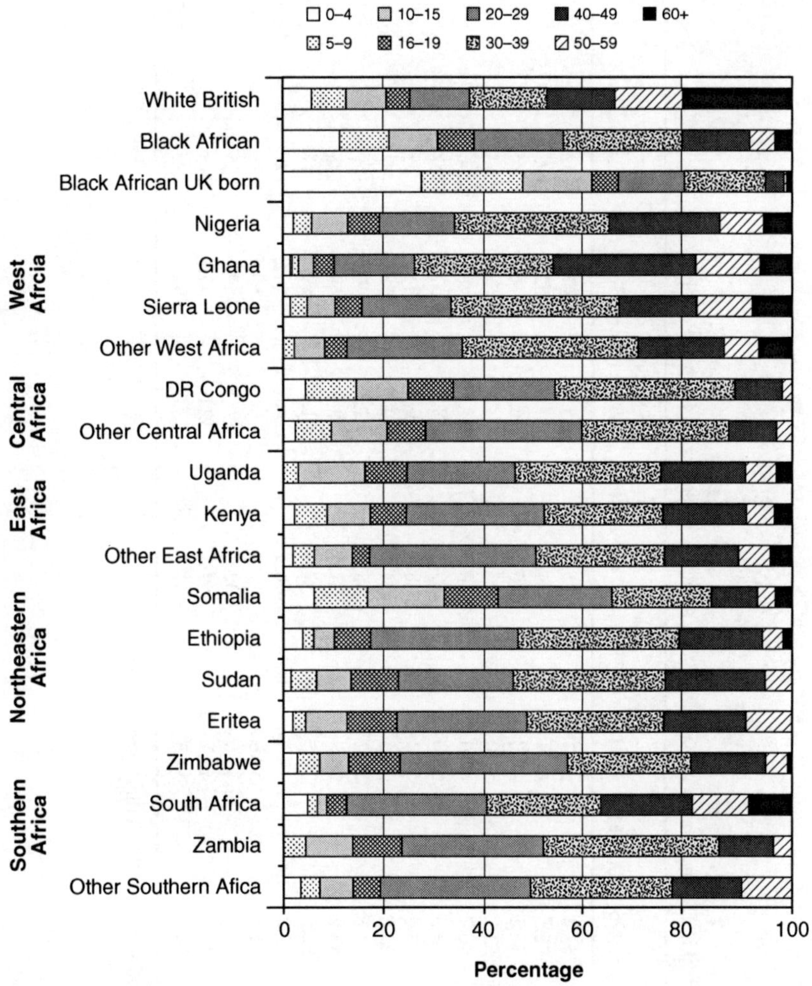

Fig. 9.2 Black Africans by age group and country of birth (Source: 2001 Census, CAMS © Crown copyright, authors' calculations)

it can provide women with greater opportunities for autonomy through employment, but can also lead to social isolation for women where there is little community support.

The traditional emigration scenario was individual migration, primarily involving men looking for work, or escaping from persecution, followed gradually over time by family reunification migration, primarily involving women and children. However, among Black Africans there is a striking pattern of migration by women (Table 9.3). The traditional male-dominated pattern of migration within and from Africa is increasingly becoming feminized from some countries of origin. For instance, there is a relatively large representation of female migrants from Ghana,

Table 9.3 Year of arrival in UK by country of birth for Black Africans, by sex, within country of birth

Country of birth		2001–2005 (%)	1996–2000 (%)	1991–1995 (%)	1986–1990 (%)	1985 or earlier (%)	Total (%)	*Sample size (unweighted base)*
Ghana	Male	50.8	53.4	37.3	45.6	45.4	47.7	*162*
	Female	49.2	46.6	62.7	54.4	54.6	52.3	*192*
Kenya	Male	54.4	46.8	43.0	26.5	46.2	46.8	*36*
	Female	45.6	53.2	57.0	73.5	53.8	53.2	*45*
Nigeria	Male	52.5	46.7	42.0	40.7	51.5	48.0	*250*
	Female	47.5	53.3	58.0	59.3	48.5	52.0	*287*
Sierra Leone	Male	40.4	30.4	64.4	28.8	40.5	41.2	*29*
	Female	59.6	69.6	35.6	71.2	59.5	58.8	*41*
Somalia	Male	42.1	41.8	26.2	48.4	61.2	40.5	*159*
	Female	57.9	58.2	73.8	51.6	38.8	59.5	*248*
Uganda	Male	51.7	32.8	20.5	53.8	81.4	49.8	*44*
	Female	48.3	67.2	79.5	46.2	18.6	50.2	*49*
DR Congo	Male	56.0	31.5	59.0			50.4	*25*
	Female	44.0	68.5	41.0	100.0		49.6	*25*
Zimbabwe	Male	49.6	45.7	45.7	68.3	32.0	47.8	*118*
	Female	50.4	54.3	54.3	31.7	68.0	52.2	*133*

Sources: Labour Force Survey Q2 2005, Q3 2006 and Q4 2007, authors' calculations.

breaking the usual pattern of men in their twenties and thirties migrating, and economic motives for migration appear stronger for Ghanaian women than family-related motives (Eurostat, 2000). In some African countries, the relatively minor role of Islam and the importance attached to economic independence of women contribute to economically driven migration by women. In addition, as care work and nursing, which recruit heavily overseas, are female dominated, women have formed an important part of labour migration. According to the 2001 Census microdata, more than 20% of Black Africans from Zimbabwe are doctors or nurses.

Table 9.3 also shows that there is considerable variation by gender among different Black African groups. The proportion of women arriving in the last 10 years is high from Zimbabwe, Somalia and Sierra Leone. It could be that a portion of these women is made up of migrants who have moved independently, rather than joining a husband or other family members. On the other hand, a high proportion of recent migrants from DR Congo are male. The table illustrates 'cohort' effects by gender. For example, prior to the late 1980s, there was a higher proportion of Somali men coming to the UK, whereas since the early 1990s, women have dominated.

Black African Household and Family Structures

The household and family structures of the Black African diaspora are varied and complex. Migration circumstances can lead to the separation of close family members from one another. Elam et al. found complicated circumstances in the UK such as partners giving financial support to each other while living in separate countries, and some households containing distant relatives and long-term visitors (2001). There are notable differences in the marital status and family type of Black Africans born in different countries. According to 2001 Census data, the proportion of widows and widowers is especially high among Somalis, Ugandans, South Africans and Sierra Leoneans in England. Given the youthful profile of these subgroups in England, it is possible that their spouses were killed in conflicts overseas. It is difficult to interpret the high figures on those who are separated, as in surveys this question may have been understood by some respondents as a temporary separation due to force of circumstances, to earn and save before returning to the country of origin, or awaiting family reunification, rather than a separation because of relationship breakdown. Reported separation in the 2001 Census is highest among Congolese (14.1%), Sierra Leoneans (11.3%) and Somalis (10.7%). This compares with a figure of 2.3% for White British people.

Overall, there is a lower level of cohabitation among Black Africans than White British people. Cohabitation is highest for Sierra Leoneans and Zimbabweans, and lowest among Ethiopians, Sudanese and Nigerians. This may be due to social and religious pressures on couples to marry. Divorce rates are higher than for White British people among Ghanaians, South Africans, Black Africans born outside the UK and sub-Saharan Africa and Nigerians. The high rate of single living among UK-born Black Africans is because of their young average age. Black Africans tend to have larger families than White British people. This is most striking for Somalis, 24% of whom are in families with four or more dependent children according to

2001 Census data. Congolese and Sudanese also have relatively large numbers of children. In contrast, migrants from Zimbabwe and southern Africa have the smallest families.

The 2001 Census microdata shows that there are relatively high numbers of Black African households headed by a female lone parent (18.1%) compared to White British households (7.3%) although this proportion is lower than for Black Caribbeans (23.4%). There is a particularly high proportion of lone parents among Somalis; they have the highest rate of lone parenthood among all the ethnic groups reported on here (35.3%). It might be expected that an overwhelmingly Muslim community, such as Somalis, would have rather low rates of lone parenthood, like Bangladeshis and Pakistanis. It could be that Somali families have been split up in the process of fleeing conflict. Rates of lone parenthood are also particularly high among Ugandans, Eritreans, Congolese and Black Africans born in the UK. In the case of Black Caribbeans, the high rate of lone parenthood has been explained by West Indian traditions, such as 'visiting partner' relationships. Among Black Africans, the often informal nature of marriage may be an influencing factor.

Expressions of National and Ethnic Identity

National and ethnic identity can influence the process of resettlement into a host society and so can be used as a measure of integration, because becoming a resident of a different country creates conditions that can lead to changes in identity. Some may greatly reduce their identification with their original ethnic or national identities, particularly if they intend to make the host country their permanent home. However, when national labels are attached by others, they can then influence self-concept, strengthening an affinity with the home country. On the other hand, others see their stay abroad as temporary and have little interest in identifying with the local population. For some, the experience of being a minority ethnic group in the UK actually leads them to assert their African or national identity (Elam et al., 2001) and thereby plays a role in promoting transnational movements.

Around 91% of those Black African adults born in the UK identify as British, according to the LFS. This is very different from the national identity of those Black Africans born outside the UK, as can be seen in Fig. 9.3 which shows a wide variation in the extent of British identity according to country of birth, with Kenyans, Nigerians and Ugandans identifying most strongly as British, although it is difficult to see historical reasons which might explain this pattern. Zimbabweans and other Black Africans from southern Africa have a low level of British identity, which may reflect their relatively recent arrival and possibly the intention to stay in the UK temporarily before returning to Africa. However, a drawback of this LFS data is that they do not allow us to gauge how many people have dual identities, such as British-Ghanaian, as this is not an option in the survey questionnaire.

There are generational differences in identity (Fig. 9.4). Younger generations have a greater affinity with mainstream London culture and many feel they have

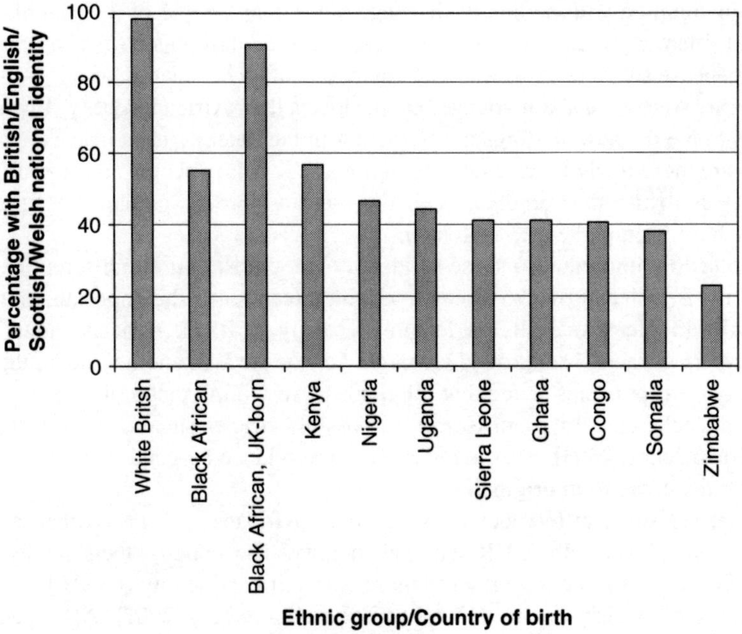

Fig. 9.3 British national identity by ethnic group/country of birth (Sources: Labour Force Survey Q2 2005, Q3 2006 and Q4 2007, authors' calculations)

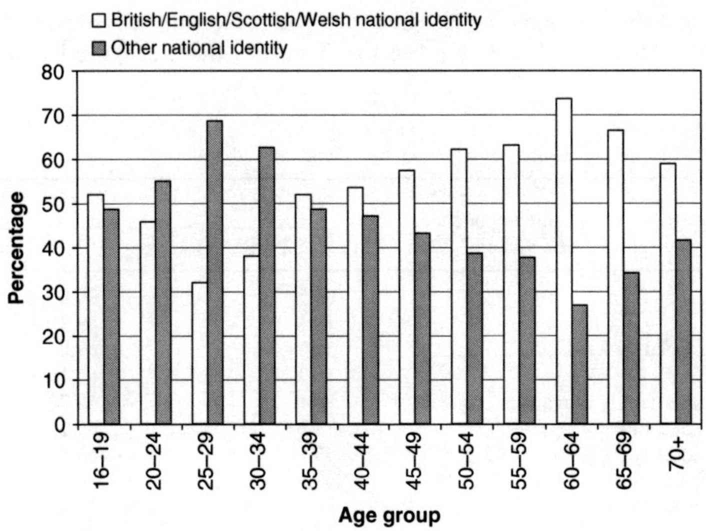

Fig. 9.4 National identity of Black Africans by age (Sources: Labour Force Survey Q2 2005, Q3 2006 and Q4 2007, authors' calculations)

more in common with people of their age rather than people of their ethnic background (Elam et al., 2001). There have been reports of younger Africans changing their names to sound more Western and there is conflict between generations as older people are concerned about younger people losing their African identity (Elam et al., 2001). Some of these findings are borne out in the data, perhaps because younger adults are more likely to have been born in the UK. Older people are more likely to identify as British than adults in their twenties and thirties, perhaps because older people have been in the UK for longer.

The factors important to sense of identity are almost entirely different between the White British and Black Africans, with the exception of the importance attached to family (Table 9.4). Religion features strongly in Black Africans' identity, as does ethnic or racial background, as might be expected. In another study, the large majority of respondents stated that religion was very important to their identity; for Muslims, adherence to Islam is seen as possibly stricter since coming to the UK (Khan and Jones, 2003). This is followed in importance by gender and the country their family came from originally.

There are some differences between Black Africans with an African national identity and those with a UK national identity. The country their family came from originally is more important to those with African identity (65.9%) compared with those of British identity (54.8%) (Citizenship Survey, 2007). Also, gender is more important to those with African identity (70.5%) compared to those of British identity (61.1%). Family is more important to those with African identity. Perhaps surprisingly, according to the Citizenship Survey, a large majority of those of Black African ethnicity feel a strong sense of belonging to Britain (Table 9.5). In 2007, 91.2% of those who reported Black African ethnicity replied to the question 'To what extent do you agree or disagree that you personally feel a part of British society?' with either 'Strongly agree' or 'Tend to agree', a figure similar to the

Table 9.4 Percentage of ethnic group answering 'Very important' to question 'What is the importance of . . . to your sense of who you are?', England and Wales

Survey question: What is the importance of . . . to your sense of who you are? (%)	Ethnic group	
	White British (%)	Black African (%)
Family	88.5	90.8
Religion	18.1	69.9
Ethnic or racial background	31.0	67.8
Gender	45.9	65.1
Country your family came from originally	38.1	62.7
Level of education	33.2	61.2
National identity	45.5	60.5
Occupation	40.1	54.9
Age and life stage	29.1	51.6
Interests	42.3	50.0
Level of income	28.4	46.7
Where you live	28.1	38.8
Social class	15.5	30.9

Source: Citizenship Survey, 2007, authors' calculations.

Table 9.5 Percentage answering question 'How strongly do you belong to Britain?', by ethnic group

	How strongly do you belong to Britain?				
Ethnic group	Very strongly (%)	Fairly strongly (%)	Not very strongly (%)	Not at all strongly (%)	*Sample size (unweighted base)*
White British	46.3	38.4	12.6	2.7	*8,004*
Black African	38.0	46.0	13.3	2.7	*808*

Source: Citizenship Survey, 2007, authors' calculations.

response of White British people. Around 84.0% said that they 'Very strongly' or 'Fairly strongly' belonged to Britain, again a figure similar to the response of White British people. What this survey data does not tell us, however, is the different meanings for people of 'belonging to Britain' (Hickman et al., 2008).

Hickman et al. (2008) explored in detailed interviews the complex meaning of belonging to Britain. They found that, in most cases, majority ethnic long-term residents found a question about the meaning they attached to belonging to Britain hard to answer. Some of their interviewees had never questioned their belonging to Britain. Minority ethnic groups tended to be more openly appreciative of belonging to Britain because of the opportunities available, the existence of the welfare state, and the legal system. New arrivals in particular were grateful for the opportunities provided by living in Britain, as well as viewing Britain as a place of security and fairness. At the same time, 37.8% of Black Africans 'Strongly agree' that it is possible to fully belong to Britain and yet maintain a separate religious or cultural identity (compared to 16.6% of White British people). This feeling does not differ by UK or non-UK national identity or by length of time spent in the UK. These responses suggest that a proportion of Black Africans believe they can integrate without sacrificing their religious or cultural identity, and are confirmed by the findings of Hickman et al. that it is possible to have diasporic ties without this being at the expense of belonging to Britain (2008).

There is a significant difference between the proportions feeling 'Very strongly' about belonging to the neighbourhood and belonging to Britain according to length of time in the UK. Those who have been in the UK longer reported a higher level of belonging, suggesting greater integration. In terms of a breakdown by national identity (British versus other national identity), there is no significant difference in very strong feelings among Black Africans with different national identities about belonging to Britain, or their neighbourhood.

Diversity of Language

Language is an important aspect of integration because disparities in occupational achievement by ethnic group are related to fluency in English (Dustmann and Fabbri, 2003; Shields and Wheatley Price, 2002). Employers may reject refugees as employees because of their level of English, or place them in lower skilled positions than their experience merits (Hurstfield et al., 2004). Lack of language can restrict economic opportunities to a local enclave. The image of Britain as hosting uniquely Anglophone Africans ceased to be true in the 1990s (Styan, 2003). For example, Francophone Congolese, Ivoirians, Togolese, and Rwandese have become established in London. A detailed indication of the increasingly diversified nature of African communities is provided by *Multilingual Capital* (Baker and Eversley, 2000), a survey of the languages spoken by London's schoolchildren.

Table 9.6 shows how frequently there were language difficulties in carrying out the interview for the National Survey of Sexual Attitudes and Lifestyles II, 2000–2001 (NATSAL II), which indicates the only moderate levels of fluency of some Black Africans, especially from Central/East Africa.

A substantial number of Black Africans speak a language other than English in their homes, although there is high variation by country of birth (Fig. 9.5). A relatively high proportion of British-born Black Africans speaking English at home, which may suggest that the second generation is becoming more integrated. Few Somalis speak English at home. On the other hand, a high proportion of those born in Nigeria, though by no means all, speak English at home. Millennium Cohort Study data from 2006 shows that many parents are not passing on their African languages to their children; in 36.5% of cases where a parent speaks a language other than English, the child does not. However, other evidence suggests that many African adults in the UK are concerned that their children will become linguistically distanced from their 'homeland' (Koser, 2003).

Somalis are particularly linguistically isolated. One study found that about 30% of Somalis could either only 'slightly write' or 'not at all write' in their main language, and about the same proportion could only 'slightly read' or 'not read at all' in their main language (Kirk, 2004). This may be because Somali only became a written language in the 1970s. Young Somalis in the UK on the other hand, often lose their ability to read in the Somali language and others born away from Somalia may never learn to read it (Olden, 1999). In some areas, the inter-generational language shift from Somali to English has been to such an extent that it has led to

Table 9.6 Difficulties with NATSAL II interview for Black Africans because of language problems by ethnic group, Great Britain

	Country of birth	
	Black African – central/east Africa	Black African – west Africa
Yes, severe (%)	1.4	1.1
Yes, some (%)	25.4	14.4
No problem (%)	73.1	84.5
Total (%)	100	100
Sample size (unweighted base)	*109*	*161*

Source: NATSAL II, 2000–2001.

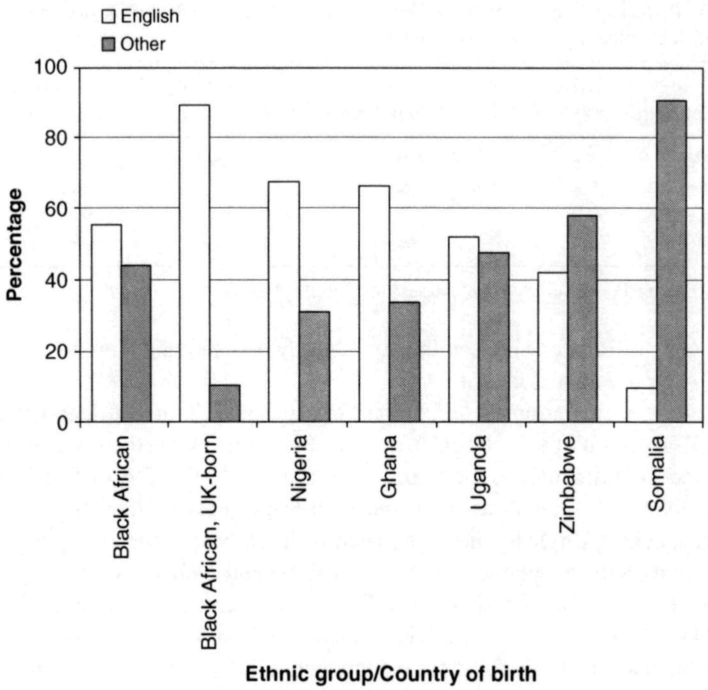

Fig. 9.5 Ethnic group of Black Africans aged 16+ by first language at home (Sources: Labour Force Survey, June–August 2003 and Q3 2006)

the establishment of Somali literacy classes to help promote the language among young Somalis (Arthur, 2004). Researchers have also found that there is a difference between Somali men and women in their level of spoken English (Bloch, 2002). Other studies have also found language to be a significant problem among Somalis, with women being far more likely than men to have language problems, and that Somalis who have arrived in the UK are likely to have language problems at an earlier age than other groups whose first language is not English (Khan and Jones, 2003). On the other hand, Hickman et al. (2008) found strategies of social cohesion among Somalis, driven by the commitment of parents to ensuring that their children learned English even where they themselves had poor or minimal English. They were concerned that their children should be literate and do well educationally.

Black Africans aged 25–34 are the adults most likely to speak African languages, probably because they tend to be the most recent migrants. Contrary to what one might expect, language spoken at home is unrelated to the length of time spent in the UK (Table 9.7). For Ghanaians, those who arrived from Ghana most recently have a greater tendency to speak English at home relative to more established migrants. For Nigerians and Zimbabweans, the length of time in the UK barely makes an impact on whether they use English at home. Finally, nearly all Somalis who have arrived subsequent to 2000 speak Somali at home, but there is a pattern of English being spoken at home by those more established in Britain. Perhaps surprisingly, there

Table 9.7 Percentage within country of birth of Black Africans who speak first language other than English at home, by year came to the UK

Country of birth	Arrived before 2000	*Sample size (unweighted base)*	Arrived 2000 or after	*Sample size (unweighted base)*
Ghana (%)	35.6	*146*	25.1	*46*
Nigeria (%)	29.6	*184*	31.9	*66*
Zimbabwe (%)	57.9	*38*	58.3	*93*
Somalia (%)	87.4	*109*	100.0	*45*

Sources: Labour Force Survey June–August 2003 and Q3 2006.

is no notable difference between those with a British national identity versus those with an African national identity.

Of course, a limitation of this home language data is that it does not indicate how well a person speaks English outside the home. Indeed, some respondents may in fact be bilingual. In the Citizenship Survey 2007, 63% of Black Africans who do not speak English as their main language reported that they were 'Very good' at speaking English when they need to in daily life, for example, to have a conversation on the telephone or talk to a professional such as a teacher or a doctor. A further 30% reported that they were 'Fairly good' at speaking English. In a study of 118 Ugandans' use of health services, each interviewer spoke English and several African languages. However, most respondents chose to conduct the interview in English, indicating a good level of fluency in English (Mcmunn et al., 1998). Further evidence of this bilingualism among some Africans is Kirk's survey of refugees, which found that although English is the official language in Zimbabwe, only 6% of her respondents considered it to be their main language – the majority of the remainder stated their main language to be either Shona (58%) or Ndebele (35%) (2004). Nevertheless, all but one considered themselves to be fluent in all aspects of the English language. One of the major factors in the comparatively good labour market outcomes for Zimbabweans is their high levels of fluency in English (Bloch, 2006). As might be expected, Somalis were the group most likely to have experienced problems in their education due to their lack of English. The community with the next largest proportion having language barriers is Ghanaians (Table 9.8).

Table 9.8 Percentage of Black Africans aged 16+ with first language at home other than English by language difficulty in education or finding or keeping a job, UK

	Language difficulty in . . .		
Country of birth	. . . Education (%)	. . . Finding or keeping a job (%)	*Sample size (unweighted base)*
Somalia	28.0	29.2	*137*
Ghana	10.4	10.5	*65*
Zimbabwe	3.3	2.3	*77*
Nigeria	2.4	1.1	*78*

Sources: Labour Force Survey June–August 2003 and Q3 2006.

LFS data demonstrates that proficiency in English is related to level of education. Around 30% of Black Africans who completed their education before the age of 16 reported language difficulty in finding or keeping a job, compared with 8.2% of those who were in education until they were over 19. This corresponds to other researchers' findings that the higher Somali refugees' educational level is, the better their command of English is likely to be, and the more likely they are to be in work. But for many, inadequate language skills put them at a severe disadvantage in the jobs market (Bloch, 2002). In summary, on language indicators, Somalis are by far the least integrated of the countries of origin studied here, followed by Ghanaians. On the other hand, Zimbabweans and Nigerians face only slight language barriers. Black Africans with higher levels of education are the most integrated on language indicators.

Employment

Employment forms a key aspect of integration policies. It is a factor influencing many issues, including economic independence, planning for the future, self-esteem and the opportunity to develop language skills. It can offer the chance to make social contacts with people from the UK. The data presented here paint a complex picture of Black African employment disadvantage. We conclude that a carefully-nuanced set of policy responses is required to meet the different problems and needs of groups from different countries of birth.

Britain's ethnic minorities face two major difficulties in the labour market. The first problem is unemployment and the second problem is those in employment tend to have lower earnings compared with similar White individuals. In this chapter we consider employment and unemployment because it can be argued that unemployment is a more serious social problem than low earnings, as earnings discrimination is easier to challenge than discrimination at the job search stage (Leslie et al., 1998). As in Blackaby et al. (1997), we justify using the employment differential on the basis that lack of jobs may ultimately be more socially damaging than an earnings differential.

The rates of unemployment vary by Black African sub-group, but are higher in all cases than for White British people (Table 9.9). Factors affecting labour market participation include: racial discrimination, age, gender, education, English language skills, lack of recognition of foreign qualifications, social networks, childcare responsibilities, length of residence and date of arrival, motivation for migrating (voluntary or involuntary), geographical mobility, health, legal status, experience in the UK labour market, length of time out of the labour market and employer attitudes.

Researchers have found that Black Africans also have high unemployment among their younger generations (Simpson et al., 2006). Berthoud (2000) found the male unemployment rate among Black African school leavers to be very high, and concluded that it is possible that some of the disadvantage experienced by men from ethnic minorities in their twenties can be explained by the difficulties they had

Table 9.9 Economic activity by ethnic group/country of birth, individuals aged 16–74 (excluding full-time students), England

	Employee (%)	Self-employed (%)	Unemployed (%)	Inactive (%)
Males				
White British	57.7	12.2	4.4	25.6
Black African	50.2	7.9	12.3	29.6
Black African UK-born	51.8	7.3	12.9	28.0
DR Congo	23.5	4.7	21.2	50.6
Ghana	64.0	7.5	7.2	21.3
Nigeria	53.2	14.0	8.0	24.8
Somalia	20.3	2.2	24.9	52.6
Zimbabwe	51.4	1.6	4.9	42.2
Females				
White British	52.7	4.3	2.3	40.7
Black African	46.5	2.2	9.8	41.5
Black African UK-born	57.0	1.9	8.4	32.7
DR Congo	15.0	0.0	20.0	65.0
Ghana	56.2	2.0	9.1	32.8
Nigeria	53.4	3.8	8.6	34.2
Somalia	6.4	0.7	11.6	81.3
Zimbabwe	55.5	1.1	8.5	34.9

Source: 2001 Census, CAMS © Crown copyright, authors' calculations.

in finding work after leaving school. Somalis have extremely high levels of inactivity, especially among women. The most common reason for this is home and family responsibilities, which applies to 40% of Somali women, probably due to the high number of lone parents. The low employment of Somalis may be linked to being refugees. Also, the proportion of Somali women who were not working previously is especially high, which might be a reflection of their Muslim culture (Kirk, 2004). Very little is known about the labour market position of refugees compared with minority ethnic groups as a whole, although the limited data show lower levels of employment among refugees (29%) than minority ethnic groups (60%) and the greater propensity of refugees, if working, to be underemployed and clustered in a few sectors with low pay and poor employment prospects (Bloch, 2002).

The other groups with high rates of inactivity are, for both males and females, Congolese and Sudanese. Data from the LFS show that most of the Black African men of working age who are inactive are students. The exception is Black Africans from outside the UK or sub-Saharan Africa who have high levels of long-term sickness or disability. Nigerians and Ghanaians experience lower unemployment levels than the average for Black Africans, and relatively high rates of self-employment. This broad pattern of different outcomes by different countries of origin is confirmed by other research; Bloch (2002) found Zimbabweans have higher average rates of employment than other refugee groups. Kirk (2004) found a difference between

Somali and Zimbabwean refugees in their occupational status prior to coming to the UK, which might affect their employability on arrival: Zimbabweans were far more likely than Somalis to have been in work prior to arrival in the UK.

Conclusion

This chapter has brought together quantitative survey data which demonstrates the contrasting characteristics and circumstances of Black Africans from different countries of birth. Using evidence on age and gender, family and household structures we have shown that the Black African community in England is indeed highly diverse. The data on national identity, use of English employment and, point to a diversity of integration experiences. In particular, Somali migrants are highly marginalised in British society, suffering from, for example, high levels of lone parenthood, a possible Islamic penalty in employment, and difficulties with the English language. Migrants from DR Congo are also highly disadvantaged. This contrasts with, for example, Zimbabweans, who, on the whole, do not face language barriers to integration even if English is not their first language at home. However, they are less likely than other Black Africans to say that they feel of British national identity, which might suggest that they see their stay in the UK as temporary. Nigerians, on the other hand, speak English at home to a greater extent and their labour market outcomes are closer to the white British average. UK-born Black Africans have lower unemployment rates than the average for Black Africans, which suggests the second generation is finding it easier to integrate.

A fuller account of integration experiences would explore many other possible indicators of integration, such as qualifications achieved, residential segregation, social interaction with other ethnic groups, health indicators and rates of victimisation to crime. Nevertheless, this selection of findings suggests that in devising integration policy close attention must be paid to the complexity of support needs of Black African migrants from different countries.

Acknowledgements The financial support of the ESRC for the research on which this chapter is based is gratefully acknowledged (grant RES-163-25-0040). The support of the Office for National Statistics, CCSR and ESRC/JISC Census of Population Programme is gratefully acknowledged. The authors alone are responsible for the interpretation of the data. Census output is Crown copyright and is reproduced with the permission of the Controller of HMSO and the Queen's Printer for Scotland.

The Labour Force Survey Office was carried out by the Office for National Statistics and the Northern Ireland Statistics and Research Agency, and was made available through the UK Data Archive, University of Essex, Colchester. The Citizenship Survey 2007 was carried out by Communities and Local Government and the National Centre for Social Research and made available through the UK Data Archive, University of Essex, Colchester. The National Survey of Sexual Attitudes and Lifestyles II (NATSAL II), 2000–2001 is copyright of the National Centre for Social Research and A. Johnson, K. Fenton, A. Copas, C. Mercer, A. McCadden, C. Carder, G. Ridgway, K. Wellings, W. Macdowall and K. Nanchahal and was made available through the UK Data Archive, University of Essex, Colchester. The Millennium Cohort Study, Third Survey, 2006, is copyright of the University of London, Centre for Longitudinal Studies and was made available through the UK Data Archive, University of Essex, Colchester.

Crown copyright material is reproduced with the permission of the Controller of HMSO and the Queen's Printer for Scotland. The original data creators, depositors, copyright holders, and the funders of the surveys, and the UK Data Archive, bear no responsibility for their further analysis or interpretation here.

References

Ager, A. and Strang, A. (2004) *Indicators of Integration: Final Report, Development and Practice Report 28*, Home Office, London.

Arthur, J. (2004) Language at the margins: The case of Somali in Liverpool. *Language Problems and Language Planning*, 28(3): 217–240.

Aspinall, P.J. and Chinouya, M. (2008) Is the standardised term 'Black African' useful in demographic and health research in the United Kingdom? *Ethnicity & Health*, 13(3): 182–202.

Atubo, M. and Batterbury, S. (2001) *Coping with Environmental Change: The Experience of Somali Refugee Women in a West London Housing Estate* (DESTIN Working Paper No. 01-11), London School of Economics, London.

Baker, P. and Eversley, J. (2000) *Multilingual Capital: The Languages of London's School Children and Their Relevance to Economic, Social and Educational Policies*. Battlebridge Publications, London.

Berthoud, R. (2000) Ethnic employment penalties in Britain. *Journal of Ethnic and Migration Studies*, 26(3): 389–416.

Blackaby, D., Drinkwater, S., Leslie, D.G. and Murphy, P.D. (1997) A picture of male and female unemployment among Britain's ethnic minorities. *Scottish Journal of Political Economy*, 44(2): 182–197.

Bloch, A. (2000) Refugee settlement in Britain: The impact of policy on participation. *Journal of Ethnic and Migration Studies*, 26(1): 75–88.

Bloch, A. (2002) *Refugees' Opportunities and Barriers in Employment and Training* (Research Report No 179), Department for Work and Pensions, London.

Bloch, A. (2006) Emigration from Zimbabwe: Migrant perspectives. *Social Policy and Administration*, 40(1): 67–87.

Castles, S., Korac, M., Vasta, E. and Vertovec, S. (2002) *Integration: Mapping the Field*, Home Office, London.

Council of Europe (1997) *Measurement and Indicators of Integration*, Council of Europe Publishing, Strasbourg.

Day, K. and White, P. (2002) Choice or circumstance: The UK as the location of asylum applications by Bosnian and Somali refugees. *GeoJournal*, 56(1): 15–26.

Dustmann, C. and Fabbri, F. (2003) Language proficiency and labour market performance of immigrants in the UK. *The Economic Journal*, 113(489): 695–717.

Dustmann, C., Fabbri, F., Preston, I. and Wadsworth, J. (2003) *Labour Market Performance of Immigrants in the UK Labour Market* (Home Office Online Report 05/03), Home Office, London.

Elam, G. and Chinouya, M.; Joint Health Surveys Unit (2000) *Feasibility Study for Health Surveys Among Black African Populations Living in the UK: Stage 2 Diversity Among Black African Communities*. National Centre for Social Research and Joint Health Surveys Unit of University College London, London.

Elam, G., McMunn, A., Nazroo, J., Apwonyoke, M., Brookes, M., Chinouya, M., et al. (2001) *Feasibility Study for Health Surveys Among Black African People Living in England Final Report – Implications for the health survey for England 2003*. Joint Health Surveys Unit of University College London and National Centre for Social Research, London.

Eurostat (2000) *Push and Pull Factors of International Migration: A Comparative Report*. Office for Official Publications of the European Communities, Luxembourg.

Fimbo, M., Kikaka Mokala, F., Pakasa, J., Mukiendi Maguy, J., Songa, J., Motondo, A., et al. (2001) *Report of the Needs Assessment Carried out by Congolese Refugee Women's Association into the Needs of the Congolese Community People of Hackney and Newham*, Department of Health, London.

Griffiths, D.J. (2000) Fragmentation and consolidation: The contrasting cases of Somali and Kurdish refugees in London. *Journal of Refugee Studies*, 13(3): 281–302.

Harding, S. and Balarajan, R. (2000) Limiting long-term illness among Black Caribbeans, Black Africans, Indians, Pakistanis, Bangladeshis and Chinese born in the UK. *Ethnicity and Health*, 5(1): 41–46.

Hickman, M., Crowley, H. and Mai, N. (2008) *Immigration and Social Cohesion in the UK: The Rhythms and Realities of Everyday Life*, Joseph Rowntree Foundation, York.

Home Office (2004) *Integration Matters: A National Strategy for Refugee Integration* (Draft Consultation), Home Office, London.

Home Office (2008) *Asylum Statistics, United Kingdom 2007*, Home Office, Croydon.

Hopkins, G. (2006) Somali community organisations in London and Toronto: Collaboration and effectiveness. *Journal of Refugee Studies*, 21(3): 361–380.

Hurstfield, J., Pearson, R., Hooker, H., Ritchie, H. and Sinclair, A. (2004) *Employing Refugees: Some Organisations' Experiences*, Employability Forum, London.

IPPR (2007) *Britain's Immigrants: An Economic Profile*, IPPR, London.

Khan, S. and Jones, A. (2003) *Somalis in Camden: Challenges Faced by an Emerging Community*, Refugee Forum in Camden, London.

Kirk, R. (2004) *Skills Audit of Refugees*. Home Office Online Report 37/04.

Koser, K. (2003) New African diasporas: An introduction in Koser, K. (ed.), *New African Diasporas*, Routledge, London.

Large, P. and Ghosh, K. (2006) Estimates of the population by ethnic group for areas within England. *Population Trends*, 124: 6–17.

Leslie, D., Drinkwater, S. and O'Leary, N. (1998) Unemployment and earnings among Britain's ethnic minorities: Some signs for optimism. *Journal of Ethnic and Migration Studies*, 24(3): 489–506.

Mcmunn, A.M., Mwanje, R., Paine, K. and Pozniak, A.L. (1998) Health service utilization in London's African migrant communities: Implications for HIV prevention. *AIDS Care*, 10(4): 453–462.

National Statistics (2009) nomis. Office for National Statistics Official Labour Market Statistics web site. Accessed 8 May 2010.

Okitikpi, T. and Aymer, C. (2000) The price of safety: Refugee children and the challenge for social work. *Social Work in Europe*, 71(1): 51–61.

Olden, A. (1999) Somali refugees in London: Oral culture in a western information environment. *International Journal of Libraries and Information Services*, 49: 212–224.

Phillimore, J. and Goodson, L. (2008) Making a place in the global city: The relevance of indicators of integration. *Journal of Refugee Studies*, 21(3): 305–325.

Pillai, R., Kyambi, S., Nowacka, K. and Sriskandarajah, D. (2007) *The Reception and Integration of New Migrant Communities*, IPPR, London.

Rutter, J., Cooley, L., Reynolds, S. and Sheldon, R. (2008) *From Refugee to Citizen: 'Standing on my Own Two Feet'*, IPPR, London.

Shields, M.A. and Wheatley Price, S. (2002) The English language fluency and occupational success of ethnic minority immigrant men living in English metropolitan areas. *Journal of Population Economics*, 15(1): 137–160.

Simpson, L., Purdam, K., Tajar, A., Fieldhouse, E., Gavalas, V., Tranmer, M., et al. (2006) *Ethnic Minority Populations and the Labour Market: An Analysis of the 1991 and 2001 Census* (Department for Work and Pensions Research Report No 333), Corporate Document Services, London.

Spencer, S. and Cooper, B. (2006) *Social Integration of Migrants in Europe: A Review of the European Literature 2000–2006*, COMPAS, Oxford.
Styan, D. (2003) La nouvelle vague? Recent Francophone African settlement in London in Koser, K. (ed.), *New African Diasporas*, Routledge, London.
UKvisas (2008) *Entry clearance statistics financial year 2006–2007*, ukvisas, Croydon.
Walters, N. and Freda, B. (1999) *Combating Social Exclusion: Integra the Refugee Partnership Project Report: A Comparative Study of Bosnian, Kurdish Somali and Senegalese Communities in the UK, Germany, Denmark and Italy*. University of Surrey, Guildford.

Chapter 10
Ethnic Differences in Physical Activity and Obesity

Vanessa Higgins and Angela Dale

Introduction: Obesity as a Policy Issue

What is seen as desirable in terms of body shape and image has changed over time and differs between societies. However, until recent decades, very few groups in western societies enjoyed a lifestyle that allowed them to become overweight or obese. The physical demands of everyday life (heavier manual work, housework with few modern aids, limited access to cars) combined with limited availability of pre-prepared or convenience foods provided little opportunity for obesity. However, recent decades have seen a much more sedentary lifestyle for most people, an increase in leisure time and supermarkets with an abundance of tempting food products at relatively low prices. The rapid rise in obesity over a similar time period has now resulted in widespread concern over its implications for public health. Obesity has been identified as a risk factor in many health problems, including arthritis, stroke, heart disease, cancer and diabetes (Gensini et al., 1998; Jonsson et al., 2002; Kopelman, 2000; Lee et al., 1999; Stevens et al., 2004). In England, around a quarter of all adults are classified as obese (Craig and Mindell, 2008) and projections estimate that this will rise to one third by 2012 (Zaninotto et al., 2009).

There is a well established link between low levels of physical activity, poor diet and obesity (WHO, 2002, 2003; Department of Health, 2004). Over the past decade the UK Government has set recommended guidelines and a series of action plans to encourage the population to eat a healthier diet and participate in more physical activity. For example, the Department of Health's 5-a-day campaign (2000) aims to increase the consumption of fruit and vegetables, whilst the Food Standards Agency is working to reduce the consumption of salt (DH, 2000; Food Standards Agency, 2003). The UK Government has set physical activity guidelines for adults

V. Higgins (✉)
The Cathie Marsh Centre for Census and Survey Research (CCSR), School of Social Sciences, The University of Manchester, Manchester M13 9PL, UK
e-mail: vanessa.higgins@manchester.ac.uk

J. Stillwell, M. van Ham (eds.), *Ethnicity and Integration*, Understanding Population Trends and Processes 3, DOI 10.1007/978-90-481-9103-1_10,

to participate in moderate or vigorous intensity physical activity on at least 5 days a week for at least 30 min per day either in one session or through a number of shorter sessions of 10 min or longer (The Chief Medical Officer, 2004).

The importance of the imbalance between energy consumed through food and energy expended through physical activity is recognized in the UK's recent cross-government strategy, *Healthy Weight, Healthy Lives,* which identifies five areas for tackling excess weight – two of which are the promotion of healthier food choices and building physical activity into our lives (Cross-Government Obesity Unit, Department of Health, Department for Children & Schools and Families, 2008). Although ethnic differences in obesity in the UK and US are fairly well documented, the various UK Government strategies do not make any distinction by ethnic group. In this chapter we aim to examine ethnic differences in obesity and physical activity. First we review some of the literature relating to these issues.

Ethnicity and Obesity

In western countries, women of higher socio-economic status are less likely to be obese than women of lower socio-economic status (Sobal and Stunkard, 1989). However, in less affluent societies there is often a positive relationship between body weight and socio-economic status (Tovee et al., 2006) and, in some traditional, non-western societies, body fat is deemed an indicator of wealth, prosperity, femininity and sexual capacity (Ghannam, 1997; McGarvey, 1991; Nasser, 1988). Cross-cultural studies suggest that young women from culturally English backgrounds dislike body fat more than peers from Black Caribbean and Black African backgrounds (Furnham and Alibhai, 1983; Furnham and Baguma, 1994; Wardle and Marsland, 1990).

Migration to a more affluent society may result in a change of lifestyle which, in turn, may lead to increased body weight (Goel et al., 2004; Mellin-Olsen and Wandel, 2005). Jackson et al. (2007) have shown that levels of obesity among populations of African origin in Cameroon, Jamaica and the UK were higher in those who had migrated to the UK than those who live in Cameroon or Jamaica. Similarly Patel et al. (2005) have shown that British Gujeratis had higher mean body mass indexes (BMIs) than Gujeratis in India. Thus we may expect obesity levels for minority ethnic groups to be related to the time since they migrated to the UK. International migration may affect physical activity levels, although there is mixed evidence of this in the literature (Dawson et al., 2005; Hayes et al., 2002; Williams et al., 1996). Migration to the UK, and length of time since migration may also play a significant role in dietary change among ethnic minority populations with the adoption of the 'unhealthy' aspects of the British diet upon migration (Anderson and Lean, 1995; Anderson et al., 2005; Kassam Khamis et al., 1995; Landman and Cruickshank, 2001; Lawrence et al., 2007; Simmons and Williams, 1997; Wandel, 1993).

The extent of physical activity is expected to be a major influence on obesity. A number of studies have shown low levels of physical activity among ethnic minority groups within the UK, particularly South Asians (Carrington et al., 1987; Chambers et al., 2006; Dhawan and Bray, 1997; Hayes et al., 2002; Johnson, 2000; Lean et al., 2001; Pomerleau et al., 1999; Sproston and Mindell, 2006a; Williams et al., 1994). Some of these studies provide comparative information on separate South Asian groups and suggest that Bangladeshis have markedly lower levels of physical activity than other South Asian groups, while Indians have the highest levels (Hayes et al., 2002; Rudat, 1994). There may be particular barriers to physical activity among South Asian women which include dress code, modesty, lack of single sex facilities and disease perceptions (Grace et al., 2007; Scraton et al., 1999, 2005; Sriskanthatrajah and Kai, 2006). However, other factors such as racial harassment and discrimination and the relatively closed nature of some sports (e.g. golf) will affect all minority groups. Ethnic differences in the occupational structure will also affect physical activity with those groups more heavily represented in manual work more likely to be physically active.

In contrast, many minority ethnic groups have healthier eating patterns than the population as a whole or the White majority (Dowler and Calvert, 1995; Erens et al., 2001; Gibbens and Julian, 2006; Lip et al., 1995; McKeigue and Chaturvedi, 1996; McKeigue et al., 1985; Miller et al., 1988; Sharma and Cruickshank, 2001; Sharma et al., 1998; 2002; Sproston and Mindell, 2006a; Williams et al., 1994). However, diet varies with religious and cultural background and it is important to note that ethnic minority groups are not a homogenous group and that there are dietary differences within ethnic groups (Smith et al., 1995; Williams et al., 1994; Wyke and Landman, 1997). Cultural beliefs and traditions play an important role in dietary habits as culture is often expressed through food (Bush et al., 1998; Kalka, 1988; Lawrence et al., 2007; Scott, 1998). Also, for most minority ethnic groups, fruit and vegetable consumption is highest amongst the older age-groups (Sproston and Mindell, 2006a). This raises the question of whether older people retain more traditional eating patterns that may not be followed by younger generations.

Finally, unhealthy lifestyles are associated with socio-economic factors such as social class, education, deprivation and income (Marmot et al., 1991; Pill et al., 1995; Wardle and Steptoe, 2003) and this is indeed the case with obesity, diet and physical activity (Craig and Mindell, 2008; Hunt et al., 2000; Pratala et al., 2003; Shelton, 2005; Sobal and Stunkard, 1989; Sproston and Mindell, 2006a). By comparison with the majority White group, minority ethnic groups tend to have higher levels of unemployment, experience less upward social mobility; have lower incomes and are more likely to live in areas of high deprivation within the UK (Blackaby et al., 2002; Clark and Drinkwater, 2007; Modood et al., 1997; Platt, 2007). However, the extent to which ethnicity is related to obesity independently of these socio-economic characteristics is not well established (Dawson et al., 2005; Saxena et al., 2004). Similarly, little is known about the independent effects of diet and physical activity upon obesity for different ethnic groups.

We begin by providing a detailed breakdown of differences in levels of obesity and physical activity for men and women in eight major ethnic groups for a nationally representative sample of the adult population of England. We then go on to use modelling methods to ask whether additional factors related to the individual or the locality explain the differences between ethnic groups on both these outcome measures.

Data and Methods

The Health Survey for England

This research uses the Health Survey for England (HSE) to examine ethnic differences in diet, physical activity and obesity in adults. The HSE is a large-scale, nationally representative, cross-sectional survey which has been carried out annually since 1991 and is commissioned by the Health and Social Care Information Centre and conducted by the National Centre for Social Research. The 2004 survey covers adults and children living in private households and focuses on the health of ethnic minority groups. The ethnic boost increased the number of Black Caribbean, Black African, Indian, Pakistani, Bangladeshi, Chinese and Irish participants and contains approximately 10,000 ethnic minority participants (Sproston and Mindell, 2006a). The 2004 HSE has a nationally representative, multi-stage, stratified probability sampling design with three components: the core (which provides a nationally representative sample); the minority ethnic group boost sample and the Chinese special boost sample.

The survey comprises two stages: (i) an interviewer-administered questionnaire to all individuals and (ii) a nurse visit to informants from the specified minority ethnic groups. The 2004 questionnaires collected information on cardio-vascular disease and related risk factors such as physical activity, diet (fruit and vegetables, fat and salt intake), smoking, drinking and height/weight measurements to measure obesity (BMI). The nurse visit collected information such as medication, blood and saliva samples, blood pressure, waist and hip measurement. Both stages translated all materials and questionnaires into seven languages: Urdu, Punjabi, Gujarati, Hindi, Bengali, Mandarin and Cantonese. Informants who could not carry out an interview in English were provided with an interviewer who could speak the appropriate language (Sproston and Mindell, 2006a, 2006b). The physical activity questionnaire records physical activity in the previous 4 weeks and includes heavy housework, heavy manual work, continuous walks of 30 min or more and sports/exercise. The questionnaire asks about the number of times the respondent has done each type of activity in the last 4 weeks and it also collects information on occupational activity.

The 2004 HSE survey includes sections on fruit and vegetable consumption and fat intake. The questions are designed to monitor consumption in line with the ‘5-a-day’ programme – which means that information related to the ‘5-a-day’ specified portions is collected. The ‘diet’ aspect of the survey is limited in that it only presents a partial measure of diet, for example there is no information available about the consumption of sugar, fizzy drinks or carbohydrates. The fat consumption data are particularly limited for measuring the link between diet and obesity because they do not provide information on portion sizes – so there is no indication of the volumes of fat consumed. For this reason, the fat data have been excluded from the analysis reported here. However, fruit and vegetable consumption has been included in the obesity model, although it does not give an overall indication of eating habits and cannot, therefore, provide any indication of overall calorie intake.

The response rate to the survey interview achieved 66% for eligible adults (63% for the ethnic minority boost) and about 56% for weight and height (51% for the ethnic minority boost). Whilst the HSE has formed the main source of our analysis we have also held three focus groups of Pakistani and Kashmiri women in Rochdale during July 2008. A total of 10 women attended the focus groups; all were under 30, most born overseas, and all were contacted through their participation in community organisations. Analysis of the transcripts from these focus groups has been used to inform our understanding of the survey results.

Analysis Strategy

Obesity is measured by body mass index (BMI) which is an internationally recognised measurement of obesity and overweight. BMI is defined as weight (kg)/height (metres)^2 and is highly correlated with adiposity. In extreme cases, BMI may lead to misclassification, for example, athletes may be classified as obese because they have high muscle mass which weighs more than fat (International Diabetes Institute, 2002). However, the BMI measurement is generally used as an indicator of adiposity and is widely used in epidemiological studies and clinical settings. The analyses used a dichotomous variable of obese/not obese with obese defined as a BMI $\geq$ 30 kg/m. Moderate intensity physical activity includes:

- walks of 30 min or more at a fairly brisk or fast pace;
- heavy housework such as moving furniture, carrying heavy shopping or scrubbing floors for at least 30 min at a time;
- heavy gardening/DIY such as digging or bricklaying for at least 30 min at a time;
- sports and exercise that lasted 30 min or more. Activity is classified according to the type of sport/exercise and the respondent's own assessment of the effort involved; and
- occupational activity, based on the respondent's own assessment of how active they are at work combined with information on whether they work full-time or part-time and the nature of their occupation using the Standard Occupational Classification 1990 (OPCS, 1990).

A summary measure has been used which indicates whether or not the respondent has met the weekly physical activity guidelines of at least five occasions of moderate intensity activity, each lasting for at least 30 min.

The 2004 HSE sampling scheme, described above, was designed to give adequate numbers for analysis of the following minority ethnic groups: Black Caribbean,

Black African, Indian, Pakistani, Bangladeshi, Chinese and Irish. Although the general population sample contains a representative spread of all ethnic groups, only the minority groups listed here have a boosted sample size and they therefore form the focus of this analysis. Ethnic minority groups are defined as in the 2001 Census, except for the Irish who were defined as Irish if either the respondent, or their mother or father, had been born in the Republic of Ireland or Northern Ireland. Informants of mixed origin, which included one of the groups listed above, are included in that group (Sproston and Mindell, 2006a).

All analyses are performed in STATA using the SVY commands to account for the complex sample design and are weighted to account for unequal probabilities of selection and non-response. Exploratory analysis examines ethnic differences in physical activity and obesity among adults separately by sex and age within each ethnic group. Age is divided into three categories for the exploratory analysis (16–34, 35–55 and 55 years and over). The two binary outcomes of interest – meeting physical activity guidelines and obesity – are then modelled separately by gender using logistic regression. Each ethnic group is included as a dummy variable and other explanatory variables are also included. Age (in single years) and age-squared are included to control for differences between and within ethnic groups for both physical activity and obesity (see later section). A 'migrant status' variable is included because the literature, as mentioned earlier, suggests that migration may have an impact on obesity and physical activity. The migrant status variable is divided into three categories: British born, adult migrant (came to GB aged 16 or over) and child migrant (came to GB before 16 years old). Socio-economic factors may influence obesity and physical activity levels as we have also discussed earlier, so a number of socio-economic indicators are included in the models, namely highest educational qualification, economic status and equivalised household income. Disaggregation by National Statistics Socio-Economic Classification (NS-SEC) is available from the dataset but it is not significant in initial models so has been excluded from the final analysis in order to make the models more parsimonious. Current literature on obesity focuses on the influences of the built environment (for example, Cummins and Macintyre, 2006; Stafford et al., 2007; Cross-Government Obesity Unit et al., 2008; Cummins et al., 2008) therefore a number of area-level variables are included in the models. These include a rural/urban/suburban indicator (based on the interviewer's observations of the area), quintiles of the 2004 Index of Multiple Deprivation (a ranking of area according to levels of deprivation) based on 2001 Census Super Output Areas (SOAs), and the respondents' views of the local area in terms of leisure facilities, public transport and access to a supermarket.

Finally, physical activity (defined as meeting/not meeting the 5×30 min of at least moderate intensity physical activity per week) and fruit and vegetable intake (defined as eating/not eating five or more portions of fruit or vegetables a day) are included in the obesity model to examine the effect of these two factors on obesity when holding all other factors constant.

Exploratory Analysis

Physical Activity

Figures 10.1 and 10.2 show the percentage of respondents meeting the physical activity guidelines (at least 5 days of moderate intensity exercise lasting 30 min, per week) by ethnic group by age group for men and women separately. For all groups, men are more likely to meet the guidelines than women and younger age groups are more likely to do so than older groups. The one exception is the Chinese group where there is very little variation by age for either men or women.

Among men, the Irish, White and Black Caribbean groups are the most likely to meet the physical activity recommendations – about 50% of the youngest age group do so. Levels are significantly lower for South Asian and Chinese males with around 30% of the youngest age-group meeting the activity guidelines. Among women, the Black Caribbean, Black African and Irish groups have the highest levels of activity whilst Pakistani, Bangladeshi and Chinese women all have significantly lower rates of activity, and these are particularly low for the oldest Bangladeshi age-groups (2% for the over 55 s). Overall, Pakistani, Bangladeshi, Chinese, Irish and White men are significantly more likely than their female counterparts to meet the recommended physical activity guidelines. Among the Pakistani, Bangladeshi and Chinese groups, the gender differences are only significant for the 16–34 and 35–54 age-groups but

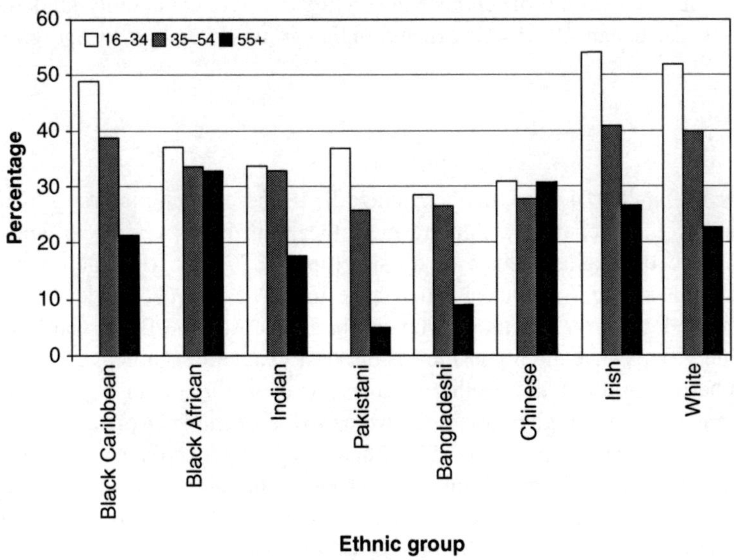

Fig. 10.1 Percentage meeting physical activity guidelines by age group by ethnic group, males aged 16+ (Source: 2004 Health Survey for England)

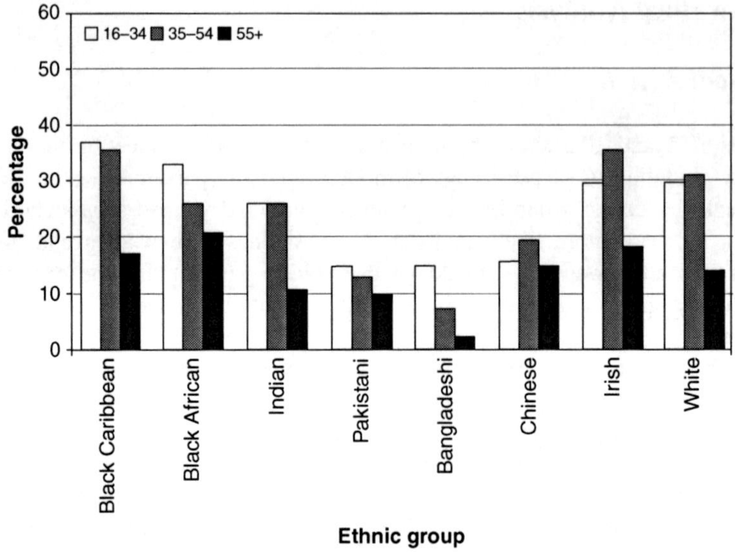

Fig. 10.2 Percentage meeting physical activity guidelines by age group by ethnic group, females aged 16+ (Source: 2004 Health Survey for England)

within the White group the gender difference is significant across all ages and within the Irish group only the 16–34 age group have significant gender differences. There are no significant gender differences in meeting the physical activity guidelines for the Black Caribbean, Black-African and Indian groups overall or by age-group.

Obesity

Figures 10.3 and 10.4 show the percentage BMI obese by ethnic group by age for men and women separately. Among men, the Irish, Black Caribbean and White groups have the highest levels of obesity (up to 37% for Irish men aged 55+), whilst Chinese and Bangladeshi men have the lowest levels (under 5% for the 55+ Bangladeshi group). Among women, the Black African, Black Caribbean and Pakistani groups have the highest levels of obesity and are significantly more likely to be obese than those in all other groups. For these three ethnic groups, obesity levels are markedly higher for older women (for example, over 50% for Black African women aged 35–54 and 55+) than for younger women (16–34). As for the men, Chinese and Bangladeshi women have significantly lower levels of obesity than women within each of the other ethnic groups and the Chinese women have significantly lower levels than the Bangladeshi women.

Black African, Bangladeshi and Pakistani females are significantly more likely than their male counterparts to be BMI-obese but for the Pakistani group these differences are only significant for those aged 34–55 and 55+. No significant gender differences are detected within the other ethnic groups.

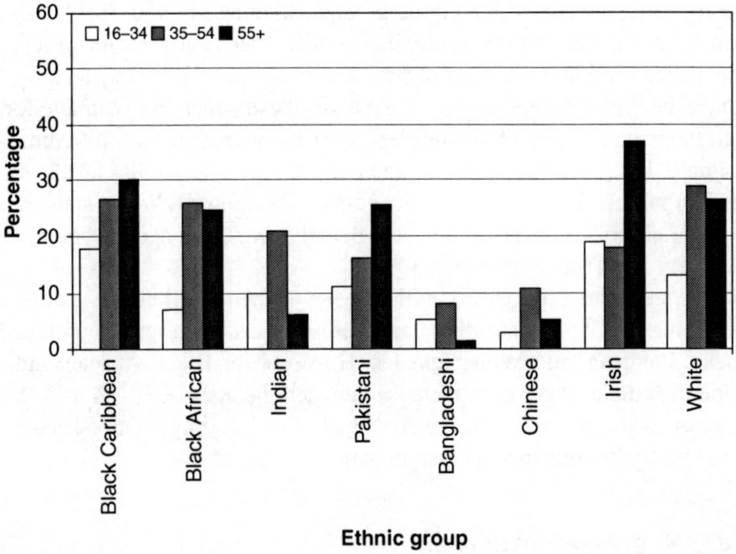

Fig. 10.3 Percentage obese by age group by ethnic group, males age 16+ (Source: 2004 Health Survey for England)

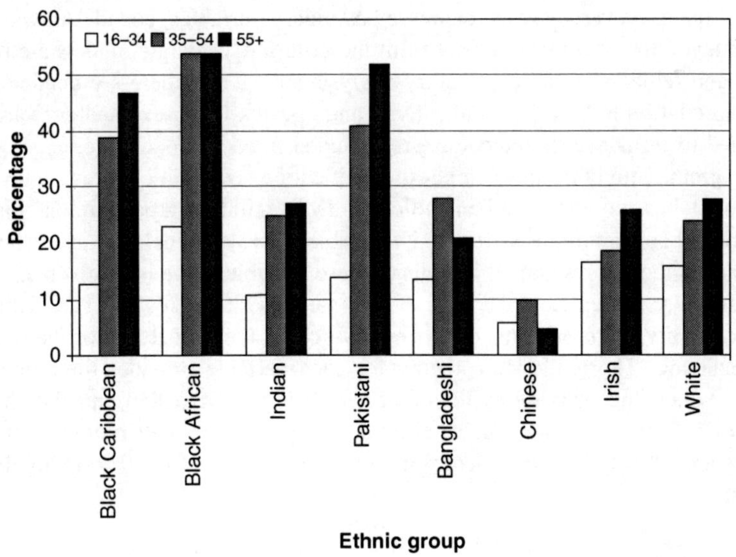

Fig. 10.4 Percentage obese by age group by ethnic group, females age 16+ (Source: 2004 Health Survey for England)

Obesity varies by age within ethnic groups. Bangladeshi and Chinese men have very low levels of obesity with no significant differences between age groups. Black Caribbean men have high levels of obesity within each age-group with no significant differences between the age groups. Levels of obesity increase with age for Black African, Pakistani, Irish and White men but these increases vary by ethnic group. For example, Irish males aged 16–34 and aged 35–54 have similar levels of obesity but this is significantly higher (37%) at age 55+. By contrast, White males aged 16–34 are significantly less likely to be obese than the two older age-groups which have similar levels of obesity – at almost 30%.

There is an increase in obesity with age for women in all ethnic groups, except for the Chinese. Obesity steadily increases with each age-group among Black-Caribbean, Pakistani and White females. However for Black African, Indian and Bangladeshi females there is an increase between the ages of 16–34 and 35–54 but this increase stops at 55+. Irish females aged 16–34 and aged 35–54 have similar levels of obesity but this increases significantly at age 55+.

Logistic Regression Analysis

Logistic regression models are used to assess ethnic differences in, firstly, physical activity (defined as meeting moderate physical activity guidelines) and, secondly, obesity (defined as a BMI of 30 kg/m^2). Logistic regression is appropriate because the two outcome variables are expressed as binary variables, coded 1/0, where the respondent either does or does not fulfil the criterion. Separate models are run for males and females as the exploratory analysis shows that there are gender differences in relation to both physical activity and obesity. Other explanatory variables, expected to influence the outcome, are included in each model: age, age squared, ethnic group, migrant status, highest qualification, economic status, equivalised household income tertile, urban indicator, IMD quintile, area opinion. Physical activity and consumption of fruit and vegetables were also included as explanatory variables in the obesity model. Details of these variables have been given earlier.

Results are presented in the form of odds ratios. Odds ratios (OR) are defined as the probability of an outcome occurring divided by the probability of the outcome not occurring. The reference category for each variable provides the comparator against which the odds ratios for other categories are assessed and thus has the value of 1. Tables 10.1 and 10.2 present the fully adjusted odds ratios for physical activity and obesity. The statistically significant odds ratios ($p<0.05$) are highlighted in bold.

Physical Activity

Model 1 in Table 10.1 (age and ethnic group) confirms the results in Figs. 10.1 and 10.2. For men, all minority groups are less likely to meet the physical activity guidelines than the white reference group, except for Black Caribbean and Irish men

Table 10.1 Logistic regression (odds ratios), physical activity

	Model 1		Model 2	
	Males	Females	Males	Females
Age (single years)	1.02	**1.08**	**0.97**	**1.07**
Age squared	**0.999**	**0.998**	1.00	**0.999**
Ethnic group				
White	1.00	1.00	1.00	1.00
Black Caribbean	0.92	1.24	1.08	1.31
Black African	**0.65**	0.95	0.91	0.82
Indian	**0.61**	**0.75**	0.77	**0.65**
Pakistani	**0.50**	**0.38**	**0.55**	**0.48**
Bangladeshi	**0.43**	**0.31**	**0.49**	**0.48**
Chinese	**0.56**	**0.50**	0.82	**0.35**
Irish	1.09	1.18	1.20	0.99
Migrant status				
GB born			1.00	1.00
Adult migrant			0.74	1.21
Child migrant			0.95	1.30
Highest qualification				
Degree			1.00	1.00
Higher education below degree			**1.59**	1.22
A-level equiv			**1.73**	1.28
O-level/CSE/Foreign/Other			**1.79**	1.02
No qualifications			**2.25**	1.03
Economic status				
In employment			1.00	1.00
Unemployed			**0.50**	1.28
Retired/other econ. inactie			**0.32**	**0.70**
Equivalised household income tertiles				
Highest income tertile			1.00	1.00
Middle income tertile			0.96	0.87
Lowest income tertile			1.05	0.86
Urban indicator				
Urban			1.00	1.00
Suburban			0.91	0.96
Rural			1.12	0.99
IMD quintiles				
IMD (1) Least deprived quintile			1.00	1.00
IMD (2)			1.17	1.07
IMD (3)			1.36	1.04
IMD (4)			1.25	0.94
IMD (5) Most deprived quintile			1.41	0.92
Good leisure facilities in area				
Agree			1.00	1.00
Disagree			1.16	1.19

Table 10.1 (continued)

	Model 1		Model 2	
	Males	Females	Males	Females
Good local transport in area				
Agree			1.00	1.00
Disagree			0.83	1.06
Unweighted number of cases	*5,540*	*7,068*	*3,832*	*4,863*

$P < 0.05$.
Source: Health Survey for England, 2004.

who are not significantly different. For women, South Asian and Chinese women are significantly less likely to meet the physical activity guidelines whilst the Black and Irish groups are not significantly different from the white reference category. Age is entered into the model as a continuous variable in single years. For women only activity initially increases with age and then, for both men and women, declines with age. The decline with age is captured using the polynomial age^2 term which expresses a change in the relationship with age in later years.

Model 2 includes the other explanatory variables expected to influence physical activity, again with separate models for men and women. Highest educational qualification is a significant predictor of physical activity for men but not for women. For men, those with qualifications below degree-level have increased odds of meeting the physical activity guidelines. Men who are in employment also have increased odds of meeting the physical activity guidelines when compared with those who are unemployed or economically inactive, whilst for women this was only the case for the economically inactive. Migrant status, household income, urban indicator, IMD quintile, leisure facilities in the area and local transport are not significantly associated with meeting the physical activity guidelines when controlling for other factors. Once these additional factors are included in the model we find that, for men, only Pakistanis and Bangladeshis remain less likely to be physically active than the white reference group. For Black African, Indian and Chinese men, the lower level of physical activity is no longer significant once other factors (e.g. qualifications and economic activity) are included in the model. For women, the same ethnic groups remain less likely to meet the physical activity guidelines – Indian, Pakistani, Bangladeshi and Chinese – as in model 1. None of the additional factors which we hypothesised might affect levels of physical activity – with the one exception of economic inactivity – have any significant effect on this measure of physical activity and the odds ratios for each ethnic group by comparison with white women, remain very similar.

Obesity

Model 1 in Table 10.2 shows that, for men, Indian, Pakistani, Bangladeshi and Chinese men have significantly lower odds of being obese than the White

Table 10.2 Logistic regression (odds ratios), obesity

	Model 1		Model 2	
	Males	Females	Males	Females
Age (single years)	**1.16**	**1.10**	**1.19**	**1.11**
Age squared	**1.00**	**1.00**	**1.00**	**1.00**
Ethnic group				
White	1.00	1.00	1.00	1.00
Black Caribbean	1.10	**1.68**	0.91	**2.03**
Black African	0.76	**2.64**	0.70	**3.18**
Indian	**0.53**	0.87	**0.47**	0.93
Pakistani	**0.65**	**1.59**	**0.54**	1.47
Bangladeshi	**0.23**	0.92	**0.12**	0.68
Chinese	**0.24**	**0.29**	**0.25**	**0.36**
Irish	0.99	0.82	0.75	0.92
Migrant status				
GB born			1.00	1.00
Adult migrant			0.87	0.72
Child migrant			1.04	0.85
Highest qualification				
Degree			1.00	1.00
Higher education below degree			1.21	1.38
A-level equiv			1.28	**1.54**
O-level/CSE/Foreign/Other equiv			**1.41**	**1.65**
No Qualifications			**1.51**	**2.08**
Economic status				
In employment			1.00	1.00
Unemployed			1.09	0.76
Retired/other economically inactive			0.99	0.92
Equivalised household income tertiles				
Highest income tertile			1.00	1.00
Middle income tertile			1.13	**1.35**
Lowest income tertile			1.28	**1.36**
Urban indicator				
Urban			1.00	1.00
Suburban			0.94	0.87
Rural			1.00	0.84
IMD quintiles				
IMD (1) Least deprived quintile			1.00	1.00
IMD (2)			0.91	0.96
IMD (3)			1.01	1.05
IMD (4)			1.11	1.30
IMD (5) Most deprived quintile			0.97	1.14
Good leisure facilities in area				
Agree			1.00	1.00
Disagree			**0.75**	0.98
Good local transport in area				
Agree			1.00	1.00
Disagree			1.07	**0.75**

Table 10.2 (continued)

	Model 1		Model 2	
	Males	Females	Males	Females
Ease of getting to supermarket				
Easy			1.00	1.00
Difficult			0.68	1.01
Meeting physical activity guidelines				
No			1.00	1.00
Yes			**0.72**	**0.65**
Eating 5 day				
No			1.00	1.00
Yes			1.17	1.16
Unweighted number of cases	*4,638*	*5,661*	*3,470*	*4,200*

P <0.05.
Source: Health Survey for England, 2004.

reference group. Black Africans, Black Caribbean and Irish men are not significantly different from the White group. Women show a rather different pattern, with Black Caribbean, Black African and Pakistani women significantly more likely to be obese than White women and Chinese women significantly less so. For both men and women, the odds of being obese initially increase with age and then decline. This decrease with age was not captured in Figs. 10.1 and 10.2 which were unable to provide fine breakdowns with age for each ethnic group.

Model 2 adds other explanatory variables into the model to establish whether the observed ethnic differences are, in fact, explained by other factors. For men, the only explanatory factors that have a significant effect on the likelihood of being obese (by comparison with the reference categories) are having no qualifications, which increases the odds of being obese by about 50%, having poor leisure facilities in the area and meeting the physical activity guidelines. The ethnic differences between men, identified in model 1, remain largely unchanged once all these additional factors have been included.

For women, those with no qualifications are twice as likely to be obese as women with a degree-level qualification and women with qualifications at NVQ level 3 or below are about 50% more likely to be obese. Unlike men, household income level is also a predictor of obesity when holding other factors constant – those in the middle and lowest income tertiles have higher odds of being obese than those in the highest tertile. Women also differ from men in that good leisure facilities do not predict obesity whilst good transport facilities are a significant negative predictor. As for men, meeting the physical activity guidelines reduces the odds of being obese by comparison with those who do not meet the guidelines. For both men and women, migrant status, urban indicator, IMD quintile, supermarkets in the local area and consumption of fruit and vegetables are not significantly associated with obesity when controlling for other factors.

The odds of obesity by comparison with white women are higher for Black Caribbean and Black African women (odds ratios of 2 and 3 respectively) once the full set of controls are added to the model, whilst Chinese women remained nearly three times less likely to be obese than White women.

Despite the strong inverse relationship between physical activity and obesity for both men and women, it was apparent from Figs. 10.1 and 10.2 that some ethnic groups with low levels of physical activity also have low levels of obesity, for example Chinese women and Bangladeshi men. We have therefore tested an interaction term between ethnic groups and physical activity for both men and women to establish whether the relationship shown in Table 10.2 varies between ethnic groups. However, no terms are significant for either men or women and therefore we have not reported them here.

Discussion

Current UK Government guidelines for tackling obesity include steps to increase physical activity and encourage healthy eating habits. Although there is evidence of ethnic differences in obesity there is limited evidence of the independent effects of ethnicity, physical activity, diet, age, sex and socio-economic characteristics upon obesity and likewise the independent effects of ethnicity, socio-demographic and socio-economic factors upon physical activity.

Ethnicity, Physical Activity and Obesity

Ethnicity differences in obesity and physical activity remain after holding constant socio-demographic, socio-economic and area characteristics but these differences vary between ethnic groups and by gender. Black Caribbean and Black African women have odds ratios of 2 and 3, respectively by comparison with White women, but obesity among Black Caribbean and Black African men is not significantly different to White men. Chinese men and women both have significantly lower odds of being obese than their White counterparts whilst South Asian men have lower odds of being obese than White men but South Asian women are not significantly different from White women. This suggests that there is no straightforward relationship between ethnicity and obesity and that we need to examine in more depth factors that influence the lifestyle and behaviour of different groups and, in particular, gender differences. The relationship between physical activity and obesity is also far from straightforward. Although our models show that meeting moderate physical activity guidelines is a significant predictor of reduced levels of obesity, both Chinese men and women and Bangladeshi men are less likely to be obese than the white comparator group and also less likely to meet the physical activity guidelines – although formal tests for an interaction failed to reach significance.

The lower levels of physical activity for South Asian women are consistent with other research (Hayes et al., 2002; Pomerleau et al., 1999; Sproston and Mindell,

2006a) and with literature that suggests that cultural or religious barriers may have a role in participation in physical activity (Grace et al., 2007; Scraton et al., 1999, 2005; Sriskanthatrajah and Kai, 2006). The presence of cultural or religious barriers is consistent with our focus groups interviews of Pakistani and Bangladeshi women aged between 18 and 30. These women recounted being restricted in doing physical sports, and outdoor activities generally, by their parents at the time of transition to secondary school/puberty. Some of these women imposed similar restrictions on their daughters and all felt that swimming, for example, was only possible in women-only sessions in the local pool. However, these women-only sessions, including women-only gym sessions and dance classes in a female setting, seemed to be very popular. Whilst these results suggest that there may be cultural barriers to physical activity for Pakistani and Bangladeshi women, our regression models shows that Chinese women have even lower odds of physical activity once control variables have been added to the model. Also, Pakistani and Bangladeshi men have lower odds of meeting the physical activity guidelines than any other ethnic groups. Therefore, whilst cultural restrictions may well influence physical activity for Pakistani and Bangladeshi women in particular, this can only provide a partial explanation.

Migration, Physical Activity and Obesity

Migration is not a significant predictor of obesity or physical activity when holding other factors constant. These findings support the research of Hayes et al. (2002) who have shown little difference between the physical activity levels of British-born Asians and their migrant peers and contradicts other literature (for example, Goel et al., 2004 and Dawson et al., 2005) which suggests that migration affects lifestyle which in turn affects obesity. However, the odds ratios in the obesity model (although not significant) suggest that both female adult and child migrants and male adult migrants are less likely to be obese than those who are born in Britain.

Again, the Pakistani and Bangladeshi women who took part in our focus groups provided some evidence of lifestyle differences between themselves and their (first-generation) parents that suggested a process by which changes may influence obesity level. For example, they described ways in which they and their children were adopting more 'western' food, e.g. pasta, lasagne, shepherd's pie, chips, pizza, whilst their parents preferred more traditional food. However, traditional food uses a lot of ghee (clarified butter) and thus highlights the difficulty of making any simplistic assumptions about the impact of traditional versus western diets on obesity.

Socio-Demographic and Socio-Economic Determinants of Physical Activity and Obesity

Only a few of the socio-demographic and socio-economic characteristics included in the logistic regression models are independent predictors of obesity and physical activity when controlling for other factors. For both men and women, obesity increases with age and then decreases at the oldest end of the age spectrum. Men and women with no qualifications or low level qualifications have higher odds of being obese than those with degree-level qualifications. This may reflect an increased willingness amongst the more highly qualified to respond to public health messages – and, in this regard, parallels smoking patterns. For men, those with qualifications lower than degree-level have higher odds of meeting the physical activity guidelines than those with degrees or equivalent but this may reflect higher levels of occupational activity among those less qualified. Women on middle or low equivalised incomes have higher odds of being obese when compared with those on high incomes (although the odds are not significantly different for different income groups among men, they are in the same direction as women). This supports the findings of many other research studies which suggest a relationship between deprivation and obesity (for example, Craig and Mindell, 2008; Diez Roux et al., 2000; Pickett et al., 2005; Sobal and Stunkard, 1989; Sproston and Mindell, 2006a). Economic status is related to physical activity (but not obesity) when controlling for other factors; unemployed men and economically inactive men and women have lower odds of meeting the physical activity guidelines than men and women in employment, probably reflecting the role of travel to work and occupation itself in providing exercise. Mutrie and Hannah (2004) have shown that exercise obtained through manual work is important for men and, on retirement, it is not fully replaced by alternative forms of activity (Berger et al., 2005).

Area is not generally an important predictor of obesity or physical activity when controlling for other factors. None of the area indicator variables are significant predictors of physical activity for men or women. Only two of the area indictor variables are significant predictors of obesity and both have an effect in the opposite direction to that expected. For men, a perception of poor leisure facilities in the area is associated with a significant reduction in the odds of obesity, whilst, for women, poor transport facilities similarly predict lower odds of obesity, holding constant other factors.

The role of transport facilities in the area can only be understood in the context of whether the respondent has access to a car and, in the HSE, this information is only available for the household as a whole, rather than the individual. It may be that women with poor transport facilities walk more than those with better transport, but we cannot test this.

Diet and Physical Activity as Predictors of Obesity

As one might expect, those who meet the physical activity guideline have lower odds of being obese than those who do not meet the guidelines, when controlling for other factors. However, fruit and vegetable consumption is not a significant predictor of obesity – and the model results, although not significant, show an inverse relationship with fruit and vegetable intake and obesity. This can be explained by the fact that fruit and vegetable consumption is only a partial measure of diet and it does not reflect eating habits as a whole. We do not have information on the extent to which other types of food are consumed, such as fizzy drinks, or on the total calorific intake of the respondent. One cannot assume that eating 5 or more fruit and vegetables a day is a predictor of a healthy diet in general.

Conclusions

These results highlight the importance of recognising differences in both levels of exercise and obesity not just between ethnic groups but also between men and women. The relatively weak association between obesity and meeting moderate exercise guidelines (meeting the exercise guidelines increases the odds of *not* being obese by about 40%) demonstrates that exercise, of itself, does not provide a sufficient explanation for obesity levels. Whilst manual work associated with employment has been shown to be an important component of physical activity for some men, the steady decline in occupations requiring heavy manual work suggests this will play a decreasing role over time.

Differences in levels of obesity between Black Caribbean and Black African men and women remain unexplained and require more work to establish the various roles of lifestyle and eating patterns, occupation or body-image preferences.

The very low levels of obesity for Chinese men and women – with no indication of an increase amongst younger generations – is not readily explained by levels of physical activity and, again, needs research in more depth to identify whether diet plays a major role or whether additional factors are at play. Similarly, the low levels of physical activity amongst Pakistani and Bangladeshi women *and men* cannot be simply explained by cultural barriers for women.

Obesity is much more complicated than just trying to tell people to eat more healthily and exercise more! Much more detailed work is needed to understand the range of different factors that explain the ethnic and gender differences observed here.

Acknowledgements We are grateful to ESRC for funding this research (RES 163-25-003); to the Economic and Social Data Service for supplying the Health Survey for England and to the Health and Information Centre for supporting the survey.

References

Anderson, A.S., Bush, H., Lean, M., Bradby, H., Williams, R. and Lea, E. (2005) Evolution of atherogenic diets in South Asian and Italian women after migration to a higher risk region, *Journal of Human Nutrition Dietetics*, 18: 33–43.

Anderson, A.S. and Lean, M.E.J. (1995) Healthy changes? Observations on a decade of dietary change in a sample of Glaswegian South Asian migrant women, *Journal of Human Nutrition and Dietetics*, 8: 129–136.

Berger, U., Der, G., Mutrie, N. and Hannah, M.K. (2005) The impact of retirement on patterns of physical activity, *Ageing and Society*, 25: 181–195.

Blackaby, D.H., Leslie, D.G., Murphy, P.D. and O'Leary, P.C. (2002) White/ethnic minority earnings and employment differentials in Britain: Evidence from the LFS, *Oxford Economic Papers*, 54: 270–297.

Bush, H., Williams, R., Bradby, H., Anderson, A. and Lean, M. (1998) Family hospitality and ethnic tradition among South Asian, Italian and general population women in the West of Scotland, *Sociology of Health and Illness*, 20(3): 351–380.

Carrington, B., Chivers, T. and Williams, T. (1987) Gender, Leisure and sport: A case-study of young people of South Asian descent, *Leisure Studies*, 6(3): 265–279.

Chambers, J.C., Elliott, P., Scott, J. and Kooner, J.S. (2006, October 31) *Physical activity and risk of Type 2 diabetes in UK Asian Indian and Northern European subjects in the London life sciences population (LOLIPOP) study*, Proceedings of the 79th annual scientific session of the American-Heart-Association, 114, pp. 894–895.

Clark, K. and Drinkwater, S. (2007) Segregation preferences and labour market outcomes, *Economics Letters*, 94(2): 278–283.

Craig, R. and Mindell, J. (eds.) (2008) *Health Survey for England 2006: Volume 1 Cardiovascular Disease and Risk Factors in Adults*, The Information Centre, London.

Cross-Government Obesity Unit, Department of Health, Department for Children, Schools and Families (2008) *Healthy Weight, Healthy Lives: A Cross-Government Strategy for England*, Department of Health and Department for Children, Schools and Families, London.

Cummins, S., Findlay, A., Higgins, C., Petticrew, M., Sparks, L. and Thomson, H. (2008) Reducing inequalities in health and diet: Findings from a study on the impact of a food retail development, *Environment and Planning A*, 40: 402–422.

Cummins, S. and Macintyre, S. (2006) Food environments and obesity – neighbourhood or nation? *International Journal of Epidemiology*, 35: 100–104.

Dawson, A.J., Sunquist, J. and Johansson, S. (2005) The influence of ethnicity and length of time since immigration on physical activity, *Ethnicity and Health*, 10(4): 293–309.

Department of Health (2004) *Choosing Health. Making Healthy Choices Easier*, Department of Health, London.

Department of Health *5 A DAY* (2000) http://www.dh.gov.uk/PolicyAndGuidance/HealthAndSocialCareTopics/FiveADay/fs/en

Dhawan, J. and Bray, C.L. (1997) Asian Indians, coronary artery disease and physical exercise, *Heart*, 78: 550–554.

Diez Roux, A.V., Link, B.G. and Northridge, M.E. (2000) A multilevel analysis of income inequality and cardiovascular disease risk factors, *Social Science and Medicine*, 50: 673–687.

Dowler, E. and Calvert, C. (1995) *Nutrition and Diet in Lone Parent Families in London*, Family Policy Studies Centre, London.

Erens, B., Primatesta, P. and Prior, G. (eds.) (2001) *Health Survey for England 1999 – The Health of Minority Ethnic Groups, Volume 1: Findings*, The Stationary Office, London.

Food Standards Agency (2003) *Salt – Eat no more than 6g a day.* http://www.salt.gov.uk/index.html

Furnham, A. and Alibhai, N. (1983) Cross-cultural differences in the perception of female body shapes, *Psychological Medicine*, 1: 829–837.

Furnham, A. and Baguma, P. (1994) Cross-cultural differences in the evaluation of male and female body shapes, *International Journal of Eating Disorders*, 15: 81–89.

Gensini, G.F., Comeglio, M. and Colella, A. (1998) Classical risk factors and emerging elements in the risk profile for coronary artery disease, *European Heart Journal*, 19(Suppl A): A53–A61.

Ghannam, F. (1997) *Fertile, Plump and Strong: The Social Construction of Female Body in Low Income Cairo* (Monographs in Reproductive Health Number 3), Population Council Regional Office for West Asia and North Africa, Cairo.

Gibbens, C. and Julian, G. (eds.) (2006) *Family Spending: A Report on the 2004–05 Expenditure and Food Survey*, The Stationary Office, London.

Goel, M.S., McCarthy, E.P., Phillips, R.S. and Wee, C.C. (2004) Obesity among US immigrant subgroups by duration of residence, *The Journal of the American Medical Association*, 292: 2860–2867.

Grace, C., Begum, R., Subhani, S., Frost, G., Greenhalgh, T. and Kopelman, P. (2007, May) Understanding roadblocks to physical activity participation in a UK South Asian community: Cultural and religious perspectives, *International Journal of Obesity*, 31(Suppl. 1): S194–S194.

Hayes, L., White, M., Unwin, N., Bhopal, R., Fischbacher, C., Harland, J., et al. (2002) Patterns of physical activity and relationship with risk markers for cardiovascular disease and diabetes in Indian, Pakistani, Bangladeshi and European adults in a UK population, *Journal of Public Health Medicine*, 24(3): 170–178.

Hunt, C.J., Nicholas, R.N. and Pryer, J.A. (2000) Who complied with national fruit and vegetable population goals? Findings from the dietary and nutritional survey of British adults, *European Journal of Public Health*, 10: 178–184.

International Diabetes Institute (2002) *The Asia-Pacific Perspective: Redefining Obesity and Its Treatment*, International Diabetes Institute, Victoria.

Jackson, M., Walker, S., Cruickshank, J.K., Sharma, S., Cade, J., Mbanya, J.C., et al. (2007) Diet and overweight and obesity in populations of African origin: Cameroon, Jamaica and the UK, *Public Health Nutrition*, 10(2): 122–130.

Johnson, M.R.D. (2000) Perceptions of barriers to healthy physical activity among Asian communities, *Sport, Education and Society*, 5(1): 51–70.

Jonsson, S., Hedglad, B., Engstrom, G., Nilsson, P., Berglund, G. and Janzon, L. (2002) Influence of obesity on cardiovascular risk. Twenty-three year follow-up of 22,025 men from an urban Swedish population, *International Journal of Obesity and Metabolic Disorders*, 8: 1046–1053.

Kalka, I. (1988) The changing food habits of Gujaratis in Britain, *Journal of Human Nutrition and Dietetics*, 1: 329–335.

Kassam-Khamis, T., Judd, P., Thomas, J.E., Sevak, L., Reddy, S. and Ganatra, S. (1995) Frequency of food consumption and nutrient consumption of composite dishes commonly consumed by South Asians originating from Gujarat and the Punjab, *Journal of Human Nutrition and Dietetics*, 8: 265–277.

Kopelman, P.G. (2000) Obesity as a medical problem, *Nature*, 404: 635–643.

Landman, J. and Cruickshank, J.K. (2001) A review of ethnicity, health and nutrition-related diseases in relation to migration in the United Kingdom, *Public Health Nutrition*, 4(2B): 647–657.

Lawrence, J.M., Devlin, E., Macaskill, S., Kelly, M., Chinouya, M.,, Raats, M.M., et al. (2007) Factors that affect the food choices made by girls and young women, from ethnic minority groups, living in the UK, *Journal of Human Nutrition & Diet*, 20: 311–319.

Lean, M.E.J., Han, T.S., Bush, H., Anderson, A.S., Bradby, H. and Williams, R. (2001) Ethnic differences in anthropometric and lifestyle measures related to coronary heart disease and risk between South Asian, Italian and general-population British women living in the west of Scotland, *International Journal of Obesity*, 24: 1800–1805.

Lee, C.D., Blair, S.N. and Jackson, A.S. (1999) Cardiorespiratory fitness, body composition, and all-cause and cardiovascular disease mortality in men, *American Journal of Clinical Nutrition*, 69: 373–380.

Lip, G.H.Y., Malik, I., Luscombe, C., McCarry, M. and Beevers, G. (1995) Dietary fat purchasing habits in Whites, Black and Asian peoples in England – implications for heart disease prevention, *International Journal of Cardiology*, 48: 287–293.

Marmot, M.G., Smith, G.D., Stansfeld, S., Patel, C., North, F., Head, J., et al. (1991) Health inequalities among British civil servants; The Whitehall II Study, *The Lancet*, 337(8754): 1387–1393.

McGarvey, S. (1991) Obesity in Samoans and a perspective in its aetiology in Polynesians, *American Journal of Clinical Nutrition*, 53: 86–94.

McKeigue, P.M. and Chaturvedi, N. (1996) Epidemiology and control of cardiovascular disease in South Asians and Afro-Caribbeans in Ahmed, W., Sheddon, T. and Stuart, O. (eds.), *Ethnicity and Health: Review of Literature and Guidance for Purchasers in the Areas of Cardiovascular Disease, Mental Health and Haemoglobinopathies* (CRD Report 5), NHS Centre for Review and Dissemination, York.

McKeigue, P.M., Marmot, M.G., Adelstein, A.M., Hunt, S.P., Shipley, M.J., Butler, S.M., et al. (1985) Diet and risk factors for coronary heart disease in Asians in Northwest London, *The Lancet*, 2(8464): 1086–1090.

Mellin-Olsen, T. and Wandel, M. (2005) Changes in food habits among Pakistani immigrant women in Oslo, Norway, *Ethnicity and Health*, 10(4): 311–339.

Miller, G.J., Kotecha, S., Wilkinson, W.H., Wilkes, H., Stirling, Y., Sanders, T.A.B., et al. (1988) Dietary and other characteristics relevant for coronary heart disease in men of Indain, West Indian and European descent in London, *Atherosclerosis*, 70: 63–72.

Modood, T., Berthoud, R. and Lakey, J. (1997) *Ethnic Minorities: Diversity and Disadvantage* (Fourth PSI study), PSI, London.

Mutrie, N. and Hannah, M.K. (2004) Some work hard while others play hard: The achievement of current recommendations for physical activity levels at work, at home, and in leisure time in the West of Scotland, *International Journal of Health Promotion & Education*, 42: 109–117.

Nasser, M. (1988) Eating disorders: The cultural dimension, *Social Psychiatry and Psychiatric Epidemiology*, 23: 184–187.

OPCS (1990) *Standard Occupational Classification Cols 1–3*, HMSO, London.

Patel, J.V., Vyas, A., Cruikshank, J.K., Prabharkaran, D.A., Hughes, E., Reddy, K.S., et al. (2005) Impact of migration on coronary heart disease risk factors: Comparison of Gujaratis in Britain and their contemporaries in villages of origin in India, *Atherosclerosis*, 185(2): 297–306.

Pickett, K.E., Kelly, S., Brunner, E., Lobstein, T. and Wilkinson, R.G. (2005) Wider income gaps, wider waistbands? An ecological study of obesity and income inequality, *Epidemiology and Community Health*, 59: 670–674.

Pill, R., Peters, T.J. and Robling, M.R. (1995) Social class and preventative health behaviour: A British example, *Journal of Epidemiology and Community Health*, 49: 28–32.

Platt, L. (2007) *Poverty and Ethnicity in the UK*, The Policy Press, Bristol.

Pomerleau, J., McKeigue, P.M. and Chaturvedi, N. (1999) Factors associated with obesity in South Asian, Afro-Caribbean and European women, *International Journal of Obesity*, 23: 25–33.

Pratala, R.S., Groth, M.V., Olderstorf, U.S., Roos, G.R., Sekula, W. and Tuomainen, H.M. (2003) Use of butter and cheese in 10 European Countries, a case of contrasting educational differences, *European Journal of Public Health*, 13: 124–132.

Rudat, K. (1994) *Black and Ethnic Minority Groups in England*, Health Education Authority, London.

Saxena, S., Ambler, G., Cole, T.J. and Maheed, A. (2004) Ethnic group differences in overweight and obese children and young people in England: Cross sectional survey, *Archives of Disease in Childhood*, 89: 30–36.

Scott, P. (1998) Lay beliefs and the management of disease amongst West Indians with diabetes, *Health and Social Care in the Community*, 6(6): 407–419.

Scraton, S., Caudwell, J. and Holland, S. (2005) Bend it like Patel. Centring 'race', ethnicity and gender in feminist analysis of women's football in England, *International Review for the Sociology of Sport*, 40(1): 71–88.

Scraton, S., Fastings, K., Pfister, G. and Bunuel, A. (1999) It's still a man's game? The experience of top-level European women footballers, *International Review for the Sociology of Sport*, 34: 99–111.

Sharma, S., Cade, J., Griffiths, S. and Cruickshank, J.K. (1998) Nutrient intakes among a UK African-Caribbean population – transition in coronary heart disease risk? *Lancet*, 352: 114–115.

Sharma, S., Cade, J., Landman, J. and Cruickshank, J.K. (2002) Assessing the diet of the British Afro-Caribbean population: Frequency of consumption of foods and food portion sizes, *International Journal of Food Sciences and Nutrition*, 53: 439–444.

Sharma, S. and Cruickshank, J.K. (2001) Cultural differences in assessing dietary intake and providing relevant dietary information to British African-Caribbean populations, *Journal of Human Nutrition Dietetics*, 14: 449–456.

Shelton, N.J. (2005) What not to eat: Inequalities in healthy eating behaviour, evidence from the 1998 Scottish Health Survey, *Journal of Public Health*, 27(1): 36–44.

Simmons, D. and Williams, R. (1997) Dietary practices among Europeans and different South Asian groups in Coventry, *British Journal of Nutrition*, 78: 5–14.

Smith, Z., Knight, T., Sahota, P., Kernohan, E. and Baker, M. (1995) Dietary patterns in Asian and Caucasian men in Bradford: Differences and implications for nutrition education, *Journal of Human Nutrition and Dietetics*, 6: 323–334.

Sobal, J. and Stunkard, A.J. (1989) Socioeconomic status and obesity: A review of the literature, *Psychological Bulletin*, 105: 2260–2275.

Sproston, K. and Mindell, J. (eds.) (2006a) *Health Survey for England 2004. Volume 1: The Health of Minority Ethnic Groups*, The Information Centre, London.

Sproston, K. and Mindell, J. (eds.) (2006b) *Health Survey for England 2004, Volume 2: Methodology and Documentation*, The Information Centre, London.

Sriskanthatrajah, J. and Kai, J. (2006) Promoting physical activity among South Asian women with coronary heart disease and diabetes: What might help? *Family Practice*, 24(1): 71–76.

Stafford, M., Cummins, S., Ellaway, A., Sacker, A., Wiggins, R.D. and Macintyre, S. (2007) Pathways to obesity: Identifying local, modifiable determinants of physical activity and diet, *Social Science & Medicine*, 65: 1882–1897.

Stevens, J., Evenson, K.R. and Thomas, O. (2004) Associations of fitness and fatness with mortality in Russian and American men in the lipids research clinics study, *International Journal of Obesity*, 28: 1463–1470.

The Chief Medical Officer (2004) *At Least Five a Week: Evidence on the Impact of Physical Activity and Its Relationship to Health*, Department of Health, London.

Tovee, M.J., Swami, V., Furnham, A. and Mangalparsad, R. (2006) Changing perceptions of attractiveness as observers are exposed to a different culture, *Evolution and Human Behaviour*, 27: 443–456.

Wandel, M. (1993) Nutrition-related diseases and dietary change among third world immigrants in Northern Europe, *Nutrition and Health*, 9: 117–133.

Wardle, J. and Marsland, L. (1990) Adolescent concerns about weight and eating: A social-developmental perspective, *Journal of Psychosomatic Research*, 34: 377–391.

Wardle, J. and Steptoe, A. (2003) Socio-economic differences in attitudes and beliefs about healthy lifestyles, *Journal of Epidemiology and Community Health*, 57: 440–443.

Williams, R., Bhopal, R. and Hunt, K. (1994) Coronary risk in a British Punjabi population: Comparative profile of non-biochemical factors, *International Journal of Epidemiology*, 23(1): 28–37.

Williams, R., Bush, H., Anderson, A., Lean, M. and Bradby, H. (1996) *Dietary Change in South Asian and Italian Women in the West of Scotland* (Annual Report to the ESRC Glasgow), MRC Medical Sociology Unit, Glasgow.

World Health Organisation (2002) *World Health Report*, WHO, Geneva.

World Health Organization (2003) *Diet, Nutrition and the Prevention of Chronic Diseases: Report of a Joint WHO/FAO Expert Consultation* (WHO Technical Report Series 916), WHO, Geneva.

Wyke, S. and Landman, J. (1997) Healthy eating? Diet and cuisine amongst Scottish South Asian people, *British Food Journal*, 99(1): 27–34.

Zaninotto, P., Head, J., Stamatakis, E., Wardle, H. and Mindell, J. (2009) Trends in obesity among adults in England from 1993 to 2004 by age and social class and projections of prevalence to 2010, *Journal of Epidemiology and Community Health*, 63: 140–146.

Chapter 11
Racial Discrimination and Health: Exploring the Possible Protective Effects of Ethnic Density

Mai Stafford, Laia Bécares and James Nazroo

Introduction

The work described in this chapter aims to widen the focus of research on ethnicity and health to highlight how the residential context can shape the everyday experiences and health of ethnic minority groups. Ethnic inequalities in health are well documented, with both a poorer economic position and exposure to racism leading to poorer health for several of the UK's ethnic minority groups (Davey Smith et al., 2000; Erens et al., 2001; Nazroo, 1997, 2001, 2003). However, there is an emerging literature that suggests that an increasing proportion of ethnic minority people in local areas may mitigate some of these effects. Although ethnic density has often been treated as an indicator of disadvantage in an area, there may in fact be health benefits to living in a more ethnically dense area once deprivation has been controlled for. The main objective of the work described here is to investigate possible protective pathways linking greater ethnic density to better health for ethnic minorities. The chapter begins by briefly summarizing some existing studies which relate ethnic density to health and reviewing the theory and evidence for some of these protective pathways. After setting out the hypotheses to be tested, we describe the study design, which is based on secondary analysis of the Citizenship Survey, formerly the Home Office Citizenship Survey. Limitations of this work and the implications of our findings are discussed in the final sections.

Several disciplines have an interest in describing and understanding the determinants and impact of the proportion of residents in a given area that are from a particular ethnic group, as evidenced by other chapters in this volume. Various labels have been given to this phenomenon, including ethnic heterogeneity, ethnic concentration and, within the field of epidemiology, ethnic density. Although not always explicit, the phrase ethnic density usually refers to ethnic minority density, i.e. the proportion of residents from a particular ethnic minority group in a given area, rather than to an interest in the majority ethnic group.

M. Stafford (✉)
Department of Epidemiology and Public Health, University College London, London WC1E 6BT, UK
e-mail: m.stafford@ucl.ac.uk

J. Stillwell, M. van Ham (eds.), *Ethnicity and Integration*, Understanding Population Trends and Processes 3, DOI 10.1007/978-90-481-9103-1_11,

Existing Studies

Ethnic Density and Health

The ethnic density effect proposes that ethnic minority people residing in areas where they form a greater proportion of the population have better health than ethnic minority residents in areas of lower ethnic concentration (Faris and Dunham, 1939; Halpern and Nazroo, 1999). This is supported by several, but not all, studies in the US and Europe which suggest that an increasing proportion of co-ethnics in an area is associated with lower rates of psychosis, suicide, common mental disorders, psychiatric admissions, self-rated health and mortality for ethnic minority groups (Boydell et al., 2001; Eschbach et al., 2004; Fagg et al., 2006; Fang et al., 1998; Franzini and Spears, 2003; Halpern and Nazroo, 1999; Neeleman and Wessely, 1999; Neeleman et al., 2001; Pickett et al., 2005; Rabkin, 1979; Veling et al., 2008; Wickrama et al., 2005). However, findings are mixed and several other studies have found no association or even statistically significantly elevated levels of poor self-rated health, infant and adult mortality, hypertension and chronic conditions among other outcomes (Abada et al., 2007; Ecob and Williams, 1991; Ellen, 2000; Karlsen et al., 2002; LeClere et al., 1997; White and Borrell, 2006; Yankauer, 1950).

An inverse association between ethnic density and good health would perhaps not be surprising given that areas of higher ethnic density are more likely to be economically and socially deprived on several indicators. In the UK, areas with high proportions of ethnic minorities have been shown to be more densely populated, with more social housing and unemployment, lower proportions of households with cars and central heating and lower proportions of individuals in professional and managerial occupations (Clark and Drinkwater, 2002). Deprived areas are also more likely to have lower quality and quantity of leisure facilities and poorer transport, housing, physical environment, food shopping opportunities, and primary and secondary health services (Cummins et al., 2005). Overwhelming evidence demonstrates that residence in a more deprived area is associated with poorer health across a whole range of health outcomes (Davey-Smith et al., 1998; Diez-Roux et al., 1997; Haan et al., 1987; Krieger, 1992; Roberts, 1997; Pickett and Pearl, 2001; Riva et al., 2007). Yet it appears that ethnic minorities living in areas of higher ethnic density do better, at least on some health outcomes, than those living in areas of lower ethnic density and lower levels of multiple deprivation.

Possible explanations for a protective association between ethnic density and health have been suggested. These include the possibility that exposure to racism and discrimination is lower in areas of higher ethnic density (Bécares et al., 2009; Halpern and Nazroo, 1999), and that higher ethnic density promotes enhanced social cohesion, mutual social support and a stronger sense of community and belongingness, which in turn provide protection from the consequences of discrimination and racial harassment (Bhugra and Becker, 2005; Daley, 1998; Halpern and Nazroo, 1999; Smaje, 1995), as well as from the detrimental effects of low status stigma (Pickett and Wilkinson, 2008). It has also been suggested that greater ethnic density may provide access to amenities and services, both because of higher demand/reduced opportunity costs and because of increased civic engagement by ethnic minorities which facilitates community organization to secure access to resources (Karlsen et al., 2002). These pathways will be described more fully in the following sections.

Ethnic Density and Experience of Racial Discrimination

Racial discrimination is detrimental to health (Halpern and Nazroo, 1999); Harris et al., 2006a, b; Krieger and Sidney, 1996; Krieger, 1990; 1999, 2000; Paradies, 2006; Williams and Mohammed, 2009; Williams and Neighbors, 2001; Williams, 1999; Williams et al., 1997). Few prior studies have examined whether ethnic minorities living in areas where they constitute a greater proportion of the population experience less racial discrimination (Bécares et al., 2009; Halpern and Nazroo, 1999; Whitley et al., 2006). A reduced number of potential perpetrators and/or prevailing norms which are intolerant of racial discrimination may well be found in areas of higher ethnic density. In line with these studies, we hypothesise that ethnic minorities will report lower levels of worry about becoming the victim of racism as well as fewer actual experiences of racism in areas of higher ethnic density. It is worth noting here that indicators of ethnic density in the UK have usually been based on fairly crude categorisations of ethnicity, for example grouping all South Asians together into a single category and not distinguishing between Black Africans and Black Caribbeans but using instead a crude measure such as proportion Black. In some cases, ethnic density has been measured as the number of residents from any ethnic minority as a ratio of the total number of residents. However, since racial discrimination can occur between individuals from two ethnic minorities, we cannot assume that higher overall ethnic minority density is associated with a reduction in the number of potential perpetrators. Therefore we also wish to explore alternative indicators of ethnic density and hypothesise that a lower likelihood of racial discrimination will be more strongly associated with co-ethnic density than with overall ethnic minority density.

Ethnic Density and Social Cohesion

Residence with co-ethnics may also enhance opportunities for accessing mutual social support through shared culture, customs and values. When people share values and norms, the community is said to be more socially cohesive. Kawachi and Berkman (2000) described social cohesion as the absence of latent social conflict and the presence of social bonds such as trust and norms of reciprocity, although many definitions of the concept can be found. A small section of literature supports the idea that ethnic density can enhance social cohesion and a sense of community and belongingness (Daley, 1998; Halpern and Nazroo, 1999; Smaje, 1995; Bhugra and Becker, 2005), although here we have to distinguish social cohesion within and between ethnic groups. For example, there is concern that special interest groups and groups with a strong group identity can be exclusive leading to the formation of in-groups and out-groups (Durlauf, 1999; ODPM, 2004; Portes, 1998; Stolle and Rochon, 1998). Whilst a strong group identity could be beneficial for the sense of belonging and psychological and even material well-being of group members, it could be detrimental in creating a sense of 'otherness' and in pulling resources away from those outside the group. Indeed, some recent theoretical and empirical work maintains that ethnic diversity undermines a sense of community and social cohesion, positing that individuals prefer to interact with others that are similar to themselves and so as ethnic concentration increases in an area, social cohesion decreases (Alesina and La Ferrara, 2002; Costa and Kahn, 2003; Glaeser et al., 2000; Putnam, 2007). Whilst this argument relates to ethnic diversity rather than to ethnic minority density, the operationalisation of ethnic diversity is such that its indicators are highly positively correlated with ethnic density. In this context, we consider that notions of social cohesion should encapsulate tolerance and understanding of diversity as well as a sense of belonging, trust and reciprocity.

A positive association between social cohesion and health is well-documented (Boreham et al., 2002; Echeverría et al., 2008; Kawachi and Kennedy, 1997). Based on this, we propose that one of the pathways linking ethnic density to better health is through increased social cohesion. Again, we suggest that the association between ethnic density and social cohesion will be stronger when ethnic density is captured by the proportion of co-ethnics in the area rather than by overall ethnic minority density. This is based on the fact that culture, customs and values can vary greatly between ethnic minority groups and we suggest that the greatest degree of identification will be amongst those from the same specific ethnic group.

Ethnic Density and Civic Engagement

Evidence from the US suggests that a third explanation for a protective effect of ethnic density is through increased civic engagement. In other words, ethnic density is hypothesised to be positively associated with political mobility and participation in community volunteering and organizations. One motivation for this political and civic engagement is the desire to attract and preserve resources for one's own group. In more ethnically dense areas, ethnic group becomes more salient and so theory suggests that engagement should be greater (Anderson and Paskeviciute, 2005). In addition, where participation depends on face-to-face contact, members of ethnic minority groups have the choice of joining a group where they are the minority or not joining at all. In areas of higher ethnic density, there is the possibility of finding groups in which they are less of a minority or indeed not a minority at all (Costa and Kahn, 2003).

The US literature suggests that in highly ethnically segregated areas, political empowerment attenuates, but does not eradicate, the negative consequences of segregation on health (LaVeist, 1993). In fact, studies have suggested that African Americans are more successful at attaining political power in highly segregated cities (LaVeist, 1993; p. 51). In the UK, studies exploring the association between ethnic density, civic engagement and political participation have found mixed results. One study found increased voter turnout in areas of high ethnic density (Fieldhouse and Cutts, 2008). Another found no statistically significant association between ethnic density and civic engagement or formal volunteering (Pennant, 2005).

It has been suggested, with some supportive evidence, that ethnic minorities with greater political participation and political power are better placed to influence decisions about resource allocation to improve relevant welfare and services (La Veist, 1992). In addition ethnic minority community infrastructure, in the form of civic and social institutions and neighbourhood associations, is also theorised to be stronger where ethnic minority political power is greater (La Veist, 1992). Welfare provision, public services and community infrastructure are then thought to have an impact on the health of that ethnic group (La Veist, 1992). Links between facets of community infrastructure, including voluntary and civic activities, and better health have been documented (Boreham et al., 2002; Harris and Thoresen, 2005; Musick et al., 1999) although the direction of causality remains poorly defined as much of that work is based on cross-sectional data. On the basis of these studies, we hypothesise that higher ethnic density will be associated with higher levels of formal and informal volunteering and greater participation in civic activities.

This synopsis of existing studies provides a context for the work described in this chapter which aims to examine:

- the associations between the residential ethnic density of an area and health, experiences of racism and discrimination, social cohesion and civic engagement;
- whether these associations vary by ethnic group; and
- whether these associations vary when alternative measures of ethnic density are used.

Data

Data for the study come from two sources, namely the 2001 UK Census (for information on ethnic density) and the Citizenship Survey (for information on all other variables of interest).

Ethnic Density Data from the 2001 Census

The areal unit chosen to measure ethnic density in the 2001 Census was Middle Super Output Area (MSOA) of which there are 6,780 in England and 413 in Wales. The minimum population of an MSOA is 5,000 and the mean is 7,200 (Office for National Statistics, 2004). Concerns over confidentiality and respondent identification did not allow us to use lower levels of disaggregation. Higher levels were not considered appropriate because the literature has argued that larger areas fail to capture local group density with accuracy (Franzini and Spears, 2003; Halpern, 1993). The 2001 Census data on ethnicity (Office for National Statistics, 2008) were geocoded to the Citizenship Survey through respondent's MSOA identifier. This step potentially allows identification of respondents and so it was performed by the Data Custodian (the National Centre for Social Research) and area identifiers were not supplied to the research team. The data linkage request was approved by the Data Custodian with the constraint that 5% random error be added to each ethnic density variable. This additional random error reduced the precision of the estimates, but it did not bias them. The percentage of the MSOA population made up by each ethnic minority group is summarised in Table 11.1.

Table 11.1 Proportion of MSOA population in each ethnic minority group

Ethnic group	Percentage of MSOA population Mean (Standard deviation)	Median	Range
Caribbean	1.14 (2.69)	0.16	0–24.14
African	0.97 (2.73)	0.11	0–41.11
Indian	2.04 (5.21)	0.45	0–71.29
Pakistani	1.38 (4.90)	0.15	0–73.14
Bangladeshi	0.56 (2.89)	0.06	0–60.99
Overall ethnic minority density	8.94 (14.31)	2.78	0–88.92

Source: 2001 Census: Key Statistics Table KS006.

Operationalising Ethnic Density

Ethnic density based on 2001 Census data was operationalised as co-ethnic density and overall ethnic minority density. Co-ethnic density was calculated by dividing the number of residents from the respondent's own ethnic group in an area by the total population in that area. This was conducted separately for Black Caribbean, Black African, Indian, Pakistani and Bangladeshi people. Residents of mixed ethnicity (14.6% of those who classified themselves as having an ethnic minority background) were excluded from the numerators. It was also calculated for Whites (with the numerator including all people who classified themselves as White British, White Irish and Other White). Overall ethnic minority density was calculated by dividing the sum of residents from any ethnic minority background (including all the ethnic minority groups listed above plus Chinese, Other Asian, Other Black and Mixed, but excluding Irish) by the total population in that area.

Data from the Citizenship Surveys were gecoded to data on ethnic density from the 2001 Census through the respondent's postcode. This data linkage was undertaken by the Data Custodian to ensure respondent confidentiality. In addition to these objective measures of ethnic density, we were able to use a subjective ethnic density measure from the Citizenship Survey. Respondents were asked what proportion of all the people in their local area were of the same ethnic group as themselves. Possible responses were 'all the same', 'more than half', 'about a half' or 'less than a half'. The local area was defined as the area within 15/20 minute walking distance. Unlike the objective measures from the 2001 Census, perceived ethnic density does not refer to an administrative boundary; nor does it refer to ethnic groupings based on pre-defined categories as used in the 2001 Census. Therefore this measure reflects subjective perceptions of ethnic density rather than externally imposed categorisations.

The Citizenship Survey

The Citizenship Survey (CS) is a biennial survey that started in 2001 and provides an evidence base for the work conducted by the Department of Communities and Local Government (DCLG). It includes questions on attitudes regarding one's neighbourhood, family and friendship networks, civic renewal and civic participation, trust between neighbours, perceived levels of racial and religious discrimination and formal and informal volunteering. Demographic information such as age, gender, ethnicity, religion, educational background, occupational status and income are also collected.

In order to increase statistical power, this study used a merged file of the 2005 and 2007 Citizenship Surveys. The 2005 Citizenship Survey consisted of two separate components: a core representative sample of the general adult population of England and Wales of around 10,000 individuals, and an ethnic minority boost sample of approximately 4,000 individuals. The core sample was obtained from residential addresses selected from the Royal Mail's Postcode Address File (PAF). A two-stage sampling approach was used to select the addresses. At the first stage, a random sample of Census Area Statistics (CAS) wards was selected. At the second stage, addresses were sampled from within the selected wards. The ethnic minority boost sample was chosen from wards selected for the core sample as well as from an additional boost sample of 150 wards, using screening and focused enumeration (Michaelson et al., 2005). The 2007 Citizenship Survey consists of 14,095 people aged 16 and over residing in England and Wales. A total of 9,336 respondents were surveyed for the core sample, and 4,759 people were surveyed for the ethnic boost sample, following a similar sampling strategy to that of the 2005 Citizenship Survey.

Ethnicity was measured as a self-reported variable, and was categorised using the same definitions as the 2001 Census into White, Black Caribbean (henceforth referred to as Caribbean), Black African (henceforth African), Indian, Pakistani and Bangladeshi. Other ethnic groups covered too few respondents to be considered in the analyses presented here.

Health was measured using two items capturing limiting long-term illness (LLTI). Participants who reported that they suffered from an illness that had troubled them for some time and that this illness limited their daily activities were classified as having a LLTI. Although not ideal, LLTI is associated with increased risk of mortality and health service use (Lyyra and Heikkinen, 2006).

Two different racism measures were analysed in this study: fear of racial/religious attacks and expected organisational discrimination. Fear of racial/religious attacks was measured by asking respondents how worried they were about being subject to a physical attack because of skin colour, ethnic origin or religion. The variable was dichotomised as 'not very worried or not worried at all' and 'fairly or very worried'. Organisational discrimination was analysed as a dichotomous variable that measured whether the respondent felt that he/she would be treated better, worse or the same as other races by members of any of the following organisations (categorised into 'expects to be treated better or same', and 'expects to be treated worse'): a local doctor's surgery, a local hospital, the health service generally, a local school, the education system generally, a council housing department or housing association, a local council, a private landlord, the Courts, the Crown Prosecution Service, the Police, the local police, the immigration authorities, the Prison Service and the Probation Service.

Social cohesion was measured in the 2005 Citizenship Survey by seven items capturing whether the respondent: agreed that people in their neighbourhood pulled together to improve the neighbourhood; agreed that this is a close-knit community; agreed that many of the people in their neighbourhood could be trusted; agreed that people in the neighbourhood were willing to help their neighbours; agreed that people in the neighbourhood share the same values; agreed that the local area (within 15/20 min walking distance) is a place where people from different backgrounds get on well together; and agreed that the local area is a place where residents respect ethnic differences between people. The item capturing whether people in the neighbourhood share the same values did not correlate well with the other items and was omitted from these analyses. Principal components analysis indicated that a single component was sufficient to capture the remaining six items and this was verified for each ethnic group separately. Component scores were approximately equal so a summary social cohesion score was calculated as the sum of these six items which, after transformation, ranged from 0 to 100 with higher values indicating greater cohesion. Some changes were made to these items in the 2007 survey and so analysis of social cohesion is limited to the 2005 data in this chapter.

Civic engagement captured whether respondents had participated in any formal or informal volunteering in the past 12 months and whether they had participated in any civic activity in the last 12 months which was not related to their jobs. Information on formal volunteering activities in an extensive list of groups, clubs and organisations (including youth activities, sport or hobby groups, and religious, political or environmental organizations) and informal volunteering activities (including shopping, transporting and babysitting) was included. Involvement in various civic activities included having been a local councillor or having been a member of a decision-making group. A summary variable capturing involvement in any formal and informal volunteering or civic activities was also analysed.

Other explanatory variables were respondent's age, sex, individual socioeconomic position, nativity (UK or abroad), number of years living in the neighbourhood and area deprivation. Socioeconomic position based on respondent's occupation was classified according to the NS-SEC into seven groups (higher/lower managerial and professions; intermediate occupations/small employer; lower supervisory and technical/semi-routine; routine occupations; never worked/long-term unemployed; full-time students; not stated/classified). Area deprivation was measured with the 2004 Index of Multiple Deprivation summary score.

Statistical Analysis

To address the first aim, namely to examine the association between co-ethnic density and health, perceived racial discrimination, social cohesion and civic engagement, regression modelling was used. Co-ethnic density was included as a continuous variable. Additional terms allowing for non-linearity were tested but did not improve model fit and are not presented here. LLTI, perceived racial discrimination and civic engagement measures were dichotomised and modelled using logistic regression. Social cohesion scores were approximately normally distributed and were modelled as a continuous variable using linear regression. Age, sex, individual socioeconomic position, number of years living in the neighbourhood and area deprivation were included as covariates.

To explore whether these associations depended on the operationalisation of ethnic density, we repeated the models described above using two alternative measures of ethnic density (namely overall ethnic minority density and perceived ethnic density) in place of co-ethnic density. Although formal comparisons of these models were not undertaken, we examined the magnitude of the ethnic density effect size across the different ethnic density measures. Since it cannot be assumed that the association between ethnic density and outcomes is the same across different ethnic groups, we stratified all analyses by ethnic group.

Description of the Citizenship Survey Participants

Table 11.2 presents the demographic characteristics of the ethnic minority groups of interest in the merged dataset. Among ethnic minorities, Caribbean people were older and Indian respondents were in higher socio-economic positions. More than half of all respondents in all ethnic minority groups were born abroad. This was most important for African (87.5%), Bangladeshi (78.7%), and Pakistani (66.2%) respondents. Bangladeshi people had the highest proportion living in areas of high deprivation whereas Indian people had the least. Over 60% of ethnic minority respondents reported living in an area where half or fewer of the residents were from the same ethnic background. In contrast, more than 80% of white respondents reported living in an area where half or more residents were from the same ethnic background.

Table 11.2 Characteristics of CS participants

	Caribbean (n=1,644) %	African (n=1,536) %	Indian (n=2,687) %	Pakistani (n=1,503) %	Bangladeshi (n=536) %	White (n=16,532) %
Female	58.6	59.0	50.1	48.6	51.5	56.4
Registrar's class (NS-SEC)						
Higher and lower man'ment	30.0	29.7	33.4	19.6	13.5	34.7
Intermed. and small emp's	28.0	19.6	25.6	25.1	21.9	31.9
Semi-routine and routine	34.8	31.4	29.1	28.4	37.7	29.4
Never worked, long-term unemployed	7.2	19.3	11.9	26.9	26.9	4.0
Foreign born	54.7	87.5	73.1	66.2	78.7	2.6
Years in neighbourhood						
Less than a Year	3.3	13.3	7.0	6.7	5.8	4.6
1–5 years	26.3	49.2	30.0	29.5	30.5	21.5
5–10 years	18.3	17.6	14.2	19.1	23.3	14.9
10+ years	52.1	19.9	48.8	44.7	40.4	59.0
Index of Multiple Deprivation						
1 Most deprived	40.3	39.3	27.1	48.0	71.5	10.8
2	28.4	27.9	24.0	25.1	11.6	13.9
3	20.6	21.6	24.5	16.1	8.6	22.3
4	6.7	5.9	12.4	5.4	3.7	18.9
5	2.2	3.2	6.1	3.1	3.3	16.1
6 Least deprived	1.8	2.1	5.9	2.3	1.3	18.0
Perceived ethnic density						
All the same	0.9	1.4	2.2	2.0	2.3	29.9
More than half same	12.1	10.6	26.5	32.4	30.6	53.7
About half same	24.4	14.6	23.0	27.7	19.8	8.8
Less than half same	62.7	73.5	48.2	38.0	47.4	7.7
Mean Age (Stand. dev.)	46.2 (16.5)	37.5 (12.5)	42.4 (15.8)	36.9 (14.0)	35.1 (13.0)	51.2 (18.5)

Source: Citizenship Surveys 2005 and 2007 combined.

Table 11.3 summarises the distribution of co-ethnic density at the MSOA level by ethnic group among the Citizenship Survey sample. Caribbean respondents were the least concentrated, with only 4.5% of their population living in areas of 20+% co-ethnic density. Indian people, in contrast, were the most concentrated, with over 45% of respondents living in areas of 20+% co-ethnic density. Caribbean, African and Bangladeshi respondents had around 50% of their population in areas with less than 10% co-ethnic density. It is also evident from Table 11.3 that Caribbean and African respondents lived in areas with lower overall ethnic minority density (around 40% of respondents in areas of 40+% density) compared with South Asian respondents (around 50 to 60% in areas of 40+% density). For all ethnic groups, perceived and measured co-ethnic densities were positively correlated, although ethnic minority participants tended to overestimate the proportion of co-ethnics in their area (Stafford et al., 2009).

Ethnic Density and Long-Term Limiting Illness

The prevalence of LLTI for Caribbean, African, Indian, Pakistani and Bangladeshi participants was 23.7, 10.5, 16.2, 16.6 and 17.2% respectively. After accounting for participant's age and sex, the likelihood of having a LLTI remained elevated (compared with White participants) for Caribbeans, Pakistanis and Bangladeshis. Statistically significant associations between co-ethnic or overall ethnic minority density and LLTI were not found (Table 11.4). In contrast, perceived ethnic density appeared to be more consistently associated with a reduced likelihood of LLTI, indicated by an odds ratio (OR) for LLTI of less than 1 at the highest levels of perceived ethnic density for all except Caribbeans.

The fact that these associations seems to depend on the operationalisation of ethnic density has been discussed more fully elsewhere (Stafford et al., 2009). Briefly, these findings suggest that perceived ethnic density is associated with reduced likelihood of reporting LLTI but that measured ethnic density, whether co-ethnic or overall ethnic minority density, is not. This may be due to the fact that perceived ethnic density refers to respondent-based perceptions of ethnic group within self-defined area boundaries rather than external categorisations. Findings highlight the importance of capturing exposures at the appropriate geographical level and could inform future studies of the ethnic density effect.

Racism Prevalence and Association with Ethnic Density

Experiences of racial discrimination among the ethnic minority population of the Citizenship Survey sample are presented in Table 11.5. Bangladeshi people were the most worried about racial/religious attacks, followed by Indian, Pakistani and African people. Caribbean people reported the highest prevalence of expecting to be treated worse than other races by a range of organisations.

Table 11.3 Distribution of co-ethnic density and overall ethnic minority density by MSOA

	Caribbean (n=1,644) %	African (n=1,536) %	Indian (n=2,687) %	Pakistani (n=1,503) %	Bangladeshi (n=536) %
Caribbean ethnic density					
0–0.9%	7.4	13.4	30.4	32.2	18.5
1–4.9%	25.9	35.9	48.8	44.6	53.4
5–9.9%	28.6	24.4	12.3	13.4	17.0
10–19.9%	33.6	24.3	7.8	9.1	10.2
20% or more	4.5	2.0	0.7	0.7	0.9
African ethnic density					
0–0.9%	19.7	15.5	41.9	51.0	22.2
1–4.9%	29.4	31.4	42.8	34.4	45.9
5–9.9%	25.9	24.0	11.9	11.2	18.7
10–19.9%	19.0	21.7	3.2	3.1	10.8
20% or more	6.0	7.4	0.2	0.3	2.4
Indian ethnic density					
0–0.9%	14.5	17.1	6.5	14.3	12.5
1–4.9%	50.1	49.6	18.4	36.5	63.1
5–9.9%	13.6	12.4	10.5	13.9	7.4
10–19.9%	11.6	11.8	19.5	15.9	7.1
20–39.9% or more	9.0	7.6	27.2	16.0	8.8
40% or more	1.2	1.4	17.9	3.5	1.1
Pakistani ethnic density					
0–0.9%	39.2	45.6	22.2	9.8	47.6
1–4.9%	33.2	34.7	39.3	16.8	19.9
5–9.9%	15.3	10.1	19.2	18.8	9.0
10–19.9%	7.8	6.8	12.6	22.1	11.2
20–39.9% or more	3.8	2.4	5.8	20.5	8.4
40% or more	0.7	0.4	0.9	12.0	6.0
Bangladeshi ethnic density					
0–0.9%	56.9	55.6	75.4	56.4	16.2
1–4.9%	34.5	36.1	17.0	24.6	21.6
5–9.9%	4.9	4.5	4.4	12.0	15.5
10–19.9%	2.2	2.1	2.5	4.9	12.9
20–39.9% or more	1.2	0.9	0.5	1.9	1.4
40% or more	0.3	0.8	0.2	0.3	19.4
Overall ethnic minority density					
0–9.9%	7.2	10.4	10.5	7.5	6.5
10–19.9%	8.8	9.2	10.1	10.2	6.7
20–39.9%	40.2	38.9	27.8	28.9	21.1
40–59.9%	29.3	31.9	21.0	24.2	34.9
60 or more	14.6	9.6	30.7	29.3	30.8

Source: Citizenship Surveys 2005 and 2007 combined.

Table 11.4 LLTI and ethnic density among the ethnic minority sample, adjusted for gender, age, socioeconomic position and area deprivation

	Caribbeans (n=820) OR (95% CI)	Africans (n=690) OR (95% CI)	Indians (n=1,299) OR (95% CI)	Pakistanis (n=678) OR (95% CI)	Bangladeshis (n=233) OR (95% CI)
Co-ethnic density (per 10% increase)	0.96 (0.51,1.81)	0.92 (0.44,1.93)	0.94 (0.80,1.11)	1.09 (0.86,1.37)	1.09 (0.80,1.49)
Overall ethnic minority density (per 10% increase)	1.02 (0.84,1.23)	1.00 (0.76,1.31)	0.95 (0.83,1.08)	1.03 (0.88,1.21)	0.95 (0.70,1.29)
Perceived ethnic density					
Less than half same	1	1	1	1	1
About half same	0.78 (0.25,2.46)	0.60 (0.12,3.07)	0.86 (0.44,1.71)	1.18 (0.50,2.78)	0.94 (0.26,3.42)
More than half same	1.10 (0.48,2.47)	0.83 (0.18,3.84)	0.75 (0.35,1.62)	1.00 (0.40,2.48)	0.73 (0.14,3.97)

CI = Confidence limit.
Source: Citizenship Survey 2005.

Table 11.5 Experiences of racial discrimination among the ethnic minority sample

	Caribbean (n=1,644) %	African (n=1,536) %	Indian (n=2,687) %	Pakistani (n=1,503) %	Bangladeshi (n=536) %
Fear of racial/religious attack					
Fairly or very worried	25.1	36.5	40.7	39.3	42.7
Organisational racism					
Expects to be treated worse than other races	43.9	37.4	24.1	29.1	30.2

Source: Citizenship Surveys 2005 and 2007 combined.

Table 11.6 summarises the relationship between the three measures of ethnic density and racism. Co-ethnic density and perceived ethnic density were statistically significantly associated with lower likelihood of fear of racial or religious attack amongst Indian and Pakistani people. In contrast, perceived ethnic density was associated with increased likelihood of fear of racial or religious attack amongst Caribbean participants. All three measures of ethnic density were also associated with lower likelihood of expected organisational racism amongst Indian participants. These findings point to a possible protective effect of ethnic density, irrespective of the choice of measure for both interpersonal and institutional racism for Indian participants. For other ethnic groups the results were less consistent and it is not possible to identify clear patterns.

Table 11.6 Relationships between ethnic density and racism among the ethnic minority sample, adjusted for gender, age, socioeconomic position, area deprivation and length of residence in neighbourhood

	Caribbean (n=1,644) OR (95% CI)	African (n=1,536) OR (95% CI)	Indian (n=2,687) OR (95% CI)	Pakistani (n=1,503) OR (95% CI)	Bangladeshi (n=536) OR (95% CI)
Fear of racial/religious attack					
Co-ethnic density (per 10% increase)	0.93 (0.75,1.15)	1.07 (0.91,1.27)	0.94 (0.90,0.99)*	0.89 (0.83,0.96)**	1.00 (0.90,1.11)
Overall ethnic minority density (per 10% increase)	0.96 (0.90,1.03)	1.02 (0.96,1.09)	0.96 (0.92,0.99)*	0.98 (0.93,1.03)	0.87 (0.78,0.97)*
Perceived ethnic density					
Less than half same	1	1	1	1	1
About half same	1.28 (0.97,1.68)	0.92 (0.67,1.27)	0.88 (0.72,1.08)	0.97 (0.74,1.27)	0.98 (0.60,1.62)
More than half same	1.50 (1.06, 2.11)	1.56 (1.12,2.18)	0.72 (0.59,0.88)	0.70 (0.53,0.91)	0.90 (0.58,1.39)
p-value (across all categories)	*		**	*	
Organisational racism					
Co-ethnic density (per 10% increase)	0.97 (0.79,1.18)	0.97 (0.82,1.15)	0.92 (0.87,0.97)**	1.03 (0.95,1.12)	1.00 (0.89,1.13)
Overall ethnic minority density (per 10% increase)	0.96 (0.91,1.03)	0.96 (0.90,1.02)	0.94 (0.90,0.98)**	1.02 (0.97,1.08)	0.92 (0.82,1.03)
Perceived ethnic density					
Less than half same	1	1	1	1	1
About half same	0.84 (0.65,1.09)	0.67 (0.48,0.93)	0.81 (0.64,1.02)	0.71 (0.53,0.96)	1.52 (0.89,2.58)
More than half same	0.77 (0.55,1.08)	1.02 (0.73,1.44)	0.69 (0.55,0.88)	0.79 (0.59,1.05)	0.85 (0.52,1.39)
p-value (across all categories)		*	**		

*p<0.05, **p<0.01
Source: Citizenship Surveys 2005 and 2007 combined.

Note that the racism measures available within the Citizenship Survey capture fear of racism and expectations of experiencing racism but not actual discriminatory experiences. The Fourth National Survey of Ethnic Minorities, in contrast, included indicators of both fear and experience of racist attacks. Briefly, this survey was conducted in 1993–1994 and provided information on the experiences of a nationally representative sample of ethnic minorities living in England and Wales. Further information is provided by Modood et al. (1997). Data from the Fourth National Survey suggest that co-ethnic density and overall ethnic minority density are associated with experiences of racism as well as with fear of experiencing racism (Bécares et al., 2009). Despite differences in the measurement and survey design, the odds ratios summarizing the relationship between ethnic density and fear of racist attack are very similar for both surveys. For example, the odds ratio of reporting fear of racial attack was 0.94 (95% CI: 0.72, 1.23) per 10% increase in co-ethnic density for Caribbean participants. The corresponding odds ratio for experiencing racial attack was 0.89 (CI: 0.59, 1.37).

Levels of Social Cohesion and Association with Ethnic Density

Social cohesion did not vary across ethnic minority groups although it was statistically significantly higher for White participants ($p < 0.001$) (Table 11.7). In line with previous work (Boreham et al., 2002; Coulthard et al., 2001), social cohesion increased with age and was lower in more deprived areas (data not shown) and subsequent analyses were adjusted for these covariates, along with gender, socioeconomic position and length of residence in the neighbourhood.

There was a trend for greater social cohesion in areas of higher co-ethnic density and overall ethnic minority density for all ethnic groups, indicated by positive regression coefficients in Table 11.8 (although these did not attain statistical significance in all cases). Respondents reporting higher perceived ethnic density also reported greater social cohesion, with the exception of Caribbeans. We had expected that measured co-ethnic density would be more strongly and clearly associated with social cohesion than was overall ethnic minority density but there was no evidence to support this. In fact, the effect of a 10% increase in overall ethnic minority density was greater than that for co-ethnic density. Compared with the reference group,

Table 11.7 Social cohesion by ethnic group

	Caribbean (*n*=832)	African (*n*=706)	Indian (*n*=1,314)	Pakistani (*n*=685)	Bangladeshi (*n*=240)	White (*n*=8,915)
Mean social cohesion score (0–100)	52.6	53.6	53.6	52.9	52.6	58.0
Standard deviation	14.6	15.2	14.0	14.2	13.6	14.3

Source: Citizenship Survey 2005.

Table 11.8 Estimates for social cohesion regressed on ethnic density among the ethnic minority sample, adjusted for gender, age, socioeconomic position, area deprivation and length of residence in neighbourhood

	Caribbean (n=832) Coeff. (s.e.)	African (n=706) Coeff. (s.e.)	Indian (n=1,314) Coeff. (s.e.)	Pakistani (n=685) Coeff. (s.e.)	Bangladeshi (n=240) Coeff. (s.e.)
Co-ethnic density (per 10% increase)	0.007 (0.089)	0.063 (0.086)	0.074 (0.019)†	0.055 (0.037)	0.141 (0.048)**
Overall ethnic minority density (per 10% increase)	0.223 (0.098)*	0.125 (0.119)	0.256 (0.067)†	0.074 (0.092)	0.091 (0.148)
	Mean (SE) difference	Mean (SE) difference	Mean (SE) difference	Mean (SE) difference	Mean (SE) difference
Perceived ethnic density					
Less than half same	Ref	Ref	Ref	Ref	Ref
About half same	–0.30 (1.19)	2.73 (1.64)	1.91 (0.99)	–0.06 (1.39)	1.62 (2.70)
More than half same	–2.04 (1.53)	2.08 (1.86)	2.88 (0.92)	3.64 (1.34)	3.28 (2.19)
p-value (across all categories)			**	**	

*p<0.05, **p<0.01, †p<0.001
Source: Citizenship Survey 2005.

those who perceived more than half of the people in the area to be of the same ethnic density had social cohesion scores around two to three points higher. The almost zero regression coefficient for co-ethnic density and the negative coefficients for perceived ethnic density amongst Caribbeans are intriguing and could represent a real difference in the effect of Caribbean density on social outcomes in this ethnic group. With the exception of Caribbean participants, Table 11.8 shows a consistent positive relationship between social cohesion and ethnic density on all three of the density measures, although possibly due to lack of statistical power these relationships are not statistically significant in every case.

Prevalence of Civic Engagement and Association with Ethnic Density

Volunteering and civic activity were less common among Indian, Pakistan and Bangladeshi respondents than amongst Caribbeans, Africans and Whites (Table 11.9). Note that the Citizenship Survey does not distinguish between civic engagement in groups and organisations for ethnic minorities specifically although it does distinguish engagement undertaken within versus outside the local area.

Table 11.9 Prevalence of civic engagement by ethnic group

	Caribbean (n=1,644) %	African (n=1,536) %	Indian (n=2,687) %	Pakistani (n=1,503) %	Bangladeshi (n=536) %	White (n=16,536) %
Any civic participation	12.6	11.1	7.7	7.2	7.3	9.4
Any informal volunteering	64.3	60.6	55.0	52.8	45.0	65.8
Any formal volunteering	40.5	42.1	34.8	26.2	25.2	43.6
Any civic engagement (any of the above)	75.5	73.6	67.5	64.1	60.6	80.1

Source: Citizenship Surveys 2005 and 2007.

Table 11.10 shows no evidence of a protective association between any of the ethnic density measures and either volunteering or civic engagement. The direction of the odds ratios suggests that formal volunteering is less likely in areas of higher overall ethnic minority density and indeed associations were statistically significant for all groups except Bangladeshis. There was no clear evidence that volunteering in informal activities was associated with the three measures of ethnic density. The direction of association was dependent on the ethnic group under consideration. There was a tendency for decreasing likelihood of informal volunteering with increasing ethnic density for Caribbeans and Indians and some indication that informal volunteering was more likely in areas of higher ethnic density for Bangladeshis. The odds ratios for civic engagement (which combines volunteering and participation in civic activities) were below 1 for some ethnic groups and above 1 for others and also varied across choice of ethnic density measure.

Thus there is no evidence to support the hypothesis that ethnic density is associated with greater civic engagement. It is possible that the indicators of civic engagement included in the Citizenship Survey are capturing western ideas, forms and ideals of engagement (Skocpol, 1996) and that alternative indicators or in-depth work could portray a different picture. However, these findings were mirrored for informal volunteering as captured in the Citizenship Survey.

Limitations of the Study

These analyses are based on cross-sectional data from an observation study and leave open the possibility of self-selection of people into different types of areas. However, it seems unlikely that the observed association between ethnic density and racism would be driven by self-selection since the literature suggests that fear of and experiences of racism are one motivation for people to remain in higher density areas (Whitley et al., 2006). Halpern and Nazroo (1999) tested the possibility that the ethnic density effect was due to social selection or drift rather than social

Table 11.10 Relationship between co-ethnic density and civic engagement among the ethnic minority sample, adjusted for socioeconomic position, nativity, area deprivation and length of residence in neighbourhood

	Caribbean OR (95% CI)	African OR (95% CI)	Indian OR (95% CI)	Pakistani OR (95% CI)	Bangladeshi OR (95% CI)
Any formal volunteering					
Co-ethnic density (per 10% increase)	0.91 (0.73,1.15)	0.99 (0.83,1.19)	0.92 (0.86,0.98)**	0.86 (0.76,0.98)*	0.98 (0.82,1.17)
Overall density (per 10% increase)					
Perceived ethnic density	0.91 (0.84,0.98)*	0.91 (0.85,0.98)**	0.89 (0.85,0.94)†	0.91 (0.84,0.99)*	0.97 (0.83,1.13)
Less than half same	1	1	1	1	1
About half same	0.76 (0.59,0.98)	0.97 (0.71,1.33)	0.89 (0.72,1.11)	0.68 (0.49,0.92)	0.70 (0.39,1.25)
More than half same	0.98 (0.71,1.36)	1.03 (0.73,1.46)	0.69 (0.56,0.85)	0.51 (0.38,0.70)	0.78 (0.46,1.32)
p-value (across all categories)			†	†	
Any informal volunteering					
Co-ethnic density (per 10% increase)	0.93 (0.74–1.17)	1.15 (0.94,1.41)	0.97 (0.91,1.04)	1.04 (0.95,1.13)	1.08 (0.96,1.22)
Overall density (per 10% increase)	0.91 (0.85,0.98)*	0.93 (0.86,1.00)	0.94 (0.89,0.99)*	0.99 (0.94,1.06)	0.99 (0.89,1.02)
Perceived ethnic density					
Less than half same	1	1	1	1	1
About half same	0.77 (0.60,1.00)	1.01 (0.74,1.38)	0.93 (0.76,1.15)	0.89 (0.68,1.18)	1.42 (0.85,2.40)
More than half same	0.88 (0.63,1.22)	1.12 (0.79,1.57)	0.78 (0.65,0.96)	0.91 (0.70,1.19)	1.41 (0.88,2.25)
p-value (across all categories)			*		
Any civic engagement					
Co-ethnic density (per 10% increase)	0.96 (0.74,1.23)	1.12 (0.90,1.40)	0.94 (0.88,1.01)	1.02 (0.93,1.11)	1.12 (0.96,1.29)
Overall density (per 10% increase)	0.91 (0.84,0.98)*	0.93 (0.85,1.00)	0.91 (0.86,0.96)†	0.98 (0.93,1.04)	1.01 (0.89,1.15)
Perceived ethnic density					
Less than half same	1	1	1	1	1
About half same	0.75 (0.57,1.00)	0.76 (0.55,1.06)	0.88 (0.70,1.10)	0.96 (0.72,1.28)	1.30 (0.77,2.20)
More than half same	1.06 (0.73,1.55)	1.04 (0.71,1.52)	0.70 (0.57,0.87)	0.87 (0.66,1.14)	1.38 (0.87,2.19)
p-value (across all categories)			**		

*$p<0.05$, **$p<0.01$, †$p<0.001$.
Source: Citizenship Surveys 2005 and 2007.

causation and acculturation. They argue that the ethnic density effect cannot be fully explained by either of these phenomena, and that the effect found reflects the benefits of group density, which notably reduce the exposure to racial harassment and provide increased social support from other ethnic minority people (Halpern and Nazroo, 1999).

Analyses are based on small numbers of participants for some outcomes, notably for racism and formal volunteering, so there is low statistical power to detect small effect sizes when stratifying by ethnic group. However, there are no UK datasets with substantially larger numbers of participants to address this limitation. The data are also limited in their inclusion of participants in areas where co-ethnic density exceeded 40% so although the relationship between ethnic density and outcomes appears to be linear within the range of these data, we cannot speak about the nature of the relationship at higher levels of density. If there is a threshold at which ethnic density begins to have a notably stronger effect, then it will be missed in this study. However, the Citizenship Survey reflects the residential patterning of ethnic minorities in the UK and this limitation is not a result of the survey sampling strategy. This highlights the danger in translating findings from other countries where ethnic densities extend beyond the range seen in the UK.

Conclusions and Implications

For Indian respondents, higher ethnic density is associated with lower likelihood of fearing and expecting racism and this holds across the three measures of ethnic density considered here. Findings were less consistent for other ethnic minorities, possibly because of low statistical power although there was an indication that Caribbeans who perceived higher ethnic density in their area were more likely to fear racist or religious attack.

Social cohesion is greater in areas of higher ethnic density for all ethnic minorities on all three ethnic density measures, with the exception of Caribbeans. The relationship to social cohesion seems to be stronger for overall ethnic minority density than for co-ethnic density. This is contrary to our original hypothesis and could indicate that greater ethnic mix in the area promotes greater tolerance and appreciation of diverse ethnic identities and cultures. Alternatively, it may represent the residential choices of people who are more tolerant moving into more mixed areas. In contrast, several studies undertaken in the US appear to indicate that indices related to ethnic density are negatively correlated with markers of social cohesion. In a Chicago-based study, Sampson et al. (1997) found a negative correlation between neighbourhood immigrant concentration (derived from percent Latino and percent foreign born persons) and collective efficacy, captured by ten items, five of which capture social cohesion (four of them included in the Citizenship Survey and used here) and five of which capture informal social control. Despite some overlap in the measures used, it is not possible to directly compare our findings since the Chicago study included an additional construct of informal social control and our measure of social cohesion included additional items capturing tolerance and respect between ethnic groups. Putnam (2007) studied a different exposure, namely ethnic homogeneity, and found it to be positively correlated with trust in neighbours which is one of the elements making up the social cohesion scale studied here. Although the exposure of interest there was not ethnic density per se, ethnic homogeneity was measured using the Herfindahl index and is positively correlated with ethnic density. Similarly, Costa and Kahn (2003) found greater ethnic diversity to be associated with lower levels of trust.

It is worth noting that we have investigated the relationship between ethnic density and perceived social cohesion for ethnic minority groups separately whereas most previous studies have not conducted a stratified analysis. Our study does not include analysis of the impact of ethnic density on social cohesion for white residents. These intriguing differences in findings relating to ethnic density and social cohesion could be explained by differences in the measures used or the analytic approach taken or they could indicate real differences in the relationship between ethnic density and social cohesion in the UK compared with predominantly US-based studies. For example, a UK study by Pennant (2005) found no significant association between ethnic diversity and trust in employers, the police, the courts, or councils, nor in volunteering or civic participation (although she did find an association between ethnic diversity and generalised trust). However, US literature does suggest a positive relationship between exposure to social networks that cut across diverse political views and political tolerance (Mutz, 2002). Therefore although not directly speaking to tolerance of ethnic diversity, this provides some support for the intergroup contact hypothesis (Allport, 1954) in the US context. The determinants of tolerance, trust, social capital and social cohesion are multifactorial including the national and local context as well as socio-cultural norms within the majority and minority ethnic groups.

The finding that the association between ethnic density and outcomes varies across ethnic groups confirms Yuan's (2008) findings. She demonstrated a positive association between co-ethnic density and social support and positive well-being for Blacks, but not for Hispanics, in Illinois. However, co-ethnic density was associated with less anger amongst Hispanics (but not Blacks) and she proposed that co-ethnic density offers different benefits according to the different cultural and social resources of each ethnic group. Marschall and Stolle (2004) also questionned the appropriateness of a general model which assumes the development of trust takes place in the same way for all ethnic groups in all contexts. Their Detroit study showed that neighbourhood ethnic diversity was associated with greater generalised trust for Blacks, but that socioeconomic factors were the predominant neighbourhood level contributor to generalised trust for Whites. Clearly the development of trust and other elements of social cohesion might differ according to the experience of being in a minority or majority ethnic group, but possibly also in a more fine-grained way between ethnic minority groups.

There was a suggestion that perceived ethnic density was associated with lower social cohesion for Caribbeans. This finding, and the indication that perceived ethnic density was associated with greater fear of racist attack amongst Caribbeans, suggest that the impact of ethnic density on outomes for this ethnic group could be qualitatively different than outcomes for other ethnic minority groups. Further work might explore the characteristics of the areas in which Caribbeans reside, such as the employment situation, industrial history, urbanicity, urbanisation and crime, resulting in diffrent kinds of race relations with white residents. It might also explore the overlap of ethnic and religious density and the role of religious affiliation in explaining differential effects of ethnic density across ethnic minority groups.

There may also be differences in the meaning of ethnic identity for Caribbeans relating, for example, to the historical treatment and perception of this group. Over time, the negative stereotyping of Blacks (Apena, 2007; Freeth, 1985; Greenwald et al., 2003) may infiltrate peoples' psyche and materialize into real-life settings. These negative stereotypes about Blacks may have strong implications for self perception (Speight, 2007). We are unable to explore the relevance of variations in the meaning of ethnic identity for differences in the ethnic density effect across ethnic minority groups further given the current data but it may be an idea worth pursuing in future research.

We found no support for the possibility that ethnic density promotes civic engagement. This could be due to limitations in the measures, as discused previously. Extant literature is divided and Anderson and Paskeviciute (2006) discuss why a higher proportion of ethnic minority residents might be positively related to some forms of citizenship behaviour whilst being negatively related to some other forms. This is confirmed by empirical studies showing, for example, that people in more racially mixed communities are less likely to participate in social and civic activities (Alesina and La Ferrara, 2000 Costa and Kahn, 2003) and others showing increased political participation in more ethnically dense areas (LaVeist, 1993).

Our starting premise was that associations between ethnic density and the outcomes of interest may vary across the ethnic groups considered. The stratification of analyses by ethnic group clearly reduces the statistical power to detect effects because of small numbers but has allowed us to identify possible differences between Caribbeans and other groups which are worthy of further investigation. We contend that an approach which assumes that different ethnic minority groups can be combined is often not appropriate and should be avoided where possible.

Our findings illustrate that there are some social benefits for ethnic minorities living in more ethnically dense areas, despite these areas being more materially deprived. Official reports show that racism and worry about racism are not uncommon among ethnic minorities in the UK. Residential choices are complex, but if fear of racism is one of the contributing factors then we need to continue to tackle racism and worry about racism in order to enable ethnic minorities greater choice about where they live.

It is interesting to note that levels of social cohesion seem to increase with increasing ethnic density. More detailed understanding about the nature of social cohesion and its formation and preservation amongst ethnic minorities in areas of high ethnic concentration may inform more general work on the promotion of cohesive communities. This will require detailed consideration of the types and quality of social contact, within and between ethnic and other socio-demographic groups, using longitudinal methods which capture processes and changes over time.

Acknowledgements This work was supported by the United Kingdom Economic and Social Research Council (grant RES-163-25-0043). M. S. was supported by a United Kingdom National Institute for Health Research personal award. We would like to thank John D'Souza at the National Centre for Social Research for his assistance with data linkage on this project.

References

Abada, T., Hou, F. and Ram, B. (2007) Racially mixed neighborhoods, perceived neighborhood social cohesion, and adolescent health in Canada, *Social Science Medicine*, 65(10): 2004–2017.

Alesina, A. and Ferrara, E.L. (2000) Participation in heterogeneous communities, *Quarterly Journal of Economics*, 115: 874–904.

Alesina, A.F. and La Ferrara, E. (2002) Who trusts others? *Journal of Public Economics*, 85(2): 207–234.

Allport, G.W. (1954) *The Nature of Prejudice*, Addison-Wesley, Reading, MA.

Anderson, C.J. and Paskeviciute, A. (2005) Macro-politics and micro-behavior: Mainstream politics and the frequency of political discussion in contemporary democracies in Zuckerman, A.S. (ed.), *The Social Logic of Politics*, Temple University Press, Philadelphia, PA, pp. 228–248.

Anderson, C.J. and Paskeviciute, A. (2006) How linguistic and ethnic heterogeneity influence the prospects for civil society: A comparative study of citizenship behaviour, *Journal of Politics*, 68(4): 783–802.

Apena, F. (2007) Being black and in trouble: The role of self-perception in the offending behaviour of black youth, *Youth Justice*, 7(3): 211–228.

Bhugra, D. and Becker, M. (2005) Migration, cultural bereavement and cultural identity, *World Psychiatry*, 4(1): 18–24.

Boreham, R., Stafford, M. and Taylor, R. (2002) *Health Survey for England 2000: Social Capital and Health*, The Stationery Office, London.

Boydell, J., van Os, J., Mckenzie, K., Allardyce, J., Goel, R., McCreadie, R.G., et al. (2001) Incidence of schizophrenia in ethnic minorities in London: Ecological study into interactions with environment, *British Medical Journal*, 323: 1336.

Bécares, L., Nazroo, J. and Stafford, M. (2009) The buffering effects of ethnic density on experienced racism and health, *Health Place*, 15(3): 670–678.

Clark, K. and Drinkwater, S. (2002) Enclaves, neighbourhood effects and employment outcomes: Ethnic minorities in England and Wales, *Journal of Population Economics*, 15: 5–29.

Costa, D.L. and Kahn, M.E. (2003) Civic engagement in heterogeneous communities, *Perspectives on Politics*, 1(1): 103–112.

Coulthard, M., Walker, A. and Morgan, A. (2001) *Assessing People's Perceptions of Their Neighbourhood and Community Involvement (Part 1)*, Health Development Agency, London.

Cummins, S., Stafford, M., Macintyre, S., Marmot, M. and Ellaway, A. (2005) Neighbourhood environment and its association with self rated health: Evidence from Scotland and England, *Journal of Epidemiology and Community Health*, 59: 207–213.

Daley, P. (1998) Black Africans in Great Britain: Spatial concentration and segregation, *Urban Studies*, 35(10): 1703–1724.

Davey Smith, G., Chaturvedi, N., Harding, S., Nazroo, J.Y. and Williams, R. (2000) Ethnic inequalities in health: A review of the UK epidemiological evidence, *Critical Public Health*, 10: 375–408.

Davey-Smith, G., Hart, C., Watt, G., Hole, D. and Hawthorne, V. (1998) Individual social class, area-based deprivation, cardiovascular disease risk factors, and mortality: The Renfrew and Paisley study, *Journal of Epidemiology and Community Health*, 52: 399–405.

Diez-Roux, A.V., Nieto, F.J., Muntaner, C., Tyroler, H.A., Comstock, G.W., Shahar, E., et al. (1997) Neighborhood environments and coronary heart disease: A multilevel analysis, *American Journal of Epidemiology*, 146: 48–63.

Durlauf, S. (1999) The case "against" social capital, *Focus*, 20: 1–5. Downloaded on 1 May, 2004, from http://www.ssc.edu/econ/archive/wp9929.pdf

Echeverría, S., Diez-Roux, A.V., Shea, S., Borrell, L.N. and Jackson, S. (2008) Associations of neighborhood problems and neighborhood social cohesion with mental health and health behaviors: The Multi-Ethnic Study of Atherosclerosis, *Health Place*, 14(4): 853–865.

Ecob, R. and Williams, R. (1991) Sampling Asian minorities to assess health and welfare, *Journal of Epidemiology and Community Health*, 45(2): 93–101.

Ellen, I.G. (2000) Is segregation bad for your health? The case of low birth weight, *Brookings-Wharton Papers on Urban Affairs*, 2000: 203.

Erens, B., Primatesta, P. and Prior, G. (2001) *Health Survey for England 1999: The Health of Minority Ethnic Groups*, The Stationery Office, London.

Eschbach, K., Ostir, G.V., Patel, K.V., Markides, K.S. and Goodwin, J.S. (2004) Neighborhood context and mortality among older Mexican Americans: Is there a barrio advantage? *American Journal of Public Health*, 94(10): 1807–1812.

Fagg, J., Curtis, S., Stansfeld, S. and Congdon, P. (2006) Psychological distress among adolescents, and its relationship to individual, family and area characteristics in East London, *Social Science and Medicine*, 63: 636–648.

Fang, J., Madhavan, S., Bosworth, W. and Alderman, M.H. (1998) Residential segregation and mortality in New York City, *Social Science and Medicine*, 47(4): 469–476.

Faris, R.E. and Dunham, H.W. (1939) *Mental Disorders in Urban Areas: An Ecological Study of Schizophrenia and Other Psychoses*, The University of Chicago Press, Chicago/London.

Fieldhouse, E. and Cutts, D. (2008) Diversity, density and turnout: The effect of neighbourhood ethno-religious composition on voter turnout in Britain, *Political Geography*, 27: 530–548.

Franzini, L. and Spears, W. (2003) Contributions of social context to inequalities in years of life lost to heart disease in Texas, USA, *Social Science and Medicine*, 57(10): 1847–1861.

Freeth, T. (1985) Racism on television: Bringing the colonies back home in Cohen, P. and Gardner, C. (eds.), *It Ain't Half Racist, Mum – Fighting Racism in the Media*, Comedia Publishing Group, London.

Glaeser, E.L., Laibson, I., Scheinkman, J. and Soutter, C. (2000) Measuring trust, *The Quarterly Journal of Economics*, 115: 811–846.

Greenwald, A.G., Oakes, M.A. and Hoffman, H.G. (2003) Targets of discrimination: Effects of race on responses to weapon holders, *Journal of Experimental Social Psychology*, 39: 399–405.

Haan, M., Kaplan, G.A. and Camacho, T. (1987) Poverty and health: Prospective evidence from the Alameda County study, *American Journal of Epidemiology*, 125: 989–998.

Halpern, D. (1993) Minorities and mental health, *Social Science and Medicine*, 36: 597–607.

Halpern, D. and Nazroo, J. (1999) The ethnic density effect: Results from a National Community Survey of England and Wales, *International Journal of Social Psychology*, 46(1): 34–46.

Harris, A.H. and Thoresen, C.E. (2005) Volunteering is associated with delayed mortality in older people: Analysis of the longitudinal study of aging, *Journal of Health Psychology*, 10(6): 739–752.

Harris, R., Tobias, M., Jeffreys, M., Waldegrave, K., Karlsen, S. and Nazroo, J. (2006a) Effects of self-reported racial discrimination and deprivation on Māori health and inequalities in New Zealand: Cross-sectional study, *Lancet*, 367(9527): 2005–2009.

Harris, R., Tobias, M., Jeffreys, M., Waldegrave, K., Karlsen, S. and Nazroo, J. (2006b) Racism and health: The relationship between experience of racial discrimination and health in New Zealand, *Social Science and Medicine*, 63(6): 1428–1441.

Karlsen, S., Nazroo, J.Y. and Stephenson, R. (2002) Ethnicity, environment and health: Putting ethnic inequalities in health in their place, *Social Science & Medicine*, 5(9): 1647–1661.

Kawachi, I. and Berkman, L. (2000) Social cohesion, social capital, and health in Berkman, L. and Kawachi, I. (eds.), *Social Epidemiology*, Oxford University Press, New York, NY, pp. 174–190.

Kawachi, I. and Kennedy, B.P. (1997) Health and social cohesion: Why care about income inequality? *British Medical Journal*, 314(7086): 1037–1040.

Krieger, N. (1990) Racial and gender discrimination: Risk factors for high blood pressure? *Social Science & Medicine*, 30: 1273–1281.

Krieger, N. (1992) Overcoming the absence of socioeconomic data in medical records: Validation and application of a census-based methodology, *American Journal of Public Health*, 82: 703–710.

Krieger, N. (1999) Does racism harm health? Did child abuse exist before 1962? On explicit questions, critical science, and current controversies: An ecosocial perspective, *American Journal of Public Health*, 93: 194–199.

Krieger, N. (2000) Discrimination and health in Berkman, L.F. and Kawachi, I. (eds.), *Social Epidemiology*, Oxford University Press, Oxford, pp. 36–75.

Krieger, N. and Sidney, S. (1996) Racial discrimination and blood pressure: The CARDIA study of young black and white adults, *American Journal of Public Health*, 86: 1370–1378.

LaVeist, T.A. (1992) The political empowerment and health status of African Americans: Mapping a new territory, *American Journal of Sociology*, 97(4): 1080–1095.

Laveist, T.A. (1993) Segregation, poverty, and empowerment: Health consequences for African Americans, *Milbank Quarterly*, 71(1): 41–64.

LeClere, F.B., Rogers, R.G. and Peters, K.D. (1997) Ethnicity and mortality in the United States: Individual and community correlates, *Social Forces*, 76: 169–198.

Lyyra, T.M. and Heikkinen, R.L. (2006) Perceived social support and mortality in older people, *Journals of Gerontology Series B: Psychological Sciences and Social Sciences*, 61(3): S147–S152.

Marschall, M.J. and Stolle, D. (2004) Race and the city: Neighborhood context and the development of generalized trust, *Political Behavior*, 26(2): 125–153.

Michaelson, J., Pickering, K., Wood, N. and Scholes, A. (2005) Home office citizenship survey, *Technical Report*, Downloaded on 08/06/2006 from http://www.esds.ac.uk/findingData/snDescription.asp?sn=5367

Modood, T., Berthoud, R., Lakey, J., Nazroo, J.Y., Smith, P., Virdee, S., et al. (1997) *Ethnic Minorities in Britain: Diversity and Disadvantage*, Policy Studies Institute, London.

Musick, M.A., Herzog, A.R. and House, J.S. (1999) Volunteering and mortality among older adults: Findings from a national sample, *Journals of Gerontology Series B: Psychological Sciences and Social Sciences*, 54(3): S173–S180.

Mutz, D.C. (2002) Cross-cutting social networks: Testing democratic theory in practice, *American Political Science Review*, 96(1): 111–126.

Nazroo, J.Y. (1997) *The Health of Britain's Ethnic Minorities: Findings from a National Survey*, Policy Studies Institute, London.

Nazroo, J.Y. (2001) *Ethnicity, Class and Health*, Policy Studies Institute, London.

Nazroo, J.Y. (2003) Patterns of and explanations for ethnic inequalities in health in Mason, D. (ed.), *Explaining Ethnic Differences in Health*, Policy Press, Bristol, pp. 87–103.

Neeleman, J. and Wessely, S. (1999) Ethnic minority suicide: A small area geographical study in south London, *Psychological Medicine*, 29(2): 429–436.

Neeleman, J., Wilson-Jones, C. and Wessely, S. (2001) Ethnic density and deliberate self harm; a small area study in south east London, *Journal of Epidemiology and Community Health*, 55(2): 85–90.

ODPM (2004) *Housing, Planning, Local Government and the Regions Committee Social Cohesion Sixth Report of SESSION 2003–04 Volume I*, The Stationery Office, London.

Office for National Statistics (2004) *Geography, an important factor in data analysis*. Downloaded on 29 May, 2009, from http://www.neighbourhood.statistics.gov.uk/HTMLDocs/images/CaseStudies_Geography_tcm97-51119.pdf

Office for National Statistics (2008)*2001 Census: Standard area statistics (England and Wales)*. ESRC/JISC Census Programme, Census Dissemination Unit, Mimas University of Manchester, Manchester.

Paradies, Y. (2006) A systematic review of empirical research on self-reported racism and health, *International Journal of Epidemiology*, 35: 888–901.

Pennant, R. (2005) *Diversity, Trust and Community Participation in England*, Research, Development and Statistics Directorate, Home Office, London.

Pickett, K.E., Collins, J.W., Masi, C.M. and Wilkinson, R.G. (2005) The effects of racial density and income incongruity on pregnancy outcomes, *Social Science and Medicine*, 60(10): 2229–2238.

Pickett, K. and Pearl, M. (2001) Multilevel analyses of neighbourhood socioeconomic context and health outcomes: A critical review, *Journal of Epidemiology and Community Health*, 55(2): 111–122.

Pickett, K.E. and Wilkinson, R.G. (2008) Minorities and health: The effect of ethnic group density, *Ethnicity and Health*, 13(4): 321–334.

Portes, A. (1998) Social capital: Its origins and applications in modern sociology, *Annual Review of Sociology*, 24: 1–24.

Putnam, R. (2007) E Pluribus Unum: Diversity and community in the twenty-first century. The 2006 Johan Skytte Prize Lecture, *Scandinavian Political Studies*, 30: 137–174.

Rabkin, J.G. (1979) Ethnic density and psychiatric hospitalization: Hazards of minority status, *American Journal of Psychology*, 136(12): 1562–1566.

Riva, M., Gauvin, L. and Barnett, T.A. (2007) Toward the next generation of research into small area affects on health: A synthesis of multilevel investigation published since July 1998, *Journal of Epidemiology and Community Health*, 61(10): 853–861.

Roberts, E.M. (1997) Neighbourhood social environments and the distribution of low birthweight in Chicago, *American Journal of Public Health*, 87: 597–603.

Sampson, R.J., Raudenbush, S.W. and Earls, F. (1997) Neighbourhoods and violent crime: A multilevel study of collective efficacy, *Science*, 277: 918–924.

Skocpol, T. (1996) Unravelling from above, *The American Prospect*, 25: 20–25.

Smaje, C. (1995) Ethnic residential concentration and health: Evidence for a positive effect? *Policy and Politics*, 23(5): 251–269.

Speight, S.L. (2007) Internalized racism: One more piece of the puzzle, *The Counseling Psychologist*, 35(1): 126–134.

Stafford, M., Becares, L. and Nazroo, J. (2009) Objective and perceived ethnic density and health: Findings from a UK general population survey, *American Journal of Epidemiology*, 170(4): 484–493.

Stolle, D. and Rochon, T.R. (1998) Are all associations alike? Member diversity, associational type, and the creation of social capital, *American Behavioral Scientist*, 42: 47–65.

Veling, W., Susser, E., van Os, J., Mackenbach, J.P., Selten, J.P. and Hoek, H.W. (2008) Ethnic density of neighborhoods and incidence of psychotic disorders among immigrants, *American Journal of Psychology*, 165(1): 66–73.

White, K. and Borrell, L.N. (2006) Racial/ethnic neighborhood concentration and self-reported health in New York City, *Ethnicity and Disease*, 16(4): 900–908.

Whitley, R., Prince, M., McKenzie, K. and Stewart, R. (2006) Exploring the ethnic density effect: A qualitative study of a London electoral ward, *International Journal of Social Psychology*, 52(4): 376–391.

Wickrama, K.A.S., Noh, S. and Bryant, C.M. (2005) Racial differences in adolescent distress: Differential effects of the family and community for blacks and whites, *Journal of Community Psychology*, 33(3): 261–282.

Williams, D. (1999) Race, SES, and health: The added effects of racism and discrimination, *Annals of the New York Academy of Science*, 896: 173–188.

Williams, D. and Mohammed, S. (2009) Discrimination and racial disparities in health: Evidence and needed research, *Journal of Behavioral Medicine*, 32: 20–47.

Williams, D. and Neighbors, H. (2001) Racism, discrimination and hypertension: Evidence and needed research, *Ethnicity and Disease*, 11: 800–816.

Williams, D., Yu, Y., Jackson, J. and Anderson, N. (1997) Racial differences in physical and mental health: Socioeconomic status, stress, and discrimination, *Journal of Health Psychology*, 2: 335–351.

Yankauer, A. (1950) The relationship of fetal and infant mortality to residential segregation: An inquiry into social epidemiology, *American Sociology Review*, 15: 644–648.

Yuan, A.S.V. (2008) Racial composition of neighborhood and emotional well-being, *Sociological Spectrum*, 28: 105–129.

Chapter 12
Ethnic Variation in Crime-Related Experiences: A Statistical Comparison of Asian and Black Responses on the British Crime Survey 2001–2007

Paula Kautt

Introduction

Given current public and policy interest in immigration and the emergence of new minority identities in the United Kingdom, a public perception exists that Black and Minority Ethnicities (BMEs) have substantively different experiences of victimisation, fear of crime and the criminal justice system than their non-ethnic minority counterparts (Webster, 2007). Prominent examples such as recurring ethnic riots in the past 50 years or the police handling of the Stephen Lawrence case accentuate and reinforce this view. Such riots in Britain have often been triggered by heavy-handed police interventions coupled with longstanding tensions between the police and minority communities (Keith, 1993; Whitfield, 2007). Likewise, the London Metropolitan Police (Met) assumption that the 1993 racially-motivated murder of young black student, Stephen Lawrence, was drug-related cascaded into a series of significant procedural and evidential errors which resulted in the crime remaining unsolved to this day. Such events demonstrate the discriminatory treatment ethnic minorities can receive from the criminal justice system in England and Wales.

With such history, it is not surprising that ethnic minorities are less likely to report criminal victimisation to the police than the white majority (Avakame et al., 1999). Although it is common knowledge that not all crimes are brought to their attention, the rate of informing police is significantly lower amongst ethnic minorities. Since 1982, the British Crime Survey (BCS) has attempted to capture this 'dark figure' of unreported crime by asking participants about the victimisation experiences (Hough et al., 2007). In addition, it solicits information regarding their fear of crime and perceptions of the criminal justice system. These characteristics make BCS data ideal for assessing differences in criminological experiences and perceptions between the different ethnic groups of England and Wales.

As such, it may be surprising to learn that BCS data have only rarely been used to investigate the possible connections between ethnic minority status, victimisation,

P. Kautt (✉)
UCL Jill Dando Institute of Crime Science, University College London, London, WC1E 7HN, UK
e-mail: p.kautt@ucl.ac.uk

J. Stillwell, M. van Ham (eds.), *Ethnicity and Integration*, Understanding Population Trends and Processes 3, DOI 10.1007/978-90-481-9103-1_12,

fear of crime and perceptions of the criminal justice system. Given the availability of very recent BCS data, it is perhaps even more astonishing that existing research based on the BCS largely relies on older (pre-2001) data. This chapter gives a brief overview of research that uses recent (2001–2007) BCS data to examine not only how these outcomes vary across ethnicities but also whether the factors predicting those outcomes also fluctuate between BME groups. It aims to discern whether assuming that the influential factors apply equally to ethnic minorities is valid or instead misrepresents the relevant issues, possibly exacerbating pre-existing tensions. The findings suggest that the common practice of treating 'White' as the 'normal' status and the many distinct BME groups as interchangeable can distort results, leading to erroneous conclusions (Garland et al., 2006). This becomes particularly problematic when such results are used to inform or formulate criminal justice policy.

Background and Literature

Differential treatment of BME groups has been well-documented in several areas of social policy, including the criminal justice system (e.g. Hood, 1992; Paul, 1997). Research consistently shows that BME group members experience higher victimisation rates than 'White British' (Grant et al., 2006; Mason, 1995) and that these levels vary significantly between minority ethnicities (Clancy et al., 2001; Osborn and Tseloni, 1998; Trickett et al., 1995). At the same time, factors related to victimisation predict fear of crime (Hough, 1995) and regions with larger minority populations report higher levels of fear (Kershaw and Tseloni, 2005). Likewise, public opinion of the police and their ability to control crime directly influences fear of crime, linking it to perceived criminal justice system performance (Jackson, 2004; Tseloni, 2007). Such assessments of the criminal justice system vary chronically between ethnicities (Allen et al., 2006), some contend because of differences in the treatment received by Whites, Asians and Afro-Caribbeans (Bhui, 2009; Bucke, 1997; FitzGerald, 1998; Mason, 1995).

Existing BCS-based victimisation research largely focuses on the effect of individual or household characteristics over crime-related outcomes (Hope et al., 2001; Osborn and Tseloni, 1998; Osborn, Ellingworth et al., 1996); Trickett et al., 1992; Tseloni and Pease, 1998, 2005; Tseloni et al., 2002). Such studies identify several factors highly correlated with respondent ethnicity that influence risk of victimisation (Clancy et al., 2001; Osborn and Tseloni, 1998; Trickett et al., 1995). These include: single-parent status, living in the inner city, type of residence (such as terraced or semi-detached), employment status, respondent age, income, education and previous victimisation (as well as offence type). Such results strongly indicate that respondent ethnicity indirectly influences the likelihood of criminal victimisation at both the household and the individual level. Other BCS studies identify area-level factors correlated with area ethnic composition that influence victimisation rates such as: area economic status, residential stability, area levels of family disruption, urbanisation, strength of community ties and most notably ethnic heterogeneity (Lowenkamp et al., 2003; Markowitz et al., 2001; Sampson and Groves, 1989).

Recent research incorporates both sets of factors into statistical analyses by using multilevel modelling techniques to simultaneously account for these distinct levels of influence (Tseloni, 2006). The subsequent results effectively demonstrate not only that factors associated with ethnicity wield significant influence over victimisation but also that the impact of these factors varies by area.

Victimisation, in turn, increases fear of crime (Tseloni, 2007). Although studies show that such fear generally overestimates the likelihood of victimisation (Ditton and Chadee, 2006; Farrall and Gadd, 2004), strong connections exist between the two (Gabriel and Greve, 2003; Hale, 1996; Hollway and Jefferson, 1997). Most factors predicting victimisation also predict fear of crime (Clancy et al., 2001). Likewise, the constellation of factors influencing fear levels varies both by crime type and area (Hough, 1995). For example, greater BME populations are associated with greater reported fear of crime (Kershaw and Tseloni, 2005).

Finally, perceived control over crime also influences fear of crime, directly linking fear levels to criminal justice system performance (Jackson, 2004). However, respondent perceptions of the criminal justice system are rarely assessed via multivariate techniques. The two existing BCS studies yield disparate results. For example, one not only finds that BMEs have different perceptions of criminal justice agencies as compared to Whites (Clancy et al., 2001) but that factors associated with ethnicity (e.g. having been stopped or searched by the police, reporting a crime, residing in a neighbourhood with high levels of incivilities and being employed) also impact these assessments. Yet, the other (Jansson, 2006) finds no such effects. Clearly, further work is needed to excavate the relationship between ethnicity and perceptions of the criminal justice system.

That most multivariate BCS studies rely on data from before 2001, further accentuates this need for additional research. Specifically, subsequent events and policies (9/11, Criminal Justice Act 2003, 7/7) are likely to influence criminological perceptions and experiences, perhaps in different ways between the ethnicities, making reliance on older data problematic at best. The larger research project, only partially reported here, remedies the above shortcomings by employing the most recent BCS data available (2001–2007) as well as multivariate and multilevel analyses to statistically compare BME respondents in selected experiences of victimization, fear of crime and perceptions of the criminal justice system (hereafter CJS). Beyond this, it expands upon the geographic variation uncovered by previous research (Tseloni, 2006) by using more refined measures (the 43 Criminal Justice Areas (CJAs) as opposed to the 12 regions) to represent geographic area in multilevel analyses.

The key questions examined are:

- What theoretically relevant factors significantly predict BCS respondent/household reported victimisation, fear of crime or perceptions of the CJS?
- To what extent do these factors vary with the ethnicity of the respondent?

- How does the effect strength (magnitude) of significant factors change significantly from one ethnic group to another?
- To what extent does the direction of effect for significant predictors vary by respondent ethnicity?
- How do the assessed outcomes vary by the CJA within which the respondent is situated?
- To what extent does CJA affect any of the previously uncovered ethnic differences?

These questions are based not only on research evidence but also on two key theoretical assumptions. First, ethnic experience is more individualised and context-dependent than empirical research generally takes into account (e.g. with simple White/non-White dichotomies or ethnicity 'dummy' variables). Commentators strongly maintain that any research attempting to assess the impact of ethnicity must embrace and incorporate different minority perspectives to better discern *the role of ethnicity ('Whiteness', 'Blackness', 'Asianess', or some 'otherness') in explaining offendings, victimization and criminal justice practices* (Phillips and Bowling, 2003, p. 271). Their arguments firmly establish a need to separately analyse the experiences of each BME group, not only from the indigenous White majority, but also from each other.

Second, victimisation, fear of crime and perceptions of the CJS are inextricably tied not only to one another but also to culture, locale and ethnicity. Specifically, in relation to locale and views of crime *…public attitudes toward crime express and gather meaning within a context of judgements, beliefs and values regarding law and order and the social make-up of one's community and society* (Jackson, 2004, p. 948). Moreover, this is directly tied to culture and ethnicity since *incivility may also symbolize the presence of a variety of sub-cultural groups whose behaviour is seen as different or foreign, with differing values, norms and behaviour* (Jackson, 2004, p. 948). Thus, location is directly related to both perceptions and experiences of the CJS as well as the impact that ethnicity may have over them. This demonstrates a clear need to take factors from both the individual and the area into account in any investigations of ethnic differences in criminological experiences and perceptions.

Data and Methods

The current analyses are quantitative, relying on data from the 2001–2007 BCS sweeps to provide individual-level information as well as from the 2001 Census to furnish CJA-level data. Both multivariate and multilevel techniques are deployed via a multistage strategy. Specifically, traditional 'pooled' analyses (all ethnicities analysed together with only 'dummy' indicators to differentiate by ethnicity) are followed by separate analyses for each ethnic group. Then, where possible, both pooled and ethnicity-specific multilevel models assess whether the CJA and its characteristics impact any uncovered ethnic effects. This strategy enables not only an assessment of the direct effects of ethnicity but also permits the gauging of its indirect effects and how those might vary by location.

Capturing Ethnicity

The BCS employs the same criteria as the 2001 Census to capture respondent ethnicity. As such, only Whites can be simply British (e.g. the White-British category). For Black or Asian respondents, an additional ethnicity is always attached (e.g. Black or British-Black Caribbean; Asian or British-Asian Indian). Thus, no non-White ethnicity can be simply 'British', even though this categorisation may actually apply in reality (Paul, 1997). This anomaly, however, is analytically useful. It enables the current research to legitimately partition the data into subsets at two ethnic tiers. The first tier, 'general ethnicity', is composed of larger groups differentiated mainly by the traditional racial groupings (e.g. White, Black, Asian and Other). The second tier, 'specific ethnicity', differentiates further between all persons falling within a given general ethnicity category. For example, under the general ethnicity category 'Asian' exist the sub-groups Indian, Pakistani, Bangladeshi and Chinese that can subsequently be compared to each other to assess any variation within the Asian general ethnic group. Figure 12.1 illustrates this breakdown as well as provides the overall frequency distribution for each ethnic group[1] – both general

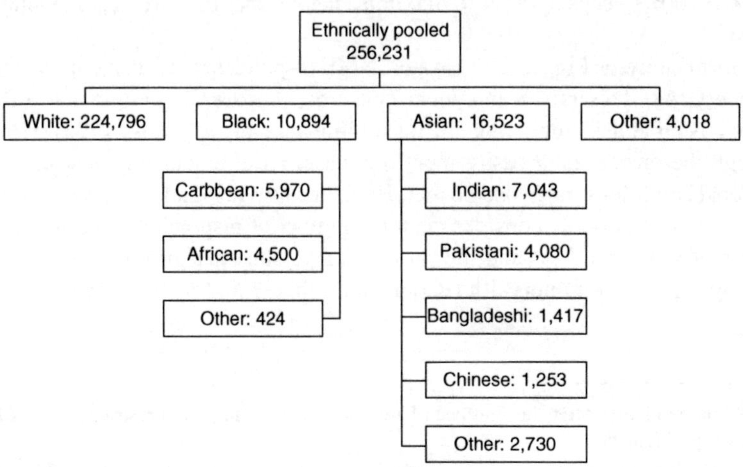

Fig. 12.1 Nested ethnicities and total ethnicity frequencies in 2001–2007 BCS sweeps

[1] The current research does not examine the available White ethnicities. Notably, the BCS does not capture White ethnicities beyond British, Irish and Other. For Other, the only options are English, Scottish and Welsh. Different White ethnicities (e.g. Polish) are not captured. Given the influx of

and specific. This chapter is predominantly concerned with comparisons by general ethnicity (see below).

Notably, the BCS captures 'Other' ethnic categories at both the General and Specific levels. However, because the number and proportion of different ethnicities comprising these groups is unknown, there is no meaningful way to discuss them. Thus, this research omits the general Other category from General Ethnicity analyses as well as the Black-Other and Asian-Other categories from the Specific Ethnicity analyses. Similarly, several Mixed ethnicity categories are present in the data (Mixed White and Black Caribbean, Mixed White and Black African, Mixed White and Asian and Mixed with any other mixed background). Unfortunately, due to small numbers, Mixed cases cannot be analysed independently. Rather, based on the supposition that such respondents will likely appear to be a member of the specifically-named BME group to a third party (e.g. offender, police), they are merged (where applicable[2]) into that ethnic group for analysis. This is done, in part, to address problems with sample size.

Sample Size Issues

Figure 12.1 shows that most BCS respondents are ethnically White. BMEs comprise approximately 10% of the sample, roughly commensurate with their representation in the overall population of England and Wales. Thus, although each year of BCS data includes roughly 1,000 cases per CJA, it is necessary to pool the data across the 2001–2007 sweeps in order to maximise the number of BME cases available for analysis.[3]

Unfortunately, as Fig. 12.2 illustrates, BME respondents are unevenly distributed between CJAs. This raises analytical concerns. An overall sample size of 3,500 has long been considered sufficient for multilevel analysis (Mok, 1995). However, although the current data easily meet this basic requirement for most ethnicities, additional conditions must also be met. Here, because respondents are nested within CJAs, one must not only consider the total number of respondents but also both the number of groups (CJAs) and the number of persons per group (respondents per CJA). Specifically, for interval-level outcomes, there must be 30 groups (CJAs) with

---

other White ethnicities after the European Union loosened immigration restrictions, this lack of diversity is problematic.

[2]Whilst the Black Mixed groups can be employed at both ethnicity levels, the Asian Mixed group can only be used in the general ethnicity analyses because there is no specific ethnicity information appended. Moreover, for the reasons articulated above regarding Other ethnic categories, the Other Mixed group cannot be used in any analyses.

[3]Notably, the decision to pool by year necessitates that an indicator of the 'year of interview' be included in the analyses. Moreover, such pooling also means that only those indicators available for all years (2001–2007) can be used. This precludes inclusion of some theoretically salient factors (e.g. respondent religion) that were captured only in later sweeps.

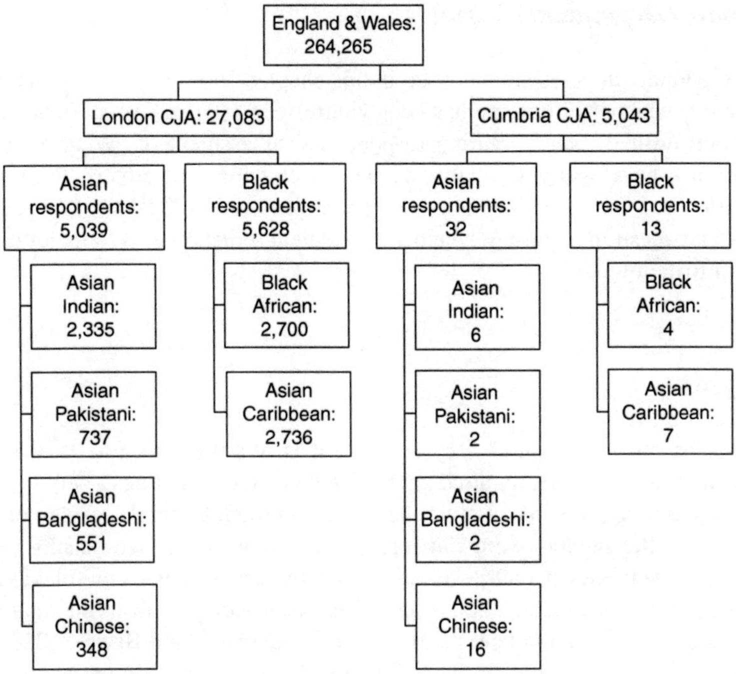

Fig. 12.2 Frequency comparison by ethnicity for London and Cumbria criminal justice areas (Specific ethnicity counts exclude the Other category)

30 cases (respondents) per group to assess contextual effects via multilevel analysis (Maas and Hox, 2005). Even more stringent, when dealing with dichotomous and ordinal outcomes, the prescribed minimums are 50 groups (CJAs) with 50 cases (respondents) per group (Hedeker, 2008; Moineddin et al., 2007). If these conditions are not met, standard errors will be significantly underestimated and the coefficients biased.

Also unfortunate, cross-tabulations by ethnicity and CJA reveal that several CJAs have insufficient numbers for ethnicity-specific multilevel analyses. For interval-level variables, only the general ethnicity categories (e.g. Asian and Black) meet the 30/30 requirement. Even worse, for dichotomous and ordinal outcomes, only the White and Asian general ethnicity groups meet the minimums articulated above. This problem is further exacerbated by the fact that some key outcomes are captured for only a fraction of respondents. For example, questions concerning perceptions of the CJS are asked of only a quarter of respondents. This further reduces the number of CJAs with sufficient numbers to support ethnicity-specific multilevel analyses. Moreover, due to 2001 changes to the BCS, data from previous sweeps cannot be used to augment the BME sample. As a result, insufficient sample size renders many multilevel statistical comparisons impossible with the current data. In such instances, only the single-level, individual-based analyses can be compared.

Outcome (Dependent) Variables

Three separate outcomes are analysed in this chapter. Victimisation, is captured by *prevalence*, whether or not one has been victimised. 'Fear of Crime' is denoted by a 10 point ordinal scale capturing respondents' assessment of 'What effect does fear of crime have over your quality of life?' (1 equalling 'no effect'; 10 indicating 'total effect'). Finally, 'Perceptions of the Criminal Justice System' is represented by a yes/no question regarding whether 'too lenient sentencing' is 'a major cause of crime in Britain today'.

Analyses

Because the above outcomes vary in form, it is important to note that different statistical techniques are required to model them (see 'findings' below for further specifics). Prior to constructing the multilevel models, single-level pooled and ethnicity-specific models were run for each outcome, with their results forming the basis for subsequent multilevel analyses.[4] Importantly, with multilevel analyses, protocol dictates the deletion of non-significant variables from the final model (unless they are key theoretical factors – see Raudenbush and Bryk, 2002). To do otherwise risks serious bias in the estimators. As such, the different ethnic multilevel models are often not identical; some have fewer independent variables than others. However, due to insufficient sample size, very few comparative multilevel models could be run, meaning that only single-level models could be compared. Fortuitously, the single-level models have no protocol requirements of deleting insignificant variables and are identical across the different ethnicities (thereby enabling them to be directly compared). To discern whether these single-level effects differ significantly between the different ethnic groups, a Z-test for equality of coefficients (Allison, 1999; Clogg et al., 1995; Paternoster et al., 1998) is employed.

Importantly, these statistical models can only show a statistical association between the measured outcome and any particular influence or factor; they do not imply causation. In addition, given the sheer number of models examined in the original project (over 50), only a selection of outcomes are discussed here. Specifically, pooled model results are reported, followed by comparisons between the Asian and Black respondents' results. The other results are described in more detail elsewhere (see for example Kautt and Tankebe, 2010).

[4]Unless otherwise specified, the multilevel error terms are fixed, the independent variables uncentred and the outcome variables continuous (Raudenbush and Bryk, 2002).

Control (Independent) Variables

Several control variables are common across the different outcomes. These are broken into four categories: respondent, 'routine activities'[5] (Cohen and Felson, 1979), area and household. Apart from BME status, respondent features include: age, sex, marital status, professional occupation, health, paid work, educational qualifications as well as number of years lived in the area and at the current address. The routine activities factors are: the number pub visits per week; number club visits per week; and the number of hours spent away from home daily. Area conditions (captured via ordinal Likert-type indicators) include problems with: public drunkenness; noisy neighbours; teens loitering; litter; vandalism; skin colour attacks; drug problems; as well as a composite index of interviewer-perceived area conditions. Finally, household characteristics include: rented accommodation; inner city location; type of residence (e.g. flat, terraced housing); child present; adult male present; single adult household; as well as a composite security measures index.

Depending upon the outcome under examination, some additional factors are included in the explanatory model. For example, past victimisation and contact with the CJS (e.g. being arrested by the police, having been a defendant in criminal court) are included as explanatory factors in statistical models of fear of crime and perceptions of the CJS respectively. However, in the simplified results tables, only those control factors that are significant for at least one of the two ethnic groups are reported.

Findings

Victimisation Prevalence

This outcome measures whether or not the respondent has been the victim of a crime in the past 12 months. Because it is dichotomous (binary), the multilevel analyses employ the Bernoulli specification and the single-level statistical tool is logistic regression (logit). The CJA variance term ($\sigma^2 = 0.042$) is significant ($p < 0.001$) in the fully unconditional, ethnically-pooled multilevel model, indicating that the likelihood of victimisation varies significantly by CJA. The pooled multilevel model shows no differences in victimisation likelihood between Black and White respondents but Asians are 40% less likely to be victimised than Whites. However, the ethnic composition of the CJA affects these results. As BME presence in the CJA population increases, the likelihood of victimisation decreases for Black respondents but increases for Asian respondents. Moreover, the Asian-specific multilevel model indicates that Pakistanis are more likely but Chinese are less likely to

[5]Routine Activities refers to the activities that an individual engages in on a regular basis (such as going to work, shopping, et cetera). Routine activities theory posits that it is via these regular activities that victims and offenders converge, enabling crime to occur.

be victimised than Indians, with the precise amount varying by CJA. Specifically, Pakistani respondents range from being 14–34% more likely than Indian respondents to be victimised depending upon the CJA in which they reside. Unfortunately, due to insufficient cases per CJA, single-level logistic regression analyses are the only way to compare the likelihood of victimisation for the remaining ethnicities.

As presented in Table 12.1, the simplified results show a number of differences between the Asian and Black general ethnicities in the factors associated with general criminal victimisation. Being female is associated with decreased likelihood of victimisation for Black but not Asian respondents. In contrast, having paid work as well as perceiving drug or noisy neighbour problems is associated with increased victimisation for Asian but not Black respondents. Likewise, taking more security precautions and perceiving local area problems with litter reduce the chances of

Table 12.1 Logit analysis of general victimisation prevalence by respondent general ethnicity

	Simplified Logistic Regression Results		
	Black	Asian	Z-test result
Security index	NS	–	Effect A only
Age respondent	+	+	ND
Female respondent	–	NS	Effect B only
Child present	+	+	Larger effect B
Fear home dark	+	+	Larger effect B
Teens problem	+	+	Larger effect A
Litter problem	NS	–	Effect A only
Vandalism problem	+	+	ND
Skin colour att.	+	+	ND
Drug problem	NS	+	Effect A only
Noise problem	NS	+	Effect A only
Pub visits	+	+	ND
Club visits	+	+	ND
Health	–	–	ND
Paid work	NS	+	Effect A only
Education quals	+	+	Larger effect B
Inner city househ'ld	–	–	ND
Married	NS	–	Effect A only
Cohabiting	NS	+	Effect A only
H. prof. occupation	NS	+	Effect A only
Hours away	+	+	ND
2002	–	NS	Effect B only
2003	NS	NS	
2004	NS	–	Effect A only
2005	NS	–	Effect A only
2006	NS	–	Effect A only
2007	NS	–	Effect A only
N	8,807	13,615	
Variance explained	12.0%	14.5%	

+ = increases victimisation odds; – = decreases victimisation odds; NS = No significant effect. B = Black; A = Asian; ND =No difference.

criminal victimisation for Asian respondents with no effect for Black respondents. Finally, marital status and being in a higher professional occupation are associated with victimisation for Asian respondents only.

Other factors, whilst significant for both groups, have different effect sizes between them. The presence of a child in the household, fear of being home alone after dark and having higher educational qualifications all increase victimisation odds more for Black than Asian respondents. At the same time, perceiving a local problem with teens hanging about is associated with greater likelihood of victimisation for Asians than Black respondents.

Beyond this, some factors have virtually identical effects across the two ethnic groups. For example, the worse the health of the respondent, the lower the odds of victimisation, regardless of ethnicity. Likewise, increases in the number of pub and club visits per month are equally associated with an increased chance of victimisation. The same is true for the number of hours spent away from home. However, as the foregoing shows, this comparability is not the norm for the factors influencing the likelihood of victimisation.

Fear of Crime – Impact on Quality of Life

This outcome is measured on a 10-point ordered scale, necessitating the employment of ordinal models. The fully unconditional, multilevel ordinal model indicates that the CJA level ($\sigma^2 = 0.074$) is significant ($p < 0.001$), meaning that how fear of crime affects respondents' quality of life changes from one CJA to the next. The ethnically-pooled multilevel model indicates that fear of crime adversely affects the quality of life more for Black and Asian respondents than White respondents. Unfortunately, this outcome is only captured for roughly 10% of respondents, forcing these analyses to rely on a much smaller sample (30,641 cases) than the victimisation analyses. In total, there are only 477 Black and 789 Asian respondents in this sub-sample, making it impossible to conduct independent multilevel models by general ethnicity.

That being said, comparison of the simplified, general ethnicity single-level ordinal logistic regression (employing the negative log-log link function) results shown in Table 12.2 indicate that the predictor effects vary significantly across all 10 outcome increments for Black respondents but only the last three for Asian respondents. Because each increment is essentially compared to the likelihood of the previous ones in ordinal logit, insignificant predictors must be eliminated from the final model or else risk biased estimates (Hildebrand et al., 1977). This produces non-identical models between ethnicities and precludes the use of the previously employed Z-test.

However, given the comparative nature of these analyses, such differences remain theoretically important. For example, having been a victim in the past 12 months, having an adult male present in the household, being afraid to be home alone after dark and perceiving a drug or noisy neighbour problem were associated with lower impact of fear of crime on Asian respondents' quality of life but had no influence for

Table 12.2 General ethnic comparison of ordered logit results for how quality of life is affected by fear of crime

		Black estimate	Asian estimate
Threshold (Quality of life)			
	1 = No effect	NS	NS
	2	+	NS
	3	+	NS
	4	+	NS
	5	+	NS
	6	+	NS
	7	+	+
	8	+	+
	9	+	+
Independent variables			
	Victim in timeframe?		–
	Female respondent	–	
	Male adult in household		–
	Afraid to be home alone after dark?		–
Years in area	Less than one	NS	
	Between 1 and 2	+	
	Between 2 and 5	NS	
	Between 5 and 10	NS	
	Between 10 and 20	NS	
Years at address	Less than one	–	+
	Between 1 and 2	–	+
	Between 2 and 5	–	NS
	Between 5 and 10	NS	+
	Between 10 and 20	NS	+
Drug users	1 Not a problem at all		–
	2 Not a big problem		–
	3 Fairly big problem		–
Drunken behaviour	1 Not a problem at all	NS	NS
	2 Not a big problem	NS	+
	3 Fairly big problem	NS	NS
Noisy neighbours	1 Not a problem at all		–
	2 Not a big problem		–
	3 Fairly big problem		–
Monthly pub visits	None	+	
	Between 1 and 3 times (Less than once a week)	+	
	Between 4 and 8 times (Once to twice a week)	+	
	Between 9 and 12 times (About 3 times a week)	+	
Monthly club visits	None		NS
	Between 1 and 3 times (Less than once a week)		NS
	Between 4 and 8 times (Once to twice a week)		NS
	Between 9 and 12 times (About 3 times a week)		+

Table 12.2 (continued)

		Black estimate	Asian estimate
General health	1 Very bad		+
	2 Bad		NS
	3 Fair		NS
	4 Good		+
Daily hours spent away from home	None	NS	NS
	Under 1	–	NS
	1 but under 3	NS	NS
	3 but under 5	NS	NS
	5 but under 7	NS	+
Worried about break-in	1 Not at all worried	–	–
	2 Not very worried	–	–
	3 Neutral or N/A	+	
	4 Fairly worried	NS	NS
Worried about being mugged	1 Not at all worried		–
	2 Not very worried		NS
	3 Neutral or N/A		
	4 Fairly worried		NS
Confidence in CJS	1 Not at all confident	NS	+
	2 Not very confident	+	+
	3 Don't know	NS	NS
	4 Fairly confident	NS	+
Police performance	1 Very poor	NS	
	2 Poor	+	
	3 Fair	NS	
	4 Good	NS	
	Variance explained	16%	27%

Link function: negative log–log; NS = No significant effect; '+ = positive effect; – = negative effect; blank spaces indicate that the factor was not included in the final model.

Black respondents. Likewise, both very good and bad health increases the impact fear of crime has over Asian respondents' quality of life whilst low confidence in the CJS increases it for Black respondents. Perhaps most interesting, the more frequently Black respondents visit a pub during the month, the more likely fear of crime is to have a large impact on their quality of life. In contrast, visiting nightclubs nine or more times a month is associated with significantly increased impact of fear of crime on Asian respondents' quality of life. Intriguingly, pub visits have no effect for Asian respondents whilst club visits have no impact for Black respondents.

At the same time, some factors are significant for both groups but have different effects. Notably, living at the current address for less than 5 years is related to lower impact of fear of crime of Black respondents' quality of life but increases the impact for Asian respondents. These diverse results suggest that the mechanism of what causes fear levels to affect quality of life differs substantially across these ethnicities and is more complex than can be unravelled here. They demonstrate the problems inherent in assuming that the mechanisms of how fear of crime impacts quality of life are identical across different ethnicities.

Perceptions of the Criminal Justice System

These analyses utilise the subset of cases (176,156) that contain responses to questions concerning whether respondents view the leniency of the courts as a major cause of crime in Britain. As this variable is dichotomous, the multilevel analyses employ the Bernoulli specification and the single-level are logistic regression (logit). Unfortunately, because there are not enough CJAs with sufficient BME cases to permit independent multilevel analysis, only the ethnically pooled multilevel analysis can be conducted and the remaining comparisons are made via single-level analyses.

The fully unconditional multilevel model indicates that the variance component for the CJA level ($\sigma^2 = 0.018$) is significant ($p < 0.001$) in explaining whether respondents felt that too lenient sentencing by the courts was a major cause of crime in England and Wales. Moving to the full ethnically pooled model, the likelihood of a 'yes' is lower for Asian and Black respondents than White, with the degree varying moderately by CJA. Moreover, as the non-White population of a CJA increases, so too does Asian respondents' likelihood of saying 'yes'.

Table 12.3 provides the simplified results of the single-level Asian and Black respondent models, revealing a number of differences. Perhaps the most striking

Table 12.3 Simplified ethnic logit comparison of the 'Too lenient sentences' cause of crime

	Black	Asian	Z test
Respondent is female	+	–	Opposite effect
Children present in the household?	NS	+	Effect A only
Time lived in area	NS	+	Effect A only
Teens hanging about problem?	NS	+	Effect A only
Noisy neighbour problem	–	NS	Effect B only
Pub visits in last month	NS	+	Effect A only
Any paid work in last week?	+	+	ND
Educational qualifications?	+	+	ND
Accommodation is a flat	–	NS	Effect B only
Respondent is married	+	NS	Effect B only
More than one adult in household	+	NS	Effect B only
Confident the CJS respects accused rights?	NS	+	Effect A only
Confident the CJS is effective in bringing people to justice?	–	–	ND
Confident that the CJS meets the needs of crime victims?	–	NS	Effect B only
Confident that the CJS deals with cases promptly/efficiently?	+	NS	Effect B only
CJS effective in reducing crime?	NS	–	Effect A only
CJS effective in dealing with young offenders?	–	–	ND
How good a job are the police doing?	+	NS	Effect B only
Variance Explained	10.5%	13.6%	

– = decreases odds; + = increases odds; NS = not significant; ND = no difference.

result is that Asian females are less likely than Asian males to perceive lenient sentences to be a cause of crime whilst Black females are more likely than Black males to have this view. In addition, a number of factors increase the likelihood of this perception for Asian but not Black respondents. These include: the presence of children in the household; the length of time lived in the area; a perceived problem with teens hanging about; confidence that the CJS respects the rights of the accused; and the number of pub visits in the past month. In contrast, for Black respondents, being married, having more than one adult in the household, being confident that the CJS deals with cases efficiently and believing that the police are doing a good job all are associated with believing that lenient sentencing is a major cause of crime in Britain today. These factors, however, have no impact for Asian respondents.

Notably, only four factors have the same influence for both Asian and Black respondents: paid work; educational qualifications; confidence that the CJS is effective in bringing offenders to justice; and belief that the CJS is effective in dealing with young offenders. Such results again make clear that distinct constellations of factors influence the crime-related perceptions of different ethnic groups.

Conclusions

The research described here empirically shows the presence of several significant differences between Asian and Black respondents in their BCS-reported perceptions and experiences of the CJS. The findings demonstrate that the relevant factors wield different influence over those responses between the ethnic groups. Such findings effectively show the dangers of assuming White British is the 'normal' perspective (Garland et al., 2006) as well as of treating the minority groups as interchangeable, particularly when making policy decisions.

Thus, these quantitative results confirm previous theoretical expectations and qualitative findings (Gilroy, 2002; Paul, 1997; Phillips and Bowling, 2003; Rutter and Tienda, 2005), suggesting that perhaps cultural factors alongside those relating to being an ethnic minority in Britain today play a significant role in respondents' crime-related experiences and assessments. As such, what works for White British may not work for Black or Asian British. In other words, if such ethnic differences are not taken into account, strategies effective with the largely homogenous, dominant majority could either have no impact or make the situation worse (and possibly alienating) for ethnic minorities.

Importantly, the current results also show that ethnicity-based differences are not universal; they vary by location and environment. Thus, it would seem crucial that the ethnic composition and overall context of communities be taken into consideration before a strategy is deployed. Based on the current findings, a 'national rollout' of any intervention designed to improve, for example, community perceptions could be ill-advised.

The current research also has implications for the quantitative methods employed to examine ethnic variation in CJS outcomes. As shown above, the commonly used ethnically-pooled approach masks the differences uncovered by ethnically independent analyses. Thus, separate analyses for each ethnic group are preferable for assessing whether there are differences between the ethnicities on any given outcome. Unfortunately, as this research has also shown, low counts of BME respondents can make such analyses impossible with BCS data, rendering the pooled approach the only viable option. Similarly, although multilevel and contextual analyses are useful for assessing whether social milieu affects how ethnicity influences salient criminal justice outcomes, the utility of this technique for assessing ethnic differences via BCS data is limited by low numbers of BME respondents or when the BME populations are spread unevenly across geographic units (CJAs).

Still, despite the limitations and work that remains to be done, this complex study highlights the importance of thinking about the different ethnic groups as distinct and independent rather than as mere deviations from the White norm. As this research shows, ethnicity wields important independent effects that vary both by location and with the influence of other factors. Acknowledging and incorporating such distinctions into both policy and research is crucial to advancing our knowledge on the relationship between ethnicity and criminological experiences.

Acknowledgements This work was supported by the Economic and Social Research Council, grant number RES 163-25-0051. Material from Crown copyright records made available through the Home Office and the UK Data Archive has been used by permission of the Controller of Her Majesty's Stationery Office and the Queen's Printer for Scotland.

References

Allen, J., Edmonds, S., Patterson, A. and Smith, D. (2006) *Policing and the Criminal Justice System – Public Confidence and Perceptions: Findings From the 2004/05 British Crime Survey*, The Home Office, London.

Allison, P.D. (1999) Comparing logit and probit coefficients across groups, *Sociological Methods and Research*, 28: 186–208.

Avakame, E.F., Fyfe, J.J. and McCoy, C. (1999) Did you call the police? What did they do? An empirical assessment of Black's theory of mobilization of law, *Justice Quarterly*, 16: 765–792.

Bhui, H.S. (ed.) (2009) *Race and Criminal Justice*, Sage Publications, London.

Bucke, T. (1997) *Ethnicity and Contacts with the Police: Latest Findings From the British Crime Survey*, Research and Statistics Directorate, Home Office, London.

Clancy, A., Hough, M., Aust, R. and Kershaw, C. (2001) *Crime, Policing and Justice: The Experience of Ethnic Minorities Findings from the 2000 British Crime Survey*, Research, Development and Statistics Directorate, Home Office, London.

Clogg, C.C., Petkova, E. and Haritou, A. (1995) Statistical methods for comparing regression coefficients between models, *American Journal of Sociology*, 100: 1261–1293.

Cohen, L.E. and Felson, M. (1979) Social change and crime rate trends: A routine activity approach, *American Sociological Review*, 44: 588–608.

Ditton, J. and Chadee, D. (2006) People's perceptions of their likely future risk of criminal victimization, *British Journal of Criminology*, 46: 505–518.

Farrall, S. and Gadd, D. (2004) Research note: The frequency of the fear of crime, *British Journal of Criminology*, 44: 127–132.

Fitzgerald, M. (1998) 'Race' and the criminal justice system in Blackstone, T., Parekh, B. and Sanders, P. (eds.), *Race Relations in Britain: A Developing Agenda*, Routledge, London.

Gabriel, U. and Greve, W. (2003) The psychology of fear of crime: Conceptual and methodological perspectives, *British Journal of Criminology*, 43: 600–614.

Garland, J., Spalek, B. and Chakraborti, N. (2006) Hearing lost voices: Issues in researching 'hidden' minority ethnic communities, *British Journal of Criminology*, 46: 423–437.

Gilroy, P. (2002) *There Ain't no Black in Union Jack: The Cultural Politics of Race and Nation*, Routledge, London.

Grant, C., Harvey, A., Bolling, K. and Clemens, S. (2006) *2004–05 British Crime Survey (England and Wales): Technical Report Research, Development and Statistics – Strategic Data Flows*, Crime Reduction and Community Safety Group, Home Office, London.

Hale, C. (1996) Fear of crime: A review of the literature, *International Review of Victimology*, 4: 79–150.

Hedeker, D. (2008) Multilevel models for ordinal and nominal variables in De Leeuw, J. and Meijer E. (eds.), *Handbook of Multilevel Analysis*, Springer, New York, NY.

Hildebrand, D.K., Laing, J.D. and Rosenthal, H. (1977) *Analysis of Ordinal Data*, Sage, Newbury Park.

Hollway, W. and Jefferson, T. (1997) The risk society in an age of anxiety: Situating fear of crime, *The British Journal of Sociology*, 48: 255–266.

Hood, R. (1992) *Race and Sentencing*, Clarendon Press, Oxford.

Hope, T., Bryan, J., Tricckett, A. and Osborn, D.R. (2001) The phenomena of multiple victimization: The relationship between personal and property crime risk, *British Journal of Criminology*, 41: 595–617.

Hough, M. (1995) *Anxiety About Crime: Findings From the 1994 British Crime Survey*, Research, Development and Statistics Directorate, The Home Office, London.

Hough, M., Maxfield, M., Morris, B. and Simmons, J. (2007) British crime survey after 25 years in Hough, M. and Maxfield, M. (eds.), *Surveying Crime in the 21st Century: Crime Prevention Studies*, Willan Publishing, Cullompton.

Jackson, J. (2004) Experience and expression: Social and cultural significance in the fear of crime, *British Journal of Criminology*, 44: 946–966.

Jansson, K. (2006) *Black and Minority Ethnic Groups' Experiences and Perceptions of Crime, Racially Motivated Crime and the Police: Findings from the 2004/2005 British Crime Survey* (Home Office Online Report 25/06), The Home Office, London.

Kautt, P. and Tankebe, J. (2010) Confidence in the criminal justice system of England and Wales: A test of ethnic and area effects, Under review.

Keith, M. (1993) *Race, Riots and Policing: Lore and Disorder in a Multi-Racist Society*, UCL Press Limited, London.

Kershaw, C. and Tseloni, A. (2005) Predicting crime rates, fear and disorder based on area information: Evidence from the 2000 British Crime Survey, *International Review of Victimology*, 12: 293–311.

Lowenkamp, C.T., Cullen, F.T. and Pratt, T.C. (2003) Replicating Sampson and Groves's test of social disorganization theory: Revisiting a criminological classic, *Journal of Research in Crime and Delinquency*, 40: 351–373.

Maas, C.J.M. and Hox, J.J. (2005) Sufficient sample sizes for multilevel modeling, *Methodology*, 1: 86–92.

Markowitz, F.E., Bellair, P.E., Liska, A.E. and Liu, J. (2001) Extending social disorganization theory: Modeling the relationships between cohesion, disorder and fear, *Criminology*, 39: 293–320.

Mason, D. (1995) *Race and Ethnicity in Modern Britain*, Oxford University Press, Oxford.

Moineddin, R., Matheson, F. and Glazier, R.H. (2007) A simulation study of sample size for multilevel logistic regression models, *BMC Medical Research Methodology*, 7: 1–10.

Mok, M. (1995) Sample size requirements for 2-level designs in educational research, *Multilevel Modelling Newsletter*, 7: 11–15.

Osborn, D.R., Ellingworth, D., Hope, T. and Trickett, A. (1996) Are repeatedly victimised households different? *Journal of Quantitative Criminology*, 12: 223–245.

Osborn, D.R. and Tseloni, A. (1998) The distribution of household property crime, *Journal of Quantitative Criminology*, 14: 307–330.

Paternoster, R., Brame, R., Mazerolle, P. and Piqquero, A. (1998) Using the correct statistical test for the equality of regression coefficients, *Criminology*, 36: 859–866.

Paul, K. (1997) *Whitewashing Britain: Race and Citizenship in the Postwar Era*, Cornell University Press, Ithaca.

Phillips, C. and Bowling, B. (2003) Racism, ethnicity and criminology: Developing minority perspectives, *British Journal of Criminology*, 43: 269–290.

Raudenbush, S.W. and Bryk, A.S. (2002) *Hierarchical Linear Models: Applications and Data Analysis Methods*, Sage Publications, Thousand Oaks.

Rutter, M. and Tienda, M. (eds.) (2005) *Ethnicity and Causal Mechanisms*, Cambridge University Press, Cambridge.

Sampson, R.J. and Groves, W.B. (1989) Community structure and crime: Testing social disorganization theory, *The American Journal of Sociology*, 94: 774–802.

Trickett, A., Osborn, D.R. and Ellingworth, D. (1995) Property crime victimisation: The roles of individual and area influences, *International Review of Victimology*, 3: 273–295.

Trickett, A., Osborn, D.R., Seymour, J. and Pease, K. (1992) What is different about high crime areas? *British Journal of Criminology*, 32: 81–89.

Tseloni, A. (2006) Multilevel modelling of the number of property crimes: Household and area effects, *Journal of the Royal Statistical Society*, 169: 205–233.

Tseloni, A. (2007) Fear of crime, perceived disorders and property crime: A multivariate analysis at the area level in Farrell, G., Bowers, K.J., Johnson, S.D. and Townsley, M. (eds.), *Imagination for Crime Prevention: Essays in Honour of Ken Pease*, Willan Publishing, Cullompton.

Tseloni, A., Osborn, D.R., Trickett, A. and Pease, K. (2002) Modelling property crime using the British Crime Survey: What have we learnt? *British Journal of Criminology*, 42: 109–128.

Tseloni, A. and Pease, K. (1998) Nuisance phone calls to women in England and Wales, *European Journal on Criminal Policy and Research*, 6: 91–111.

Tseloni, A. and Pease, K. (2005) Population inequality: The case of repeat crime victimisation, *International Review of Victimology*, 12: 75–90.

Webster, C. (2007) *Understanding Race and Crime*, Open University Press, Maidenhead.

Whitfield, J. (2007) The historical context: Policing and black people in post-war Britain in Rowe, M. (ed.), *Policing Beyond Macpherson: Issues in Policing, Race and Society*, Willan Publishing, Cullompton.

Chapter 13
Exploring the Links Between Population Heterogeneity and Perceptions of Social Cohesion in England

Joanna Taylor, Liz Twigg and John Mohan

Introduction

There are extensive debates about the measurement and extent of ethnic heterogeneity and segregation, which have formed the basis of much research in the UPTAP programme and elsewhere. However, the focus of this chapter is on debates about the consequences of heterogeneity specifically, whether or not ethnic heterogeneity has an identifiable effect on social cohesion at the neighbourhood scale. We are therefore concerned with investigating neighbourhood heterogeneity as an area influence or area effect on such outcomes. There is a long tradition of research on this topic. This can be traced back at least as far as the work by Shaw and McKay in Chicago (1942); they, and their modern successors Sampson and Raudenbush (1999), argued that low levels of social cohesion were found in urban neighbourhoods characterised by low socio-economic status, a high degree of population turnover, and ethnic heterogeneity. These features contributed to a decline in informal social control and thus to various indicators of social disorganisation. Sampson et al. (1999) have extended this tradition of analysis with their work on the beneficial effects of community-level 'collective efficacy' on a range of outcomes such as child development.

Our interest in this question was also sparked by more immediate concerns and debates. Firstly, enquiries into the causes of disorder in some urban centres in northern England drew attention to the combination of socio-economic disadvantage and ethnic heterogeneity in the affected communities (Amin, 2002; Cantle, 2001). This prompted a wider debate about whether or not the UK was 'sleepwalking to segregation' (Phillips, 2005); see also Commission on Integration and Cohesion, 2007; Finney and Simpson, 2009). Secondly, the political commentator David Goodhart (2004) argued that immigration to the UK posed a threat to the welfare state because the indigenous population was unwilling to share resources with newcomers. Goodhart's contentions prompted former Home Secretary David

J. Taylor (✉)
Department of Geography, University of Portsmouth, Portsmouth PO1 3HE, UK
e-mail: Joanna.Taylor@port.ac.uk

J. Stillwell, M. van Ham (eds.), *Ethnicity and Integration*, Understanding Population Trends and Processes 3, DOI 10.1007/978-90-481-9103-1_13,

Blunkett to observe that *this is an important argument and it is important that we examine it* (Blunkett, 2004), p. 4). In one sense, this is an argument about the sustainability of the welfare state at the national level. However, we are interested in whether it is plausible at a more local scale: we are interested in whether perceived social tensions are heightened in locations characterised by ethnic heterogeneity. Thirdly, Robert Putnam (2007) has suggested that inhabitants of heterogeneous places are, in the short term, more inclined to do what he terms 'hunkering down'; that is, retreat into a private world rather than interact with their neighbours.

What these arguments have in common is a concern with the impact of heterogeneity on a range of socio-economic outcomes. This is a subject on which previous findings do not point unequivocally in one direction (Sturgis et al., 2010). Much work concentrates on trust (Nannestad, 2008); several US-based studies have found negative associations at the state level between heterogeneity and the provision of public goods and between levels of trust and ethnic diversity (Alesina and La Ferrara, 2000; Hero, 1998), 2003). Of course, these are large spatial units. Putnam (2007) investigated the relationships between heterogeneity and trust for a sample of communities which varied greatly in size. He claimed that once allowance had been made for socio-economic circumstances, there remained evidence of a negative effect of heterogeneity on trust. However, his critics pointed to several weaknesses in his argument. Dawkins (2008) argued that the substantive significance and impact of heterogeneity demonstrated by his study were trivially small and did not justify the importance he attached to it. Other findings have been at best equivocal. Coffe and Geys (2006) used the number of political parties competing in Flemish municipal elections as an index of community heterogeneity and a composite index of social capital and concluded that there was a negative relationship with social capital, but did not attribute this directly to ethnic-cultural differences (see also Coffe, 2009). Guest et al. (2008) argued, on the basis of their survey-based work in Seattle, that the effect of heterogeneity on harmony was at best a minor one. Heterogeneity had a slight effect on responses to questions about desire to leave the community and on whether respondents would miss their neighbourhood, but these effects were small compared to those of the individual and area characteristics, and were mediated via residential stability and population turnover, echoing the earlier conclusions of Shaw and McKay.

Other studies are more positive about the impacts of ethnic heterogeneity, such as Anderson and Paskeviciute (2006) who argue that greater ethnic heterogeneity should aid in recruiting members of voluntary associations, not least because – as previously suggested by Weisbrod (1988) – the formation of such associations is more likely in heterogeneous societies since individual ethnic groups cannot command majority support, and are therefore likely to develop voluntary provision of various kinds. However, this might not translate into wider social benefits, if the organisations established were largely inward-looking and devoted to the interests of the ethnic groups in question, a matter which was not explored by these authors.

British work on the impact of heterogeneity has produced limited or contradictory findings. For example, Page et al. (2004) report reduced levels of satisfaction with local public services in areas of ethnic diversity, but their analysis was based largely on correlations. Ford (2004) found limited evidence in the British Social Attitudes study for an association between diversity and level of support for the welfare state once allowance was made for individual and area characteristics. Pennant (2005) investigated the relationship between the diversity of an area, in terms of socio-economic status and ethnicity, and levels of generalised trust as reported in the Citizenship Survey. Whilst she found no statistically significant relationship between diversity and trust in a range of institutions, nor between diversity and either civic participation or formal volunteering, there was a suggestion that an increase in ethnic diversity is associated with a reduction in the probability that people will trust others within that area. Letki (2008) also used the Citizenship Survey but found that once allowance was made for local socio-economic conditions, ethnic diversity was not associated with an erosion of social capital. Laurence and Heath (2008) argue that diverse areas generally are more cohesive but the nature of the relationship depends on the ethnic mix in an area. Fieldhouse and Cutts (2008) contend that diversity is not damaging to participation (expressed in terms of voter turnout) even amongst majority populations, and is associated with higher participation among minority populations.

We sought to add to these findings by examining the relationship between ethnic heterogeneity and various outcome measures captured by the British Crime Survey. In particular, following the arguments of sociologists such as Shaw and McKay (1942), we hypothesise that if heterogeneity has negative outcomes then these would be evident in heightened perceptions of antisocial behaviour in neighbourhoods, to the extent that these can be taken as an index of disorder. We also explore whether heterogeneity is related to perceptions of the levels of collective efficacy in neighbourhoods. This concept refers to expectations about whether or not the residents of one's neighbourhood can either be trusted or can be relied upon to intervene in response to minor neighbourhood problems. We are particularly interested in assessing the relative importance of heterogeneity as an area effect on these outcomes in comparison to other important contextual influences, such as the socio-economic make-up of a neighbourhood or the level of population stability. We investigate these questions using a large-scale social survey, the British Crime Survey (BCS), to which small area census data have been linked. This allows us to conduct a much more fine-grained analysis of the relationship between heterogeneity and social cohesion than previously possible with this data.

We begin the chapter by outlining the data source that we use, i.e. the BCS. We then explain how indicators of perceptions of anti-social behaviour (ASB) and collective efficacy, our dependent variables, were constructed. We also discuss the selection and construction of independent variables including measures of ethnic heterogeneity before moving on to describe the modelling strategy adopted. The BCS is a large-scale clustered survey which lends itself to multilevel modelling, a technique which is also appropriate to the simultaneous investigation of individual and area effects. After describing our analytical methods and presenting the results, the concluding section of the chapter explores the broader implications of these findings alongside the study's limitations and ways in which our work may be developed in the future.

Data Sources

Our principal source is the 2006/07 sweep of the British Crime Survey (BCS), a victimisation survey in which adults (aged 16 or above) living in private households are asked about their experiences of and views on crime and criminal justice issues. Data were collected between April 2006 and March 2007 by the British Market Research Bureau (BMRB) on behalf of the Home Office. Although the BCS covers England and Wales, some of our key independent variables were not available for Wales and therefore our analysis and results are based on England only with a resultant sample size of 43,115 individual respondents.[1] Full technical details on the survey's design can be found at Bolling et al. (2007).

Our other main sources of data are the 2001 UK Census (Office for National Statistics, 2004a), the 2007 Indices of Deprivation (Department for Communities and Local Government, 2007) and the cross-government rural and urban area classification indicator (The Countryside Agency, Department for Environment Food and Rural Affairs, Office of the Deputy Prime Minister & Office for National Statistics and Welsh Assembly Government, 2004). This project is amongst the first to utilise the Home Office's trial of attaching UK 2001 Census area codes to the BCS dataset, allowing us to link in area level characteristics derived from the Census and other datasets for the local areas within which the BCS respondents are located.

Dependent Variables: Perceptions of Anti-social Behaviour and Collective Efficacy

Our first dependent variable is perceptions of anti-social behaviour. The BCS asks a series of questions which explore respondents' perceptions of several different types of anti-social behaviour (ASB). Respondents are asked whether any of the following are a problem in the area: 'noisy neighbours or loud parties'; 'teenagers hanging around on the streets'; 'rubbish or litter lying around'; 'vandalism, graffiti and other deliberate damage to property or vehicles'; 'people using or dealing drugs'; 'people being drunk or rowdy in public places'; and 'abandoned or burnt out cars'. The respondent is asked whether they feel that the issue in question is a 'very big problem,' or a 'fairly big problem', compared to 'not a very big problem' or 'not a problem at all'.

We followed the scoring rationale adopted by previous studies such as Kershaw and Tseloni (2005) and Upson (2006), whereby the responses were scaled from three ('a very big problem') to zero ('not a problem at all'). The scores were then summed across these seven issues to generate an indicator of the combined level of ASB, resulting in a composite score which ranged from zero to 21. Exploratory work

[1] Some of our independent variables are derived from the 2007 English Indices of Deprivation (Noble et al., 2008). The Welsh index is not constructed in the same way as the English version and therefore the two indices cannot be used together.

using principal components analysis (Bartholomew and Knott, 1999) suggest that it is fair to consider these scores as unidimensional, i.e. measuring the same underlying concept, and that each question should carry a similar weighting. Furthermore, we checked the reliability of this scale using Cronbach's α (Cronbach, 1951) which is an additional test to ensure that the scale is consistently reflecting the construct that it is measuring; with an index of 0.84 we can conclude that the scale is reliable (Field, 2005). We then dichotomised this variable, so those scoring 11 or above, which represents those scoring more than one standard deviation above the mean, were classed as perceiving 'high' levels of ASB. This cut-off point is also consistent with the approach taken by the Home Office for its Statutory Performance Indicator (Nicholas et al., 2007), apart from the way in which missing data are dealt with. A small number (5%) of respondents were missing from the scale – the majority because they answered 'don't know' to the 'people using or dealing in drugs' question. Rather than ignore all those respondents who failed to answer one (or more) of the ASB questions, we used their available responses (where there was certainty) to assign them to one side of the dichotomy. This process reduced the number of respondents excluded from our modelling to just 444, or slightly over 1%, and led to 17% of adults in England being classified as having high levels of perceived ASB.

For our second measure of perceptions of the local area explored in this research – namely collective efficacy – we took Sampson et al.'s (1997) definition as our starting point. They defined collective efficacy as *social cohesion among neighbours combined with their willingness to intervene on behalf of the common good* and measured it by combining two Likert scales measuring 'informal social control' and 'social cohesion and trust' (Sampson et al., 1997, p. 918).

Due to the fact that very similar questions to those used by Sampson et al. were asked in the 2006/07 sweep of the BCS, we were also able to construct scales for these two dimensions of collective efficacy. For our measure of 'informal social control', respondents were asked for their views on the probability that people in their neighbourhood would: 'do something about a group of local children who were playing truant from school and hanging around on a street corner'; 'do something about children who were spray-painting graffiti on a local building'; 'do something about a fight near their home and someone was being beaten up or threatened'; 'tell off a child who was being rude to an adult'; and 'participate if they were asked by a local organisation to help solve a community problem'. Individuals could choose between the responses of 'very likely' (scoring zero), 'likely' (scoring one), 'unlikely' (scoring two) or 'very unlikely' (scoring three). We checked the reliability of this scale using Cronbach's α (Cronbach, 1951); with an index of 0.78 we can conclude that it is reliable (Field, 2005).

Our Likert scale for 'social cohesion and trust' also consisted of five questions scoring from zero for the most positive response through to three for the most negative response. The BCS asked respondents how much they agreed or disagreed with each of these statements about their local area: 'people are willing to help their neighbours' (previously researched by Letki, 2008 and Livingston et al., 2008); 'theirs is a close knit community' (Livingston et al., 2008); 'people do not share the same values' (Livingston et al., 2008); 'different backgrounds get on well together' (Laurence and Heath, 2008) and 'how many people in the neighbourhood can be trusted' (also analysed by Letki, 2008; Livingston et al., 2008; Pennant, 2005; Putnam, 2007; Sturgis et al., 2010). Once again, reliability analysis showed that these questions or factors could be meaningfully combined (Cronbach's α of 0.79).

Both scales – social cohesion and trust (SC&T) and informal social control (ISC) – range from zero to 15 with the higher the score the lower the levels of SC&T and ISC. The mean score for SC&T is 5.1 with a standard deviation of 2.6, and the corresponding values for ISC are slightly larger at 5.9 and 3.2, respectively.

A fundamental departure from Sampson et al. (1997) is that we report the findings from these two dimensions of collective efficacy separately. Our rationale for this was both technical and substantive. First, although the combined scale achieved an acceptable Cronbach's α score, principal component analysis suggested a two dimensional solution. The two dimensions grouped the questions into those measuring (i) SC&T and (ii) ISC. How we modelled these two separate dimensions of collective efficacy simultaneously is covered in depth later in this chapter. Second, we were also interested in revealing potential differences in the relationship between each of our independent variables and these two dimensions of collective efficacy.

Independent Variables

As regards independent variables, we were primarily interested in the covariates of the adverse social consequences outlined earlier at the area level. However, we also included a broad range of individual and household level characteristics in the models to take account of the socio-demographic make-up of an area's residents. All the individual and household level variables included in the models had been found in previous research to be correlated with perceptions of one's local area (Laurence and Heath, 2008; Letki, 2008; Livingston et al., 2008; Millie et al., 2005; Moley, 2008; Putnam, 2007; Sampson et al., 1997; Sturgis et al., 2010). These were: gender, age, ethnicity, marital status, educational attainment, health status, socio-economic classification, household income, accommodation type, tenure and length of time at current address. Alongside these usual socio-demographic variables, the BCS collects information on the respondent's experiences of crime in the last 12 months or so.

Neighbourhood covariates in which we were interested were primarily those concerned with ethnic heterogeneity or homogeneity and levels of deprivation. Other area variables previously related to negative perceptions of the local area, namely population turnover, settlement size, levels of crime and proportional size of the teenage population (aged 10–19), were also included. Because this project is amongst the first to utilise the Home Office's trial of attaching UK 2001 Census codes to the BCS dataset, we could link BCS results to the 2001 Census and other data in order to calculate these measures at a small-area scale. Although the codes were available for Lower Super Output Areas (LSOA), we decided to aggregate these to the larger geography of Middle Super Output Areas (MSOA) to use in the delineation of neighbourhood or local area.[2] The reasons for choosing MSOAs are threefold. First, at least in urban areas, they are similar in size to the definition of 'local area' used in the wording of the ASB questions in which 'local area' is defined as a 15 min walk from the respondent's home. Second, the choice is consistent with similar research on the BCS fear of crime questions (Brunton-Smith, 2007), and finally, there is insufficient clustering at the LSOA level to employ multilevel modelling techniques (see Maas and Hox, 2005). The average number of respondents per LSOA[3] is 5.4 (standard deviation of 3.5 and range from 1 to 29). Moreover, there are 2,559 (out of 12,049) LSOAs that contain only one individual and so, for these observations, individual and area effects cannot be separated.

Before describing the modelling process it is important to define how each of our area level independent variables is measured. Taking ethnic heterogeneity first, there is extensive debate – what Peach (2009) characterises as 'index wars' – about the nature of segregation and heterogeneity, and which aspects of them are captured by specific measures. We were not primarily concerned with measurement of the presence, absence, growth or distribution of a particular ethnic group and so we do not use – as do some other studies, such as Kershaw and Tseloni (2005) or McCulloch (2003) – a measure of the proportion of residents of a particular ethnic background as an index of heterogeneity. Instead, we emphasised the degree to which different ethnic groups are mixed, in residential terms, with other groups, our supposition being that the more heterogeneous the area, the more difficult it might prove for residents to generate a sense of shared norms. For these purposes, the index we have chosen – the Theil index (Theil and Finizza, 1971) – is widely regarded as being appropriate. It is extensively used in the calculation of indices of segregation and isolation in the literature on social geography and demography. It is usually standardised so that the value for each sub-regional unit, e.g. wards within a city, for which it is calculated is compared with the index for the region as a whole. For our purposes we are simply interested in the degree of heterogeneity at the local level, and not in how it compares with a regional or national average. Therefore we have used the Theil entropy score (Massey and Denton, 1988) which is computed according to the following formula:

$$E_i = \sum\nolimits_{r=1}^{r} (\pi_{ri}) \ln \left[\frac{1}{\pi_{ri}} \right] \tag{13.1}$$

where i stands for a neighbourhood area and r stands for the following ethnic groups (i) white, (ii) mixed, (iii) Asian or Asian British, (iv) Black or Black British, and

[2]LSOAs relate to UK Census geography and have a minimum population of 1,000 and a mean of 1,500. They are built from groups of smaller census output areas (OAs) and constrained by the boundaries of the Standard Table wards used for 2001 Census outputs. Typically four to six OAs are aggregated to form LSOAs. In contrast, MSOAs have a minimum population of 5,000 and mean of 7,200. They are built from groups of LSOAs constrained by the 2003 local authority boundaries used for 2001 Census outputs (Office for National Statistics, 2008b).

[3]Based on the entire 43,115 2006/07 BCS England sample.

(v) Chinese or Other. Term π_{ri} represents the proportion of group r in area i as measured by the 2001 Census (Office for National Statistics, 2004a). The higher the Theil score, the more diversity there is in an area. The maximum level of entropy is given by the natural log of the number of groups used in the calculations – in this case ln(5) or 1.6 – and the maximum score occurs when all groups have equal representation in a geographical area (Iceland et al., 2002).

Although the Theil entropy score tells us about the ethnic diversity of areas, it does not tell us about their ethnic make-up. For example, an area with an almost exclusively White population would have the same score as an area with almost entirely Asian residents. To be able to model for these differences, a typology based on the ethnic mix of a MSOA was created using cluster analysis which aims to allocate individuals, or in this case MSOAs, to a set of mutually exclusive, exhaustive groups such that individuals in the same group or cluster are similar. For more information on cluster analysis, see Chatfield and Collins (1980). Complete linkage (an agglomerative hierarchical technique) suggested a seven cluster solution (Fig. 13.1).

These two measures of ethnic mixing (Theil and the cluster analysis) are describing different dimensions of heterogeneity but are highly collinear and for this reason are tested separately (Spearman's r = 0.506, p = <0.000). The Theil score can be regarded as a 'pure' measure of heterogeneity whereas the cluster groups tell us more about the degree to which a particular group is dominant in a specific locality. If there is any evidence that heterogeneity per se influences perceptions of one's locality, then we would expect perceptions to worsen with higher Theil scores reflecting higher levels of diversity, irrespective of the nature of that diversity. In

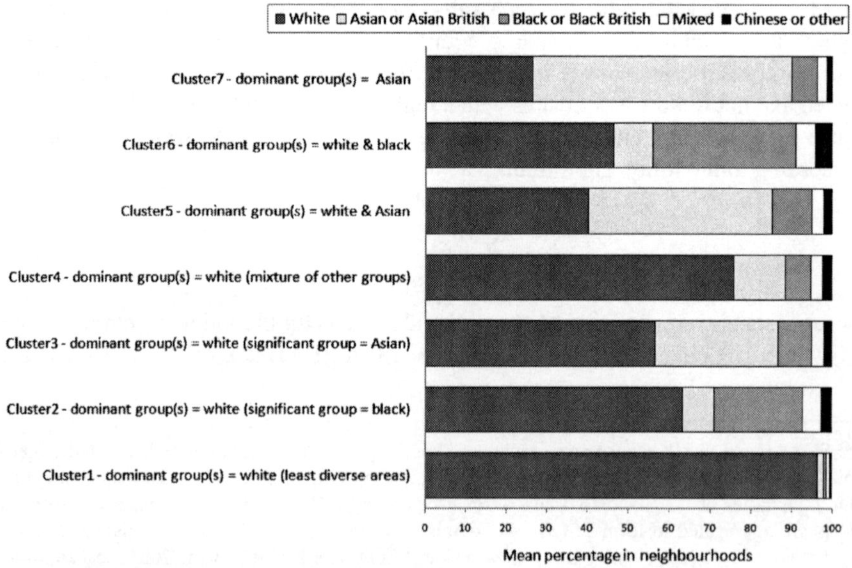

Fig. 13.1 Seven cluster solution for MSOAs

contrast, if there is a relationship between individual ethnicity and the majority or dominant ethnicity in an area, we would expect more negative perceptions of a person's local area for those living in areas with the characteristics of clusters 3, 5, and 6 (where the dominant ethnicity proportion is just over or below half of the total neighbourhood population).

Data from the 2007 Indices of Deprivation (IMD 2007) were also attached to our working dataset (Department for Communities and Local Government, 2007). These data are only available at the LSOA level, therefore weighted population averages were calculated to aggregate the data up to MSOAs. The overall IMD combines seven domains, chosen to cover a range of economic, social and housing issues. We isolated the crime domain which represents the rate of recorded crime for four major volume crime types (burglary, theft, criminal damage and violence). In the case of perceptions of ASB this was used separately as a proxy for local crime levels in MSOAs.[4] On the other hand, for the collective efficacy models the crime domain was excluded completely. The rationale for this was that in contemporary work on heterogeneity and disorder, much of which is actually conducted in Chicago, collective efficacy is seen as a mediator to crime and disorder (for a review, see Kubrin and Weitzer, 2003). Accordingly, we did not want to include crime as a potential explanatory variable in our model. The IMD was then re-calculated based on the other six domains only.[5]

Apart from the measures of ethnic heterogeneity and deprivation outlined above, three further area level variables were included in all the models, namely population turnover, percentage of young people and settlement size. The level of population turnover (in other words, a measure of the number of people moving into, out of, or within an area during a 1 year period) was quantified using the formula adopted by Livingston et al. (2008).[6] Natural logarithmic transformations were applied to the Census measures of both turnover and Theil to improve their skewness and kurtosis.[7] All the continuous area variables were also standardised

[4]At present, police recorded crime figures are not available for all Super Output Areas nor can the BCS produce accurate estimates for such small geographical localities (Walker et al., 2009).

[5]A further complication was that one of the remaining six domains – the living environment domain – consists of two sub-domains which focus on deprivation within the 'indoors' and the 'outdoors' living environment (Noble et al., 2008). High levels of ASB beyond the home naturally adversely affect the quality of the local outdoor living environment. Because of the circular relationship between our dependent variable and this potential independent variable, we decided to exclude this sub-domain from our measure of deprivation for the ASB models.

[6]There are some issues with this measure of turnover. The Office for National Statistics does not produce 2001 Census migration statistics for super output areas (Office for National Statistics, 2008a). Therefore migration counts were aggregated from output area level (Office for National Statistics, 2004b). Consequently 'movers' are defined as those moving in, out or within the OA as opposed to the MSOA. However, despite this scale mismatch, the turnover figure does give an indication of the amount of movement in the vicinity of the respondent's address.

[7]This approach is consistent with other relevant papers such as Sampson and Raudenbush (2004) who transformed the violent crime rate and Tseloni (2007) who performed power or logarithmic transformations which best improved skewness and kurtosis on the area characteristics from the

(with mean = 0 and standard deviation = 1). The percentage of people aged 10–19 years was derived from the 2001 Census and our measure of settlement size was the cross-government rural and urban area classification which divides the MSOAs into three types; 'urban' (defined as urban settlements with a population greater than 10,000), 'small town and fringe' and 'village, hamlet and isolated dwellings' (The Countryside Agency, Department for Environment Food and Rural Affairs, Office of the Deputy Prime Minister & Office for National Statistics and Welsh Assembly Government, 2004). Before moving on to describe the methods used in this analysis it is useful to summarise the research questions that are being explored. In essence, we are investigating whether there is a significant, independent effect for neighbourhood ethnic heterogeneity (as measured via the Theil entropy score and the cluster analysis) on perceptions of ASB and collective efficacy, after controlling for important individual, household and other area level variables. Moreover, we are specifically interested in the relative importance of such heterogeneity compared to contextual levels of urban development, deprivation, population turnover, and teen populations. We also investigate the possibility that heterogeneity mediates the relationship between our outcome measures (ASB and collective efficacy) and these additional contextual measures.

Methods

To investigate the research questions set out above, we employed multilevel modelling (Goldstein, 2003; Snijders and Bosker, 1999). Such techniques have been applied to the BCS (Brunton-Smith, 2007; Tseloni, 2006), though not in the analysis of perceptions of ASB or collective efficacy. Multilevel methods are advantageous for two reasons. First the BCS data uses a multi-stage, stratified design which results in a clustered sample and in this instance we have three levels – individuals (n = 43,115), nested within MSOAs (n = 4,002), which in turn are nested within 38 Police Force Areas.[8,9] A failure to recognise clustering at this and other levels will result in the underestimation of standard errors and increase the risk of committing a Type I error. With multilevel approaches, standard errors are adjusted accordingly, thus reducing such risk. Second, we are interested in modelling geographical and individual characteristics simultaneously. Multilevel methods distinguish between the variation associated with individuals and the variation relating to higher spatial levels, thus avoiding incorrect inferences based on ecological or atomistic fallacies.

1991 Census. Other continuous area variables were not transformed as they already followed a normal distribution.

[8] Based on the entire 2006/07 BCS England sample.

[9] Whilst we do not include any covariates in our models that relate to PFAs, we retain them in the hierarchy to reflect the design of the survey which is stratified by PFA with unequal probability of selection between PFAs.

All the models were initially estimated using iterative generalised least squares (IGLS) based on a first order marginal quasi-likelihood (MQL) approximation using the software package MLwiN (Rasbash et al., 2009).[10] The ASB models had a binary response variable and the model coefficients were checked for stability using Markov Chain Monte Carlo (MCMC) simulation – a Bayesian estimation method again conducted in MLwiN (Browne, 2004).[11] On the other hand, the collective efficacy models – namely social cohesion and trust and informal social control – were both continuous dependent variables modelled simultaneously using a technique known as multivariate multilevel modelling (i.e. a multilevel model with more than one outcome variable) (Snijders and Bosker, 1999). By extending the multilevel framework to a multivariate model it becomes possible to assess the degree to which the two dimensions of collective efficacy are connected. Because the BCS collects information on each dimension, we can create a multilevel structure in which level one includes the two response or dependent variables, one for social cohesion and trust and one for informal social control. Level 1 is nested within individuals at level two which in turn is nested within areas (MSOAs at level three and Police Force Areas at level four).

This modelling strategy provides a number of advantages over using separate multilevel models for one or more of the dimensions individually. Firstly, as already suggested, the relative influence of any one independent variable can be assessed simultaneously for each dimension of collective efficacy (Twigg et al., 2000). Further, the tests of specific effects for single independent variables are more powerful, with the improvement being visible in the form of smaller standard errors (Snijders and Bosker, 1999). Second, the approach allows for joint statistical significance testing of the same explanatory variable on more than one dependent variable (Tseloni, 2007). Whilst varying effects for any one explanatory or independent variable could be obtained from separate models, the statistical significance of any differences can only be gauged when the models are run simultaneously (Twigg et al., 2000).

For both the ASB and the collective efficacy outcomes, two sets of multilevel models were developed. First, the neighbourhood Theil entropy score was added to a base model that contained all pertinent individual, household and areal level variables. In the second model, Theil was removed and the cluster analysis information was added. This allowed us to determine whether there was a significant, independent effect for each of these measures of neighbourhood heterogeneity.

---

[10] In all the models presented in Table 13.1 we allowed random intercepts but not random slopes.

[11] The default prior distributions applied in MLwiN are 'flat' or 'diffuse' for all the parameters (for details see Browne, 2004). Information on the conditional posterior distributions can also be found in Browne (2004). The MCMC models were each run through 100,000 iterations (with a burn in period of 5,000 iterations). The Raftery-Lewis diagnostic (Raftery and Lewis, 1992) confirmed that this Markov chain length was sufficiently long (Browne, 2004).

Table 13.1 Area level influences on perceptions of the local area

	Perceptions of anti-social behaviour			Perceptions of social cohesion and trust		Perceptions of informal social control	
	β	SE(β)	Exp(β)	β	SE(β)	β	SE(β)
Observed crime levels	0.25	0.03	1.29[a]	NA	NA	NA	NA
Rural and urban area classification (base = greater than 10,000)							
Town and fringe	0.07	0.07	1.07	−0.43	0.10[a]	−0.43	0.13[a]
Village, hamlet & isolated dwellings	− 0.69	0.09	0.50[a]	−0.91	0.10[b]	−1.30	0.13[b]
Teenagers (% aged 10–19)	0.08	0.02	1.08[a]	0.08	0.03[a]	0.06	0.04
ln(Population turnover)	0.02	0.02	1.02	0.08	0.03[a]	0.04	0.04
Level of deprivation	0.25	0.03	1.28[a]	0.36	0.03[a]	0.35	0.04[a]
Ethnic heterogeneity							
ln(Theil)	− 0.02	0.03	0.98	0.15	0.04[a]	0.22	0.06[a]

NA indicates the independent variable was not included in the model.
All models also take into account pertinent individual and household level independent variables.
[a]Indicates statistically significant result at the 5% level.
[b]Indicates a statistically significantly different result between SC&T and ISC.
Source: Authors' calculations based on the 2006/07 British Crime Survey.

Results

For reasons of brevity and because our focus centres on assessing the impact of neighbourhood heterogeneity on perceptions of ASB and collective efficacy, we do not include the results for individual and household level variables in Table 13.1. It should be noted however that the area level results shown in the table have been adjusted for these socio-demographic characteristics of the respondents within the neighbourhood. Information on the influence of individual and household level factors on perceptions of ASB and collective efficacy can be found at Taylor et al. (2010) and Twigg et al. (2010) respectively.

In line with other research (Laurence and Heath, 2008; Pennant, 2005; Putnam, 2007), living in a less built-up area was strongly associated with higher levels of collective efficacy but we can also note that the effect of living in a rural area was significantly stronger statistically in relation to informal social control (ISC) than for social cohesion and trust (SC&T). Residence in villages, hamlets or isolated dwellings (i.e. rural locations) also significantly reduces the odds of having high levels of perceived anti-social behaviour (ASB) compared with those living in urban settlements (with a population greater than 10,000). However, unlike in the case of collective efficacy, there appears to be no significant effect for those living in 'town and fringe' areas.

There was also a relatively strong effect for the proportion of young people in the area whereby higher levels of 10–19 year-olds increase the odds of perceiving high levels of ASB. We also found that the proportion of residents in a neighbourhood aged 10–19 years had a detrimental, albeit much weaker, effect on SC&T. Levels of population turnover also had a small negative effect on SC&T. This finding highlights the advantage of treating the two dimensions of collective efficacy separately. Sampson et al. (1997), for example, found a statistically significant relationship between residential stability and collective efficacy but here we show more specifically that the association in this instance is due to the social cohesion and trust dimension only. Once all other area and individual factors have been accounted for, population turnover does not influence levels of informal social control in a neighbourhood. Further, population turnover did not have an independent effect on perceptions of ASB.

As expected, based on the findings of Sampson and Raudenbush (2004), the results indicate that observed crime levels increase an individual's propensity to perceive high levels of ASB (regardless of whether they themselves have been a recent victim of crime).

At the neighbourhood level, when personal background characteristics were controlled for, deprivation (as measured here by the 2007 Indices of Deprivation) was strongly negatively associated with both dimensions of collective efficacy, a finding which is consistent with all other research in this field. Area deprivation also increases the odds of perceiving high levels of ASB, thus supporting the results of Wood (2004) (based on the BCS) and Ipsos MORI (2007) (based on the Best Value Performance Indicator Surveys). This finding is also consistent with the arguments of Shaw and McKay (1942) and these are key observations that we revisit later.

Most pertinent to this chapter is the contested relationship between ethnic heterogeneity and potential adverse social consequences. Do our models support an argument that high levels of ethnic heterogeneity lead to negative perceptions of one's local area? Table 13.1 indicates that ethnic heterogeneity (as measured by the Theil entropy score) is associated with reduced levels of both dimensions of collective efficacy. It should be noted though that the standardised regression coefficients are substantially smaller than those for deprivation.

On the other hand, with respect to perceptions of levels of anti-social behaviour we do not find significant results. The level of ethnic heterogeneity, as measured by the Theil entropy score, was not important in explaining high levels of perceived ASB. When Theil was substituted in the models with the ethnic cluster typology, none of the clusters were found to be significant (results not given here). In other words which ethnic group is dominant in a neighbourhood does not affect perceptions of the local area on the part of its residents.

We now return to the crucial relationship outlined earlier between deprivation and diversity. The results presented above indicate that both deprivation and ethnic diversity have a statistically significant negative effect on the two dimensions of collective efficacy. However, a statistically significant finding does not necessarily imply a substantively important one (Cohen, 1994). Having controlled for pertinent individual and area level variables, the Theil entropy score only explains 1% of the MSOA level variation for social cohesion and trust and does not explain any of the MSOA level variation in the case of informal social control. This is not an impressive effect when compared with the influence of the level of deprivation in the local area which explains substantially more variation – 19% in the case of SC&T and 7% for ISC.

Further, the creation of an interaction term between diversity and deprivation suggests that the effect of ethnic diversity on levels of social cohesion and trust is dependent on the level of deprivation in an area. The coefficient (of the interaction term between deprivation and ethnic diversity) is significant ($\beta = -0.09(0.03)$) but in the opposite direction to our a priori expectation – as deprivation increases, the negative relationship between diversity and SC&T diminishes. This is unexpected if we adhere to a conflict theory, since we would expect perceptions of negative effects to be greatest in deprived areas where there was greatest competition for resources. However, the result is consistent with Sturgis et al. (2010) who found the same relationship to hold when researching trust, and Laurence and Heath (2008, p. 41) who found that areas with both high levels of disadvantage and high ethnic diversity record higher average cohesion scores than highly disadvantaged White areas, leading them to conclude it is *deprivation that undermines cohesion, not diversity*.

Although looking for causal pathways with a cross-sectional survey is inherently problematic, we employ a further modelling strategy to try and unpick whether it is diversity or deprivation that drives negative perceptions of one's neighbourhood by focusing on any possible mediating effect of ethnic heterogeneity. Here we employ the modelling strategy explained in detail in Raudenbush and Sampson (1999) which involves looking at the total effect of deprivation in a model that does not contain a measure of heterogeneity. When the Theil entropy score is introduced, the resultant coefficients represent the direct effects, and the indirect effects can be derived by subtracting the direct effects away from the total effects. The coefficients for deprivation (0.36, 0.35 and 0.25 for SC&T, ISC and ASB respectively) remain unchanged in models with and without the Theil index, suggesting that ethnic heterogeneity does not mediate the relationship between either of the dimensions of collective efficacy or anti-social behaviour and neighbourhood deprivation. In other words, pure ethnic heterogeneity does not influence the observed significant associations between deprivation and negative perceptions of the local area.

Conclusions

The broad conclusions of our work can be simply stated: using these outcome measures of social cohesion, and at this geographical scale, we find very little evidence in support of the proposition that, after allowing for socio-economic characteristics of both individuals and areas, there is an independent effect – whether positive or negative – of heterogeneity on people's perceptions of the degree of disorder (measured by perceived levels of ASB) and cohesion (measured by indicators of collective efficacy) in their neighbourhoods. This is generally consistent both with earlier sociological findings from the USA, with the more recent work of Sampson et al. and contemporary British findings cited in our review of the relationship between deprivation and diversity. In particular, along with the findings of Sturgis et al. (2010), our work provides a strong challenge to Putnam's views about the negative impacts of heterogeneity and the contention that it causes groups to 'hunker down'. Because our measure of ethnic heterogeneity does not capture effects of recent immigration from the EU, our work may not be regarded as a strict test of the so-called 'Goodhart hypothesis', but our findings do not suggest (as Goodhart implies) that we intrinsically distrust those who are different from ourselves.

There are three possible limitations of this work which we cannot resolve with existing data sources. The first is the question of causality: segregation may represent a response to social tensions rather than perceptions of social tensions being a response to segregation. This is inevitable with cross-sectional data although the census data antedates our survey data by several years. The second is that we do not have objective measures of local levels of antisocial behaviour and collective efficacy, since there are no measures of these which are gathered – or are publicly available – independently. Thirdly, MSOAs may, or may not, represent good approximations to the communities within which people live, but these are the only small-area spatial units with which we are able to work at the present time. There are, consequently, several ways in which this work might be developed which would improve our understanding. One would be to add small area socio-economic data to previous versions of the British Crime Survey, so that we can explore whether the relationships we have identified are consistent over time. A second would be to explore whether 'bespoke neighbourhoods' could be created around the residential locations of survey respondents, in the manner developed by Johnston et al.

(2004), but this would have to be done under conditions of strict confidentiality to protect anonymity of respondents. A third would be linkage of other appropriate datasets such as those relating to the distribution of voluntary and community organisations, which may have a mediating effect on relationships between socio-economic conditions and perceptions of community. A final improvement would be to develop, in a British context, an equivalent of the 'systematic social observation' of neighbourhood dynamics practiced by the Project on Human Development in Chicago Neighbourhoods (Sampson et al., 1997), which captures a much wider range of neighbourhood conditions and which has followed individuals over many years.

Reflecting on wider debates, we would argue that the findings of this work offer only one perspective on the relationship between heterogeneity and social cohesion. We agree with Perry (2008, p. 64) that there is a need for a more *complex local perspective* on these matters, and we endorse the Hudson et al. (2007, p. 113) argument that *an overemphasis on residential segregation leads to the exclusion of the complex dynamics of separation/interaction in highly diverse neighbourhoods.*

More in-depth local investigations would therefore be required to tease out these dynamics. Nevertheless, our broad conclusion is in line with that of Sturgis et al. (2010) and Laurence and Heath (2008) namely that the question should be better phrased as 'deprivation, not diversity'; put another way, there is much stronger evidence that perceived social tensions are a response to socioeconomic disadvantage than they are a function of the degree to which neighbourhoods are, or are not, ethnically heterogeneous.

Acknowledgements We are grateful to the Home Office and the Office for National Statistics for allowing us access to the British Crime Survey data and results from the UK 2001 Census, respectively. We would also like to thank the Economic and Social Research Council for funding this work through the 'Understanding Population Trends and Processes' programme (Award number: RES-163-25-0046).

References

Alesina, A. and La Ferrara, E. (2000) Participation in heterogeneous communities, *Quarterly Journal of Economics*, 115: 847–904.

Amin, A. (2002) Ethnicity and the multicultural city: Living with diversity, *Environment and Planning A*, 34(6): 959–980.

Anderson, C. and Paskeviciute, A. (2006) How ethnic and linguistic heterogeneity influence the prospects for civil society: A comparative study of citizenship behavior, *Journal of Politics*, 68(4): 783–802.

Bartholomew, D. and Knott, M. (1999) *Latent Variable Models and Factor Analysis* (2nd ed.), Arnold, London.

Blunkett, D. (2004, 7 July) *New Challenges for Race Equality and Community Cohesion in the 21st Century.* Speech by the Rt. Hon. David Blunkett MP, Home Secretary, to the Institute of Public Policy Research.

Bolling, K., Grant, C. and Sinclair, P. (2007) *2006–07 British Crime Survey (England and Wales) Technical Report*, Vol. I, BMRB, London.

Browne, W. (2004) *MCMC Estimation in MLwiN*, Centre for Multilevel Modelling, Insitute of Education, University of London, London.

Brunton-Smith, I. (2007) *New and Old Measures of the Fear of Crime: A Multilevel Assessment of Measures of Intensity and Frequency*, British Society of Criminology Conference, London.

Cantle, T. (2001) *Community Cohesion: A Report of the Independent Review*, Home Office, London.

Chatfield, C. and Collins, A. (1980) *Introduction to Multivariate Analysis*, Chapman and Hall, London.

Coffe, H. (2009) Social capital and community heterogeneity, *Social Indicators Research*, 91(2): 155–170.

Coffe, H. and Geys, B. (2006) Community heterogeneity: A burden for the creation of social capital? *Social Science Quarterly*, 87(5): 1053–1072.

Cohen, J. (1994) The Earth is round ($p < 0.05$). *American Psychologist*, 49(12): 997–1003.

Commission on Integration and Cohesion (2007) *Commission on Integration and Cohesion – Our Shared Future*, Communities and Local Government Publications, Leeds.

Cronbach, L. (1951) Coefficient alpha and the internal structure of tests, *Psychometrika*, 16: 297–334.

Dawkins, C.J. (2008) Reflections on diversity and social capital: A critique of Robert D. Putnam's E Pluyibus Unum: Diversity and community in the twenty-first century The 2006 Johan Skytte Prize Lecture, *Housing Policy Debate*, 19(1): 208–217.

Department for Communities and Local Government (2007) *Indices of deprivation 2007*. Retrieved April 22, 2008, from http://www.communities.gov.uk/communities/neighbourhood renewal/deprivation/deprivation07/

Field, A. (2005) *Discovering Statistics Using SPSS*, Sage, London.

Fieldhouse, E. and Cutts, D. (2008) Diversity, density and turnout: The effect of neighbourhood ethno-religious composition on voter turnout in Britain, *Political Geography*, 27(5): 530–548.

Finney, N. and Simpson, L. (2009) *Sleepwalking to Segregation? Challenging Myths About Race and Migration*, The Policy Press, Bristol.

Ford, R. (2004) *Local Diversity, Prejudice and White Majority Welfare Attitudes in the UK*. MSc thesis, University of Oxford, Oxford.

Goldstein, H. (2003) *Multilevel Statistical Models* (3rd ed.), Hodder, London.

Goodhart, D. (2004) Too diverse? *Prospect*, 95.

Guest, A., Kubrin, C. and Cover, J. (2008) Heterogeneity and harmony: Neighbouring relationships among whites in ethnically diverse neighbourhoods in Seattle, *Urban Studies*, 45(3): 501–526.

Hero, R. (1998) *Faces of Inequality: Social Diversity in Amercian Politics*, Oxford University Press, Oxford.

Hero, R. (2003) Diversity in American politics, *Perspectives on Politics*, 1: 113–122.

Hudson, M., Phillips, J., Ray, K. and Barnes, H. (2007) *Social Cohesion in Diverse Communities*, Joseph Rowntree Foundation, York.

Iceland, J., Weinburg, D. and Steinmetz, E. (2002) *Racial and Ethnic Residential Segregation in the United States: 1980–2000*, US Government Printing Office, Washington, DC.

Ipsos MORI (2007) *Anti Social Behaviour; People, Place and Perceptions*, Ipsos MORI, London.

Johnston, R., Jones, K., Sarker, R., Burgess, S. and Bolster, A. (2004) Party support and the neighbourhood effect: Spatial polarisation of the British electorate, 1991–2001, *Political Geography*, 23(4): 367–402.

Kershaw, C. and Tseloni, A. (2005) Predicting crime rates, fear and disorder based on area information: Evidence from the 2000 British Crime Survey, *International Review of Victimology*, 12(3): 293–311.

Kubrin, C. and Weitzer, R. (2003) New directions in social disorganization theory, *Journal of Research in Crime and Delinquency*, 40(4): 374–402.

Laurence, J. and Heath, A. (2008) *Predictors of Community Cohesion: Multi-level Modelling of the 2005 Citizenship Survey*, Department for Communities and Local Government, London.

Letki, N. (2008) Does diversity erode social cohesion? Social capital and race in British neighbourhoods, *Political Studies*, 56(1): 99–126.

Livingston, M., Bailey, N. and Kearns, A. (2008) *People's Attachment to Place – The Influence of Neighbourhood Deprivation*, Published for the Joseph Rowntree Foundation by the Chartered Institute of Housing, Coventry.

Maas, C. and Hox, J. (2005) Sufficient sample sizes for multilevel modelling, *Methodology*, 1(3): 86–92.

Massey, D. and Denton, N. (1988) The dimensions of residential segregation, *Social Focus*, 67(2): 281–315.

McCulloch, A. (2003) An examination of social capital and social disorganisation in neighbourhoods in the British household panel study, *Social Science and Medicine*, 56(7): 1425–1438.

Millie, A., Jacobson, J., McDonald, E. and Hough, M. (2005) *Anti-social Behaviour Strategies Finding a Balance*, Policy Press, Bristol.

Moley, S. (2008) Public perceptions in Kershaw, C., Nicholas, S. and Walker, A. (eds.), *Crime in England and Wales 2007/08* (Home Office Statistical Bulletin 07/08), Home Office, London, pp. 117–142.

Nannestad, P. (2008) What have we learned about generalized trust, if anything? *Annual Review of Political Science*, 11: 413–436.

Nicholas, S., Kershaw, C. and Walker, A. (2007) *Crime in England and Wales 2006/07* (Home Office Statistical Bulletin 11/07), Home Office, London.

Noble, M., McLennan, D., Wilkinson, K., Whitworth, A., Barnes, H. and Dibben, C. (2008) *The English Indices of Deprivation 2007*, Communities and Local Government, London.

Office for National Statistics (2004a) *Census 2001*. Key Statistics and Univariate tables for Super Output Areas. Crown Copyright 2004. Crown Copyright material is reproduced with the permission of the Controller of HMSO.

Office for National Statistics (2004b) *Neighbourhood statistics topics* (KS 24 migration). Retrieved 17 June, 2008, from http://www.neighbourhood.statistics.gov.uk/dissemination/Download1.do

Office for National Statistics (2008a) *Key statistics for super output areas in England and Wales*. Retrieved July 15, 2008, from http://www.statistics.gov.uk/census2001/product_ks_soas.asp

Office for National Statistics (2008b) *Super Output Areas (SOAs)*. Retrieved April 2, 2008, from http://www.statistics.gov.uk/geography/soa.asp

Page, B., Ames, A., Pask, R. and Palenicek, A. (2004) *What Drives Public Satisfaction with Local Government*? (Local Government Research Report 20/04), LGA Publications, London.

Peach, C. (2009) *Slippery Segregation: Discovering or Manufacturing Ghettos?* (Institute for Social Change Working Paper), University of Manchester, Manchester.

Pennant, R. (2005) *Diversity, Trust and Community Participation in England* (Home Office Research Findings 253), Home Office, London.

Perry, J. (2008) Comments on a 'critical examination of the recommendations of the Commission on Integration and Cohesion', *People, Places and Policy Online*, 2(3): 163–171.

Phillips, T. (2005) *After 7/7: Sleepwalking to segregation, speech given by Trevor Philips at the Manchester Council for Community Relations, 22 September 2005*. Retrieved October 6, 2009, from http://83.137.212.42/sitearchive/cre/Default.aspx.LocID-0hgnew07s.RefLocID-0hg00900c002.Lang-EN.htm

Putnam, R. (2007) E Pluribus Unum: Diversity and community in the twenty-first century The 2006 Johan Skytte Prize Lecture, *Scandinavian Political Studies*, 30(2): 137–174.

Raftery, A. and Lewis, S. (1992) How many iterations in the Gibbs sampler? in Bernardo, J., Berger, J., Dawid, A. and Smith, A. (eds.), *Bayesian Statistics Four*, Oxford University Press, Oxford, pp. 763–773.

Rasbash, J., Steele, F., Browne, W. and Goldstein, H. (2009) *A User's Guide to MLwiN Version 2.10*, Centre for Multilevel Modelling, Bristol.

Raudenbush, S. and Sampson, R. (1999) Assessing direct and indirect effects in multilevel designs with latent variables, *Sociological Methods and Research*, 28(2): 123–153.

Sampson, R., Morenoff, J. and Earls, F. (1999) Beyond social capital: Spatial dynamics of collective efficacy for children, *American Sociological Review*, 64(5): 633–660.

Sampson, S. and Raudenbush, S. (1999) Systematic social observation of public spaces: A new look at disorder in urban neighbourhoods, *American Journal of Sociology*, 105: 603–651.

Sampson, R. and Raudenbush, S. (2004) Seeing disorder: Neighborhood stigma and the social construction of "broken windows", *Social Psychology Quarterly*, 67(4): 319–342.

Sampson, S., Raudenbush, S. and Earls, F. (1997) Neighbourhoods and violent crime: A multilevel study of collective efficacy, *Science*, 277: 918–924.

Shaw, C. and McKay, H. (1942) *Juvenile Delinquency and Urban Areas*, University of Chicago Press, Chicago, IL.

Snijders, T. and Bosker, R. (1999) *Multilevel Analysis – An Introduction to Basic and Advanced Multilevel Modeling*, Sage, London.

Sturgis, P., Brunton-Smith, I., Read, S. and Allum, N. (2010) Does ethnic diversity erode trust? Putnam's 'hunkering-down' thesis reconsidered, *British Journal of Political Science*, Forthcoming.

Taylor, J., Twigg, L. and Mohan, J. (2010) Investigating perceptions of antisocial behaviour and neighbourhood ethnic heterogeneity in the British Crime Survey, *Transactions of the Institute of British Geographers*, 35(1): 59–75.

The Countryside Agency, Department for Environment Food and Rural Affairs, Office of the Deputy Prime Minister, Office for National Statistics and Welsh Assembly Government (2004) *Rural and Urban Area Classification 2004: An Introductory Guide*, Office for National Statistics, London.

Theil, H. and Finizza, A. (1971) Note on measurement of racial integration of schools by means of informational concepts, *Journal of Mathematical Sociology*, 1(2): 187–193.

Tseloni, A. (2006) Multilevel modelling of the number of property crimes: Household and area effects, *Journal of the Royal Statistical Society Series A (Statistics in Society)*, 169(2): 205–233.

Tseloni, A. (2007) Fear of crime, perceived disorders and property crime: A multivariate analysis at the area level, *Crime Prevention Studies*, 21: 163–185.

Twigg, L., Moon, G., Duncan, C. and Jones, K. (2000) Consumed with worry: 'unsafe' alcohol consumption and self-reported problem drinking in England, *Health Education Research Theory and Practice*, 15(5): 569–580.

Twigg, L., Taylor, J. and Mohan, J. (2010) Diversity or disadvantage? Putnam, Goodhart, ethnic heterogeneity and collective efficacy, *Environment and Planning A*, Forthcoming.

Upson, A. (2006) *Perceptions and Experience of Antisocial Behaviour: Findings From the 2004/05 British Crime Survey* (Home Office online report 21/06), Home Office, London.

Walker, A., Flatley, J., Kershaw, C. and Moon, D. (2009) *Crime in England and Wales 2008/09: Volume 1 Findings from the British Crime Survey and Police Recorded Crime*, Home Office, London.

Weisbrod, B. (1988) *The Non Profit Economy*, Harvard University Press, Boston, MA.

Wood, M. (2004) *Perceptions and Experience of Antisocial Behaviour: Findings From the 2003/04 British Crime Survey* (Home Office online report 49/04), Home Office, London.

Chapter 14
Ethnic Group Populations: The Components for Projection, Demographic Rates and Trends

Paul Norman, Philip Rees, Pia Wohland and Peter Boden

Introduction

A population projection provides an indication of the age-sex structure of future populations. Providing projections with an ethnic group dimension can inform the planning of the provision of relevant goods and services, such as appropriate housing and language support, and can help set targets for take-up of equal opportunities. Projections by ethnic group can also inform policy debates on international migration and diversity. These types of need led Haskey (2002, p. viii) to conclude that *for a wide range of purposes, projections of the population by ethnic group are a necessary element in the armoury of available national demographic data, rather than a discretionary 'optional extra'*. Even if outputs are not needed by ethnic group, Simpson (1997) believes that the inclusion of an ethnic group dimension will improve the precision of total population forecasts when population sub-groups are changing in different ways. In terms of demographic behaviour, for different ethnic groups, this is likely to be the case (Penn, 2000).

A range of methods exist through which to project a population (see Booth, 2006; Wilson and Rees, 2005 for reviews). The most common approach is the cohort-component method in which age-specific fertility, mortality and migration rates are applied to an area's base population to estimate the population at a future time point. Rees (2002) outlines the conventional cohort-component method used for the current UK national projections and shows how the model can be extended to provide projections by separate ethnic groups. For subnational areas, this reveals the need for robust estimates of ethnic group specific fertility and mortality rates and for migration rates between subnational areas and different countries. Further developments proposed by Rees (2002) allow groups to evolve as people of different ethnicities form households and have mixed origin children and for ethnicity to change from that assigned to children by their parents to an adult's self-identification (Simpson and Akinwale, 2007).

P. Norman (✉)
School of Geography, University of Leeds, Leeds LS2 9JT, UK
e-mail: p.d.norman@leeds.ac.uk

J. Stillwell, M. van Ham (eds.), *Ethnicity and Integration*, Understanding Population Trends and Processes 3, DOI 10.1007/978-90-481-9103-1_14,

This chapter reports on a range of innovative data usages and methods to estimate ethnic-group specific demographic rates within the UK for input to a projection of the UK's ethnic group populations. A difficulty to be overcome is that few data sources exist which directly inform about geographically referenced demographic behaviour by ethnic group. We begin by defining the ethnic group categorisations of the population by age and sex used in the study. We then work through each demographic component and outline how rates and recent trends of each have been estimated by ethnic group and the geography of interest. Finally, we describe how scenarios might be applied to explore alternative future populations.

In this research the coverage of the projections is the whole of the UK and the geography is the local government system for which data from the 2001 Census were disseminated. We use local authorities (LAs) in England and Wales, together with Scotland and Northern Ireland as single zones because of their small non-White ethnic minority populations. Projections are made on an annual basis up to 2051. To match the age-time plan of the model, data inputs are required with single year of age detail although, in some instances, this will be interpolated from grouped age information.

Ethnic Group Populations

A base population provides the start point for a projection and this is often the previous census. The age-sex structure of this base population is the result of previous demographic processes and in itself, is highly predictive of the future population. Population age structures vary considerably by ethnic group (Dunnell, 2008). The ethnic group categories utilised here are the 16 groups used for the dissemination of the 2001 Census. Table 14.1 lists these for England. Slightly different ethnic

Table 14.1 2001 Census ethnic groups, England

Broad grouping	Detailed group
White	White – British
	White – Irish
	White Other – White
Mixed	Mixed – White and Black Caribbean
	Mixed – White and Black African
	Mixed – White and Asian
	Mixed – Other Mixed
Asian or Asian British	Asian or Asian British – Indian
	Asian or Asian British – Pakistani
	Asian or Asian British – Bangladeshi
	Asian or Asian British – Other Asian
Black or Black British	Black or Black British – Black Caribbean
	Black or Black British – Black African
	Black or Black British – Other Black
Chinese or Other Ethnic Group	Chinese or Other Ethnic Group – Chinese
	Chinese or Other Ethnic Group – Other Ethnic Group

Source: 2001 Census, England.

categorisations were used in the UK's other countries. Note that the 1991 Census, the first in the UK to ask all respondent's about their ethnicity, used different groups from those in 2001 and that these groups are not necessarily comparable over time (Simpson, 2002). The applicability of ethnic classifications is the subject of a wide and ongoing debate (Ahmad, 1999) with the groups used in these projections perhaps becoming less applicable over time. We use the detailed groups in the right hand column of Table 14.1 rather than the broad groupings in the left hand column, because we observe considerable heterogeneity within broad groupings. In particular, we retain the Mixed groups because they have been the most rapidly expanding in the recent past, although most analyses of trends between 1991 and 2001 assigned these Mixed groups back to their parent groups (e.g. Rees and Butt, 2004).

Demographic Components

Fertility

A cohort-component model uses age-specific fertility rates (ASFRs) applied to the population of women of child-bearing age to estimate the number of births in the next time period of the projection. Overall fertility level is summarised using a total fertility rate (TFR). Calculating a time-series of ASFRs and TFRs from the 1980s to 2006 has been achieved here for all women using vital statistics on births and official mid-year estimates as denominators with all data allocated to the LA geography by the national statistics agencies (see Tromans et al., 2008 for trends in England and Wales). Figure 14.1 illustrates ASFRs in Bradford and in Leeds, both of which are

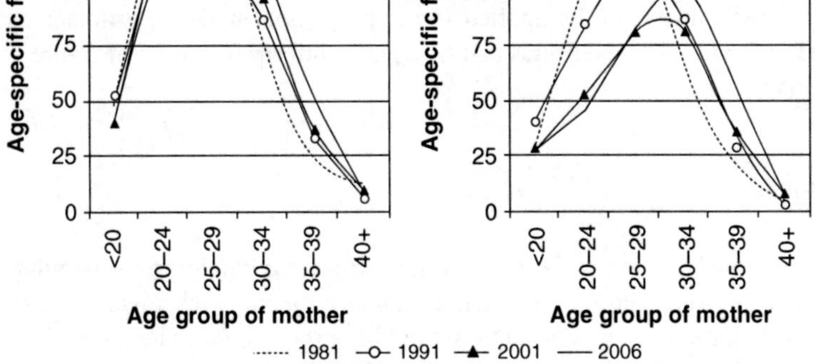

Fig. 14.1 Age-specific fertility trends, Bradford and Leeds, 1981–2006
(Source: Authors' calculations based on vital statistics and population data from ONS)

multicultural, university LAs but evidently have rather different fertility trends since 1981. In both, the curves move down and to the right as fertility gradually falls over time and as women in general 'postpone' births to have children somewhat later in their childbearing years. Leeds overall has lower fertility than Bradford with the latter having a somewhat 'younger' ASFR profile. Both LAs experienced a rise in fertility between 2001 and 2006, which has continued to 2008.

The need in this research is to estimate ASFRs and fertility trends by ethnic group. Here a variety of population and sample data sources are used to estimate rates since the necessary ethnic group information is not necessarily available by time-point, data source and geography. Table 14.2 summarises the sources used here and outlines the relevant geographical and demographic detail which each provides. TFRs by ethnic group and LA are estimated from 1991 and 2001 Census data using child to woman ratios (CWRs) which are assumed to emulate family size by ethnic group (Sporton and White, 2002). Annual trends in national level ASFRs by ethnic group are derived from the Labour Force Survey (LFS) by modelling the probability of a woman having a child based on her age and ethnicity.

Using CWRs in Bradford and Leeds, ethnic-specific TFRs have been estimated with examples illustrated in Fig. 14.2. Higher fertility rates are shown for Pakistani and Bangladeshi women. Rates for Indian women are closer to the White group TFRs, particularly in Leeds. The local ASFRs for all women (Fig. 14.3) have been adjusted for overall level using these TFRs by ethnic group and for shape of curve using the LFS-derived national estimate of each group's ASFR. In 2001 in Bradford, the Bangladeshi group have high fertility with the peak age of giving birth for women in their early 20s. The Pakistani curve is similar and a little lower. Whilst the TFR for Indian women is just a little lower than for the Pakistani group, the curve is somewhat older, resembling that of the White ethnic group. In Leeds, fertility levels for all groups are lower than in Bradford and the ASFR curves much flatter with the peak ages of fertility for women in their late 20s and early 30s

For each year from the early 1980s to 2006, fertility trends for all women have been identified for each LA and by ethnic group at national level using the LFS. The UK's Census provides indicators of changes in family size by ethnic group between 1991 and 2001. In combination, these sources have underpinned the calculation of ASFRs and trends for all LAs across the UK by ethnic group, as appropriate to each country. These rates can be applied in the projection model to estimate births in the next time period. The trends can be used to inform scenarios of future fertility directions.

Mixing

One important decision to be taken when projecting ethnic group populations is the extent to which groups interact. In some projections by country of birth or nationality, foreign born or foreign nationality groups contribute native born children or children of host country nationality, although this depends on the nationality law in place (Coleman, 2006). In other projections, the racial groups remain

Table 14.2 Sources to estimate fertility by ethnic group

Source	Time point	Geography	Ethnicity	Fertility measure	Notes
Census area statistics	1991 2001	LAs LAs	10 groups 16 groups	Child to woman ratios to estimate TFRs by ethnic group	1991 Ethnic group categories can be aligned with the 2001 categories by assuming that eight are equivalent over time (Simpson, 2002, p. 77) 1991 data can be adjusted to the 2001 geography (Norman et al., 2003) Children not directly linked with mothers
Census samples of anonymised records	1991 2001	National National	10 groups 16 groups	Child to woman ratios to estimate TFRs by ethnic group	Provides national level fertility estimates by ethnic group and acts as a control for LA estimates Children are directly linked with mothers
Labour force survey	Annually from 1980s to date	National	A variety of different groups over time	Modelled probability of child provides ASFRs by ethnic group	Small numbers and changing ethnic information mean that information for only five broad ethnic group can be estimated reliably

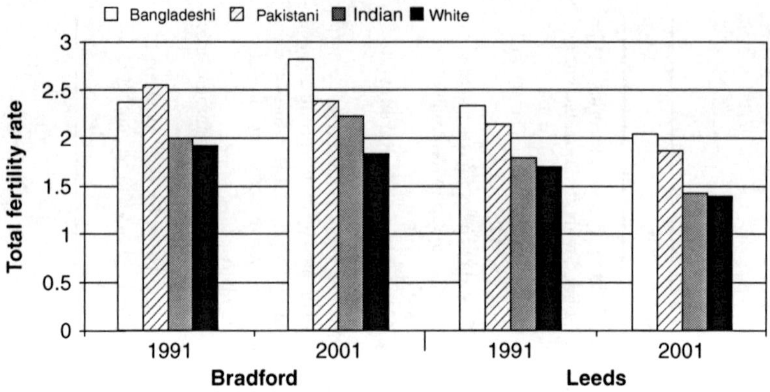

Fig. 14.2 Estimated TFRs, Bradford and Leeds, 1991 and 2001

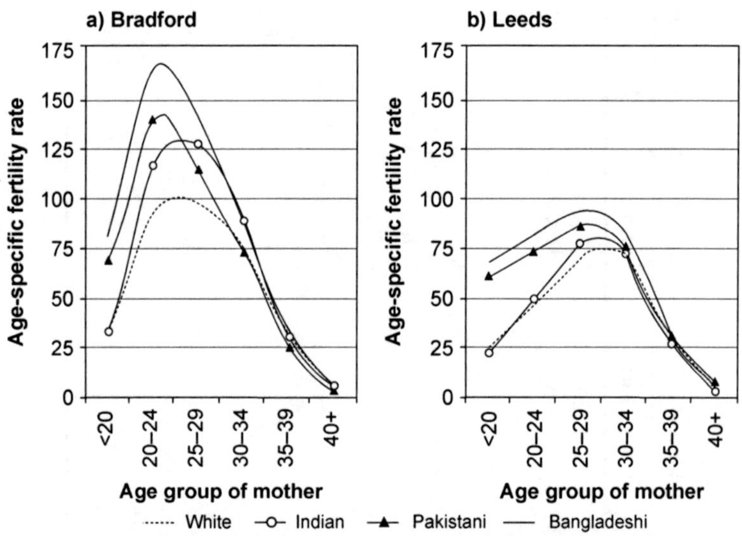

Fig. 14.3 Estimated ASFRs by ethnic group, Bradford and Leeds, 2001
(Source: Authors' calculations based on vital statistics, census, population and survey data from ONS)

independent (US Bureau of the Census, 2008). In one unusual ethnic population projection model, the offspring of mixed parentage are assigned to the ethnic group of the populations of both parents (Statistics New Zealand, 2008b). The consequence of this approach is that the sum of ethnic group populations exceeds the national all group projections.

Here we adopt a different approach. Ethnic groups are projected independently with one exception: births to mothers in each ethnic group are distributed across all ethnic groups using ethnic mixing probabilities that a mother of one ethnic group has a child of her own or another ethnic group (Table 14.3). These probabilities are computed from commissioned Table CO431 from the 2001 Census of England, which cross-classifies children under one in households by the ethnicity of their mother and that assigned by their parent(s) in the census return. Ethnic groups thus both 'receive' new recruits born to mothers of other ethnicities and 'send' children into other ethnic groups. The main process behind these flows is marriage or partnership between men and women of different ethnicities together with decisions by parents about the ethnicity assigned to their offspring on the census form.

Table 14.3 reports the statistics from the mother's viewpoint and shows the ethnic membership of the infant by mother's ethnicity. So, for example, only 25.4% of children of White Irish mothers are assigned White Irish ethnicity. The majority (64.3%) are given White British ethnicity, indicating that White Irish mothers have husbands or partners who are White British. The sending percentages, in the form of probabilities summing to 1 rather than 100, are used to assign the ethnicity of a newborn within the projection model. We use mixing matrices for each Government Office Region in England for the constituent LAs. Since we have no alternative evidence, we assume that the England sending probabilities will serve for Wales, Scotland and Northern Ireland and will check the impact of this in alternative projection models.

What effect will this process of ethnic mixing have on the future population of the ethnic groups? In Table 14.3 we have computed the percentage net gain or loss to an ethnic group as the ratio of the number of children under one in an ethnic group to the number of children under one of mothers of that ethnicity. The statistics indicate a very rapid mixing process: the mixed groups have gains of 150–250%. Small losses are experienced by the Asian groups; larger losses are experienced by the Chinese group, Other Ethnic group and the White Irish group. Other White and Other Black groups experience gains as well. Over two generations of projection (2001–2051), the mixing process is likely to result in substantial shifts in the ethnic composition of the population towards the Mixed groups a result of the mixing process. There will, of course, be compensating effects as a result of fertility, mortality and migration differentials.

Mortality

Mortality is a vital component for projecting populations, particularly at older ages. Figure 14.4 shows spatial variations of life expectancy across the UK: characteristically life expectancy in the South is higher compared to the North, and within those regions, rural areas usually experience higher life expectancy than urban areas (Brown and Rees, 2006).

Figure 14.5 illustrates the time series of mean life expectancies at birth from 1991 to 2007 for men and women by deprivation quintiles (Townsend, 1987) weighted by population. The least deprived quintile is illustrated by black lines and symbols and the most deprived socioeconomic quintile is represented by grey lines and

Table 14.3 Sending percentages of ethnic group of child under one by ethnic group of mother 2001 Census, England

2001 Census, England		White			Mixed				Asian				Black			Chinese Or Other	
Ethnic group of mother: percentages	Totals	British	Irish	Other White	White and Black Caribbean	White and Black African	White and Asian	Other Mixed	Indian	Pakistani	Bangladeshi	Other Asian	Black Caribbean	Black African	Other Black	Chinese	Other Ethnic Group
Totals	100.0	100.0	100.0	100.0	100.0	100.0	100.0	100.0	100.0	100.0	100.0	100.0	100.0	100.0	100.0	100.0	100.0
White: British	83.4	96.8	64.3	49.7	21.0	23.5	40.2	33.5	2.6	2.9	3.8	7.8	3.5	2.7	7.8	5.9	12.8
White: Irish	0.4	0.1	25.4	0.3	0.0	0.0	0.3	0.2	0.1	0.0	0.0	0.2	0.1	0.1	0.0	0.1	0.1
White: Other White	2.2	0.4	4.4	40.1	2.2	4.9	3.0	6.1	0.3	0.2	0.2	1.7	0.6	0.6	1.9	0.8	3.1
Mixed: White and Black Caribbean	1.5	1.1	1.7	1.5	48.1	3.5	2.7	3.4	0.2	0.1	0.2	0.6	15.2	0.3	7.0	0.4	0.7
Mixed: White and Black African	0.5	0.3	0.7	1.6	2.0	38.9	1.1	1.7	0.1	0.1	0.1	0.4	0.3	5.5	1.1	0.0	0.4
Mixed: White and Asian	1.2	0.6	1.5	2.3	0.9	0.9	39.1	4.0	7.4	1.9	1.7	7.1	0.5	0.2	0.4	5.8	18.5
Mixed: Other Mixed	0.9	0.3	0.9	2.2	12.1	11.6	5.9	41.2	0.8	0.3	0.6	3.9	2.1	0.8	11.1	16.1	14.4
Asian or Asian British: Indian	2.1	0.0	0.1	0.2	0.5	0.3	1.1	0.8	83.2	1.6	1.2	4.6	0.2	0.4	0.3	0.4	0.7
Asian or Asian British: Pakistani	2.4	0.1	0.1	0.2	0.5	0.0	2.4	1.1	2.3	90.0	2.4	4.3	0.2	0.3	0.3	0.2	0.8
Asian or Asian British: Bangladeshi	0.9	0.0	0.0	0.2	0.1	0.3	0.9	0.4	0.4	0.6	87.3	1.5	0.0	0.2	0.0	0.0	0.3
Asian or Asian British: Other Asian	0.6	0.0	0.1	0.4	0.4	1.3	1.7	1.2	2.0	1.9	1.6	65.1	0.3	0.6	0.6	0.3	2.0
Black or Black British: Black Caribbean	1.0	0.0	0.2	0.1	8.8	1.2	0.3	1.7	0.1	0.1	0.1	0.2	65.8	1.9	7.2	0.1	0.2
Black or Black British: Black African	1.7	0.0	0.2	0.6	0.7	10.7	0.2	1.1	0.2	0.1	0.1	0.6	4.0	80.8	6.5	0.2	0.8
Black or Black British: Other Black	0.4	0.0	0.1	0.2	2.6	2.4	0.2	1.7	0.0	0.0	0.1	0.4	7.2	5.6	55.4	0.1	0.5
Chinese or Other Ethnic Group: Chinese	0.4	0.0	0.1	0.1	0.0	0.0	0.3	0.7	0.1	0.1	0.1	0.1	0.1	0.0	0.0	68.3	1.1
Chinese or Other Ethnic Group: Other Ethnic Group	0.4	0.0	0.2	0.3	0.2	0.6	0.6	1.3	0.2	0.2	0.5	1.6	0.0	0.1	0.4	1.2	43.6

Key to percentage classes: >=80% | 50%-<80% | 25%-<50% | 1%-<25% | <1%

Source: Authors' computations from 2001 Census, Commissioned Table CO431.

Fig. 14.4 Life expectancy in the UK for all persons, 2001 (Source: Authors' calculations based on vital statistics and population data from ONS, GROS and NISRA)

symbols. This reveals important details about UK life expectancies: the continuous and considerable increase in life expectancy over recent decades for both men and women. Women, as in most countries, experience higher life expectancy, but men are recently starting to catch up. We also see how life expectancy is related to deprivation, the more deprived, the lower the life expectancy. This effect is more pronounced in men than in women, with the difference in life expectancy between the two socioeconomic groups much larger than the difference between sexes. Despite overall increases in life expectancy, the gap between socioeconomic groups slightly widened from 1991 to 2007.

If there are different life expectancies by sex and by geographical area, we might expect variations between ethnic groups. Previous UK population projections by ethnic group only used all-person mortality rates (Coleman and Scherbov, 2005; Coleman, 2006; Rees and Parsons, 2006, 2009; Rees, 2006, 2008), even though data from other countries suggest differences in ethnic group mortality. For example,

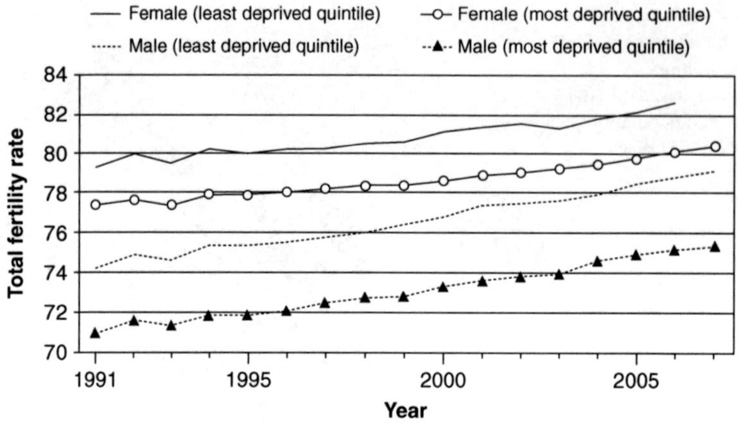

Fig. 14.5 Life expectancy for men (♂) and women (♀), 1991–2007. Note: *Black* represents the least deprived group according to the Townsend (1987) index and *grey* the most deprived group (Source: Authors' calculations based on vital statistics, census and population data from ONS, GROS and NISRA)

in 2003, White men in the US had a period life expectancy at birth of 75.3 years, while for Black men life expectancy was 68.9 years (NCHS, 2007). In New Zealand, during 2005–2007, Māori life expectancy at birth was 8.2 years lower than for non-Māori persons (Statistics New Zealand, 2008a).

In the UK, mortality data by ethnic groups are not readily available since a person's ethnic group or race is not registered when they die. Even though a place of birth has been noted on English death certificates since 1969, this only indicates mortality for first generation immigrants and is potentially biased, for example, by White British born in India before independence. A direct source for ethnic group mortality is the ONS Longitudinal Study (LS) but this only represents 1% of the England and Wales population and has considerable loss to follow-up of LS members, up to 30% at older ages (Harding and Balarajan, 2002). The LS is not a reliable enough mortality source for ethnic groups and cannot provide local mortality information.

Various studies using panel or longitudinal data find that self-reported health is a strong predictor for subsequent mortality, for total populations as well as subgroups (e.g. Burström and Fredlund, 2001; Heistaro et al., 2001; Helweg et al., 2003; McGee et al., 1999). Thus, with no adequate ethnic mortality data available, we use a proxy measure for which data existed by UK LA level and ethnic group: answers to the 2001 Census question, 'Do you have any long-term illness, health problem or disability which limits your daily activities or the work you can do?'

To estimate mortality by ethnic group, we use a suite of census, official mid-year population estimates and vital statistics data to estimate ethnic group life expectancy. As outlined in Fig. 14.6, first we calculated standardised illness ratios (SIRs) for each LA by sex with data from the 2001 Census. We also calculated standardised mortality ratios (SMRs) for all local areas and both sexes from mid-year population estimates and vital statistics mortality data. Next, we use these ratios to define all-person SMRs as a function of all person SIRs. This all-person

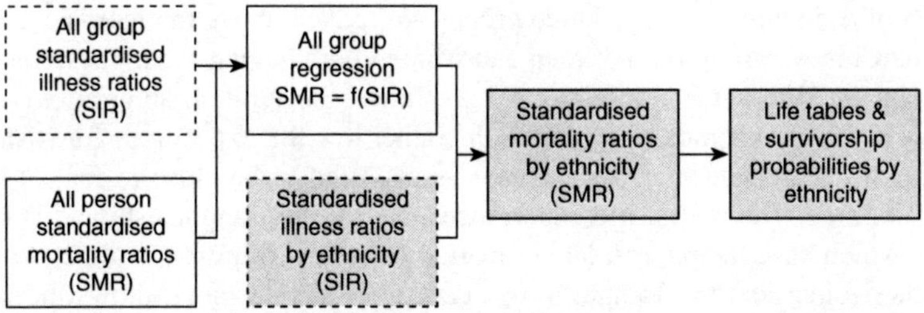

Fig. 14.6 Method to estimate life tables and survivorship probabilities from self reported illness, combining 2001 Census data with mid-year estimates and vital statistics

function is then applied to each ethnic group's local area SIR to calculate an ethnic group-specific SMR. These ethnic group SMRs are used to adjust upwards or downwards age-sex specific mortality rates (ASMRs) for each local area. These ASMRs are fed into life tables to derive survivorship probabilities for our projection model. During this procedure, we found men reporting less illness than women but experiencing higher mortality. We also found different SIR/SMR relationships for the UK's constituent countries.

Thus, we estimated life expectancies and survivorship probabilities for all ethnic groups defined in the UK 2001 Census for each local authority, by single year of age and sex. Below we present examples of life expectancies at birth in England. Table 14.4 shows a gender combined rank for each ethnic group in life expectancy at birth, together with the population weighted mean life expectancy for men and

Table 14.4 Ranks of life expectancy at birth (e_0) in England, for the total population of each ethnic group and mean life expectancies at birth for men and women of each group, 2001

		Mean e_0	
Total rank	Ethnic group	Women	Men
1	Chinese	82.1	78.1
2	Other White	81.3	76.9
3	Other Ethnic	81.5	76.2
	All groups	80.5	76.0
4	Black African	80.4	76.1
5	White British	80.5	75.9
6	White-Irish	80.3	74.9
7	White-Asian	80.0	75.1
8	Indian	79.3	75.5
9	Other Asian	79.5	75.2
10	Other Mixed	79.9	74.6
11	White-Black African	79.5	74.2
12	Black Caribbean	79.1	74.4
13	White-Black Caribbean	78.7	73.4
14	Other Black	78.5	73.4
15	Bangladeshi	77.7	72.7
16	Pakistani	77.3	73.1

Source: Rees et al. (2009)

women of each ethnic group. Three groups are ranked above the national average, with the Chinese group on top, men and women both having the highest mean life expectancies. Within the White group, we estimate the White Irish group to occupy the lowest rank. This ranking is due to the rather low life expectancy for Irish men, whereas life expectancy of Irish women is expected to be close to that of White British women. The lowest life expectancies are for the Bangladeshi and Pakistani groups which have the poorest labour market positions (Simpson et al., 2006). That the Other Asian and the Indian groups occupy moderate ranks shows the importance of having well-defined subgroups. We also find a strong contrast in the Black group, where the Black African group is one rank below the total population, in contrast to the Black Caribbean group which occupies rank 12. The Black African estimate is reasonable considering the so-called healthy migrant effect (Fennelly, 2005) whereby persons moving countries are advantaged in various ways (compared with their origin and/or their destination populations) including good health which thereby enables their move. The Black African group is a much younger – and therefore healthier – migrant community compared with the Black Caribbean group which is longer established in the UK.

We are cautious about the origins of the differences between the group estimates, though preliminary analyses suggest the most important socioeconomic influence is the level of higher education attainment in the group (Rees and Wohland, 2008). The healthy migrant effect is also likely to be important. Migration selects for individuals who are healthy because they have the resources and energy to move and because immigration rules prevent people with long term limiting illness from entry to a destination country. At older ages migration may be associated with the transition to various grades of disability, when older persons move to locations where health care or family support is better. This probably only affects the White British group (return to the UK to benefit from NHS care) and the Black Caribbean group (older cohorts have retired back to the West Indies).

Spatial distributions of life expectancy for women from example ethnic groups (one from each racial group) are given in Fig. 14.7. The dark shade on the maps denotes areas in the 25% highest life expectancies (81.2–85.9 years), the light shade denotes the 25% lowest local areas (73.8–78.9 years) and the mid-shade the 50% between these. We find pronounced differences between the ethnic groups. Most extreme differences are found between the Chinese women with most areas in the top 25% distribution and the Pakistani women with the largest numbers of areas in the bottom 25%. Most groups also reflect the North-South gradient mentioned above. Note that the Mixed group, Black and White Africans, has more areas in the bottom of the distribution compared to either of the separate ethnic groups, White British or Black African. A full account of methods and results is provided in Rees et al. (2009).

To establish recent trends, before ethnic mortalities are introduced into the population projection, they are updated to 2007. Since there is no comprehensive source of local ethnic illness data beyond the 2001 Census, we will update ethnic mortality in line with the mortalities for all groups. We analyse life expectancy trends in the total populations, by following deprivation or other group characteristics

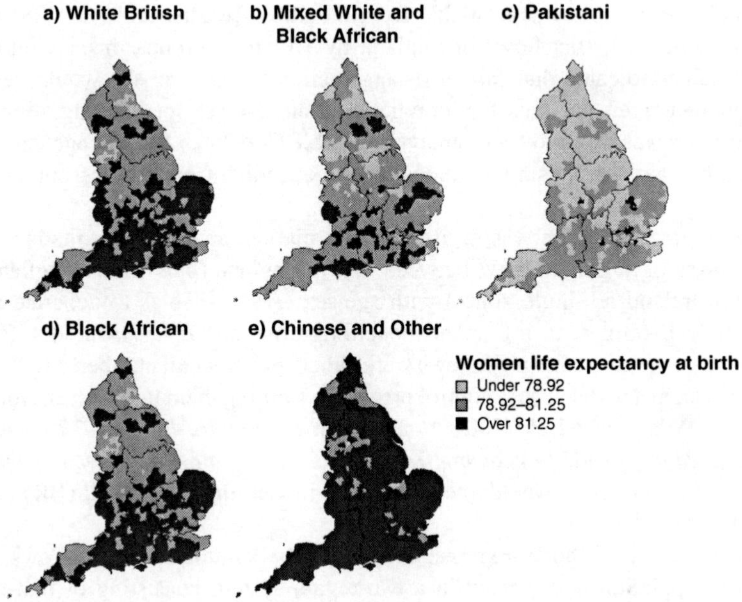

Fig. 14.7 Spatial distribution of female life expectancy at birth for five example ethnic groups, England, 2001
(Source: Authors' calculations based on vital statistics, census and population data from ONS, GROS and NISRA)

through time to analyse the extent of convergence or divergence in society (as in Fig. 14.5). Finally, we will combine results from the ethnic mortality estimates and the all-group trends to create various future scenarios to inform our projection model.

Sub-national Migration

To project the populations of 16 ethnic groups for 352 local authorities in England and three countries filling out the United Kingdom we need robust estimates of internal migration, which is a very important component of population change. Data on migration by ethnic group are collected in two sources: the decennial census and the annual Labour Force Survey and its successors, the Annual Population Survey and the Integrated Household Survey. The annual household surveys have been used to understand the structure of UK migration by ethnic groups by Raymer and Giulietti (2008, 2009) and Raymer et al. (2008), while Stillwell et al. (2008) have used information from the 2001 Census Small Area Microdata. Hussain and Stillwell (2008) and Stillwell and Hussain (2008) have analysed the spatial structure of inter-district migration using 2001 Census commissioned tables. However, the data sets used by these authors did not match the input requirements of our projection model – 16 detailed ethnic groups as well as a LA spatial scale (in England). Fortunately, a commissioned table was available from the 2001 Census (table CO528) which reports the inter-district flows in England by 16 ethnic groups. Inspection of the CO528 table indicated that further disaggregation by age and sex would generate very small numbers and therefore unreliable ethnic-age-sex specific migration rates. The decision was taken to focus analysis on table CO528 and to add age and sex as independent variables, using a national age-sex profile of migration from the 2001 Census.

The original intention was to use this information, an origin-destination-ethnic (ODE) array of migration flows between LAs in England (plus Wales, Scotland and Northern Ireland as single zones) with age-sex (AS) variables to generate multi-regional probabilities: in log-linear modelling terms an ODE+AS model. Further investigation revealed that most flows were either zero or small numbers (1, 2) which had been subject to disclosure control procedure (turning them into 0 or 3). Adopting advice in Wilson and Bell (2004, p. 157) that *the POOL, BR and BR+N models were argued to provide forecasting frameworks with a balance between conceptual purity and practicality*, we adopted a reduced model, the bi-regional (BR) cohort-component model.

The structure of the bi-regional model can be summarised as follows. Each region's population is projected in a two-region system consisting of that region and the rest of the country. The model projects flows from the region of interest to the rest of the country and from the rest of the country to the region of interest as products of out-migration probabilities multiplied by the population at risk in the respective origin region. It thus captures the essential advantage of the multiregional model over the single-region model (with net migration or gross flows), namely that the migration flows respond, *ceteris paribus*, to the changing size of origin populations. The model was found by Wilson and Bell (2004) to give projection results close to the outcomes of a multiregional model applied to the states and territories of Australia. A couple of adjustments are needed to the model to ensure consistency of the projected flows. The total of outflows from the regions may differ from the total of inflows (outflows from the rest of the country). In each time interval, these totals are reconciled by adjusting the inflows to agree with the total of outflows. The second adjustment is to compute the total country populations as the sum of all the regional populations for use in the next time interval.

Because we employ census migration data between LAs, there is an opportunity to separate the processes of survival from those of migration. Migration data from the 2001 census is generated from a question on location 1 year ago, asked (by definition) of those who have survived the year. So from these data we can compute the probabilities of re-location given survival within the country covered by the census. We can compute survival probabilities using life tables from local and national mortality data (described above) and thereby estimate the probability of emigration given survival. The advantage of computing the component probabilities in this way is that it ensures that they are all well behaved, being non-negative and not exceeding unity. So the flows of internal migrants in each period-cohort, sex and ethnic group are modelled using equations set out in Table 14.5.

The projection begins with Equation (14.1) in which the start population is multiplied by a survivorship probability derived from the local area life table (see above).

Table 14.5 Equations used to estimate the out-migration probabilities for local areas

Variable		Constituent variables	Equation numbers
Total survivors	=	Survivorship probability × Start population of origin	(14.1)
Emigrant survivors	=	Square root (survivorship probability) × Emigration flow	(14.2)
Survivors within country	=	Total survivors – Emigrant survivors	(14.3)
Out-migrant survivors	=	Probability of out-migration given survival within country × Survivors within country	(14.4)
Surviving stayers	=	Census population – Total surviving in-migrants – Surviving immigrants	(14.5)
Total surviving in-migrants	=	Total migrants – Intra-zone migrant – Surviving immigrants	(14.6)
Total survivors within the UK	=	Surviving stayers + Total surviving out-migrants within the UK	(14.7)
Total surviving out-migrants within the UK	=	Total migrants within UK (with given origin) – Intra-zone migrants	(14.8)
Total probability of out-migration given survival within the UK	=	Total surviving out-migrants within the UK/Total survivors within the UK	(14.9)
Total survivors in rest of UK	=	Sum of total survivors within UK in each zone – Total survivors within UK	(14.10)
Total probability of out-migration from the rest of UK given survival in UK	=	Total surviving in-migrant to zone/total survivors in rest of UK	(14.11)

Then in Equation (14.2) the model inputs the estimate of emigration from the local area and computes the number of emigrant survivors using the square root of the survivorship probability to reflect the shorter exposure to mortality in the UK of persons who emigrate. We then subtract emigrant survivors from total survivors to yield the survivors within the country (Equation 14.3). The number of out-migrant survivors (people who migrate and survive between local areas within the country) is projected by multiplying the total survivors within the country computed in Equation (14.1) by the probability of out-migration given survival within the country in Equation (14.4). These probabilities are estimated by converting the inter-area internal migration matrix from the census into a population accounting matrix. The way this is done is best explained through an example shown in Table 14.6.

Table 14.6 contains the matrix of flows for one ethnic group, Indians, showing three of the 355 origins/destinations. The top left sub-table shows the flows from origins (rows) to destinations (columns). These derive from the census commissioned table but have been adjusted upwards by re-distributing the persons reporting ‘No usual address 1 year ago’ (NUA) using the reported migrants flows as weights (including intra-area migrants). This is a vital adjustment as NUA migrants make up 8% in the case of the Indian ethnic group. The diagonal terms in the matrix contain the intra-zone migrants (persons with a different address 1 year before the census which was in the same zone as that they lived at the time of the census).

Table 14.6 Subnational migration flows for ethnic groups, Indian ethnic group, 2001 Census[b]

Origin		Destination													
Zone No.	Zone name	City of London + Westminster	:	Leeds	:	Northern Ireland	Total migrants within UK	Intra-zone migrants	Total surviving out-migrants within UK	Surviving stayers	Total survivors within UK	Total probability of out-migration from area[a]	Total surviving in-migrants	Total Survivors in Rest of UK	Total probability of out-migration from RUK[a]
1	City of London + Westminster	405	:	3	:	1	1,015	405	610	4,463	5,073	0.120226	872	990,070	0.000881
:	:	:	:		:		:	:	:	:	:	:	:	:	:
67	Leeds	10	:	1,134	:	1	1,671	1,134	537	11,322	11,859	0.045253	707	983,285	0.000719
:	:	:	:		:		:	:	:	:	:	:	:	:	:
355	Northern Ireland	3	:	4	:	205	385	205	180	1,399	1,579	0.055575	48	992,241	0.000157
	Address outside UK	495	:	274	:	122									
	Total migrants	1,772	:	2,115	:	375									
	Intra-zone migrants	405	:	1,134	:	205									
	Total surviving in-migrants	872	:	707	:	48									
	Total surviving in-migrants & immigrants	1,367	:	981	:	170									
	Total surviving stayers	4,463		11,322	:	1,394									
	2001 Census population	5,830	:	12,303	:	1,569									
	No usual address 1 year ago	140	:	138	:	0									

[a]Given survival in the UK.

[b]Figures may not sum precisely to column or row totals because of rounding for presentation purposes.

Source: Authors' calculations based on Commissioned Table CO528, 2001 Census, Crown Copyright and census migration statistics and population data from ONS, GROS and NISRA.

They are replaced for probability calculations by the surviving stayers within a zone (within zone migrants and non-migrants). This term is not provided in the census tables but can be computed as a residual by subtracting from the census population the total of internal in-migrants plus the international immigrants ('Address outside the UK 1 year ago'). This is Equation (14.5) in Table 14.5. Total surviving in-migrants to a local area can be computed as a sum of the flows from all other areas or through subtracting intra-zone migrants and surviving immigrants from total migrants (Equation 14.6 in Table 14.5).

Consider the migration flows into the first zone, City of London plus Westminster. There are a total of 1,772 in-migrants, 405 intra-zone migrants and 495 surviving immigrants, so that the total surviving in-migrants are 872. Subtract from the census population of 5,830 there 872 surviving in-migrants and the 495 surviving immigrants and the result is 4,463 surviving stayers. This population term is essential for the computation of the total of survivors within the UK, who are located in the middle top panel of the table. They are computed as the sum of surviving stayers within the local area plus total surviving out-migrants within the UK (Equation 14.7 in Table 14.5). Total surviving out-migrants within the UK are total migrants within UK (with given origin) less intra-zone migrants (Equation 14.8 in Table 14.5). For the City of London plus Westminster, the total migrants are 1,015 and the intra-zone migrants 405, leaving 610 total surviving out-migrants within the UK. Add this number to the surviving stayers and we get 5,073 total survivors within the UK. We are now in a position to compute the migration probabilities needed in the projection model.

The total probability of out-migration given survival within the UK is computed as the total surviving out-migrants within the UK divided by total survivors within the UK (Equation 14.9 in Table 14.5). In the case of the City of London plus Westminster, this probability for the Indian group is 610/5,073 = 0.120226 or 12% for the Indian group in this London borough. The out-migration probabilities are higher for London boroughs than elsewhere because they are small parts of a much larger metropolitan housing and jobs market.

The rightmost panel in Table 14.6 reports the computation of the out-migration probabilities from the rest of the UK (the UK minus the zone of interest), which requires the computation of the total survivors in the rest of the UK. These are calculated as the sum of total survivors within UK in each zone less total survivors within UK (Equation 14.10 in Table 14.5). The total probability of out-migration from the rest of UK given survival in UK is computed as total surviving in-migrant to zone divided by total survivors in rest of UK (Equation 14.11 in Table 14.5). For the City of London plus Westminster, this probability is 872/990,070 or 0.00088.

Full versions of Table 14.6 have been developed for all 16 ethnic groups and all 355 zones in our analysis. Previous work used only broad ethnic groupings (Stillwell et al., 2008). The out-migration probabilities for ethnic groups in Leeds are plotted in Fig. 14.8. Figure 14.8a plots the probabilities of out-migration from Leeds. Compared with the White British, the Other White, all of the Mixed Groups, the Indian, Black African, Chinese and Other Ethnic Group all exhibit higher probabilities whereas the White Irish, White and Black Caribbean, Pakistani and Bangladeshi

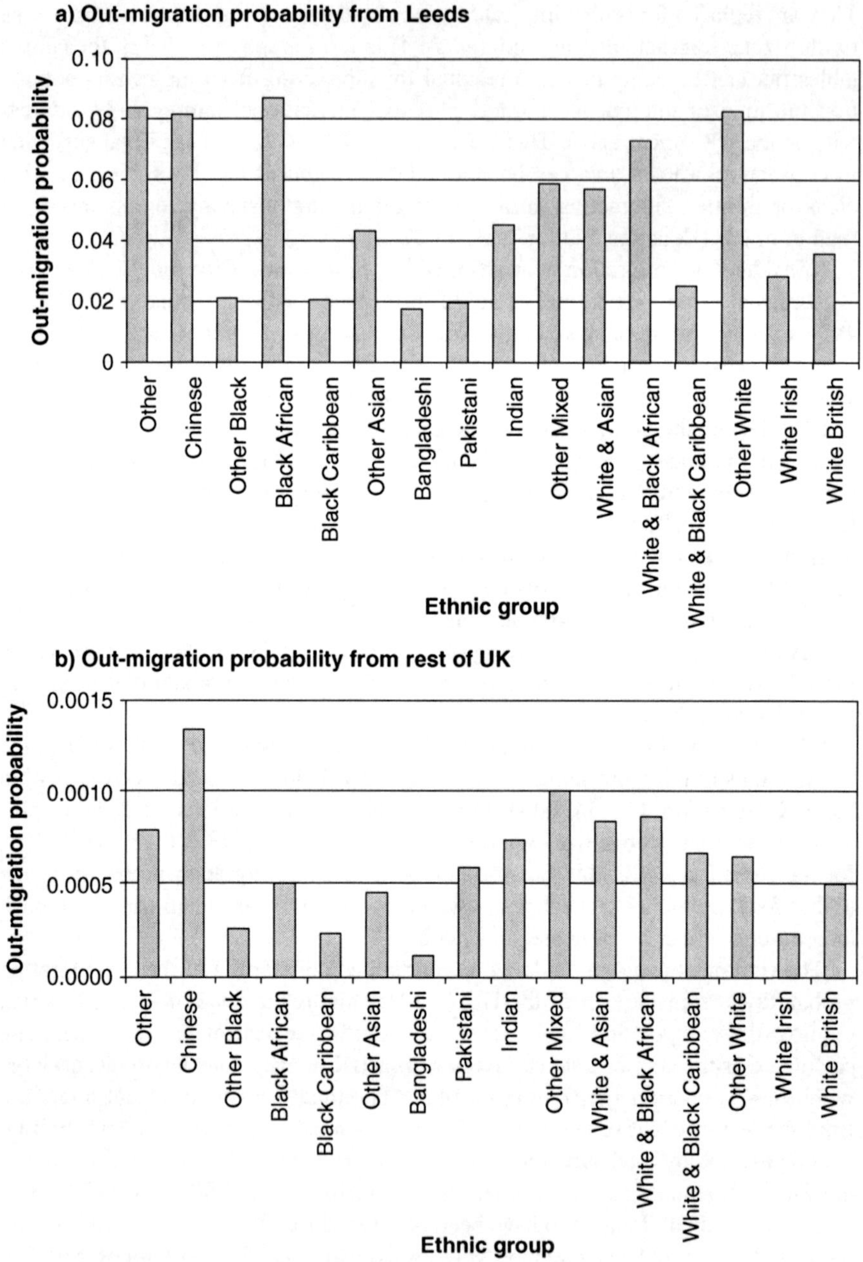

Fig. 14.8 Migration probabilities for Leeds, by ethnic group, 2000–2001
(Source: Authors' calculations based on census migration statistics and population data from ONS, GROS and NISRA)

and Other Black groups have lower probabilities. Thus, within four of the five broader groupings, there are detailed groups with low and with high migration probabilities. The picture is broadly similar in terms of highs and lows for out-migration from the rest of the UK (in-migration to Leeds), shown in Fig. 14.8b. We will carry out a more detailed analysis of all groups across all zones in the future and compare the findings with previous analyses cited earlier.

The final piece in the jigsaw of internal migration estimation is to add age-sex detail. Here we converted single year of age profiles for men and women for UK migrants as a whole into ratios of the profile means. These ratios were then multiplied by the mean probabilities generated in the analysis illustrated in Table 14.6. This estimate assumes independence of the OD pattern of migration from the AS pattern. As a first approximation this is satisfactory but further analysis comparing with broad age migration data for seven ethnic groups (Stillwell et al., 2008) will be appropriate.

International Migration

International migration is a significant driver of population change in the UK and as such is a crucial component in a subnational projection model. The methods available to estimate its true impact on local areas are constrained, however, by inadequate systems of measurement and data capture since there is no single data collection instrument for the measurement of international migration. There are various alternative sources which provide intelligence about the movement of population into and out of the UK (Rees et al., 2009). These sources include census, survey, administrative and 'composite' datasets with each having its limitations depending upon the question asked, purpose of data collection and the population covered (for more details see Rees and Boden, 2006; Green et al., 2008).

The UK's official source of data on immigration and emigration is the Total International Migration (TIM) statistics (ONS, 2008b). The TIM statistics are primarily based on the International Passenger Survey's question on each migrant's 'intentions' to stay or leave the UK. For immigration estimation the Labour Force Survey (LFS) is part of the subnational calibration process with 2001 Census data used for the proportional allocation of flows to local authority areas. Emigration estimation cannot be informed by the LFS or Census so incorporates a 'migration propensity' model to estimate the distribution of flows from each local authority. At ONS, an ongoing programme of improvement to international migration statistics includes an evaluation of the explicit use of administrative statistics (ONS, 2009; Rees et al., 2009). The results of this work are subject to consultation during 2009 with any methodological revisions to be implemented in 2010 with the release of 2008 mid-year estimates.

Here a 'New Migrant Databank' (NMD) originally recommended to the Greater London Authority to measure international migration at a local level (Rees and Boden, 2006) has been developed to produce a repository of UK-wide migration statistics from national to local authority level (Boden and Rees, 2010). The NMD aims to provide a single source of migration statistics for each LA and to facilitate the development of alternative migration estimation methods. Using the NMD repository in parallel with the ONS improvement programme, we have developed a number of alternative methods for subnational estimation incorporating intelligence from administrative datasets. An alternative methodology for distributing

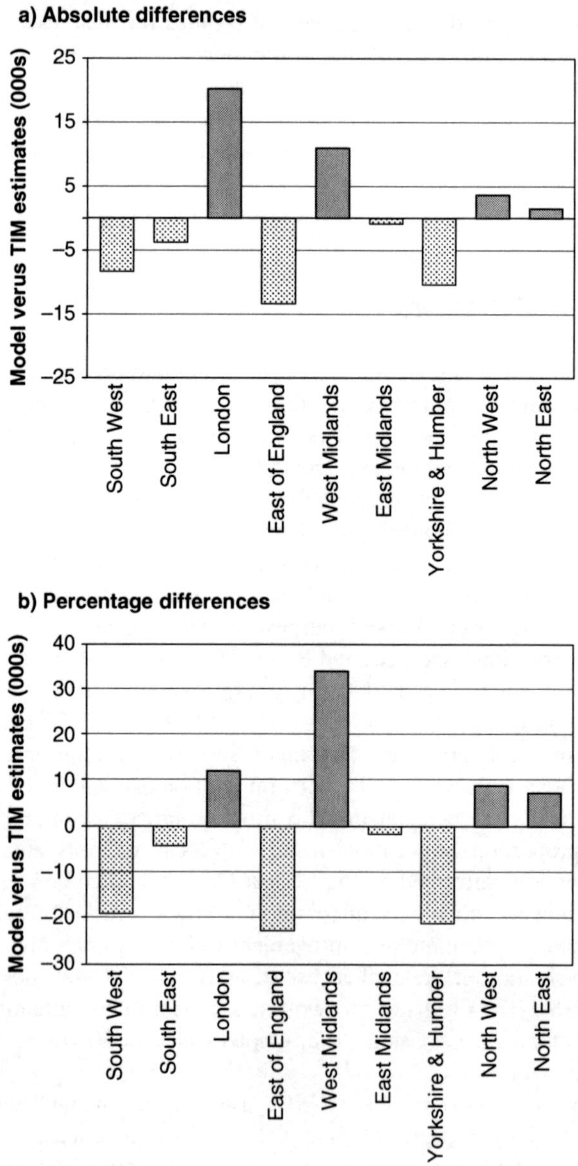

Fig. 14.9 Immigration estimation: impact of an alternative methodology (Source: Authors' calculations)

immigration flows has been derived combining TIM statistics at a national level with subnational statistics from three administrative sources: National Insurance Number (NINo) registrations by migrant workers, the registration of international migrants with a local GP and Higher Education Statistics Agency (HESA) data on international students (Boden and Rees, 2010). The methodology uses flow 'proportions' to distribute national TIM totals to subnational areas and results in a different distribution of immigration flows to that recorded in official statistics (Fig. 14.9).

Figure 14.10 illustrates a time-series of immigration flows from different sources for Leeds and Bradford. The official TIM statistics demonstrate the rise in the level of long-term migration following expansion of the EU in 2004. The registration of international migrants with GPs also increased steadily over the time period in both Leeds and Bradford. NINo registrations reveal the impact of the Accession migrants post-2004 but also that non-Accession registrations have remained fairly constant since 2001.

Given the challenge of accurately estimating international migration at all spatial scales, the robust calculation of an ethnic group dimension to migration flows is

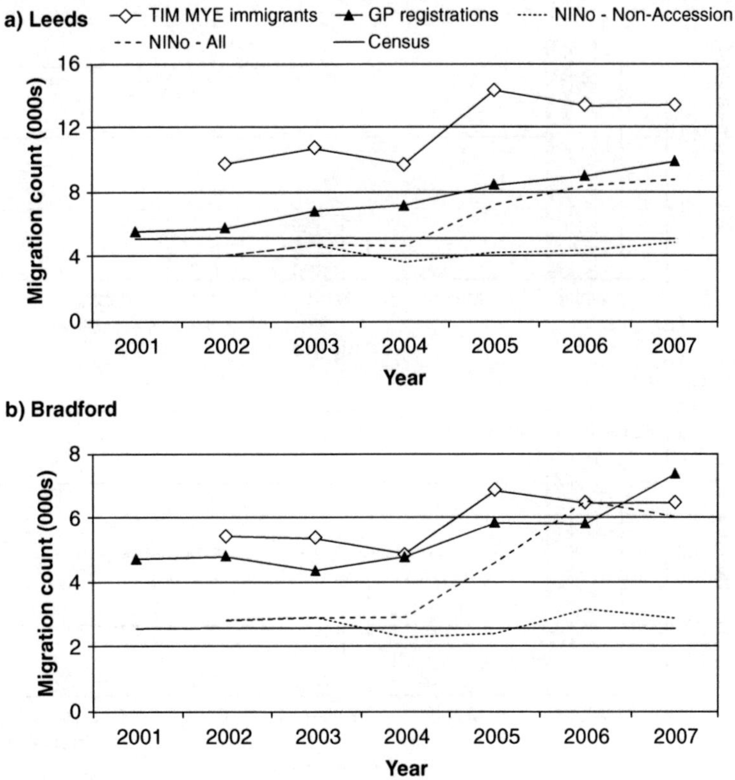

Fig. 14.10 International migration flows, Leeds and Bradford, 2001–2007
(Sources: 100% data extract from the National Insurance Recording System (NIRS): ONS Mid-year estimates; GP registration statistics provided by ONS)

even more difficult to derive. The 2001 Census provides the only direct source of data on ethnic flows and only for immigration. The ethnic profile of immigration in 2001 can be applied to flow totals for later years to produce an updated ethnic profile. As a better alternative, which captures the new migrant streams post 2001, the Department for Work and Pension's NINo registration statistics have been used here to derive ethnic profiles for immigration to each local authority area. Based on a commissioned 2001 Census table (C0880) linking ethnic group and country of origin, this has allocated an ethnic group to each NINo registration using each registrant's country of origin. Combining these sources has produced an aggregation of NINo registrations by ethnic group for each local authority (Fig. 14.11).

There are some shortcomings here since, for example, NINo statistics are associated with migrants whose length of stay is indeterminate and do not account for White-British migrants who do not require NINo registration. However, the derived ethnic profiles provide a comparison with census profiles and have been used to

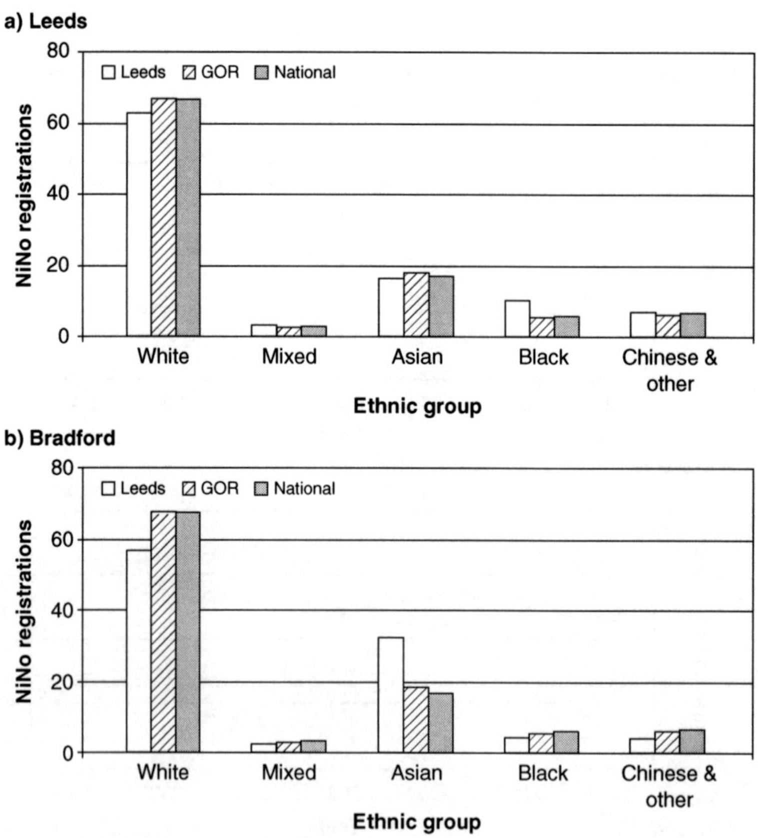

Fig. 14.11 Ethnic group profiles of immigration flows, Leeds and Bradford
(Source: Authors' calculations)

inform the estimation of updated ethnic migration profiles for local areas which better reflect the changing patterns that have been evident since 2001 and particularly since EU-expansion in 2004. The projection model can be used to explore the impact of different scenarios relating to immigration and emigration.

Conclusions

The chapter has outlined how the ingredients have been assembled for input to an ambitious model for projecting the populations of the UK's ethnic group populations at a detailed spatial scale (LAs in England with Wales, Scotland and Northern Ireland). The new projection model for the UK population has the following innovative features: (i) it is an integrated model of the whole UK, (ii) it is a bottom-up model that uses local areas within England, (iii) it uses sixteen sub-populations (ethnic groups), (iv) it uses new estimates of ethnic fertility, ethnic mortality, international migration and internal migration for ethnic groups, (v) it uses a mixing matrix to assign the ethnicity of the newborn, thus capturing the ethnic mixing process, (vi) it is specified in single year of age detail and (vii) extends the age distribution to a final age of 100+. To solve the challenges that such a model poses, we have employed a bi-regional model that captures the essential dependency of in-migration to an area on out-migration from other areas. We also use a new model structure based on making migration probabilities conditional on survival. The survival and migration processes in the model are thus de-coupled and the computations for each time step in the projection need be executed only once. This structure guarantees that both survival and migration probabilities are non-negative and means iteration is not needed.

The first experimental results have been generated using a benchmark set of inputs estimates for 2001 and assumed to be constant thereafter (Rees and Wohland, 2009). In these projections, the UK population rises to a peak of 62.4 millions in 2030 and then falls to 60.9 millions in 2051. Note that the 2006 based national population projections (NPP) anticipate much higher growth to 77.2 millions in 2051 based on higher fertility, lower mortality and higher immigration trends since 2001 and much higher assumptions into the future. In our projections, four ethnic groups experience decline before 2051: the White British population from 2011, the White Irish population from 2001, the Other White population from 2031 and the Black Caribbean population from 2041. All other groups show substantial growth (Table 14.7): the Mixed and the Chinese triple in size, the Asian groups (except Indians) double in population. The Other groups double their populations. These experimental projections anticipate a substantial shift in the ethnic composition of the UK population, as shown in Table 14.7. For example, the White British share of the population shrinks from 87 to 77% by 2051 and the non-White share increases from 8 to 19%.

From these first, experimental projections, we will develop a suite of projections that demonstrate how the ethnic and spatial variations in dynamics play out over the first half of the twenty-first century to 2051. Table 14.8 sets out the agenda for

Table 14.7 Projected ethnic shares of the UK population for an experimental benchmark projection, 2001–2051

Ethnic Group	2001	2031	2051	Percentage change 2001–2051
White	87.1	80.9	77.0	–9
White & Black Caribbean	0.4	1.0	1.4	+242
White & Black African	0.1	0.3	0.5	+249
White & Asian	0.3	0.8	1.2	+271
Other Mixed	0.3	0.6	0.9	+255
Asian	4.0	6.7	8.6	+120
Black	2.0	3.2	3.8	+98
Chinese or Other	0.8	1.9	2.5	+214
Total	100	100	100	+3
Not White British	12.9	19.1	23.0	+83
Not White	8.0	14.6	18.9	+144
Mixed & Other Groups	4.6	7.7	9.5	+111

Source: Authors' computations.

this work. We will align the component trends in 2001–2007 to published all group estimates. We will develop future trends based on 2001–2007 changes taking into account new NPP assumptions for the 2008 round. We will explore the sensitivity of future projections to different assumptions and to particular event scenarios such as convergence of vital rates across ethnic groups. Finally, we will develop a set of

Table 14.8 An agenda for ethnic projections of UK local area populations

Projection set name	Description	Purpose
Benchmark	Uses 2001 data and applies constant component rates and probabilities	To prove the validity of the projection model and component estimates
Aligned	Updates the benchmark data to 2007 using the latest demographic data	To align the projections with National Statistics estimates and projections
Trend	Develops trends in the key drivers for each component using best knowledge	To develop the most likely future trajectory for all populations
Sensitivity	Tests out the sensitivity of projections to different assumptions	To determine the most important assumptions made in the projections
Impact	Develops set of 'what if' scenarios linked to public policy	To evaluate the impact of particular events/trends and policy changes
Convergence	Develops scenarios in which ethnic and spatial differences reduce	To assess what it will take to achieve less inequality
Variant	Develops high and low variants of the trend projection	To set some upper and lower bounds on future populations

variant projections to give the user some sense of the uncertainty of the projections. Full probabilistic analysis of uncertainty must, however, await a new project.

Acknowledgements The research reported here was supported by ESRC Research Award RES-163-25-0032, 'What happens when international migrants settle? Ethnic group population trends and projections for local areas'. 1991 and 2001 Census data were obtained via the MIMAS CASWEB facility and the SARs team at CCSR and GIS boundary data via EDINA's UKBORDERS facility, all supported by ESRC and JISC. The Census, official Mid-Year Estimates, Vital Statistics and Labour Force Survey data for England and Wales, Scotland and Northern Ireland have been provided by ONS, GROS and NISRA and the digital boundary data by OSGB and OSNI. These data are Crown copyright and are reproduced with permission of the Office of Public Sector Information.

References

Ahmad, W. (1999) Ethnic statistics: Better than nothing or worse than nothing? in Dorling D. and Simpson S. (eds.), *Statistics in Society*, Arnold, London.

Boden, P. and Rees, P. (2010) International migration: The estimation of immigration to local areas in England using administrative data sources, *Journal of the Royal Statistical Society, Series A*, DOI: 10.1111/j.1467-985X.2009.00637.x.

Boden, P. and Rees, P. (2010) New migrant databank – Concept and development, Chapter 6 in Stillwell, J., Duke-Williams, O. and Dennett, A. (eds.), *Technologies for Migration and Commuting Analysis: Spatial Interaction Data Applications*, IGI Global, Hershey, pp. 112–133.

Booth, H. (2006) Demographic forecasting: 1980 to 2005 in review, *International Journal of Forecasting*, 22: 547–581.

Brown, D. and Rees, P. (2006) Trends in local and small area mortality and morbidity in Yorkshire and the Humber: Monitoring health inequalities, *Regional Studies*, 40(5): 437–458.

Burström, B. and Fredlund, P. (2001) Self-rated health: Is it as good a predictor of subsequent mortality among adults in lower as well as in higher social classes, *Journal of Epidemiology and Community Health*, 55: 836–840.

Coleman, D. (2006) Immigration and ethnic change in low-fertility countries: A third demographic transition, *Population and Development Review*, 32(3): 401–446.

Coleman, D. and Scherbov, S. (2005) *Immigration and ethnic change in low-fertility countries – towards a new demographic transition*? Presented at the Population Association of America Annual Meeting, Philadelphia. Online at http://www.apsoc.ox.ac.uk/Oxpop/publications%20files/WP29.pdf

Dunnell, K. (2008) Ageing and mortality in the UK – National Statistician's annual article on the population, *Population Trends*, 134: 6–23.

Fennelly, K. (2005) The healthy migrant effect, *Healthy Generations*, 5(3): 1–3.

Green, A.E., Owen, D. and Adam, D. (2008) *A resource guide on local migration statistics*. Report prepared for the Local Government Association. Online at http://www.lga.gov.uk/lga/publications/publication-display.do?id=1308025

Harding, S. and Balarajan, R. (2002) Mortality data on migrant groups living in England and Wales: Issues of adequacy and of interpretation of death rates in Haskey, J. (ed.), *Population Projections by Ethnic Group: A Feasibility Study*, The Stationery Office, London, pp. 115–127.

Haskey, J. (2002) Introduction in Haskey, J. (ed.), *Population Projections by Ethnic Group: A Feasibility Study* (Studies on Medical and Population Subjects No. 67), The Stationery Office, London, pp. vii–x.

Heistaro, S., Jousilahti, P., Lahelma, E., Vartiainen, E. and Puska, P. (2001) Self-rated health and mortality: A long term prospective study in eastern Finland, *Journal of Epidemiology and Community Health*, 55(4): 227–232.

Helweg, M., Kjøller, M. and Thoning, H. (2003) Do age and social relations moderate the relationship between self-rated health and mortality among adult Danes? *Social Science and Medicine*, 57(7): 1237–1247.

Hussain, S. and Stillwell, J. (2008) *Internal Migration of Ethnic Groups in England and Wales by Age and District Type*, School of Geography, University of Leeds, Leeds, Online at http://www.geog.leeds.ac.uk/wpapers/08-03.pdfWorking Paper 08/3).

McGee, D.L., Liao, Y., Cao, G. and Copper, R.S. (1999) Self-reported health status and mortality in a multiethnic US cohort, *American Journal of Epidemiology*, 149(1): 41–46.

NCHS (2007) United States life tables, 2003, *National Vital Statistics Reports*, 54(14): 1–40, National Center for Health Statistics, Centers for Disease Control and Prevention, U.S. Department of Health and Human Services, MD 20782. Online at http://www.cdc.gov/nchs/data/nvsr54/nvsr54_14.pdf

Norman, P., Rees, P. and Boyle, P. (2003) Achieving data compatibility over space and time: Creating consistent geographical zones, *International Journal of Population Geography*, 9(5): 365–386.

ONS (2009, February) *Improvements to migration and population statistics*. Office for National Statistics. Online at http://www.statistics.gov.uk/about/data/methodology/specific/population/future/imps/updates/downloads/msiwpfeb.pdf

Penn, R. (2000) British population and society in 2025: Some conjectures, *Sociology*, 34(1): 5–18.

Raymer, J. and Giulietti, C. (2008, 2 July) *Analysing structures of interregional migration in England*. Paper presented at the ESRC Research Methods Festival Session 40: Handling Migration and Commuting Flow Data, Oxford

Raymer, J. and Giulietti, C. (2009) Ethnic migration between area groups in England and Wales, *Area*, 41(4): 435–451.

Raymer, J., Smith, P. and Giulietti, C. (2008) *Combining Census and Registration Data to Analyse Ethnic Migration Patterns in England From 1991 to 2007* (Methodology Working Papers M08/09), Southampton Statistical Sciences Research Institute, Southampton.

Rees, P. (2002) New models for projecting UK populations by ethnic group at national and subnational scales in Haskey, J. (ed.), *Population Projections by Ethnic Group: A Feasibility Study* (Studies on Medical and Population Subjects No. 67), The Stationery Office, London, pp. 27–52.

Rees, P. (2006) *What is happening to the UK population in a global mobility system?* Paper presented at the ESRC/ONS Public Policy seminar series on Demographic Change and Government Policy, Third Seminar on Globalisation, population Mobility and the Impact of Migration on Population, Royal Statistical Society, London.

Rees, P. (2008) What happens when international migrants settle? Projections of ethnic groups in United Kingdom regions in Raymer, J. and Willekens, F. (eds.), *International Migration in Europe: Data, Models and Estimates*, Wiley, Chichester, pp. 329–358.

Rees, P. and Boden, P. (2006) *Estimating London's New Migrant Population. Stage 1 – Review of Methodology*, Mayor of London, Greater London Authority, London, Online at http://www.london.gov.uk/mayor/refugees/docs/nm-pop.pdf

Rees, P. and Butt, F. (2004) Ethnic change and diversity in England, 1981–2001, *Area*, 36(2): 174–186.

Rees, P. and Parsons, J. (2006) *Socio-demographic Scenarios for Children to 2020*, Joseph Rowntree Foundation, York, Online at http://www.jrf.org.uk/child-poverty/publications.asp#rees

Rees, P. and Parsons, J. (2009, January) *Child Poverty in the UK: Socio-Demographic Scenarios to 2002 for Children (2008 Update)* (Report on Datasets, Models and Results, Report to the Joseph Rowntree Foundation), School of Geography, University of Leeds, Leeds.

Rees, P., Stillwell, J., Boden, P. and Dennett, A. (2009) Part 2: A review of migration statistics literature, in UK Statistics Authority in *Migration Statistics: The Way Ahead?* Report 4, UKSA, London, pp. 53–140.

Rees, P. and Wohland, P. (2008) *Estimates of Ethnic Mortality in the UK* (Working Paper 08/04), School of Geography, University of Leeds, Leeds.

Rees, P. and Wohland, P. (2009) *What happens when international migrants settle? An analysis of the demographic future of ethnic mixing in the UK*. Presentation at the session on Migration, Mixing and Ethnic Integration at the Annual conference of the Royal Geographical Society-IBG, University of Manchester, Manchester, 26 August. Online at http://www.geog.leeds.ac.uk/fileadmin/downloads/school/research/projects/migrants/The_demographic_future_of_ethnic_mixing.pdf

Rees, P., Wohland, P. and Norman, P. (2009) The estimation of mortality for ethnic groups at local scale within the United Kingdom, *Social Science and Medicine*, 69: 1592–1607.

Simpson, S. (1997) Demography and ethnicity: Case studies from Bradford, *New Community*, 23(1): 89–107.

Simpson, L. (2002) The starting population for population projections by ethnic group in Haskey, J. (ed.), *Population Projections by Ethnic Group a Feasibility Study* (Studies on Medical and Population Subjects No. 67), The Stationery Office, London, pp. 73–80.

Simpson, L. and Akinwale, B. (2007) Quantifying stability and change in ethnic group, *Journal of Official Statistics*, 23(2): 185–208.

Simpson, L., Purdam, K., Toya, A., Fieldhouse, E., Gavalas, V., Tranmer, M., et al. (2006) *Ethnic Minority Populations and the Labour Market: An Analysis of the 1991 and 2001 Census*, Department of Work and Pensions, London, Online at http://asp.ccsr.ac.uk/dwp/info/report333.pdfResearch Report No.333).

Sporton, D. and White, P. (2002) Fertility in Haskey, J. (ed.), *Population Projections by Ethnic Group a Feasibility Study*, The Stationery Office, London, pp. 81–92, Online at http://www.statistics.gov.uk/downloads/theme_population/SMPS_67_v2.pdfStudies on Medical and Population Subjects No. 67

Statistics New Zealand (2008a) *New Zealand period life tables: 2005–07*. Online at http://search.stats.govt.nz/search?w=New%20Zealand%20Period%20Life%20Tables:%202005%e2%80%9307

Statistics New Zealand (2008b) *National ethnic population projections: 2006 (base)-2026* (Statistics New Zealand/Tatauranga Aotearoa). Online at http://www.stats.govt.nz/NR/rdonlyres/11B5CDF9-5DF0-4321-8BF2-4811595lCD97/0/nationalethnicpopulationprojections2006basehotp.pdf

Stillwell, J. and Hussain, S. (2008) *Ethnic Group Migration Within Britain During 2000–01: A District Level Analysis* (Working Paper 08/2), School of Geography, University of Leeds, Leeds.

Stillwell, J., Hussain, S. and Norman, P. (2008) The internal migration propensities and net migration patterns of ethnic groups in Britain, *Migration Letters*, 5(2): 135–150.

Townsend, P. (1987) Deprivation, *Journal of Social Policy*, 16: 125–146.

Tromans, N., Natamba, E., Jefferies, J. and Norman, P. (2008) Have national trends in fertility between 1986 and 2006 occurred evenly across England and Wales? *Population Trends*, 133: 7–19.

US Census Bureau (2008) *National population projections, released 2008* (Based on Census 2000). Online at http://www.census.gov/population/www/projections/summarytables.html

Wilson, T. and Bell, M. (2004) Comparative empirical evaluations of internal migration models in subnational population projections, *Journal of Population Research*, 21(2): 127–160.

Wilson, T. and Rees, P. (2005) Recent developments in population projection methodology: A review, *Population, Space and Place*, 11: 337–360.

Index

J. Stillwell, M. van Ham (eds.), *Ethnicity and Integration*, Understanding Population Trends and Processes 3, DOI 10.1007/978-90-481-9103-1,

Lightning Source UK Ltd.
Milton Keynes UK
08 September 2010

159561UK00002B/18/P

9 789048 191024